# Horoscopes of Europe

## An Astrological Study
## of Its Cities and Countries

### Marc Penfield

Copyright 2006 by Marc H. Penfield
All rights reserved.

No part of this book may be reproduced or transmitted in any form or by any means, electronic or mechanical, including photocopying
or recording, or by any information storage and retrieval system, without written permission from the author and publisher. Requests
and inquiries may be mailed to: American Federation of Astrologers, 6535 S. Rural Road, Tempe AZ 85283.

ISBN: 0-86690-567-7

First Printing: 2006

Cover Design: Jack Cipolla

Published by:
American Federation of Astrologers, Inc.
6535 S. Rural Road
Tempe AZ 85283.

Printed in the United States of America

# Dedication

This book is dedicated to

DONALD L. HEDRICK

who kept our home fires
burning while I was away
doing research around the
world, at discount rates
of course

# Acknowledgements

I wish to thank the following astrologers for their invaluable assistance in helping me to complete this book:

| | |
|---|---|
| Belgium | Sandy Dumont and Grietje Versatel |
| Croatia | Slaven Slobodnjak |
| Czech Republic | Jindra Johanisova and Jaroslav Mixa |
| Denmark | Karl Aage Jensen and Holger Stavnsbjerg |
| England | Nicholas Campion |
| Finland | Kyosti Tarvainen |
| France | Maurice Charvet and Luc de Marre |
| Germany | Richard Vetter |
| Greece | Antonia Peta and Demetrios Koronakis |
| Hungary | Catalin Horanyi |
| Ireland | Hans Hinrich Taeger |
| Italy | Grazia Bordoni |
| Macedonia | Simeon Atanasoski |
| Netherlands | Joyce Hoen and Tees Reitsma |
| Portugal | Pinto Moreira |
| Poland | Dariusz Proskurnicki |
| Romania | Sorin Ripa |
| Russia | Van Golay |
| Sweden | Monica Werneman |
| Switzerland | Verena Bachmann |
| Turkey | Baris Ilhan and Hakan Kirkoglu |
| Ukraine | Jacob Schwartz |

# Contents

## Countries of Europe According to Region

| | |
|---|---|
| Scandinavia | Denmark, Finland, Iceland, Norway, Sweden |
| Baltic States | Estonia, Latvia, Lithuania |
| The Low Countries | Belgium, Luxembourg, Netherlands |
| British Isles | England, Ireland, Northern Ireland, Scotland, Wales |
| Central and Western | Austria, Czech Republic, France, Germany Hungary, Liechtenstein, Monaco, Poland, Slovakia, Switzerland |
| The Balkans | Albania, Bosnia-Herzegovina, Bulgaria, Croatia, Greece, Macedonia, Montenegro, Romania, Serbia, Slovania |
| The Italian Peninsula | Italy, Malta, San Marino, Seborga, Sovereign Military Order of Malta, Vatican |
| Former Soviet Union | Armenia, Azerbaijan, Belarus, Georgia, Moldova, Russia, Ukraine |
| Middle Eastern | Turkey, Cyprus |

| | | | | |
|---|---|---|---|---|
| Albania | 1 | Tampere | 41 |
| Independence Republic | 2 | Turku | 41 |
| Tirana | 3 | France | 42 |
| Andorra | 4 | First Republic | 44 |
| Armenia | 5 | Napeolonic | 45 |
| Austria | 7 | Second Republic | 46 |
| Hapsburg Republic | 9 | Third Republic | 47 |
| Vienna | 10 | Paris | 49 |
| Innsbruck | 10 | Bordeaux | 50 |
| Linz | 11 | Clermont-Ferrand | 50 |
| Azerbaijan | 12 | Le Havre | 50 |
| Belarus | 14 | Lyon | 50 |
| Minsk | 15 | Marseille | 51 |
| Belgium | 16 | Nancy | 51 |
| Antwerp | 18 | Nantes | 51 |
| Brussels | 18 | Nice | 52 |
| Liege | 19 | Rouen | 52 |
| Bosnia-Herzgovina | 20 | Strasbourg | 53 |
| Bulgaria | 22 | Toulouse | 53 |
| Independence Republic | 23 | Georgia | 54 |
| Sofia | 24 | Germany | 56 |
| Croatia | 25 | Prussia | 58 |
| Zagreb | 26 | German Empire | 58 |
| Cyprus | 28 | Weimar Republic | 60 |
| Czech Republic | 30 | West Germany | 62 |
| Brno | 32 | East Germany | 62 |
| Prague | 32 | United Germany | 63 |
| Denmark | 33 | Berlin | 64 |
| Arhus | 35 | Bonn | 65 |
| Copenhagen | 35 | Bremen | 65 |
| Odense | 36 | Chemnitz | 65 |
| Estonia | 37 | Cologne | 66 |
| Tallinn | 38 | Dortmund | 66 |
| Finland | 39 | Dresden | 66 |
| Helsinki | 40 | Dusseldorf | 67 |

| | |
|---|---|
| Frankfurt-am-Main | 67 |
| Hamburg | 68 |
| Hannover | 68 |
| Leipzig | 68 |
| Mainz | 69 |
| Mannheim | 69 |
| Munich | 70 |
| Nuremberg | 70 |
| Greece | 71 |
| Independence Republic | 73 |
| Athens | 74 |
| Thessalonika | 74 |
| Hungary | 75 |
| Monarchy Republic | 76 |
| Budapest | 78 |
| Iceland | 79 |
| Reykjavik | 80 |
| Ireland | 81 |
| Dublin | 83 |
| Cork | 83 |
| Italy | 84 |
| Roman Republic | 84 |
| Roman Empire | 85 |
| Unification Republic | 86 |
| Italy | 88 |
| Rome | 89 |
| Bari | 90 |
| Florence | 90 |
| Naples | 91 |
| Turin | 92 |
| Venice | 92 |
| Latvia | 94 |
| Liechtenstein | 96 |
| Vaduz | 97 |
| Lithuania | 98 |
| Luxembourg | 100 |
| Luxembourg Ville | 101 |
| Macedonia | 102 |
| Malta | 104 |
| Moldova | 105 |
| Monaco | 107 |
| Montenegro | 109 |
| Netherlands | 110 |
| Amsterdam | 112 |
| The Hague | 113 |
| Rotterdam | 112 |
| Utrecht | 114 |
| Norway | 115 |
| Bergen | 116 |
| Hammerfest | 117 |
| Oslo | 117 |
| Poland | 118 |
| Krakow | 120 |
| Lodz | 121 |
| Poznan | 121 |

| | |
|---|---|
| Szczecin | 122 |
| Warsaw | 122 |
| Wroclaw | 123 |
| Portugal | 124 |
| Independence Republic | 125 |
| Lisbon | 126 |
| Oporto | 127 |
| Romania | 128 |
| Independence | 128 |
| Republic | 129 |
| Bucharest | 130 |
| Russia | 132 |
| Imperial | 132 |
| Bolshevik | 134 |
| Moscow | 138 |
| St. Petersburg | 140 |
| San Marino | 143 |
| Seborga | 144 |
| Serbia | 145 |
| Independence | 145 |
| Yugoslavia | 146 |
| Republic | 146 |
| Slovakia | 150 |
| Bratislava | 151 |
| Slovenia | 152 |
| Sovereign Military Order of Malta | 153 |
| Spain | 155 |
| Unification Republic | 158 |
| Madrid | 159 |
| Barcelona | 159 |
| Bilbao | 160 |
| Granada | 160 |
| Valencia | 161 |
| Zaragosa | 161 |
| Sweden | 162 |
| Goteborg | 164 |
| Malmo | 164 |
| Stockholm | 164 |
| Switzerland | 165 |
| Bern | 167 |
| Geneva | 167 |
| Zurich | 168 |
| Turkey | 169 |
| Byzantine Empire | 169 |
| Ottomon Empire | 170 |
| Turkey | 171 |
| Istanbul | 173 |
| Ukraine | 175 |
| Kiev | 176 |
| Odessa | 177 |
| United Kingdom | 179 |
| Norman England | 179 |
| London | 185 |
| Bath | 185 |
| Birmingham | 185 |

| | |
|---|---|
| Blackpool | 186 |
| Bournemouth | 186 |
| Bradford | 186 |
| Brighton | 187 |
| Bristol | 187 |
| Cambridge | 188 |
| Coventry | 188 |
| Derby | 189 |
| Exeter | 189 |
| Gloucester | 189 |
| Huddersfield | 190 |
| Ipswich | 190 |
| Kingston upon Hull | 190 |
| Leeds | 191 |
| Leicester | 191 |
| Liverpool | 191 |
| Manchester | 192 |
| Newcastle upon Tyne | 192 |
| Northampton | 193 |
| Norwich | 193 |
| Nottingham | 193 |
| Oxford | 194 |
| Plymouth | 194 |
| Portsmouth | 195 |
| Reading | 195 |
| Sheffield | 196 |
| Southampton | 196 |
| Stoke on Trent | 197 |
| Teeside | 197 |
| Torquay | 197 |
| Wolverhampton | 198 |
| York | 198 |
| Scotland | 200 |
| Aberdeen | 201 |
| Dundee | 201 |
| Edinburgh | 202 |
| Glasgow | 202 |
| Wales | 203 |
| Cardiff | 204 |
| Swansea | 204 |
| Northern Ireland | 205 |
| Belfast | 206 |
| Londonderry | 206 |
| Vatican | 207 |
| Appendix A—Charts of the European Union | 209 |
| Appendix B—Alternative Birth Times for European Cities | 216 |

# Introduction

I first became acquainted with Mundane, or Geopolitical, Astrology when I was hired as a cataloguer and bibliographer for a used bookstore in Hollywood, California in 1973. Prior to that time, I had read little on the subject mainly because there was a dearth of material available. There were a few books by the Church of Light, and books by Louis Macneice and Charles E. O. Carter contained some data but not nearly enough to satisfy my Scorpionic inquisitiveness. While indexing books for future catalogues, I began to take notes on the founding dates for countries and cities and then proceeded to enlarge my databank by sending hundreds of letters to various libraries, historical societies and government offices throughout Europe. The response was overwhelming and the postman groaned under the weight of the material sent to me. Before long, I was heading for Europe to do further research and meet some of those people who had been kind enough to answer my requests for information. Long hours spent in the British Library and Bibliotheque Nationale were extremely rewarding, and I still had time to see the usual tourist sights. Over the past few decades, books by Moon Moore, Glenn Malec, Doris Chase Doane and Nicholas Campion have also been published, many with conflicting data. Most astrologers aren't historians and they don't have the foggiest clue as to what might constitute the birth of a nation. I hope to rectify that situation with this book.

Much of the information on Europe was obtained from numerous astrologers living on the continent. If I had written this book three decades ago when I began my initial research, I would have had to deal with only 33 countries, not the 51 mentioned in this book. With the break-ups of the Soviet Union, Yugoslavia and Czechoslovakia, Europe is considerably more complicated and varied than it was a while back. Data on European cities was obtained directly from mayor's offices, city and university libraries and records offices of historical societies.

Some countries mentioned in this book might not be considered European by some standards. I've chosen to incorporate Turkey because it had a major role in European history and a small portion of Turkey is geographically inside Europe. Cyprus was included due to its large Greek population and because it became a member of the European Common Market. The Caucasus nations of Armenia, Azerbaijan and Georgia are continentally-split, depending on which encyclopedia or almanac you're perusing. Let's call them Eurasian. I've also decided to include two countries I'm certain you've never heard of called Seborga and the Sovereign Military Order of Malta (SMOM), two tiny enclaves inside Italy never mentioned by travel agencies and totally ignored in major reference works. Thank God for the Internet.

Horoscopes used in this book represent the uniqueness surrounding a nation. Many are for the coronation of a monarch, some for the establishment of a republic. Those countries such as France and Portugal will have a minimum of two horoscopes: one monarchial, one republican. Countries in the former Soviet bloc were problematic, as many countries like Poland, Hungary and Czechoslovakia were already republics when the Communists took over. Did the imposition of an outside force (the Soviets) necessitate a new horoscope? I'll let you be the judge of this riddle. Other Eastern European countries like Bulgaria, Romania and Albania were monarchies, so with the fall of their Heads of State, a new chart had to be erected as the form of government had indeed changed.

Russia was somewhat of an enigma to me. The original founding chart for Old Russia of 862 A.D. technically came to an end in 1598 when the old dynasty died out. After 15 years of turmoil, the Romanovs came to power in 1613, and they were themselves ousted in 1917 when Czar Nicholas II was forced to abdicate for himself as well as his heirs. The Provisional Government under Kerensky didn't last all that long, though the fact that the monarchy had ended and a republic established, I chose, instead, to concentrate on the events of the October Revolution as more indicative of the events which followed the establishment of Communism as a better indicator of subsequent history for most of the 20th century inside Russia. I chose not to analyze the chart for the Soviet Union, as I felt that it was an outgrowth of the 1917 chart already in operation, and the Soviet Union was also trying to recapture the First Russian Empire founded by Peter the Great back in 1721. With the downfall of the Soviet Union on Christmas Day 1991, ostensibly the chart for Bolshevik Russia of 1917 should still be considered in effect. Or does Russia deserve another horoscope, now that the Communists no longer occupy the majority of their legislature? To me, the Soviet Union was a government inside a government, nothing more.

Ascertaining birth times for European countries was made considerably easier thanks to *The Times* of London, *The New York Times* and *Los Angeles*

*Times*. In same instances, only an approximate time was mentioned, like Yugoslavia which stated "evening." Many historical societies gave me the same thing, like those in Belgium and Hungary. I had to rectify those horoscopes using events since their founding for accuracy. Some nations like Andorra, Liechtenstein and Luxembourg had no idea what time their nation was founded, so when in doubt, I used a noon birth time, and especially so when a coronation took place.

Then there was the problem of what time to use. Most ancient charts used Local Mean Time (LMT) even though it wasn't in general use until the 19th century. The time used prior to that was Local Apparent Time (LAT) which is the same as Sundial Time, which generally places the Sun at the Midheaven each noon. If an astrologer fails to differentiate LMT from LAT, then the Sun could be as many as four degrees away from the MC at noon, especially in November and February.

I had to correct some birth dates as well, due to the fact that most Balkan countries were still using the Julian (OS) calendar until the early 20th century. Most Catholic countries switched to the Gregorian (NS) calendar in the 16th century, but Protestant nations didn't follow suit until the mid-18th century.

Some countries like Denmark presented a real problem. I would have loved to find a book which gave me the exact date when the King founded that country, but sources could only speculate on sometime in the early 10th century. I had to do extensive rectification on Denmark's chart, and no doubt some will disagree with my conclusions. I chose the date of June 5 for its inception, as so many important historical events seem to take place on this date, including the signing of the first Constitution in 1849. Austria was another problem as I had three dates from which to choose. Belgium had three dates, as did the Netherlands and Luxembourg.

The chart for Bosnia-Herzegovina is a departure in many ways. This enclave inside Yugoslavia declared its sovereignty in October 1991, but the European Union wouldn't recognize that sovreignty until a referendum was taken. Results of the referendum were proclaimed in March 1992, which many astrologers use as the foundation of Bosnia. I tend to disagree, as the European Union didn't demand similar referendums when Croatia and Slovenia declared their independence. Besides, the October 1991 chart describes Bosnia much better than does the March 1992 horoscope.

Ireland was another dilemma. Most Irish astrologers prefer the Easter Rising chart for April 1916 instead of the chart I prefer which is for when a treaty was signed in London in December 1921, one year to the date before the Irish Free State was born. Does Ireland have Libra or Gemini rising? In either case, the Sun is in Sagittarius.

Longitudes and latitudes were obtained from the *International Atlas* published by Astro-Computing Services in San Diego. Finding a place called Rutli in Switzerland proved futile, but since I had been there on my trip to Europe in 1974, I knew precisely where it was located on the south shore of Lake Lucerne. I also had to estimate the coordinates for the enclave of Seborga in northern Italy from places mentioned in the *Los Angeles Times* article.

Most countries have checkered histories, especially France and Germany. The oldest chart I could use for France was for the formation of the Capetian Dynasty in 987 A.D., which was in force until 1792, when the monarchy was overthrown and the First French Republic established. Whether that chart is still in force or not depends on your view of history, I suppose. The French wavered back and forth for another eight decades from republic to monarchy to empire and back to republic in 1870, which in one way or another is still the horoscope one should use for France, irrespective of whether it's the Third, Fourth or Fifth Republic. Changes since 1870 have been constitutional, not governmental.

Technically, Germany didn't have a horoscope until the German Empire was founded in 1871. I had to relocate this chart from Versailles to Berlin before it would work for me. Earlier charts for Germany generally used the coronation of Charlemagne in 800 A.D., but the Pope was resurrecting the Roman Empire, nothing more. With the establishment of the Holy Roman Empire in 962 A.D., that was another matter, for that act did indeed have a major effect on German history for the next nine centuries. Germans insist Charlemagne's empire was their "First Reich" even though most of it was located inside neighboring France and the Low Countries.

With the fall of the German Empire in November 1918, a republic was proclaimed two days before the Armistice was signed. I have chosen to continue examining that chart until the end of World War II as I feel that Hitler's dictatorship and proclamation of the "Third Reich" was an outgrowth of the Weimar Republic chart of November 1918. I also differ on the generally-used dates for the foundation of West Germany in 1949. Most reference works give West Germany's inception as May 1949, when the Basic Law, or Constitution, was promulgated and signed, prior to the Allied Powers surrendering most of their powers to the new nation in September 1949.

England's horoscope is for the coronation of William the Conqueror in December 1066, which is fully-documented and analyzed in my book *Stars Over England*, published by the American Federation of Astrologers. That book also has miniature biographies of all its monarchs. Unfortunately, I could not find dates when the Scottish or Welsh kingdoms came into being.

Countries in Europe have evolved in many ways. The following nations proclaimed their independence from another country: Estonia, Latvia, Lithuania, Belarus, Moldova, Ukraine, Armenia, Azerbaijan and Georgia from the Soviet Union.

| | |
|---|---|
| Finland | from Russia |
| Bosnia, Croatia, Macedonia | |
| Montenegro and Slovenia | from Yugoslavia |
| Slovakia | from Czechoslovakia |
| The Netherlands | from Spain |
| Belgium | from the Netherlands |
| Luxembourg | from Belgium |
| Norway | from Sweden |
| Albania, Bulgaria, Greece, | |
| Romania and Serbia | from the Ottoman Empire |
| Switzerland | from the Holy Roman Empire |

Some countries were granted their independence:

| | |
|---|---|
| Cyprus, Ireland and Malta | from Great Britain |
| Iceland and Sweden | from Denmark |
| The Holy See (Vatican) | from Italy |

Spain was formed with the marriage of Ferdinand and Isabella, which united their kingdoms into one nation.

Yugoslavia was formed when Bosnia, Croatia, Macedonia, Slovenia and Montenegro merged with Serbia at the end of World War I.

Andorra was formed under joint suzerainty with France and Spain.

Gathering data on European cities was relatively easy by comparison to ascertaining the correct founding date of their respective countries. As communities in Europe are often hundreds, if not thousands, of years old, I decided to concentrate on the date when those places were first chartered by their local rulers. King Richard I of England sold charters by the truckload to finance his battles in the Holy Land. I always tried to get the date when the community was first chartered, but that was not always possible. In some cases, only the year was known, and in a few cases, only the century. Some cities in eastern Europe appear not to have been chartered at all. Due to these anomalies, I was unable to erect charts for places like Essen in Germany or most cities in Italy. Cities in Russia had governors, not mayors, until recent times. Most of them were appointed, not elected,

which sort of defeats the purpose of a charter which is to grant an elected body of officials to run the place. So I had to erect founding charts for cities in Russia, Belarus and the Ukraine.

I found the chart for the founding of Rome to be interesting and accurate. The foundation of Rome is the point from which the Roman calendar was measured, Ab Urbe Condita, or AUC. I've also included my rectified charts for London and Paris, both ascertained through research at their respective national libraries. I found it interesting that the degree most British astrologers associate with the city of London (17 Gemini 52) became the Sun of London, not its rising degree. The original charters for Prague and Budapest did not include the month day or year, so I've used the dates when those cities were consolidated: Buda with Pest and Old Prague with New Prague. Most of the data on English cities comes from Harold Wrigglesworth's pamphlet, *The Astrology of Cities & Towns*, which I purchased at a small bookstore in London three decades ago.

No doubt the future may hold many surprises for Europe during the 21st century. A few more countries may be formed, such as Montenegro, which could separate from Serbia, and some parts of Spain may decide to go their own way. With the emergence of the European Union, it's no longer a pipe dream that nations from the Atlantic to the Urals will one day be united in a common purpose. Most countries have loosened border controls and many are using a common currency, the Euro. There is a distinct possibility that this European Union will have one army, one navy and one air force and be less reliant on NATO to keep the peace. Trade and commercial transactions have made things considerably easier since the adoption of the Euro, and the future may be no more complicated than sending something here in America from New York to California. Each individual nation will undoubtedly be responsible for local issues, but major decisions involving Europe will probably be made in places like The Hague, Brussels or Strasbourg. Countries that were in the former Soviet bloc are knocking at the doors of the European Union and NATO. One must remember that Europe west of Russia is slightly larger than the USA east of the Mississippi River. Europe is much smaller than Asia, Africa or South America. It's even smaller than Australia. Individual and regional pecularities will still continue to exist and languages will still have, for a while, their peculiar dialects and idioms. Hopefully, the European Union of the future will produce peace and harmony between nations that for the past two millenia have fought one another for territory or political dominance. If America was the first truly

Aquarian country on earth, then the nations of Europe may well be its continuation and expansion in the Old World.

*Marc Penfield*
*May 2006*

## The Planets in Mundane Astrology

The Sun—Governs the will of the people and their inherent characteristics. Rules all political activities and persons in power and authority.

The Moon—Rules the common people, their personality and desire for change. Also has dominion over the basic necessities of food, clothing and shelter.

Mercury—Rules the people's ability and desire to communicate as well as their literary interests and desire for movement.

Venus—Represents the people's desire to make their community more attractive. Governs high society, the arts and culture.

Mars—Governs the energy of the people. It has dominion over manufacturing and industrial concerns. It rules the police and the military.

Jupiter—Governs the religious and moral principles of the people and their capacity for law and order. Jupiter illustrates the people's desire to elevate themselves physically, financially or spiritually.

Saturn—Rules conservatism and right-wing elements of society. It also shows the ability to accomplish a desired goal and degree of ambition. Saturn also shows the most restrictive elements which must be dealt with lest ruin and disgrace tarnish the reputation of the community.

Uranus—Has dominion over radical and progressive elements and all left-wing activities. Uranus governs riots, rebellions and all acts which upset the general equilibrium of the community.

Neptune—Governs the ideals of the people as well as their desire to communicate with outsiders. Neptune governs the mass media, all chain stores and places which are franchised.

Pluto—Represents the group effort and degree of cooperation that is to be expected to accomplish a desired goal. Pluto rules transformations, such as urban renewal, mergers, foreign alliances and treaties.

## The Houses in Mundane Astrology

First—Represents the people and the first impression one gets when viewing a particular place, as well as its disposition, temperament and personality of its populace. This house acts as a lens through which the rest of the horoscope is filtered.

Second—Represents the people's attitude towards material possessions and their sense of values. It also shows their potential wealth and assets and all places where earnings are deposited.

Third—Shows the people's ability and desire to communicate. Governs the postal service, the mass media and all forms of transportation and literary interests. Also rules lower education.

Fourth—Shows the people's desire for security, especially through the ownership of real estate. It governs houses, apartments and other places of residence, permanent or transient. This house rules agriculture, farmers, miners and those who deal with the land. It might also have something to do with the general weather patterns.

Fifth—Shows the ability of the people to amuse themselves. Governs the theatre, cinema, gambling and prostitution. Also rules the Stock Market as well as children, both forms of speculation.

Sixth—Represents the workers of the community or country, especially those in the employ of the government. All civil service workers, police and military come under its jurisdiction. Along with the first house or Ascendant, it governs general health considerations.

Seventh—Governs the people's ability to relate to outsiders and their desire to form alliances and treaties. Failure to balance and adjust results in conflict and could lead to war.

Eighth—Illustrates the debts of the people and their taxation. All forms of payment to insurance companies or credit card firms are shown by this house. Areas which need to be regenerated or destroyed in order for the entire structure to perform at maximum efficiency.

Ninth—Shows the people's desire for law and order. Governs the courts and the church and all forms of higher education such as colleges and universities. All international concerns and commercial interests come under its dominion.

Tenth—Represents the leader of the people, be it a mayor, governor, president or monarch. Also shows the people's attitude towards those in authority and the reputation of the community. Also shows the outcome of elections and referendums.

Eleventh—Represents the friends, supporters and backers of the community. Shows their legislators, congressmen, senators or aldermen. This house also governs philanthropy and bequests.

Twelfth—Illustrates the hidden ills of the community. Hospitals, asylums, jails and prisons are shown here as well as those who work in those facilities. All those on welfare and support from SSI or unemployment insurance are shown here as well.

## Aspects in Mundane Astrology

Aspects can be either soft or hard, good or bad, positive or negative It all depends on the outlook, but I prefer to think of aspects as either stating specific conditions (soft aspects) or clarifying possible obstacles with which one must learn to cope (hard aspects).

Conjunction (0 deg.)—Neither soft nor hard, it depends on the nature of the planets conjoined which blend often varying natures into a single unit.

Semi-square (45 deg.)—Often mildly irritating and vexating, like a rash that won't go away.

Sextile (60 deg.)—Presents numerous opportunities and social contacts that are highly beneficial.

Square (90 deg.)—Indicates obstacles which must be overcome and the areas of life that need the most improvement or attention.

Trine (120 deg.)—Indicates a harmonious state of being and luck but in itself is rather passive and lacking in energy.

Sesquare (135 deg.)—Indicates continual frustration and annoyance often with mental manifestations which require patience and calm.

Inconjunct or Quincunx (150 deg.)—Like mixing oil and vinegar, two forces which will never really mix and have little in common. Also the "fly in the ointment or monkey wrench" situation which requires adjustment, alteration or radical elimination.

Opposition (180 deg.)—Indicates a literal opposition as to either temperament or methodology that exists between two forces that could lead to either cooperation or conflict depending on the circumstances.

# Albania
## Republika E Shqiperise

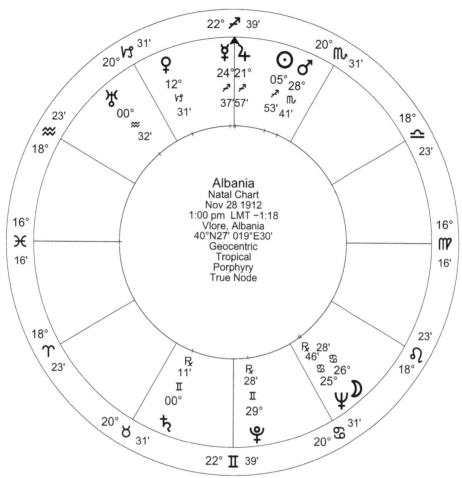

**Chart 1, November 28, 1912, 1:00 p.m. LMT, Vlore, Albania**
**Source:** *The Times* of London

Albania is situated on the eastern shore of the Adriatic Sea in the southwest part of the Balkan Peninsula. Marshy along the coast, the land rises to a plateau covered by scrub forests. The coastline is 275 miles long and the highest point is Mt. Korab (9,070 ft.) along the Macedonian border.

Population: 3,510,484; 95% Albanian, 3% Greek

Religion: 70% Moslem, 20% Orthodox, 10% Catholic

Area: 10,600 square miles (size of Maryland or Belgium); 25% arable, 41% urban

Capital: Tirana

Exports: Chromium, nickel, petroleum, tobacco and copper

Albania was known as Illyria to the Romans who conquered the region in 168 BC. After the fall of the Western Roman Empire in 476 AD, it became part of the vast Byzantine Empire. Serbian and Bulgarian tribes invaded the region in the 9th century and between 1271 and 1368, Albania was ruled by the Kingdom of Sicily. Albania fell to Ottoman armies in 1468 and was virtually ignored until November 28, 1912 (chart 1) when this tiny country declared its independence.

Albania was invaded by Italian forces in August 1914 at the beginning of what was to become World War I (progressed MC conjunct Mercury, ruler of the DESC). In 1925, a Republic was proclaimed with Ahmed Zog as president (transiting Uranus conjunct ASC). By September 1928, Zog proclaimed himself king (progressed Sun conjunct Jupiter, ruler of MC. In April 1939, Albania was forcefully annexed to Italy (transiting Neptune square MC; transiting Pluto opposition Uranus). Mussolini's troops invaded in June 1940 (progressed MC semisquare Sun; progressed ASC square Jupiter). With the fall of Italy to

1

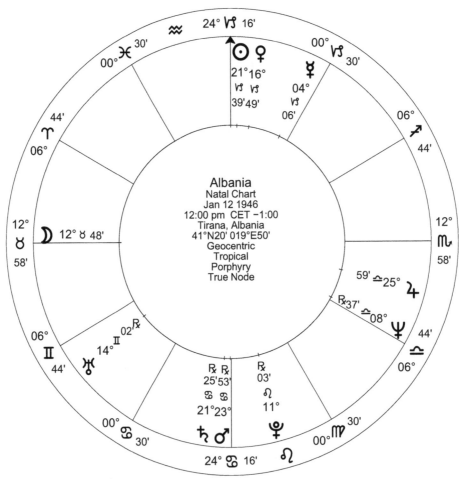

**Chart 2, January 12, 1946, noon MET, Tirana, Albania**
**Source: Encyclopedia Britannica for the date; no time found in newspapers; noon birth used.**

the Allies in August 1943, Albania was invaded by the Germans (progressed MC opposition Neptune; progressed ASC semisquare Pluto in the fourth).

On January 12, 1946 (chart 2), Albania was proclaimed a Communist People's Republic, the monarchy having been dissolved. Albania was the most obedient satellite of the Soviet Union until March 1961, when an ideological rift caused Albania to switch allegiance to Communist China (progressed Sun trine Neptune, progressed MC opposition Pluto, ruler of seventh house of alliances). By January 1967, all places of worship were closed and services were banned (progressed Sun trine Uranus). Albania left the Warsaw Pact in January 1968 (progressed MC semisquare Mercury; progressed ASC conjunct Uranus).

By July 1978, Communist China had cut off all military and economic assistance, leaving Albania to fend for itself (progressed Sun trine Jupiter, transiting Jupiter conjunct Saturn; transiting Uranus opposition Moon square Pluto). Albania was now the poorest country in Europe and remains so to this day. Enver Hoxha, ruler of Albania for nearly four de-

cades, died in April 1985 (transiting Jupiter trine Uranus). To alleviate their economic suffering, thousands of refugees left the country in a boatlift to Italy in 1991 (progressed Sun inconjunct Neptune; progressed MC sesquare Jupiter inconjunct Pluto; progressed ASC opposition Mercury). Later that year, in October 1991, Communists were ousted from the government and Albania's international isolation began to end (transiting Neptune inconjunct Uranus).

By January 1997, a financial pyramid scheme with ties to the Italian mafia collapsed, riots ensued, and most Albanians lost their life savings (progressed Sun square Uranus in the second house; progressed ASC square Neptune, the planet of scams). Transiting Neptune had been sitting on the MC for more than a year and Jupiter crossed the MC when the enormity of the financial loss was revealed. In March 1999, hundreds of thousands of ethnic Albanians from neighboring Kosovo in Serbia poured into Albania as NATO planes were bombing their homeland as Serbian troops were again "ethnically cleansing" their country (progressed Sun sextile Venus; transiting Uranus trine Uranus; transiting Pluto trine Pluto).

# Tirana

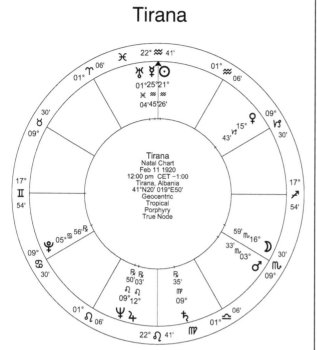

**February 11, 1920, noon MET Source: Albanian Assn. of Astrology for the date; noon presumed**

Tirana was founded in 1614 by Ottoman Turks. Capital of Albania only since 1920, it was rebuilt by King Zog during the 1930s, but construction was halted after the Italian and German invasions.

# Andorra
## Principat d'Andorra

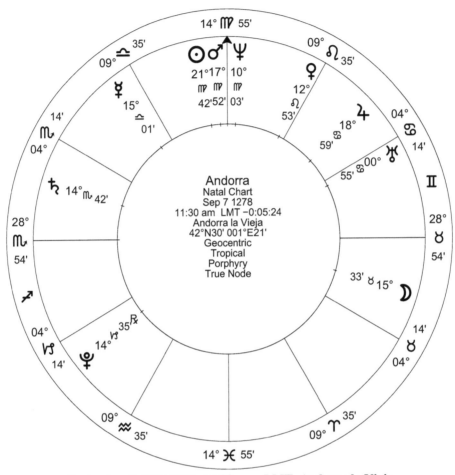

**September 7, 1278 (OS), 11:30 a.m. LMT, Andorra la Vieja**
**Source: Bibliotheque Nationale in Paris for the date; no time has been mentioned anywhere; time is rectified**

Andorra is situated in the Pyrenees mountains, a region of deep gorges and narrow valleys. The highest point is 9,500 feet.

Population: 67,627; 61% Catalan, 30% Andorran; 6% French

Religion: 99% Catholic

Area: 174 square miles (the size of of Brooklyn and Queens in New York); 93% urban, 4% arable

Economy: Over 80% of its revenue comes from tourism. Smuggling was once the most profitable business. The main export is tobacco.

Andorra was granted a charter by Charlemagne in the 9th century for its assistance in ridding France of the Muslims. In 954 A.D., Andorra passed into the hands of the Bishop of Urgel, but by 1208 Andorra had become the property of the Count of Foix in France. Joint suzerainty was established on September 7, 1278 between the Bishop of Urgel and the Comte de Foix. In 1793,

France renounced all rights to the region (progressed MC square Moon and progressed MC sesquare Uranus, ruler of third house). Fortunately, the progressed ASC was also sextile Venus, ruler of the seventh house of treaties and agreements.

Men were given the right to vote in 1933 (progressed Sun sextile Neptune in ninth) and by 1970, women were also given the right to vote (progressed Sun square Saturn inconjunct Pluto; progressed ASC trine Uranus). Andorra adopted its first income tax in 1977 (progressed MC square Moon and Saturn, rulers of the second and eighth houses). In March 1993, Andorra approved its first Constitution, thus abolishing Europe's last feudal political system and forming a parliamentary form of government (progressed MC sextile Uranus sesquare Pluto, ruler of ASC; progressed ASC sextile Mars in tenth; transiting Uranus trine Sun and Pluto was crossing the ASC).

# Armenia
## Haikakan Hanrapetoutioun

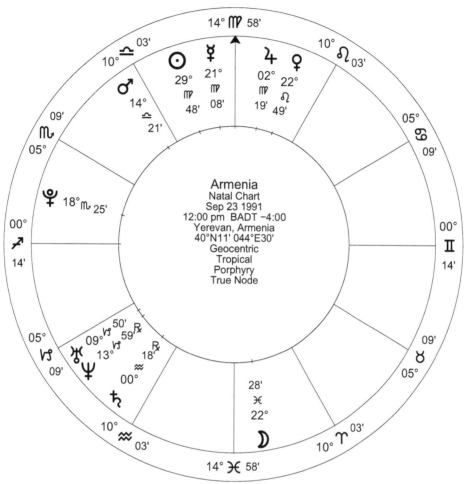

**September 23, 1991, noon BGT/DST, 8:00 a.m. GMT, Yerevan**
**Source: Book of World Horoscopes by Nicholas Campion**

Armenia is situated in the center of the Trans-Caucasus region between the Caspian and Black Seas at the juncture of Europe and Asia. Most of the region is more than 3,000 ft. in elevation, the highest point being Mt. Aragats (elev. 13,420 ft.).

Population: 3,336,100; 93% Armenian, 3% Azeri, 2% Russian

Religion: 94% Orthodox

Area: 11,506 square mi (the size of Belgium or New Hampshire); 70% urban, 17% arable

Economy: Main exports are cotton, figs, citrus fruits and grapes. Main resources are copper and zinc.

Capital: Yerevan (Erivan)

The first Armenian kingdom was established in 317 B.C., one century before the Greeks arrived in 211 B.C.; Romans came in 69 B.C. and ruled Armenia until 232 A.D. The region was partitioned between Persia and Asia Minor in 387 A.D. around the time Armenia became the first country to make Christianity its official state religion. Arab invaders came in 653 A.D. but had little overall influence in changing the status quo. Direct rule from the Byzantine capital in Constantinople began in 1046, two centuries before the Mongols laid waste to the region.

Russian occupation began in 1828 and lasted until Armenia first declared its independence in May 1918. But freedom was short-lived due to the arrival of the Bolsheviks in December 1920. Armenia joined the USSR in December 1922 as part of the Trans-Caucasus Republic and became a separate republic 14 years later.

With the break-up of the Soviet Union, Armenia

again declared its independence in September 1991. Shortly thereafter, fighting broke out with neighboring Azerbaijan over the disputed region of Nagorno-Karabakh (progressed MC sesquare Saturn; progressed ASC semisquare Mars). In October 1999, the Prime Minister was shot by terrorists during an attempted coup in Parliament (progressed Sun semisquare Venus; progressed MC opposition Moon; transiting Neptune inconjunct Jupiter). Since independence, over one-third of Armenia's people have emigrated due to a pervasive energy shortage. Many went to America.

# Yerevan (Erivan)

The capital and largest city of Armenia is one of the longest inhabited places on Earth. Situated only eight miles from the Turkish border, Yerevan lies on the crossroads of trade routes from Russia and Anatolia (Turkey) to Persia. Settled as early as the 8th century B.C., Yerevan has endured many severe earthquakes during its long history. The tremor of late 1988 killed more than 25,000 and laid waste to much of the city.

# Austria
# Republik Osterreich

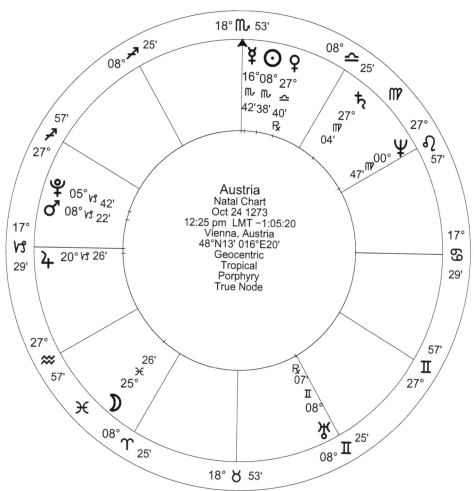

**Chart 1, October 24, 1273, 12:25 p.m. LMT, Vienna**
**Source: Encyclopedia Brittanica for the date; noontime assumed;**
**chart relocated from Aix (Aachen) Germany to Vienna, Austria**

Austria is located in the heart of Europe. Its western region, the Tyrol, is completely surrounded by the Alps; other regions include Styria, Carinthia and Burgenland, as well as Upper and Lower Austria. The highest point is Grossglockner (elev. 12,460 ft.) in the Alps.

Population: 8,150,835; 93% Germanic, 2% Yugoslavian, 2% Turkish

Religion: 78% Catholic, 6% Protestant, 4% Moslem

Area: 32,377 square miles (the size of Maine or the Czech Republic); 65% urban, 18% arable

Economy: Main exports are iron and steel, machinery, textiles, wood and paper products, chemicals. The main resource is lead.

The Romans began their conquest of this region they called Pannonia in 16 B.C., but in the 5th century A.D., the Huns and Ostrogoths drove out the Romans. By 803 A.D., Ostreich became part of Charlemagne's empire. Otto I captured the region from Hungarian invaders in 955 and by 962 was crowned as the first Holy Roman Emperor. In 976, Leopold of the Babenberg Dynasty became Count of Ostmark and his heirs ruled until 1246, when their dynasty died out shortly after an invasion by the Mongols. In 1252, Ottokar, King of Bohemia, gained possession of Austria. What followed for the next two decades was called the Interregnum.

Rudolf von Hapsburg was elected Holy Roman Emperor in Frankfurt, Germany on August 24, 1273 and was crowned in Aix (Aachen), Germany on October 24, 1273 (chart 1). Ottokar was furious and vowed revenge, but in August 1278, he was defeated, thus paving the way for total Hapsburg control of Austria. On Christmas Day 1282, two kings were crowned in Vienna whose heirs would rule most of central Europe for the next six centuries. The name Hapsburg is a corruption of the name of their family castle, Habichtsburg (which lies in Switzerland), which means "hawk's castle." By 1438, the Hapsburg had become titular rulers of the Holy Roman Empire (progressed MC trine Pluto). Hapsburg expansion into western Europe began in 1477, when Maximilian I married Mary of Burgundy and received the Netherlands in her dowry (progressed MC sesquare Venus, ruler of fourth and placed in the ninth house of foreign countries). Maximilian then arranged for his son, Philip, to marry Juana of Castile, daughter of Ferdinand and Isabella. Their son, Charles I, became king of Spain in 1516 and Holy Roman Emperor in 1519 as Charles V. He arranged for his grandson, Ferdinand, to become king of Hungary. Thus through strategically placed alliances did the Hapsburg Dynasty add territory and wealth. At one time the Hapsburgs ruled not only Austria but also Hungary, Bohemia, the Netherlands, Spain and parts of Italy, Poland and Croatia.

In 1529, Suleiman the Magnificent, Sultan of Turkey, was halted at the gates of Vienna (progressed Sun opposition Jupiter; progressed ASC inconjunct Moon, ruler of the seventh house of open enemies). The Turks again laid siege to Vienna in 1683, but were turned back with the aid of Polish troops under King John Sobieski (progressed Sun inconjunct Sun; progressed ASC square Mars inconjunct Sun).

During the 18th century Austria was involved in numerous conflicts. The War of the Spanish Succession erupted in 1701, when Louis XIV of France tried to place one of his relatives on the Spanish throne (progressed MC sesquare Uranus; progressed ASC opposition Mercury). The War of the Polish Succession began in 1773 (progressed Sun semisquare Pluto; progressed MC opposition Neptune). Napoleon, Emperor of France, dissolved the Holy Roman Empire in August 1806, after ruling central Europe for nearly a millennium (progressed Sun opposition Venus inconjunct Saturn, ruler of ASC; progressed MC opposition Sun trine Mars; progressed ASC inconjunct Juptier sesquare Pluto, ruler of MC).

Revolutions broke out all across Europe in March 1848 in reaction to the harsh policies of Prince Metternich, the Henry Kissinger of his day. A resurgence of nationalism erupted in France, which brought down the monarchy and demanded a constitution for Germany (progressed Sun conjunct Uranus; progressed MC inconjunct Mercury; progressed

ASC trine Jupiter). Austria lost Lombardy to Italy in 1859 (progressed MC square Saturn; progressed ASC conjunct Saturn) and ceded Venice to Italy in 1866 (progressed Sun sesquare Sun).

On February 2, 1867, a dual monarchy was formed with Hungary which created the largest empire in Europe, ruling more than 50 million subjects in an area of nearly 300,000 square miles (progressed Sun square Moon; progressed MC opposition Pluto). On June 28, 1914, the heir to the Austro-Hungarian throne, Archduke Franz Ferdinand, was gunned down with his wife in the Bosnian city of Sarajevo by a Serbian sympathizer named Gavrilo Princip, a student terrorist working for the Black Hand. Austria was outraged and sent steep demands to Serbia, knowing that Serbia could not comply. On July 28, 1914, the Austrians began shelling the Serbian capital of Belgrade, thus beginning World War I (progressed Sun sesquare Moon; progressed MC inconjunct Jupiter sesquare Pluto; progressed ASC conjunct Sun sesquare Moon; transiting Jupiter square MC; transiting Saturn square Saturn; transiting Uranus square Sun). Before the week was out, most of Europe had jumped into the conflict on one side or another; Germany decided to side with Austria despite its previous political and dynastic differences.

On November 21, 1916, the aged Emperor Franz Josef died at age 86 (progressed Sun semisquare Saturn; progressed MC sesquare Mars). Two years later with the empire crumbling and in ruins, Germany signed the Armistice and on November 11, 1918 the greatest conflict the world had ever seen up to that time finally ended. The following day the monarchy was abolished and the first republic proclaimed (progressed MC inconjunct Moon; progressed ASC semisquare Saturn; transiting Saturn sextile Venus; transiting Neptune square Sun; transiting Pluto opposition Pluto).

Austria (chart 2) was now a shell of its former self. Reduced over 90 percent to its present size, it was a nation of only seven million souls. Austria had lost 1.2 million soldiers in the war and 3.5 million were placed on the casualty list. Despite the fact that Austria fought on the same side as Germany, the aftermath during the 1920s was less harsh for Austria than her neighbor. During the early days of the worldwide economic depression, Austrian banks suspended payments on foreign accounts in 1931 and reverberations were felt all across Europe (progressed Sun square Moon). By 1933, with the rise of Hitler in Germany, Chancellor Dollfuss signed an alliance with Mussolini in Italy to counteract Nazism (progressed MC sextile Mercury; progressed ASC oppo-

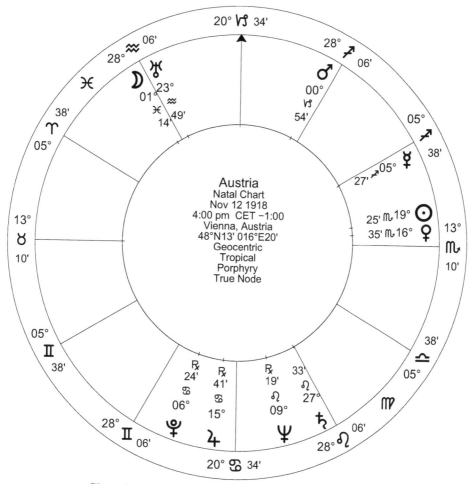

**Chart 2, November 12, 1918, 4:00 p.m. MET, Vienna**
**Source:** *Book of World Horoscopes* by Nicholas Campion. Astrologer Luc de Marre gives 3:55 p.m.

sition Mercury). The Chancellor was assassinated the next year in July 1934, possibly by Nazis seeking revenge on their Germanic brethren (progressed Sun conjunct Mercury; progressed MC inconjunct Pluto; transiting Jupiter square Jupiter; transiting Saturn opposition Saturn; transiting Uranus trine Mars). By March 1938, Hitler completely annexed Austria (the Anschluss) into the Third Reich (progressed Sun trine Neptune; progressed MC opposition Neptune; transiting Saturn square Pluto; transiting Uranus conjunct ASC; transiting Neptune trine MC). Austria's leader, von Schuschnigg, was thrown into a concentration camp.

With the end of World War II and the fall of the Third Reich, Austria was divided into four military zones of occupation by the Allies and the Soviets (progressed Sun inconjunct Jupiter, progressed MC square Venus; progressed ASC inconjunct Sun; transiting Saturn sesquare Uranus). The war had killed 280,000 Austrians and more than 350,000 were wounded. The Second Austrian Republic was formed in December 1949 (progressed ASC trine Uranus) and on May 15, 1955, Austria regained its

sovereignty with the ending of military occupation (progressed MC opposition Saturn, ruler of the MC). The new rules forbade Austria from forming a customs union with Germany, and Austria was to remain perpetually neutral (transiting Mars trine Uranus; transiting Saturn conjunct Venus; progressed Pluto opposition Uranus).

In June 1986, Kurt Waldheim became chancellor of Austria with much controversy due to his association with Nazis during the war (progressed Sun inconjunct Saturn; progressed ASC inconjunct Uranus). Despite previous obstacles and restrictions, Austria became a member of the European Union in January 1995 (progressed Sun inconjunct Pluto; progressed MC square Pluto; progressed ASC inconjunct Mars). The European Union placed sanctions on Austria from February through September 2000, due to fears that Joerg Haider's Freedom Party would gain a foothold in Parliament. Their political philosophy reminded many of the horrors of Nazi Germany, replete with hate-mongering and talk of national superiority.

# Vienna (Wien)

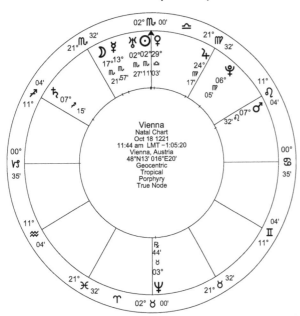

**October 18, 1221, 11:44 a.m. LMT**
**Source: Magistrat der Stadt**

The capital and largest city of Austria lies on the banks of the Danube River. Founded by the Romans and named Vindobona, the old city was built in a circle, the center of which is now St. Stephen's Cathedral, whose majestic spire towers 450 feet above the city. Vienna is known as an Imperial City due to influence ranging from the Babenbergs through the Hapsburgs. Sacked twice by the Turks (in 1529 and 1683), Vienna managed to repel the Turks from dominating central Europe once and for all. In 1850, the old walls were torn down and replaced by a series of wide boulevards called the Ringstrasse. Along this promenade are the Hofburg (royal palace) with its 2,600 rooms, the Rathaus (city hall), the university, the Austrian Parliament, the Burg Theatre and the Royal Opera House. The best example of Baroque church architecture is to be found in the Karlskirche, erected in 1713. Vienna also has two other royal palaces: the Belvedere and Schonbrunn, modeled after Versailles.

For art lovers, Vienna has the Kunsthistorisches, but Vienna is also home to those famous white stallions, the Lippanzaners, as well as the famed Vienna Boys Choir. But Vienna is known mostly for its music, the city of Mozart, Haydn, Beethoven, Brahms and Schubert. But it's those Straus waltzes that evoke memories of this highly cosmopolitan and sophisticated city at a time when it was home to the largest empire in Europe.

# Graz

Austria's second-largest city and capital of Styria is located 85 miles southwest of Vienna. During the 12th century it was a fortress town and trading and now it's the heart of Austria's iron and steel industry.

# Innsbruck

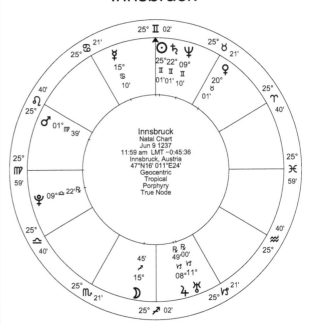

**June 9, 1237, 11:59 a.m. LMT**
**Source: Stadtmagistrat**

Austria's fifth-largest city and capital of the Tyrol is located on the River Inn about 85 miles west of Salzburg. Innsbruck hosted the Winter Olympics of 1964 and 1976. Tourism is the main industry due to the fine Alpine skiing. The main sites are the Hofburg and the Hofkirche.

# Linz

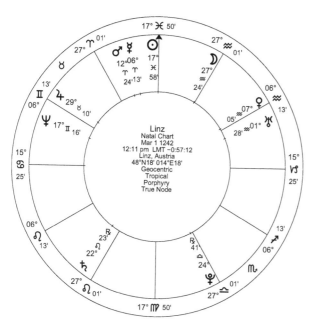

**March 1, 1942, 12:11 p.m. LMT**
**Source: Oberosterreichisches Landesarchiv**

Austria's third-largest city and capital of Upper Austria lies on the Danube River 100 miles west of Vienna. The main sights are its two cathedrals: the Alter Dom in the Baroque style and the Neuer Dom in the Gothic. Linz also has Austria's oldest place of worship, the Martinskirche, erected in the 9th century.

# Salzburg

Austria's fourth-largest city lies on the Salzach River 160 miles west of Vienna. Founded in 798 A.D., and subsequently governed by archbishops, it became part of Austria only in 1806. The Romans knew this place as Juvavum, famous for its salt, hence its current name of "salt town." Salzburg is famous for being the birth place of Mozart and hosts a music festival each summer. The main sights are the castle, Hohensalzburg, the home of the archbishops, Residenz, and its Cathedral, the Dom.

# Azerbaijan
## Azerbaijchan Cumhuriyeti

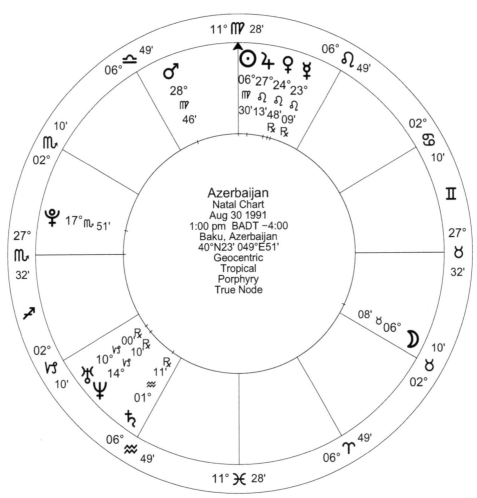

**August 30, 1991, 1:00 p.m. BGDT, 9:00 a.m. GMT**
**Source: Los Angeles Times says 9:00 a.m. GMT**

Azerbaijan is located on the western shore of the Caspian Sea. Over 40 percent of the country is lowlands and 10 percent lies below sea level. The Greater and Lesser Caucasus Mountains are separated by the fertile river valleys of the Kura and Arak.

Population: 7,771,092; 83% Azeri, 6% Armenian, 6% Russian

Religion: 93% Moslem, 5% Orthodox

Area: 33,436 square miles (the size of Maine or the Czech Republic); 59% urban, 18% arable

Economy: Oil refining and natural gas are its main industries. Major exports besides petroleum and natural gas include iron, copper, lead, zinc, cotton and textiles.

Capital: Baku

King Atropates established an independent state during the 4th century in a region known in ancient times as Scythia. Turkish armies overran the area during the 11th century to be followed by the Persians and Mongols two centuries later. Russia conquered the region in 1813, but its southern part was ceded to neighboring Iran 15 years later. A railroad to the Black Sea was completed in 1883, enabling Baku to become the world's leading oil producer of the late 19th century.

In May 1918, an independent republic was formed, but freedom was fleeting as the Soviet army entered two years later. Azerbaijan became a charter member of the USSR in December 1922 as part of the Trans-Caucasus Republic. In December 1936, it became a separate republic. In 1988, fighting with Armenia began over the ethnic enclave of Nagorno-Karabakh, which continues today.

Azerbaijan again declared its independence from

the dying Soviet Union on August 30, 1991. World attention was soon focused on oil pollution in the Caspian Sea and this country became famous for being the world's most ecologically-devastated region. In November 1995, a new constitution expanded the powers of the president (progressed ASC sextile Saturn) and in January 2001, Azerbaijan was admitted to the Council of Europe.

## Baku

The capital and largest city of Azerbaijan lies on the western shore of the Caspian Sea in the mist of one of the world's richest oil fields. A pipeline runs from Baku to the Black Sea port of Batumi. Baku was founded in the 11th century and achieved fame in the Middle Ages for its silk and saffron. Baku was part of Persia from the 16th to the 19th centuries.

# Belarus
## Respublika Belarus

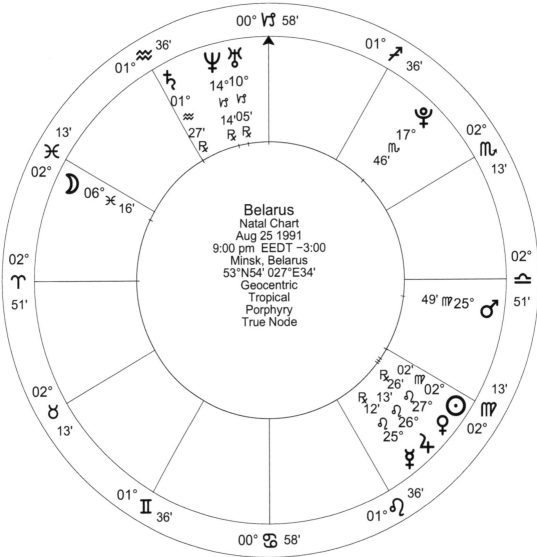

**August 25, 1991, 9:00 p.m. EET/DST, 6:00 p.m. GMT, Minsk**
**Source: Nicholas Campion, in his *Book of World Horoscopes*, states independence took place sometime between 2:54 p.m. and 6:00 p.m. GMT. The latest time is the one I selected to be the most appropriate.**

Situated in eastern Europe between Poland and Russia, Belarus is a region of hilly lowlands with numerous swamps and peat marshes. Belarus has more than 10,000 lakes within its borders. The highest point of land is only 1,135 feet above sea level.

Population: 10,350,194; 78% Belarussian, 13% Russian, 4% Polish

Religion: 80% Orthodox

Area: 80,154 square miles (the size of Nebraska or twice the size of Bulgaria); 30% arable, 71% urban

Economy: Main exports are chemicals, fertilizer, motor vehicles and machinery. Main resources are peat and timber, and the chief crop is potatoes.

Belarus was settled by Slavic tribes in the 5th century A.D. Four centuries later it came under domination from Kiev and became known as White Russia (Byelorussia). Lithuania conquered the region in 1326 and ousted the Kievans. After Poland united with Lithuania in 1569, Belarus became part of Poland. After the third and final partition of Poland in 1795, White Russia became part of the vast Russian Empire.

Independence from the Russian Empire was proclaimed in early 1918, even though the country was occupied by the Germans. Freedom lasted only until August 1920, when the Bolsheviks moved in. In December 1922, Byelorussia became a charter member of the USSR. In the opening days of World War II, in September 1939, Byelorussia recaptured territory it was forced to cede to Poland during World War I. German troops occupied the region from 1941 until the Soviets came in 1944 and rid Belarus of the Nazis. The nuclear meltdown at Chernobyl in neighboring Ukraine in 1986 forced many to evacuate as poisonous clouds from the disaster filtered over Belarus.

Independence was again proclaimed on August 25, 1991. In December 1991, Belarus became a charter member of the Commonwealth of Independent States (CIS), whose capital was to be Minsk. Due to increasing economic and financial problems, Belarus adopted the Russian ruble as its currency in 1994 (progressed Sun opposition Moon; progressed ASC sesquare Venus, ruler of the second house).

In November 1996, an authoritarian constitution granted its leader, Lukashenko, vast new powers (progressed MC sextile Moon; progressed ASC inconjunct Pluto; transiting Saturn square MC; transiting Pluto square Sun trine ASC). In April 1997, Belarus signed a treaty to integrate the political and economic systems with Russia.

## Minsk

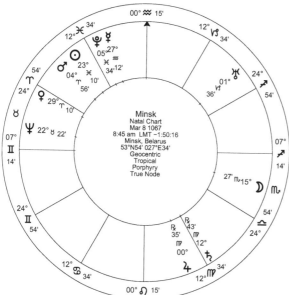

**March 8, 1067 (OS), 8:45 a.m. LMT**
**Source: Year from Lenin Library in Moscow; date rectified from numerous sources; time also rectified**

First mentioned in 1067, Minsk means "exchange" in Belarussian (Gemini rising). Sacked by Ukrainian troops in 1096 (progressed MC opposition Jupiter; progressed ASC square Mars), the city fell to Lithuanian troops in 1320 (progressed MC opposition Mars; progressed ASC square Pluto). Absorbed by Poland in 1569 (progressed MC square Saturn), it became part of Russia in 1793 (progressed MC sesquare Saturn; progressed ASC square Jupiter). Napoleon used Minsk as a supply base during his invasion of Russia in 1812 (progressed MC semisquare Uranus; progressed ASC square Sun), it was occupied by Germans during 1918 (progressed MC square Mercury, ruler of the ASC; progressed ASC opposition Pluto).

Minsk's darkest chapter occurred between July 1941 (progressed ASC trine Neptune) and July 1944 (progressed ASC opposition Sun) when the Nazis leveled the city due to its majority Jewish population. When the Russians liberated Minsk, 80 percent of the city was in ruins and half its population had died or been sent to concentration camps. By May 1945, Minsk had only 20 percent of its pre-war population.

Capital and largest city of Belarus, as well as headquarters of the CIS, Minsk is a major railroad center and industrial supplier. Gemini rising indicates the overall newness of the city with little remaining of historical interest except the Mariinsky Cathedral. With Mercury, ruler of the ASC in the tenth house, Minsk has been a railroad hub for more than a century, and with Pluto square the ASC, this city has repeatedly been overrun by invading armies. Neptune, ruler of the Sun, in the twelfth house, could indicate that this city would be a jumping-off point for Jewish emigration. Czar Nicholas I, in 1835, forced Jews to live in the region and regular pogroms caused untold horrors. Minsk is the largest city between Moscow and Warsaw.

Population: 1,671,600

# Belgium
## Koninkrijk Belgie—Royaume De Belgique

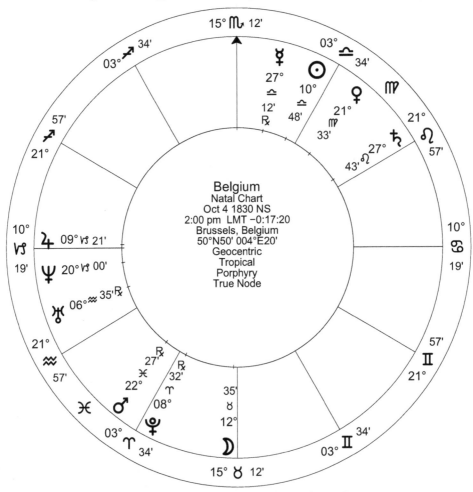

Belgium
Natal Chart
Oct 4 1830 NS
2:00 pm LMT −0:17:20
Brussels, Belgium
50°N50' 004°E20'
Geocentric
Tropical
Porphyry
True Node

**October 4, 1830, 2:00 p.m. LMT, Brussels**
**Source: Archives du Royaume states "mid-afternoon." Astrologers Sandy Dumont and Grietje Versatel prefer the date of November 18, 1830 between 3:00 and 3:15 p.m., according to Charles E. O. Carter**

Belgium is situated in northwestern Europe on the eastern shore of the North Sea. Most of its territory is flat except for a hilly region in the southeast called the Ardennes, where Botrange, its highest point at 2,290 feet, is located. The coastline is only 40 miles long and the main rivers are the Schelde, Meuse and Sambre.

Capital: Brussels

Population: 10,258.762; 55% Flemish, 33% Walloon

Religion: 70% Catholic, 25% Protestant, 4% Moslem

Area: 11,780 square miles (the size of Maryland or Albania); 25% arable, 97% urban

Economy: The main exports are chemicals, linen and textiles, iron, steel and glassware. Main resources are iron and coal. Belgium ranks second in world diamond cutting.

Roman legions conquered the Belgae in 50 B.C. and five centuries later, Prankish tribes overran the region. In 496 A.D., King Clovis of France accepted Christianity and Belgium became part of his empire. The Treaty of Verdun in 843 A.D. divided Belgium between France and Lorraine and by the 12th century, the duchies of Brabant, Liege, Hainaut and Luxembourg rose to wealth due to a large merchant class.

In 1308, the Golden Age of Belgium began as King Henry VII of Luxembourg ascended the throne. The Joyeuse Entree, Belgium's Magna Carta, was signed in 1356, but in 1384, Belgium was annexed to Burgundy and previous liberties were curbed. Liberties were restored in 1477 as Belgium passed into Hapsburg hands. Belgium was then passed to Burgundy in 1519 as a wedding gift to Maximilian by Emperor Charles V. Further repression ensued in 1556 when King Philip II of Spain took control. At the time he was married to England's Queen Mary. Belgians revolted against Spanish rule in 1566 and churches were sacked and burned. The Pacification of Ghent in November 1576 pledged eventual independence, so when the seven northern provinces of the Netherlands separated from Spain in January 1579, Belgium sought peace with Spain.

All Protestant activity was stamped out in 1621 during the early days of the Thirty Years War which pitted Catholic against Protestant. When the Treaty of Westphalia was signed in 1648 ending Europe's most horrific conflict up to that time, France grabbed territory from southern Belgium. The Treaty of Rijswijk in 1697 limited further French incursions. In 1702, however, France laid claim to the Spanish Netherlands, thus fomenting the War of the Spanish Succession. The Treaty of Utrecht in 1713 saw Belgium transferred from Spanish to Austrian rule, but still under the Hapsburgs.

Some reforms were made in the 1780s, but in 1796, Napoleon annexed the entire region into his growing empire. When Napoleon was finally defeated at the battle of Waterloo outside Brussels in June 1815, the Treaty of Vienna made Belgium part of the Kingdom of the Netherlands.

In August 1830, a revolt began in a Brussels opera house against rule from Amsterdam and by October 4, 1830, independence had been proclaimed. Formalities were worked out six weeks later in mid-November 1830. By July 1831, Prince Leopold of Saxe-Coburg-Gotha was chosen to be its first king; he was an uncle to England's Queen Victoria (progressed ASC square Sun). In April 1839, the provinces of Limburg and Luxembourg were partitioned (progressed MC semisquare Jupiter sesquare Pluto; progressed ASC conjunct Neptune; progressed Sun square Neptune). Luxembourg dates its independence from this date.

In July 1885, the Congo Free State was created in central Africa, a region of more than one million square miles with large reserves of rubber and ivory (progressed MC conjunct Jupiter square Sun; progressed Sun sextile Uranus, ruler of the second house). In 1900, unemployment and health insurance began (progressed ASC semisquare Pluto). In September 1908, the Congo was annexed as a Belgian colony (progressed ASC trine Uranus; transiting Jupiter conjunct Saturn; transiting Saturn conjunct Pluto).

World War I began in August 1914 with Belgium proclaiming its neutrality (transiting Saturn sextile Saturn), but the Germans turned a deaf ear and turned Belgium into the battleground of Europe (progressed MC sex Pluto). When the Armistice was signed in November 1918, more than 14,000 had died at the front and more than 45,000 wounded (progressed Sun conjunct Jupiter; transiting Jupiter trine MC; transiting Saturn conjunct Saturn; transiting Neptune trine Pluto).

Belgium became officially bilingual in 1932 (progressed MC trine Mercury opposition Saturn). Belgium again proclaimed its neutrality in May 1940 but again the Germans ignored and invaded (progressed MC semisquare Neptune; progressed ASC opposition Jupiter square Pluto). King Leopold decided to surrender to the Germans and was then held prisoner for the duration of the war (transiting Uranus sextile Mars; transiting Neptune opposition Mars). Belgians felt the King should have put up a stronger fight against the Nazi invaders, so when the war ended in May 1945, he was not permitted to sit on the throne again (progressed Sun conjunct Uranus; progressed MC inconjunct Sun; progressed ASC semisquare Saturn; transiting Saturn square Pluto; transiting Pluto trine Pluto). The war total included 8,000 on the battlefield and more than 55,000 wounded. A long period of reconstruction began, aided by the formation of BENELUX, a trade pact with the Netherlands and Luxembourg signed in January 1948 (progressed Sun sextile Pluto; progressed MC sextile Moon; transiting Uranus square Mars and Venus). King Leopold II tried to regain his throne in 1950, but a revolt ensued and Baudoin was chosen the new King in July 1951 (progressed Sun square Moon).

Belgium joined the European Union in January 1958 (progressed ASC sextile Venus trine Mars; transiting Jupiter sextile Saturn). By June 1960, Belgium had decided to grant freedom to the Congo as a civil war was about to erupt (progressed Sun inconjunct Venus; progressed MC inconjunct Mercury and Saturn). Higher taxes were imposed on the Belgians due to the loss of the Congo. In 1970, Belgium was divided into three sectors based on language (progressed MC sextile Uranus). In January 2002, those regional governments of Flanders, Wallonia and Brussels were now responsible for agriculture and foreign trade (progressed MC semisquare Mars; progressed ASC inconjunct Mars, natally in the second house of financial matters).

# Antwerp (Antwerpen)

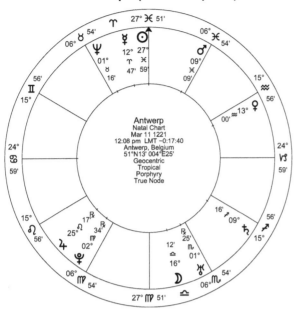

**March 11, 1221, 12:08 p.m. LMT**
**Source: Stadsarchief**

The second-largest city in Belgium and its largest port is situated on the Schelde River 55 miles from the North Sea and 30 miles north of Brussels. During the Middle Ages it was one of the wealthiest trade centers in Europe. The Spanish came in 1576 and in 1648 they closed the port which caused the city's fortunes to decline dramatically. The French came in 1795 and the Germans invaded during both World Wars in the 20th century. Antwerp was heavily bombed in 1944 and today is a major center of the diamond trade with its numerous diamond-cutting firms. Antwerp is home to the Bourse, the world's first Stock Exchange, and its port ranks as one of the top 10 on earth. Antwerp was also the home of the Flemish painter, Peter Paul Rubens.

# Brussels (Bruxxeles)

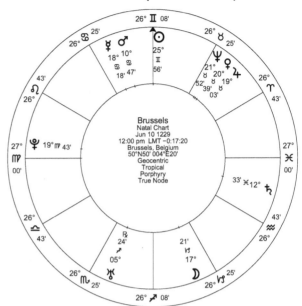

**June 10, 1229, noon LMT**
**Source: Archives du Royaume**

The capital and largest city of Belgium was founded in 580 A.D. on an island in the River Senne. During the 13th century it became seat of the Dukes of Brabant. The French burned the city in 1695 and occupied it exactly a century later. Germans invaded during both World Wars. Since 1958, when Brussels hosted a World's Fair, it has been the administrative headquarters for the EEC (European Common Market). It's also home to NATO and many view it as the capital of Europe as well. Brussels sits in an autonomous region of Belgium (the others being Flanders and Wallonie) and is bilingual and bicultural.

The main sight in Brussels is the Grand Place, which many say is the most magnificent public square in Europe. Fronting it is the Hotel de Ville (City Hall) with its 315 foot spire. A few blocks away is the Mannekin-Pis, a cute little statue of a small boy urinating; there's also a statue of a little girl doing the same thing nearby. Brussels tried to match the splendor of Paris architecturally during the 19th century by building the Bourse (Stock Exchange), the Palais de Justice (Law Courts), which in its time was the largest building in the world, the Musee de Beaux Arts and the Royal Palace. A few miles outside Brussels in the town of Waterloo, where Napoleon was defeated. Metropolitan Brussels was formed on September 27, 1942 when several villages merged to form the present city.

## Charleroi

Belgium's fourth-largest city was founded in 1666 and named to honor the King of Spain, Charles II.

## Ghent (Gent)

Belgium's third-largest city is located on several islands in the midst of the Lys and Schelde Rivers 35 miles northwest of Brussels. Founded in the 7th century, it had become a major wool-trading center for Europe by the 13th century. The city still retains its medieval aura and is a center for the flower seed and bulb industry. It's also Belgium's second port. Ghent is famous for its three towers, one a bell tower, the others spires for churches.

## Liege (Luik)

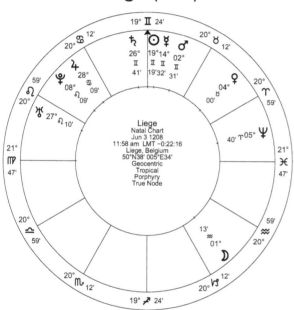

**June 3, 1208, 11:58 a.m. LMT**
**Source: Hotel de Ville**

Belgium's fifth-largest city lies on the Meuse River 60 miles east of Brussels. Capital of Wallonie, the French-speaking region of Belgium, numerous fires destroyed the city in 1792 during the French Revolution. Liege still retains much of its ecclesiastical past as it was once a state of the Holy Roman Empire. Today it's an iron and steel center.

19

# Bosnia Herzegovina
# Bosna Hercegovina

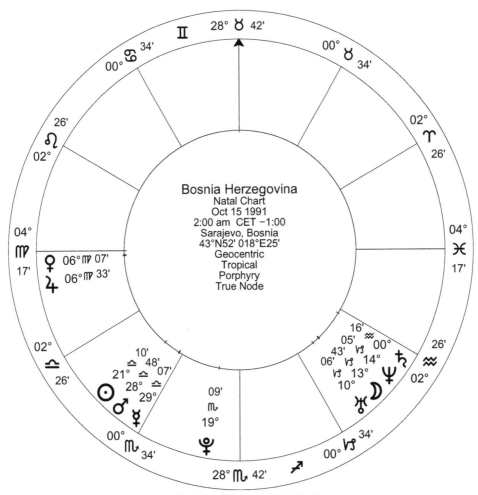

**October 15, 1991, 2:00 a.m. MET, Sarajevo**
**Source: Bosnian Embassy and local newspapers state 2:00 a.m.**

Situated on the Balkan peninsula "between Croatia and Serbia, the northern part contains the Dinaric Alps with thick forests, while the south lies on a rugged plateau. The coastline along the Adriatic Sea is a mere 13 miles long. The highest point is Cvrsnika (7,353 ft.).

Population: 3,922,205; 40% Serbian, 35% Bosnian, 22% Croatian, 38% Moslem, 31% Orthodox, 15% Catholic

Languages: Bosnian (written in either Roman or Cyrillic script), Serbian and Croatian

Area: 19,776 square miles (the size of Croatia or Vermont and New Hampshire combined); 14% arable, 43% urban

Economy: Main exports are iron ore, machinery and textiles. Chief resources are iron, coal, bauxite and manganese

Known to the Romans as Illyria, Serbians settled the region during the 7th century A.D. Three centuries later, Bosnia was ruled from neighboring Croatia and a century later, the Hungarians took over and ruled Bosnia until the Ottoman Turks captured the region in the 16th century. Even back then, religious, cultural and ethnic strife between Catholics, Orthodox Christians and Moslems threatened to tear this country asunder. The Treaty of Berlin in July 1878 granted Austria-Hungary a mandate to rule Bosnia and in October 1908 it was formally annexed into that great empire, despite the fact that it was nominally still part of the declining Ottoman Empire.

On June 28, 1914, Archduke Franz Ferdinand, heir to the throne of Austria-Hungary, was visiting Sarajevo with his wife when an anarchist named Gavrilo Princip, a terrorist working for the Serbian

Black Hand, assassinated the Archduke and his wife. Austria was outraged and sent steep demands to Serbia, knowing full well that Serbia could not, and would not, comply. One month later, on July 28, 1914, Austrians began bombing Belgrade, the opening salvo of what would be known as the Great War, or World War I. With the disintegration of the Austro-Hungarian Empire in late 1918, Bosnia agreed to become part of a new nation, known as the Kingdom of Yugoslavia on December 1, 1918. German troops invaded in 1941 and Bosnia became part of the Nazi puppet state of Croatia for the next three years.

With the secession of Slovenia and Croatia from Yugoslavia in late June 1991, and followed by Macedonia that September of 1991, Bosnia decided to proclaim its own sovereignty or independence on October 15. The European Union, however, decided not to recognize that independence from Yugoslavia until a referendum took place. On February 29 and March 1, 1992 a referendum was taken and independence was overwhelming desired. Independence was formally proclaimed on March 3, 1992.

Serbians decided not to take the referendum lying down and a month later, civil war began with Serbia, which by the end of 1992 controlled over 70% of Bosnian territory. The atrocities continued until a peace accord signed in December 1995 brought an end to the hostilities. The Republika Srpska was established in 1996 for Serbians living inside Bosnia. Nearly 60,000 NATO troops tried to keep the peace in this politically and ethnically fractious nation.

By then, the progressed ASC had already crossed Venus and Jupiter and the progressed Sun was being sextiled by transiting Jupiter. Saturn was transiting trine to Pluto in the third house of neighboring countries and transiting Uranus was trine the natal MC.

Bosnia has a very difficult and fractious chart. Mars, ruler of the eighth house of death, conjuncts Mercury, ruler of the ASC, and both of them inconjunct the MC. Venus and Jupiter form semisquares to the Sun, ruler of the twelfth house of secret enemies and self-undoing. The Moon sesquares the MC and is besieged between Uranus and Neptune, a clear indication of potential for turmoil and devastation. If one uses the 30-degree dial, one quickly sees that Pluto opposes the ASC and was itself squared by the progressed Moon when the civil war began. The Moon-Neptune conjunction also opposes Mercury and Mars on the 30-degree dial.

Other charts for Bosnia are shown in Nicholas Campion's *Book of World Horoscopes*, including those for March 3, 1992 and March *27,* 1992. Neither chart, in my opinion, works as well as does the chart I've selected for this book.

## Sarajevo

The capital and largest city of Bosnia-Herzgovina is located on the Miljacka River about 95 miles from the Adriatic coast. Sarajevo has a distinctive Oriental feeling due to its 80 mosques and Ottoman architecture. The Turks ruled this city from 1463 until 1878, when the Austrians took over. It was here, on June 28, 1914, that a Serbian sympathizer named Gavrilo Princip mortally wounded the Austrian Archduke Franz Ferdinand and his wife, an event which led to the birth of the First World War. Sarajevo also hosted the 1984 Winter Olympics. One month after a referendum was held on Bosnian independence, a civil war began which lasted from April 1992 until February 1994, which ruined this city and separated the Bosnian and Serb minorities which before had lived in relative peace.

# Bulgaria
## Republika Bulgaria

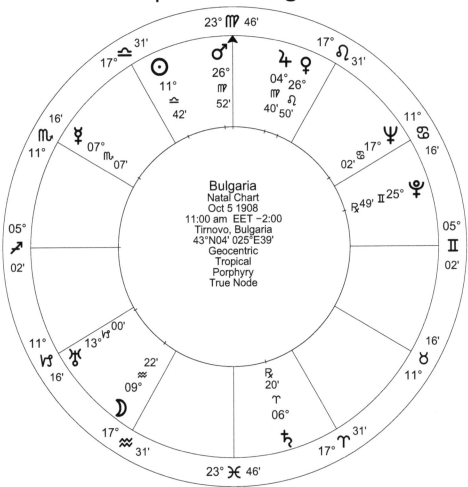

**Chart 1, April 5, 1908 (NS), 11:00 a.m. EET, Tirnovo**
**Source:** *The Times* of London says 11:00 a.m.

Bulgaria is situated on the Balkan peninsula between Turkey and Romania. Its coastline along the Black Sea is 220 miles long. The Balkan Mountains divide the country east to west, the highest point being Musala (elev. 9,655 feet above sea level). The southern part contains the plain of the Maritsa River, and in the southwest are the Rhodope Mountains.

Population: 7,707,495; 85% Bulgarian, 9% Turkish, 5% Macedonian

Religion: 85% Orthodox, 13% Moslem

Language: Bulgarian (written in Cyrillic script)

Area: 42,822 square miles (the size of Yugoslavia or Louisiana); 37% arable, 69% urban

Economy: Main exports are fruit, grain, tobacco and rose oil. Main resources are bauxite, copper, lead and zinc.

Romans invaded this region they called Moesia in the 3rd century B.C. Attila the Hun arrived in the 5th century and Bulgars from central Asia overthrew the Huns in 679 A.D., two years before the first Bulgarian Empire was founded. In 863 A.D., a monk named Cyril formulated an alphabet which today is used by Russia, Serbia and Bulgaria. Byzantine armies tried to gain a foothold in the region at the end of the 9th century but were repelled. They were successful by 1018, but were themselves repelled when the Serbs conquered the land. Bulgaria finally became part of the Byzantine Empire in 1396.

In 1876, a revolt against Turkish rule erupted but was quickly put down with Russian aid, thus making Bulgaria a puppet state of Russia. The Treaty of San Stefano in early March 1878 brought an end to the conflict, but Bulgaria grew to proportions that alarmed other European powers, so the Treaty of Berlin in July 1878 made Bulgaria an Ottoman principality while neighboring Rumelia became an Otto-

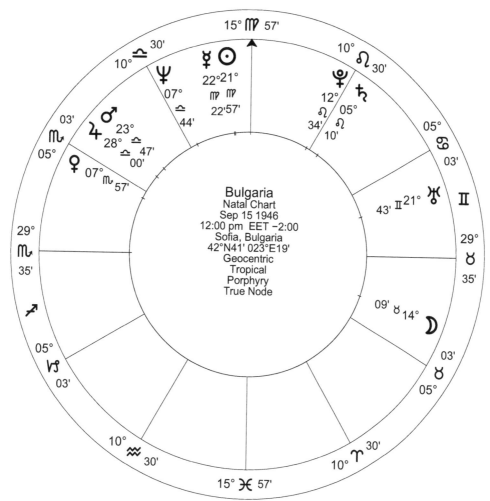

**Chart 2, September 15, 1946, noon EET, Sofia**
**Source: Bulgarian Embassy for the date and as no accurate time is known, noon is presumed.**

man province. Turkey agreed to recognize Bulgarian autonomy in September 1885, and thus were Bulgaria and Rumelia united. A prince from Germany, Ferdinand, was elected to be their first czar. Independence from Turkey was finally proclaimed by the Czar on October 5, 1908 (chart 1).

The first Balkan War broke out in October 1912 against the Turks (progressed MC conjunct Mars; transiting Saturn square Jupiter, ruler of the ASC). The second Balkan War erupted in June 1913, this time against the Serbians and Romanians (progressed Sun square Neptune; transiting Uranus square Mercury, ruler of DESC). Thus with two brief wars under its belt, when World War I began in August 1914, Bulgaria decided to sit on the sidelines until October 1915, when it sided with Germany and Austria against Britain, France and Russia, its former ally (progressed Sun semisquare Jupiter; transiting Saturn opposition Neptune). When the war ended in November 1918, Bulgaria was defeated and lost Macedonia to Serbia and Czar Ferdinand abdicated (progressed ASC sextile Sun; transiting Neptune

semisquare MC; transiting Pluto inconjunct ASC). More than 88,000 Bulgarians had died in the war and 153,000 were wounded.

In April 1934, Czar Boris III formed a dictatorship and suspended the Constitution (progressed MC semisquare Jupiter; progressed ASC opposition Pluto). One year later there was an assassination attempt on the Czar's life. In 1940, Nazi Germany took Dobruja, a region along the Black Sea, from neighboring Romania and gave it to the Bulgarians, thus allowing German troops to enter Bulgaria unopposed in June 1941 on their march to southern Russia (progressed MC sextile Venus trine Pluto; transiting Jupiter opposition ASC; transiting Saturn trine MC). Amazingly, Bulgaria somehow managed to protect most of its Jews from Nazi death camps during World War II. Czar Boris died mysteriously in 1943 (progressed Sun trine Neptune). By September 1944, the Soviet army entered Bulgaria and ousted the Nazis; Bulgaria then declared war on Germany (transiting Saturn inconjunct Moon; transiting Pluto opposition the Moon). Uranus was also inconjunct its natal position. With the proclamation of the People's Republic in September 1946, the monarchy ended and the Communists were in full control of Bulgaria (progressed ASC trine Jupiter square Saturn; transiting Saturn trine ASC; transiting Neptune opposition Saturn; transiting Pluto sextile the Sun).

With the formation of the new government on September 15, 1946 (chart 2), Bulgaria became the most loyal and obedient of Soviet satellites. Not nearly as rebellious as East Germany, Poland or Hungary in the 1950s, Bulgaria toed the line and endured few trials experienced by its more recalcitrant neighbors. With the fall of the Berlin Wall in November 1989, Bulgaria decided to replace President Zhikov, who had ruled the country for more than 35 years (progressed MC conjunct Jupiter; progressed Sun square Saturn; transiting Pluto sextile MC opposition Moon). Zhikov was imprisoned in January 1990 and was convicted of crimes against the state by September 1992, almost a year after the Communists were ousted (progressed Sun semisquare Sun; progressed ASC inconjunct Saturn). In June 2001, former King Simeon II became prime minister and Bulgarian head of state (progressed MC conjunct Venus; progressed ASC inconjunct Pluto). Bulgaria hopes to join the European Union in January 2007 (progressed Ascendant inconjunct Uranus).

## Sofia

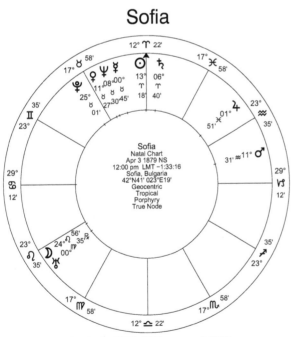

**April 3, 1879 (NS), noon LMT**
**Source: Date from St. Cyril's Library for the date when Sofia became the capital**

Capital and largest city in Bulgaria, it was founded by Romans in the 2nd century A.D. and known as Serdica, one of Emperor Constantine's favorite residences. In the 6th century, it was renamed after St. Sophia's Church. The Turks arrived in 1383 and stayed until 1878. Sofia became capital of Bulgaria on April 3, 1879. It was heavily bombed by the Allies in World War II as Bulgaria was on the side of the Axis.

Sofia has many Byzantine churches and Islamic mosques. Its 19th-century cathedral is one of the largest in the Balkans while the nine-domed Great Mosque houses the Museum of Archaeology. The oldest structure in Sofia is St. George's Church, which was built in the 4th century. Sofia is also famous for its mineral hot springs, and its skyline is dominated by the National Palace of Culture, a hideous monstrosity built in the Stalinist style.

## Plovdiv

Bulgaria's second-largest city is situated 85 miles southeast of Sofia. Founded in the 1st century B.C. as Trimontium, it became the capital of Thrace in 46 B.C. Occupied by the Turks in the late 14th century, Plovdiv had become a part of Bulgaria by 1885.

## Varna

Bulgaria's third-largest city is located on the Black Sea. Founded in the 6th century B.C. by Greeks and known as Odessus, it came under Turkish rule in 1391. A part of Bulgaria only since 1878, Varna hosts an international music festival in the summer and is a popular seaside resort for the Bulgarians.

# Croatia
# Republika Hrvatska

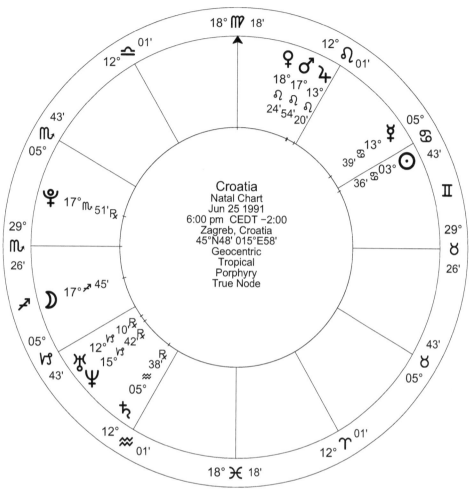

**June 25, 1991, 6:00 p.m. MEDT, 4:00 p.m. GMT, Zagreb**
**Source: Yugoslavian Embassy says 6:00 p.m. and *The Fall of Yugoslavia* by Glenny says just before 6:00 p.m.**
**Astrologer Slaven Slobodnjak prefers the time of 7:55 p.m. MEDT.**

Situated on the Balkan peninsula on the eastern shores of the Adriatic Sea, the Dinaric Alps run along the coastline, which is 1,105 miles long. The northern part of Croatia is called Slavonia, which occupies most of the Pannonian plain. The highest point is Troglav (elev. 6,280 feet).

Population: 4,334,142; 78% Croatian, 12% Serbian

Religion: 80% Catholic, 15% Orthodox

Area: 21,824 square miles (the size of Bosnia or Maryland); 21% arable, 57% urban

Economy: Main exports are machinery, plastics, chemicals, wine and olive oil. Main resources are coal and bauxite.

The Romans called this region Pannonia. Slavic tribes came in the 6th century A.D., and five centuries later, ethic warfare erupted. In 1091, Hungary conquered the region which 11 years later was united with the Magyar Empire. Ottoman Turks took eastern Croatia, or Slavonia, in 1526 on their way to Vienna. During the 17th century, Croatians opted for Austrian rule to ward off future attempts at Ottoman domination. In 1867, Croatia formally became part of the vast Austro-Hungarian Empire.

With the end of World War I, Croatia declared its independence from Austria at the end of October 1918. One month later it opted to join the new nation of Serbs, Croats and Slovenes, later known as Yugoslavia. During World War II, Croatia was harshly ruled with an iron fist by the Germans, who turned this region into a fascist puppet state from 1941 to 1944.

Croatia proclaimed its independence from Yugoslavia on June 25, 1991, half an hour before its neighbor, Slovenia. During the next six months civil war broke out against the Serbs who by the end of 1991 gained control of one-third of Croatia's territory (progressed Sun semisquare Venus and Mars in the ninth house; progressed Sun semisquare Pluto, ruler of ASC). A referendum taken in 1993 in the region of Krajina voiced a desire for integration with Bosnia and Serbia (progressed ASC semisquare Neptune, ruler of the fourth house). Further "ethnic cleansing" continued until a cease-fire in March 1994, prohibiting Krajina from joining Serbia. By August 1995, the army had recaptured former Serb-held territories (transiting Jupiter sextile Saturn). Eastern Slavonia was returned by the Serbs in January 1998 (progressed ASC inconjunct Sun; transiting Saturn trine Jupiter; transiting Neptune sextile ASC).

Ethnic warfare seems to be commonplace in this part of Europe. Looking at Croatia's chart, the Moon, which rules the people of a country, squares the MC but trines Venus and Mars. The Moon, however, sits at the midpoint of Neptune/Pluto, one ruling the ASC in late Scorpio and the other governing the fourth house of homeland and security.

## Zagreb

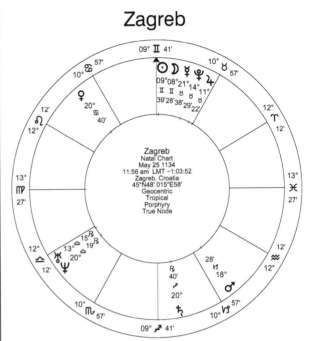

**May 25, 1134, 11:56 a.m. LMT**
**Source: Arhiv Hrvatske for the date.**

Zagreb is the capital and largest city in Croatia. Founded on the banks of the Sava River in 1094 by King Ladislav I of Hungary, it was originally two communities, Gradec and Kaptol. Zagreb was attacked by the Tatars in the 13th century but fortunately missed the Turkish invasion three centuries later. Zagreb was united as one city in 1850. After Croatia's declaration of independence from Serbia in June 1991, the entire region became a massive refugee camp. Zagreb has many Gothic and Baroque churches and palaces. The Gornji Grad (small town) and Donji Grad (lower town) are the dual hearts of this historic city.

## Rijeka (Fiume)

Croatia's third-largest city is located 80 miles southwest of Zagreb at the mouth of the Rijeka River on Bakar Bay. It was the focus of an international dispute after World War I due to its large Italian population; it was a free city until 1939 and didn't become part of Croatia until after World War II. It's Croatia's leading port and shipbuilding center. Rijeka has large paper manufacturing plants and large oil refineries.

## Split (Spalato)

Croatia's second-largest city and largest metropolis in Dalmatia is located on the Adriatic Sea. The old city sits on a promontory above the harbor and surrounds the retirement palace of Emperor Diocletian, who died here in 313 A.D. After the Avars attacked the region in the 7th century, refugees swarmed into the present city. Diocletian's mausoleum became the city's Cathedral. Byzantines ruled the city from 812 until 1089 and the Venetians held sway from 1420 until 1797. Split has many ancient places of worship and several fine museums. Today it's a major port for Croatia as well as a naval base. When the civil war broke out in 1991, Split was shelled by the Serbs but received little real damage.

## Dubrovnik

Located on a rocky headland on the Adriatic Sea, Dubrovnik has a definite medieval aura. The old city is surrounded by walls with double ramparts and 20 towers. Inside are magnificent baroque cathedrals, churches, palaces and monasteries. Dubrovnik has many fountains and its houses have red or yellow roofs. This city was an independent city-state from 1205 until 1808, when it was conquered by Napoleon. Becoming part of Austria in 1815, it became part of Yugoslavia in 1918. During the civil war of 1991, it was badly damaged by Serbian forces.

# Cyprus
## Kypriaki Dimokratia

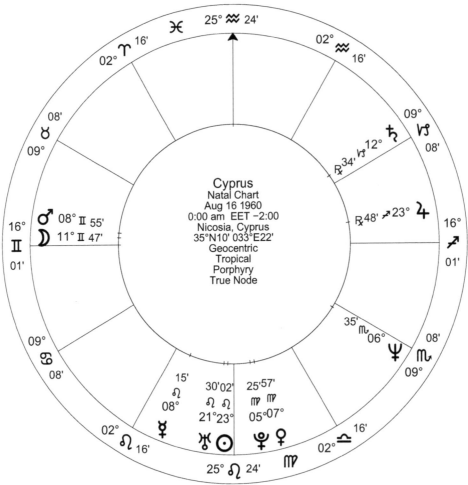

**August 16, 1960, 12:00 a.m. EET, Nicosia**
**Source:** *The New York Times* says midnight

Cyprus is the third-largest island in the Mediterranean Sea, after Sicily and Sardinia, and it's situated off the southern coast of Turkey. This island is the crossroads between Europe, Asia and Africa. Two mountain ranges border a wide central plain and the coastline is 403 miles long. The highest point is Mt. Olympus (elev. 6,401 feet)

Population: 762,887; 78% Greek, 18% Turkish

Religion: 70% Orthodox, 26% Moslem

Area: 3,572 square miles (the size of Connecticut or one-third the size of Belgium); 47% arable, 56% urban

Economy: Main exports are potatoes, citrus fruit, grapes and olives. The main resources are copper and asbestos.

Cyprus was first settled more than 10,000 years ago. By 2000 B.C., it was the center of Mycenean Greek culture and a thousand years later, the Phoeni-cians from the Levant arrived. Cyprus was annexed into the Roman Empire in 58 B.C. and to the vast Byzantine Empire in 395 A.D. In 1191, King Richard I of England married Berengaria at Limassol, and with the aid of the Knights Templar proclaimed Cyprus a crusader state. The Lusignan Dynasty ruled until 1489, when Cyprus was ceded to Venice. Ottoman Turks captured the island in 1571 and virtually ignored the place for three centuries. The Treaty of Berlin in July 1878 placed Cyprus under British administration and it was made a British Crown Colony in 1925. After World War II, Cyprus became a detention camp for illegal immigrants desiring to live in Palestine. Riots broke out in 1954 as Greeks on Cyprus desired union with their mother country (called Enosis).

Independence from Great Britain came on August 16, 1960 with Archbishop Makarios as its first leader.

The Constitution forbade either Enosis with Greece or partition. UN peacekeeping forces were called here in 1964 to quell further rioting (progressed Sun square Saturn). Makarios was ousted by a military coup in July 1974 and within days, Turkey invaded the northern part of the island (progressed Sun conjunct Venus/Pluto, progressed MC square Mars; transiting Jupiter square ASC; transiting Uranus sextile Jupiter). Makarios returned to power in December that year.

In June 1975, however, Turkey proclaimed the de facto partition of Cyprus (transiting Neptune opposition Moon/Mars; transiting Pluto semisquare Uranus) but formal declaration of independence for Northern Cyprus did not become a fact until November 15, 1983 (progressed ASC semisquare Uranus sextile Pluto trine Neptune). The "country" of Northern Cyprus is unrecognized by any country with the exception of Turkey.

Northern Cyprus has 1,295 square miles, about the size of Rhode Island or Luxembourg, and nearly all of its people are Turkish and Moslem.

In April 2003, Turkish Cypriot authorities allowed citizens from the Greek side of the island to cross the "green line" to visit relatives on the other side of the island as a goodwill gesture preparing the way for entrance into the European Union which Cyprus joined in May 2004 (progressed MC sextile Mars trine Mercury inconjunct Venus; progressed ASC semisquare Venus and Pluto).

## Nicosia

The capital and largest city of Cyprus is situated in the center of the island. Founded in the 7th century BC and known as Ledra, its present name comes from Nike, the Greek goddess of victory. The Old City is surrounded by three miles of walls, but since 1974, Nicosia has been a divided city: the north side is Turkish and Moslem, the southern part is Greek and Orthodox. Nicosia is the capital of both Cypruses. The main attractions on the north side are St. Sophia's Cathedral, which is now a mosque, and a 14th century Armenian church. The south side has the Cyprus Museum with its large archaeological collections.

# Czech Republic
# Ceska Republika

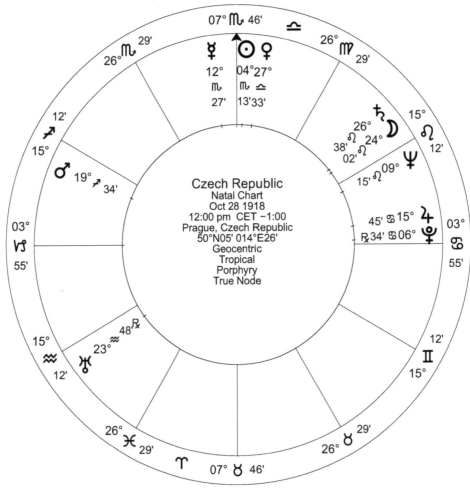

**October 28, 1918, noon MET, Prague**
Source: *Collapse of the Austro-Hungarian Empire* by Opocensky.
Astrologer Jindra Johanisova prefers the time of ll:25 a.m.

Situated in the heart of Europe, the western part is called Bohemia, a region completely surrounded by low mountains. Moravia occupies its eastern part, a hilly region of incredible beauty. The south is part of the Danube River basin. Other main rivers are the Elbe and Vltava (Moldau). The highest point is Snezka (elev. 5,285 feet) on the Polish border.

Population: 10,264,212; 94% Czech, 3% Slovaks, 2% Magyars

Religion: 39% Catholic, 5% Protestant, 3% Orthodox

Area: 30,386 square miles (the size of Scotland or South Carolina); 41% arable, 75% urban

Economy: Main exports are machinery, motor vehicles, iron, steel, chemicals, glass and, of course, beer

Slavic tribes settled this region in the 6th century; three centuries later, the first Moravian Empire was founded under Mojmir I. During the 10th century Bohemia was ruled by King Wenceslas of the Premyslid Dynasty. In 1025, Bohemia and Moravia united with Silesia in southern Poland. Mongols from central Asia invaded the region in 1241.

Further Bohemian expansion was checked by the emerging Hapsburg Empire in Austria, but with the emergence of the Luxembourg Dynasty in 1310, Bohemia's Golden Age began. By 1348, the University of Prague had been founded, the oldest seat of higher learning in central Europe. Religious strife erupted soon after, and in 1415, John Hus was burned at the stake as a heretic. His followers, called Hussites, waged war on the Crown and the Pope was forced to launch a crusade against the rebels. In 1454, peace returned when Bohemia merged with Hungary under the rule of Jiri Podebrany.

When the old dynasty ended in 1526, Bohemia asked the Hapsburgs for assistance, thus beginning nearly four centuries of rule from Vienna. The Thirty Years War began in Prague in 1618, when dissenters were thrown out windows (called defenestration) and northern Europe pitted Catholic against Protestant, one century after Martin Luther began the Reformation. When peace returned in 1648 with the Treaty of Westphalia, most of Europe was in shambles, its population decimated and starving. Bohemia lost one-third of its people and 150,000 Protestants fled, including 80 percent of the nobility. In 1621, Catholicism became the state religion and Germany became the official language. In March 1848, with Europe erupting in revolution, the Czech language was again allowed to be freely spoken.

On October 28, 1918, with the aid of U.S. President Wilson, the nation of Czechoslovakia was formed, two weeks before the Armistice was signed with Germany. Anti-Catholic riots broke out the following year, and many Catholics became Protestant. Thomas Masaryk, Czechoslovakia's first leader, died under mysterious circumstances in 1935, as tensions were rising against Nazi Germany (progressed MC square Moon and Uranus). In September 1938, the Munich Pact allowed Adolf Hitler to annex the Sudetenland (a largely German-speaking region in the northwest) with no opposition from the rest of Europe (progressed Sun square Moon and Uranus; transiting Jupiter conjunct Uranus opposition Moon; transiting Saturn square Jupiter; transiting Pluto square Sun/Venus). In March 1939, Hitler grabbed the entire country, which became a German protectorate (progressed Sun sesquare Pluto, ruler of the MC; progressed ASC inconjunct Saturn, ruler of the ASC).

By March 1942, serious revolts against Nazi occupation became stronger and Reinhard Heydrich was assassinated by the Czechs (progressed Sun square Saturn; progressed MC sesquare Jupiter; transiting Saturn square Moon and Uranus; transiting Uranus square Saturn). Hitler retaliated by leveling the town of Lidice (transiting Pluto square Sun). Soviet troops arrived in March 1945 and Ruthenia in eastern Slovakia was ceded to the Soviet Union (transiting Saturn opposition ASC). When the war ended two months later, Czechoslovakia counted more than 250,000 dead (progressed ASC inconjunct Pluto, ruler of the Sun and MC).

In 1946, a coalition government was formed and Communists received 38 percent of the vote. On February 25, 1948, a Communist coup toppled the government, and the following month Jan Masaryk was found dead. By June, Benes resigned and was dead within three months (progressed MC inconjunct Pluto).

Alexander Dubcek managed to institute numerous reforms before the Soviets invaded in late August 1968 (progressed Sun trine Moon sextile Uranus; progressed MC semisquare Mercury; progressed ASC sesquare Neptune; transiting Neptune square Moon and Uranus). A new constitution was drawn up in 1969, recognizing the equality of both Czechs and Slovaks (transiting Saturn trine Moon/Saturn).

With the fall of Communism in eastern Europe in November 1989, the "Velvet Revolution" took place in Czechoslovakia. A poet named Vaclav Havel was elected president (progressed Sun opposition Jupiter; transiting Uranus conjunct ASC; transiting Pluto trine Jupiter). By the end of June 1991, the last Soviet troops had left the country. By the middle of 1992, plans were underway to let Slovakia secede, and on New Years Day 1993, the new nation of Slovakia was born (progressed ASC inconjunct Mars; transiting Pluto square Moon and Uranus). In March 1999, the Czech Republic became a member of NATO. Devastating floods on the Vltava flooded downtown Prague in August 2002 (progressed ASC inconjunct Sun). The Czech Republic joined the European Union in May 2004 (progressed Sun sesquare Jupiter; progressed MC square Sun semisquare Mars).

# Brno

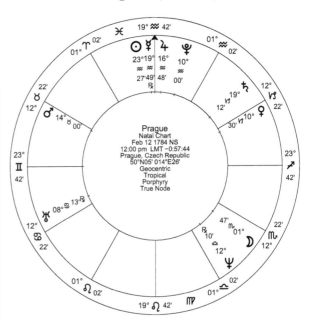

**January 18, 1243, 12:14 p.m. LMT**
**Source: Archiv Mesta Brna**

Brno is the Czech Republic's second-largest city and the biggest city in Moravia. Situated 120 miles southeast of Prague, it was founded in the 13th century and has been capital of Moravia since 1642. Chief sites are the Spilberk Castle, built in the 13th century, the main cathedral (Dom) and the Old Town Hall with its crooked central spire.

# Prague (Praha)

**February 12, 1784, noon LMT**
**Source: Town Hall**

Prague is the capital and largest city of the Czech Republic. It's built on seven hills along the Vltava (Moldau) River. Founded in the 9th century by the Premyslid Dynasty, it was chartered in 1230. A new town was begun in 1348, and by 1784, both villages were united. The Old Town (Stare Mesto) is situated on the east side of the river and contains the Town Hall built in the 14th century, and Charles University, opened in 1348, the oldest in central Europe. The Old Town also has the old Jewish ghetto. The New Town (Nove Mesto) contains Wenceslas Square, a long boulevard and heart of the central city. Towering over everything is Hradcany Hill, which contains the Royal Castle and St. Vitus' Cathedral. Below the hill is the Mala Strana (Little Quarter) housing the Wallenstein Palace and many government offices. History can be fortunate that Prague was was not seriously damaged during World War II as most of its baroque architecture has been preserved. Prague is known as the City of Spires for its numerous churches.

# Denmark
## Kongeriget Danmark

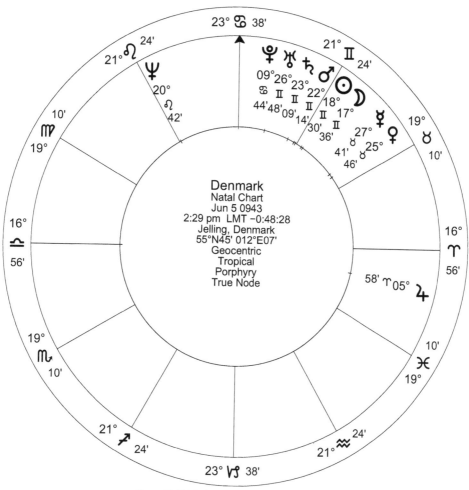

June 5, 943, 2:29 p.m. LMT, Jelling

**Source:** Date and time speculative. My reasoning is that since so many political events take place on June 5, it could be the founding date. The year was ascertained from sources which stated that Harold Bluetooth formed the monarchy sometime between 930 and 950 A.D. So if you're a stickler for charts that have "birth certificates," concentrate on the history and ignore the progressed and transiting aspects to Denmark's natal chart that I've rectified.

Denmark is the southernmost of the Scandinavian countries. The Jutland Peninsula lies between the Baltic and North Seas just above Germany. Denmark is a country of 406 islands, the largest of which are Sjaelland and Fyn. The land is relatively flat and the highest point is only 570 feet above sea level. No point is more than 30 miles from the shore and the coastline is 4,544 miles long, giving Denmark the longest beaches in Europe.

Population: 5,352,815; 91% Danish

Religion: Protestant (Lutheran), 3% Moslem

Area: 16,639 square miles (the size of Switzerland or half the size of Maine); 60% arable, 85% urban

Economy: Known as the "breadbasket of Europe," Denmark exports milk, cheese, bacon, eggs, ham, butter and fish.. Other exports are pharmaceuticals, furniture, porcelain and silverware.

Other: Denmark also has dominion over Greenland (840,000 square miles) and the Faeroe Islands (540 square miles)

The Norsemen, or Vikings, settled Denmark in the 7th century A.D. and Christianity was introduced two centuries later. King Gorm the Old began uniting the tribes in the early 10th century and unification was completed under Harold Bluetooth between 935 and 985 A.D. According to my research, the Danish Kingdom began on June 5, 943 A.D., the oldest monarchy in Europe and the world's second-oldest after

Japan. Beginning in 985, King Sweyn began warring against other Scandinavian countries and by 1014 had conquered England when his son, Knut (Canute) became king of England (progressed Sun square Mercury and Venus sextile Uranus). In 1282, the Great Charter created a Parliament and Council of Nobles to curb monarchial abuses (viz. Magna Carta) (progressed MC conjunct Uranus; progressed ASC trine Mercury). Beginning in 1332, when the progressed Sun conjuncted Pluto, the progressed MC sextiled the Moon and the progressed ASC sesquared the Moon, Denmark fought against the powerful Hanseatic League which controlled the economic and political life around the Baltic. Denmark lost in 1370 and 10 years later Iceland became part of Denmark (progressed Sun square Mercury sextile Uranus).

Scandinavia's finest moment during the Middle Ages occurred in June 1397, when Queen Margarethe formed the Union of Kalmar, uniting Denmark, Sweden and Norway into one nation (progressed MC trine Sun; progressed ASC inconjunct Pluto). The union lasted until 1523, when Sweden declared its independence (progressed Sun inconjunct Neptune; progressed MC square Venus trine Saturn; progressed ASC semisquare Neptune). Lutheranism was made the state religion in 1537 (progressed MC trine Pluto).

Over the following two centuries Denmark was involved in one conflict after another with its neighbor, Sweden. In 1563, Denmark fought to regain possessions in southern Sweden (progressed MC conjunct Jupiter; progressed ASC semisquare Sun). The war went on until 1660, when Absolutism was instituted to restore order within Denmark, albeit years of repression and a benevolent dictatorship emerged (progressed Sun sextile Jupiter; progressed MC conjunct Pluto; progressed ASC opposition Jupiter). In 1697, the Great Nordic War pitted Sweden against Denmark, Norway, Poland and Russia (progressed Sun semisquare Venus; progressed MC sextile Moon). When all conflicts ended, Denmark had lost its possessions in Skane (southern Sweden), but Sweden had lost all its overseas lands.

In 1807, the British bombarded Copenhagen, driving Denmark to seek an alliance with Napoleon (progressed Sun trine Uranus; progressed ASC inconjunct Mars). After Napoleon's downfall in 1814, Denmark was punished by the Allies for siding with France, and Norway was given to Sweden (progressed Sun sesquare Sun; progressed MC inconjunct Pluto; progressed ASC sesquare Sun).

A liberal Constitution was framed and signed on June 5, 1849 (there's that date again), a date many as-

trologers prefer to use for Denmark. It was a model for other Scandinavian countries to copy (progressed Sun inconjunct Pluto; progressed ASC semisquare Uranus sextile Pluto). German Chancellor Otto von Bismarck provoked a conflict with Denmark in January 1864 over the provinces of Schleswig and Holstein which the Germans claimed were theirs. Denmark lost to the ever-increasing military might of Germany (progressed Sun inconjunct Venus; progressed MC trine Mercury). During the late 19th century, Denmark made numerous changes to benefit its citizens. Primary schools were founded in 1842, a labor party formed in 1888 and old-age pensions and health insurance were established in 1891 (progressed MC trine Uranus).

Denmark decided to remain neutral when World War I broke out in August 1914 (progressed Sun trine Moon; progressed MC square Sun inconjunct Neptune; transiting Jupiter trine Sun). Denmark wasn't nearly as lucky in April 1940 when the Germans invaded (progressed MC sextile Moon; progressed ASC semisquare Saturn; transiting Uranus square Neptune; transiting Neptune square Saturn). During this war, however, Denmark granted Iceland its independence in June 1944 (progressed Sun square Moon; progressed MC trine Neptune; progressed ASC semisquare Uranus).

Denmark joined the European Union in January 1973 (transiting Jupiter inconjunct Sun; transiting Saturn conjunct Moon; transiting Uranus trine Mars; transiting Neptune trine Jupiter). Before long a revolt broke out protesting one of the world's highest tax rates, which was needed to fund an extremely generous welfare state. In 1979, Greenland became an autonomous province with representation in Parliament (progressed Sun trine Neptune; progressed MC conjunct Venus; progressed ASC inconjunct Jupiter). In September 2000, Denmark voted not to adopt Europe's new currency, the Euro.

In February 2006, cartoons insulting the prophet Mohammed printed in a local newspaper caused worldwide furor and riots in both Europe and the Middle East (progressed Midheaven conjunct Mars in the ninth house of publications).

# Alborg

The fourth-largest city in Denmark is located on the Limfjorden, which connects the North Sea to the Kattegat. This city, which was chartered in 1342, is a major port and trade center famous for its manufacture of akavit. Despite its charming 16th century look, the main tourist site is nearby at Lindholm Hoje, a Viking burial ground and museum that has more than 700 graves of ancient Vikings.

# Arhus (Aarhus)

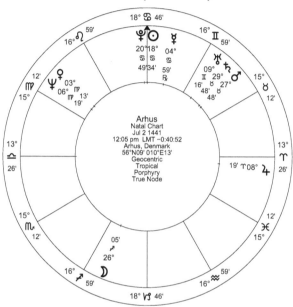

**July 2, 1441, 12:05 p.m. LMT Source: Hovedbiblioteket**

Denmark's second-largest city and capital of Jutland is situated on the Kattegat, the straight that separates Denmark from Sweden. First settled by the Vikings, it has two 13th century cathedrals an a well-preserved Old Town. Its university was founded in 1934.

# Copenhagen (Kobnhavn)

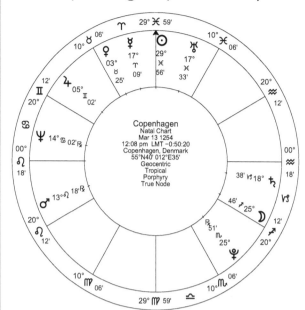

**March 13, 1254, 12:08 p.m. LMT**
**Source: Stadsarkiv**

Denmark's largest city and capital since 1445, Copenhagen is situated on the island of Zealand about 12 miles from Sweden across the Oresund. A highly cosmopolitan and sophisticated community, its liberal laws and attitudes make it a popular tourist destination. Founded in 1167 by Bishop Absalon, it's managed to retain its central core and numerous canals over the centuries. Contrasting with its numerous old structures are modern communities which practice free love and emporiums which cater to erotica.

The main tourist sights are the Amalienborg Palace, the Carlsberg brewery, Christiansborg (home of Parliament and Supreme Court) and of course the statue of the Little Mermaid, the most photographed sight in the city. There's also the Rundetarn, Europe's oldest functioning observatory and the world-famous Tivoli Gardens, the pleasure center in the heart of town.

Copenhagen has several distinctive neighborhoods such as Christiania, a community of hippies and squatters; Christianshavn, with its centuries-old homes and courtyards that reminds one of Amsterdam; and Nyhavn, the sailors district. Don't miss the Erotica Museum, not such an oddity here as Denmark legalized pornography in 1968.

# Odense

**March 2, 1477, 12:10 p.m. LMT Source:
Landerarkivet for Fyn**

Denmark's third-largest city is situated on the island of Fyn and was named by the Vikings to honor the god Odin, their god of hospitality. Famous for being the birth place of Hans Christian Andersen, it's a pleasant, but provincial, town.

# Estonia
# Eesti Vabariik

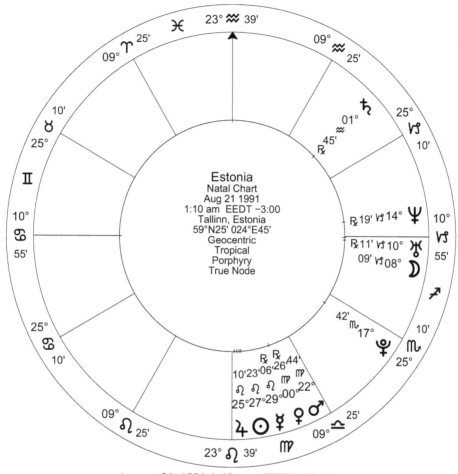

Estonia
Natal Chart
Aug 21 1991
1:10 am  EEDT −3:00
Tallinn, Estonia
59°N25' 024°E45'
Geocentric
Tropical
Porphyry
True Node

**August 21, 1991 1:10 a.m. EEDT, Tallinn**
Source: *The Guardian, The Times* of London and *USA Today* all state 1:10 a.m.

Situated on the eastern shore of the Baltic Sea, Estonia is a region of lowlands, swamps, marshes and numerous lakes. More than 1,500 islands dot the region. The highest point in Estonia (elev. 1,045 ft.) is near the border with Latvia.

Population: 1,423,316; 65% Estonian, 28% Russian

Religion: 75% Protestant (Lutheran), 20% Orthodox

Area: 17,463 square miles (the size of Denmark or Vermont and New Hampshire combined); 22% arable, 69% urban

Economy: Main exports are textiles, cement, wood products and timber. Main resources are oil, peat and phosphorous.

Estonia was conquered in the 13th century by Teutonic Knights from Germany. The northern part was taken by Sweden in 1526, and its southern part surrendered to Sweden in 1629. Peter the Great ousted the Swedes in 1721 and Estonia became part of the vast Russian Empire for the next two centuries.

In February 1918, Estonia first declared its independence from Russia, three months after the Bolshevik Revolution. Soviet forces entered in June 1940 and incorporated Estonia into the Soviet Union. German troops occupied the country from June 1941 until 1944.

Estonia again declared its independence, this time from the waning Soviet Union, in the early hours of August 21, 1991. Soviet troops were finally gone by the end of August 1994 (progressed Sun conjunct Venus; progressed MC opposition Sun; progressed ASC opposition Neptune). Today, of all the former Soviet republics, Estonia is the most economically viable and its transition to a capitalist system has shown great strides. Estonia joined the European Union in May 2004.

# Tallinn

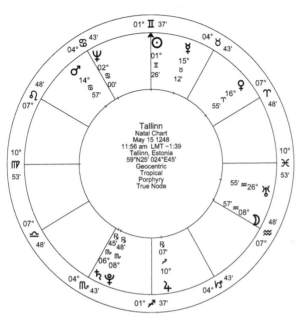

Tallinn
Natal Chart
May 15 1248
11:56 am  LMT −1:39
Tallinn, Estonia
59°N25' 024°E45'
Geocentric
Tropical
Porphyry
True Node

**May 15, 1248, 11:56 a.m. LMT**
**Source: Tallinn University Library for the date.**

Tallinn is the capital and largest city in Estonia. Situated on the Baltic Sea and the Gulf of Finland, it lies opposite the Finnish port of Helsinki. Founded in the 10th century as a trading post, it was captured by Danes in 1219 under King Waldemar III. Germans and then Swedes captured the city. After 1346, Teutonic Knights ruled Tallinn. The Russians came in 1710 and stayed until 1918, when independence was first declared. But the Soviets came in 1940 and stayed until 1991, when independence was again declared.

# Finland
## Suomen Tasavalta

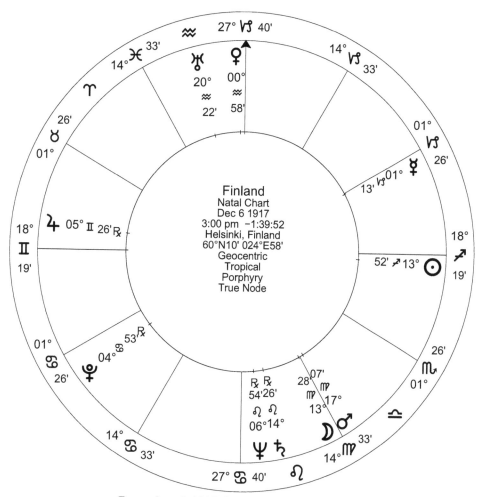

**December 6, 1917, 3:00 p.m. LMT, Helsinki**
**Source: University of Helsinki says between 2:30 and 3:00 p.m. I've chosen the**
**later time per astrologer Kyosti Tarvainen.**

Finland is situated between the Gulfs of Bothnia and Finland, bordering Russia. Many consider it part of Scandinavia despite the fact that its language is more like Hungarian (Magyar) than are the Germanic-sounding tongues of Denmark, Sweden and Norway. The south part of Finland is flat, the north mountainous. More than 80,000 islands and 200,000 lakes lie within its borders. One-third of Finland lies above the Arctic Circle, a region called Lapland. The coastline is 700 miles long, and the highest point, Halti (elev. 4,375 ft.), is on the border with Norway.

Population: 5,175,783; 93% Finnish, 6% Swedish
Religion: 70% Lutheran
Area: 130,127 square miles (the size of Norway or New Mexico); 8% arable, 67% urban
Economy: Main exports are wood and paper products. Main resources include copper, zinc and iron ore. Shipbuilding is a major industry.

During the 8th century A.D., the Fenni tribes from the Volga region of Russia ousted the indigenous Lapps to the far north. In 1155, Sweden conquered the region but treated its people as equals and by 1362, Finns had delegates in the Swedish Parliament and were able to elect Swedish kings. By 1397, Finland had its own currency and courts of appeals. In 1540, Finland became part of Sweden, but 16 years later it managed to get its own parliament, the Diet. By 1654, over 60 of Finland was in the hands of Swedish nobles.

In 1716, Peter the Great of Russia conquered Finland, largely to protect his new capital of Saint Petersburg. In 1788, Finland sided with Sweden and rid the country of Russians, but in 1807, Napoleon plotted with Tsar Alexander I to give him Finland if Alexander would attack Sweden, which refused to join a blockade against British ships. In February 1808, the Russians invaded Finland and one year later, Finland was created a Grand Duchy. The Finns were allowed to keep their Constitution and the peasants remained free. In 1835, the Kalevala, an epic poem, was published which sparked a rise for nationalism.

In 1863, Tsar Alexander II of Russia granted Finland a Parliament and Swedish and Finnish languages became equal under the law. In 1899, however, Tsar Nicholas II closed Parliament, made Russian compulsory in the schools and banned freedom of speech and the press. After the first Russian Revolution of 1905, Nicholas II eased up on his hard-line stance and granted women the vote.

One month after the Bolshevik Revolution, Finland declared its independence from Russia on December 6, 1917. Two months later, a civil war erupted and the Reds seized Helsinki and the Whites (monarchists) set up shop in Vaasa. When the conflict ended in June 1919, more than 24,000 Finns had lost their lives (progressed Sun square Moon; progressed MC sesquare Moon). After asking Kaiser Wilhelm II of Germany to send his son to become King of Finland, the Diet (Parliament) decided to form a Republic (progressed Sun semisquare Venus; progressed MC semisquare Sun; progressed ASC trine Uranus).

In June 1930, a fascist movement surfaced trying to stamp out Communism whose sympathizers were deported back to Russia (progressed ASC opposition Mercury). This movement died in February 1932. In March 1939, the Soviet Union asked for a 30-year lease on four islands in the Gulf of Finland which they needed to protect their city of Leningrad (St. Petersburg) in case war erupted with Nazi Germany (progressed Sun opposition Pluto inconjunct Jupiter). The Finns refused in November 1939, Finland was invaded by the Russians and Helsinki was bombed (transiting Uranus square Uranus; transiting Pluto semisquare ASC). Finland lost 10 percent of its territory in Karelia and 450,000 Finns were relocated to safer locales. When the war ended in early 1940, some 48,000 Finns were dead (progressed Sun inconjunct Neptune; progressed MC conjunct Uranus sesquare Pluto).

In June 1941, Finland entered World War II on the Axis side with Nazi Germany against Russia (transiting Jupiter conjunct Jupiter; transiting Uranus trine the MC). By 1943, Finland saw the way things were going with Hitler and wanted out of its alliance with Nazi Germany. German troops were asked to leave in September 1944, but they refused to budge. It took the Finns seven months to rid them-

selves of the Germans (progressed ASC inconjunct Sun). When World War II ended in May 1945, Finland had lost another 13 percent of its territory, 79,000 were dead, 50,000 wounded and nearly 400,000 had been displaced (transiting Saturn conjunct Pluto; transiting Neptune square Pluto; transiting Pluto conjunct Neptune).

In April 1953, the Soviet Union agreed to cancel the remaining debt owed by Finland (transiting Jupiter trine MC; transiting Pluto opposition Uranus). Finland joined the European Union in January 1995 (progressed MC inconjunct Mars; progressed ASC conjunct Saturn trine Sun). In 2001, Finland opted not to become part of NATO.

# Helsinki (Helsingfors)

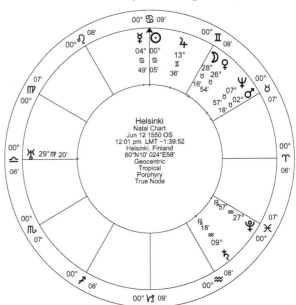

Helsinki
Natal Chart
Jun 12 1550 OS
12:01 pm LMT −1:39:52
Helsinki, Finland
60°N10' 024°E58'
Geocentric
Tropical
Porphyry
True Node

**June 12, 1550, 12:10 p.m. LMT
Source: Helsinki City Library; The Kaupiniginkirjasto in Helsinki wrote that Helsingfors was founded on June 12, 1550 and chartered in 1569**

Helsinki is the capital and largest city in Finland. Scandinavia's second-largest port is situated on the Gulf of Finland on a peninsula. With the exception of Reykjavik, it's the most northern world capital. Founded as Helsingfors in June 1550, a new city was commissioned by King Gustavus Vasa in 1642, but it was burned to the ground by the Russians in 1713. Helsinki was fortified in 1748, but was heavily bombed during the war with the Soviet Union in 1939-1940. After Helsinki became the capital in 1812, it was completely redesigned by the Russians. The heart of the city is called Senate Square, dominated by the massive Lutheran Cathedral. Two other churches, both Russian in style, are the Uspenski and

Temple. The austere-looking Parliament Building and President's Palace are also architecturally noteworthy. Probably the most interesting edifice in Helsinki is the ultra-modern railroad station. Surrounding the central city are numerous parks, including the Seurasaari and Suomelinna.

## Tampere

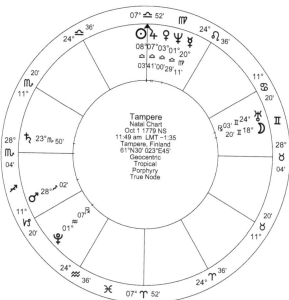

**October 1, 1779, 11:49 a.m. LMT**
**Source: Tampere City Library**

Finland's second-largest city is located 105 miles northwest of Helsinki at the edge of the lake district. Situated between lakes Nasijarvi and Pyhajarvi, it's been a center for cotton milling since the early 19th century when a Scotsman harnessed the surrounding rapids. Tampere has been known as the industrial center of Finland ever since. After the Russian Revolution of 1905, Tampere became the Communist capital due to Lenin's residence in this city.

## Turku

**September 15, 1229, 11:53 a.m. LMT**
**Source: *Gazeteer of Place Names***

The third-largest city in Finland is situated 95 miles northwest of Helsinki on the Aurajoki River where it meets the Gulf of Bothnia. Turku was the birth place of the Reformation in Finland and houses the country's oldest university, founded in 1640. Capital of Finland until 1812, a huge fire burned most of the city in 1827. The Turku Castle is the oldest structure in the city and the favorite tourist spot is the Luostarinmaki, or the artisan's quarters, which survived the 1827 fire. The huge Gothic cathedral dates from the late 13th century.

# France
## La Republique Francaise

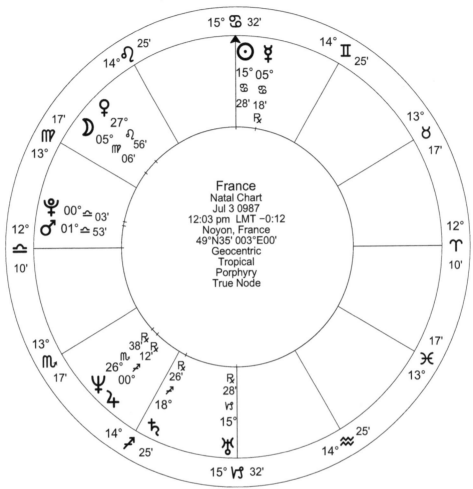

**Chart 1, July 3, 987 A.D., 12:03 p.m. LMT, Noyon**
**Source: Bibliotheque Nationale, Paris; noon presumed as that's when coronations take place**

France is the third-largest country in Europe after Russia and the Ukraine. Shaped like a hexagon, the Atlantic Ocean, Bay of Biscay and the English Channel (La Manche) and the Mediterranean Sea line its borders on the west and southeast. The Pyrenees Mountains separate France from Spain and the Alpes Maritimes and Jura Mountains divide France from Italy and Switzerland.

France has many famous and historic regions. In the north, Artois and Picardy contain the Ile de France and the metropolitan area of Paris. In the northwest lie Normandy and Brittany, while the northeast has Champagne, Burgundy and Lorraine. In the southeast are Languedoc, Provence, Dauphine and Savoie, while the southwest has Poitou, Gascony and the Aquitaine. In the center of France lies the Massif Central, which rises to a height of 6,000 feet in the province of Auvergne.

The main rivers of France are the Rhine (which separates France from Germany), Rhone, Loire, Seine and Garonne. The highest point in western Europe, Mont Blanc, rises to a height of 15,781 feet on the border with Switzerland. France's coastline is 2,130 miles long, but there are few offshore islands, the largest being Corsica.

Population: 59,551,227; 90% French, 10% Arabic

Religion: 90% Catholic, 10% Moslem

Area: 211,924 square miles (the size of Spain and Portugal or Arizona and New Mexico combined); 75% urban, 33% arable

France ranks first in world production of wine and perfume, third in iron and steel, fourth in chemicals, automobiles and aircraft and fifth in textiles and shipbuilding. France is Europe's number-one miner of aluminum, other chief resources being coal, iron ore and bauxite. France is also a center of fashion, culture, art, science and philosophy. France is also a feast for gourmets or gourmands and produces more than 400 kinds of cheese.

Greeks began colonizing land along the Mediterranean in the 6th century B.C. and a century later, Celtic tribes invaded. Romans began occupying Gaul in 121 B.C. and 70 years later, Julius Caesar had completed the conquest. Franks and Alemans invaded in the 3rd century A.D. shortly before the Burgundians and Vandals tore through the region. In 451 A.D., Attila the Hun was defeated at the Battle of Chalons.

Clovis, Mayor of the Palace and founder of the Merovingian Dynasty, was baptized a Christian on Christmas Day 496 A.D. Charles Martel halted the advance of the Moors (Muslims) at Tours in 732, one of the most decisive battles in history. Pepin founded the Carolingian Dynasty in 751 and his son, Charlemagne, ruled the region from 768 to 814. Upon the death of Charlemagne, his kingdom was divided between his three sons after the Treaty of Verdun was signed in 843.

On July 3, 987 A.D. (chart 1), Hugh Capet, the Count of Paris, became king and founded a dynasty that would rule France for the next 800 years. The Normans under William the Conqueror began their conquest of England in October 1066 (progressed MC conjunct Mars; progressed ASC square Moon). The First Crusade began at the Pope's request in November 1095 to protect pilgrims traveling to the Holy Land from Moslems (progressed MC conjunct Jupiter/Pluto; progressed ASC trine Venus). In May 1154, Eleanor of Aquitaine, the richest woman in Europe and former Queen of France, married King Henry II of England, making Eleanor and her husband the wealthiest landowners in Europe (progressed MC square Pluto, ruler of second house; progressed ASC opposition Pluto).

The Estates General, founded in 1302, was to become instrumental during the final days of the monarchy (progressed MC opposition Neptune square Venus; progressed ASC conjunct Moon sextile Mercury). Due to political strife in Italy, the Papacy moved its headquarters to Avignon in 1309 (progressed MC square Moon). Two decades later the original branch of the Capetian dynasty died out and the Valois branch took over a nation of 15 million people, the richest in Europe (progressed ASC sextile Jupiter).

In July 1337, the Hundred Years War began when King Edward III of England laid claim to the throne of France through his mother (progressed MC square Mars/Pluto; progressed ASC conjunct Mars/Pluto).

In 1377, the Papacy travelled back to Rome (progressed ASC conjunct Jupiter/Pluto). After many years, the Hundred Years War began anew with the enthronement of Henry V. England and France suffered a massive defeat at the Battle of Agincourt in 1415. The French fought on horseback with heavy armor while the English fought on foot and used a longbow (progressed MC sextile Sun trine Uranus; progressed ASC conjunct Neptune). Joan of Arc broke the English siege at Orleans in June 1429 and placed the Dauphin, Charles VII, on the throne (progressed MC sextile Jupiter; progressed ASC square Moon). The King later betrayed her and Joan was burned as a heretic in Rouen in 1431. The Hundred Years War ended in 1453 at the Battle of Castillon when England lost its last French possession at Calais.

The French Renaissance began in 1515, when King Francis I took the throne (progressed MC trine Venus; progressed ASC square Saturn). An alliance with the Turks was signed in 1520 hoping to quell Ottoman advances (progressed MC square Pluto; progressed ASC opposition Mars/Pluto). During the 16th century, many French had become Protestants (Hugenots) but 8,000 of them were brutally murdered on orders from Catherine de Medici on St. Bartholomew's Day 1572 (progressed ASC inconjunct Neptune). The Valois branch of the Capetians died out in 1589 and the Bourbons came to power under Henry IV of Navarre. Only one major problem: Henry was a Protestant and in order to become King of France, he had to convert to Catholicism by July 1593 (progressed MC trine Sun sextile Uranus; progressed ASC conjunct Sun opposition Uranus). Henry IV guaranteed religious freedom by signing the Edict of Nantes in April 1598 (progressed MC square Saturn; progressed ASC inconjunct Saturn). Twelve years later, Henry IV was assassinated and was succeeded by Louis XIII, whose chief minister was Cardinal Richelieu (progressed MC opposition Mars; progressed ASC trine Neptune). Richelieu then went to war against Spain and Austria.

In May 1643, Louis XIV (the Sun King) ascended to the throne at age five and the Golden Age of France began (progressed MC sesquare Saturn; progressed ASC semisquare Mars). Louis' policies provoked a revolt, called the Fronde, in July 1648 but it was quickly squelched. Louis revoked the Edict of Nantes in 1685 causing the Hugenots to flee to England, Holland or America (progressed MC inconjunct Uranus; progressed ASC square Saturn). Louis also got into hot water when he tried to place one of his relatives on the Spanish throne thus begin-

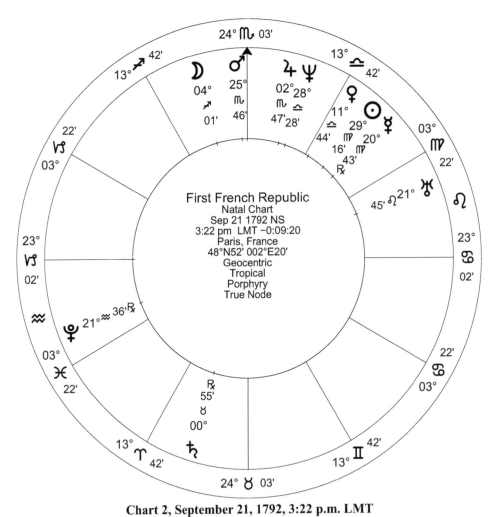

**Chart 2, September 21, 1792, 3:22 p.m. LMT**
**Source: Journal of the National Convention as cited by Campion in his book**
*Book of World Horoscopes* **prefers the time of 3:30 p.m. The chart used in this book has been rectified.**

ning what was called the War of the Spanish Succession in February 1701 (progressed MC square Pluto inconjunct Jupiter; progressed ASC conjunct Pluto sextile Jupiter). The most famous battle of this war was fought at Blenheim in 1704 and resulted in victory for the British (progressed MC square Mars; progressed ASC conjunct Mars).

In December 1720, a real-estate speculation called the Mississippi Bubble burst and caused extensive financial ruin to both England and France (progressed MC inconjunct Saturn; progressed ASC square Sun and Uranus). In May 1756, the Seven Years War began with France against Britain. The nadir came in September 1759 when the French lost Canada to the British on the Plains of Abraham outisde the city of Quebec. Both generals, Montcalm and Wolfe, were killed (progressed MC square Neptune). The formal ceding of Canada to Britain took place in February 1763 (progressed MC conjunct Venus).

France deteriorated further and further into rebellion with the rise of Louis XVI in 1774 (progressed ASC sesquare Mercury). His wife, Marie Antoinette,

provoked the French with her haughty ways and finally the residents of Paris could take no more. On the afternoon of July 14, 1789, they stormed the Bastille, an infamous prison, thus beginning the French Revolution (progressed ASC conjunct Jupiter sextile Mars and Pluto).

A republic was formed on September 21, 1792 (chart 2) and the monarchy came to an end (progressed MC sextile Neptune; progressed ASC sextile Mars).

## First French Republic

With the proclamation of the First Republic in September 1792, a new calendar also came into use with seasonal names for its months. With the monarchy now defunct, King Louis XVI was guillotined in January 1793 (progressed Sun inconjunct Saturn). France was already at war with Britain but soon had to fight Austria and Prussia as well. The infamous Reign of Terror began in September 1793 (progressed MC conjunct Mars) when Robespierre began

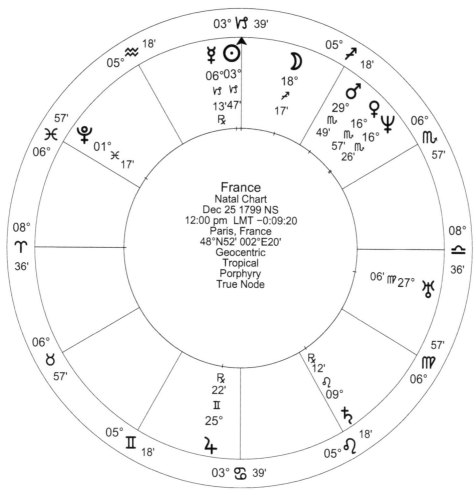

**Chart 3, December 25, 1799, noon LMT, Paris**
**Source: Encyclopedia Britannica for the date; noon assumed**

to purge France of its enemies. When the Terror ended in July 1794, Robespierre himself was executed (progressed MC semisquare Venus; progressed ASC sextile Mars).

To curtail future dictators, the Directoire was established in August 1795; its first leader was Barras. Relative peace reigned until November 1799, when Napoleon Bonaparte's coup d'etat took over the government (progressed Sun semisquare Uranus sesquare Pluto; progressed MC inconjunct Saturn; progressed ASC square Jupiter and Saturn).

## French Empire

Napoleon Bonaparte was proclaimed First Consul on Christmas Day 1799 (chart 3) and Consul for Life in August 1802 (progressed MC conjunct Mercury; progressed ASC sesquare Mars). Napoleon needed funds to wage his numerous campaigns of conquest so he sold the entire Louisiana Territory to the Americans in December 1803 (progressed ASC inconjunct Venus and Neptune). Proclaimed Emperor of the

French in May 1804, he was crowned by the Pope along with his wife, Josephine de Beauharnais, in Notre Dame Cathedral on December 2, 1804 (progressed ASC trine Moon). Thus began the First Empire (progressed MC inconjunct Saturn).

In October 1806, Napoleon occupied Berlin (progressed ASC sextile Jupiter) and soon afterwards carved out the Duchy of Warsaw. Rome was occupied in February 1808 and Spain fell to the French one month later (progressed ASC inconjunct Uranus). Vienna was taken in May 1809 (progressed ASC inconjunct Mars), and one year later Napoleon married the Archduchess Marie-Louise to strengthen ties between the two empires, and also to hopefully give Napoleon an heir (progressed MC semisquare Mars; progressed ASC sextile Pluto).

Napoleon began making preparations in 1811 for his venture to conquer Russia (progressed ASC trine Sun sesquare Moon). In June 1812, Napoleon entered Russian territory and won the Battle of Borodino two months later. But when his troops entered Moscow to claim their prize, they found the city

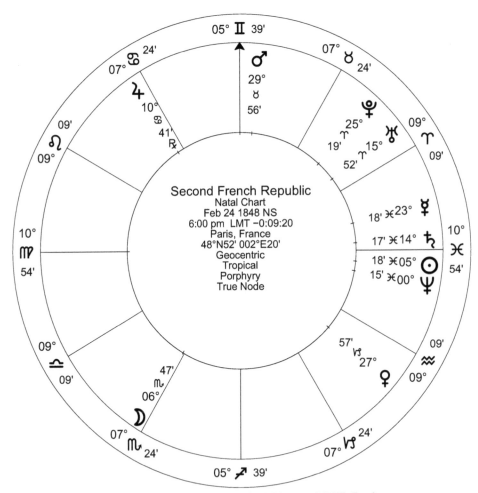

**Chart 4, February 24, 1848, 6:00 p.m. LMT, Paris**
**Source:** *The Times* of London says 6:00 p.m.

in flames and few, if any, provisions were left for the enemy. Napoleon could only retreat before the long and brutal Russian winter set in. By the time La Grande Armee returned back to France, it was a shadow of its former self (progressed MC semisquare Pluto sextile Venus and Neptune; progressed ASC trine Mercury). Napoleon had lost two-thirds of his troops in the snow.

Napoleon was forced into exile on the island of Elba in April 1814 (progressed ASC square Saturn), but Napoleon escaped his island prison, landed on the Riviera and worked his way through France to regain his position. Napoleon's dreams were dashed, however, on the plains outside Brussels at a place called Waterloo on the afternoon of June 15, 1815. The British troops under the Duke of Wellington trounced the French (progressed ASC semisquare Jupiter) and Napoleon was again exiled, this time to a small island in the South Atlantic called St. Helena where he died in May 1821. During Napoleon's 15 years in power, he cost the lives of more than two million people, military and civilian alike.

With the likes of Napoleon, the French decided to restore the monarchy they had refuted 23 years before. The Bourbon Dynasty was restored with Louis XVIII on the throne. A revolution in July 1830 necessitated a Constitutional Monarchy under Louis-Philippe, the Citizen King, of the House of Orleans. Another revolution in February 1848 threw out the monarchy again and the Second French Republic was proclaimed.

## Second Republic and Second Empire

The Second Republic was proclaimed on February 24, 1848 (chart 4) in Paris with Louis Napoleon, nephew of the former Emperor, as its leader. Republicanism, however, lasted for only four and a half years until Napoleon III (as he now called himself) seized power during a coup d'etat on December 2, 1852. Napoleon abolished the Second Republic and proclaimed the Second Empire in effect (progressed Sun trine Jupiter; progressed ASC opposition Saturn) France then began a 30 year battle to conquer Indochina in 1858 (progressed MC sextile Uranus).

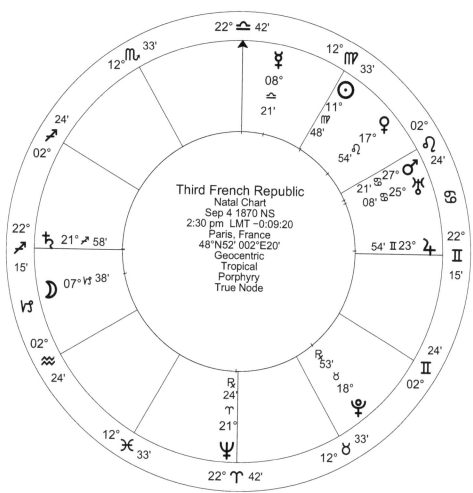

**Chart 5, September 4, 1870, 2:30 p.m. LMT, Paris**
**Source:** *The Times* **of London says 2:30 p.m.**

France also had designs in North America to expand his empire. When the Mexicans failed to repay their debts to France, French troops landed at Veracruz in December 1861. Napoleon III chose Maximilian, brother of the Austrian Emperor, to be Mexico's first monarch (progressed ASC semisquare Moon). It was an ill-fated venture from the onset and the Mexicans eventually executed Maximilian in June 1867 and his wife, Carlota, fled back to Europe (progressed MC sextile Pluto).

The French had been digging a canal through the isthmus of Suez since 1859 and by November 1869, it was finally completed. Dedication ceremonies saw much pomp and ceremony (progressed ASC trine Venus) for now it took much less time to journey to the Far East. Germany was rattling its sabers in 1870 and France foolishly thought it could beat its neighbor. Heavy losses were incurred, France surrendered at Sedan, the Second Empire had fallen and the Third Republic was proclaimed (progressed Sun sextile Venus; progressed MC inconjunct Venus).

## Third Republic

The Third Republic came into being on September 2, 1870 (chart 5) on the heels of Napoleon's defeat. Riots took place in Paris, the famed Tuileries Palace was burned and a radical group, called the Commune, ruled for a while. France had also lost the province of Alsace-Lorraine to Germany. France then settled into relative tranquillity until 1894 when a French army officer, named Alfred Dreyfus, was falsely accused of treason. Dreyfus was Jewish and a wave of anti-semitism swept over France threatening to bring down the government (progressed Sun semisquare Pluto). Dreyfus was sent off to Devil's Island, a prison located off the coast of South America, but was later cleared of all charges, much to the embarrassment of the government.

The greatest calamity to befall France in modern times began in August 1914 when Germany and Austria-Hungary declared war on the rest of western Europe. For the first time in history, France was fighting alongside its former enemy, Great Britain (progressed Sun square Uranus; progressed MC sesquare Neptune; progressed ASC sesquare Jupiter; transiting Jupiter square Pluto opposition Venus; transiting Saturn conjunct Mars). Northern France became the battlefield of Europe; carnage in places like the Marne, the Somme and Verdun exceeded one's imagination. The front lines scarcely moved from one year to the next in a deadlock of massive proportions and thousands and thousands were led to the slaughter. With the final entry of the United States of America into the war in late 1917, matters turned in favor of the Allies and the Armistice was finally signed at Compeigne on November 11, 1918 (progressed MC sesquare Uranus; progressed ASC opposition Venus). France had lost 1.5 million soldiers and 4.5 million others were put on the casualty list. France regained the province of Alsace-Lorraine when the Treaty of Versailles was signed in 1919 (transiting Saturn inconjunct Mars; transiting Uranus trine Jupiter).

A Socialist government under Leon Blum, called the Popular Front, took over during the 1930s. But France had bigger things to worry about when Hitler began occupying the Rhineland, thus repudiating the Treaty of Versailles. Eight months after Hitler invaded Poland, Nazi troops stormed into France in May 1940 (progressed Sun inconjunct Neptune; progressed ASC semisquare Pluto; transiting Uranus inconjunct ASC and MC; Neptune square ASC). The French foolishly believed that the Maginot Line, a series of trenches leftover from the previous war, would protect their nation. But the German Luftwaffe simply flew over the trenches and by June 13, 1940, the French surrendered, a puppet government was set up at Vichy under Marshal Petain, a hero from the former conflict with Germany. General Charles de Gaulle headed Free French forces from London and the resistance units cropped up all over France to oust the Nazis.

France was finally liberated by the Allies in August 1944 (progressed Sun trine Uranus) and when the Germans surrendered in May 1945, World War II had cost France not only its prestige, honor and integrity but also the lives of 200,000 lost in battle and 400,000 on the casualty list (transiting Saturn opposition Moon; transiting Uranus square Sun).

The Third Republic fell apart after World War II due to massive embarassment at having to surrender to the Germans, not to mention the ignoble Vichy government which had left a bad taste in the mouths of Frenchmen. A new Constitution was amended to focus power in the hands of the Prime Minister, and thus the Fourth Republic was born on October 30, 1946 (progressed Sun trine Mars; progressed MC conjunct Moon square Mercury; progressed ASC trine Venus) Transiting Mars was trine Uranus, Jupiter sextiled the Moon, Saturn sextiled Mercury and Uranus sextiled Neptune.

Please Note: Unlike most other astrologers, I believe that the Fourth Republic of 1946 was nothing more than a revision, or amendment, to the democratic regime set up under the Third Republic back in 1870. The Fourth Republic was a change in the French constitution, nothing more. To me, this does not constitute thinking a new country had been founded. With this in mind, I'll continue using the Third Republic chart of 1870 in my delineation through progressions and transits.

France pulled out of Indochina after its defeat at Dienbienphu in July 1954 (transiting Uranus square MC; transiting Pluto inconjunct MC). Soon afterwards, the movement for Algerian independence emerged. Beginning in March 1956, France began granting independence to its numerous African colonies. Morocco and Tunisia were first on the list (progressed MC inconjunct Venus; progressed ASC semisquare Jupiter sesquare Saturn; transiting Jupiter sextile MC).

On January 1, 1958, France became a charter member of the European Union (progressed Sun sextile Mercury; progressed MC trine Pluto; transiting Jupiter square Mars). Due to the Algerian crisis, the Fourth Republic fell in September 1958 and the Fifth Republic was proclaimed with Charles de Gaulle as President. The Constitution was again amended, this time to grant vast powers to the Chief Executive who would be responsible only to the legislature and who could rule with virtual powers of a dictator, if necessary.

France continued to loosen ties to its African colonies and beginning in July 1960, a host of new nations were born (progressed Sun square Sun; progressed MC square Neptune; transiting Jupiter inconjunct Mars and Uranus). The French Community was formed along the lines of the British Commonwealth. Algeria was finally granted its freedom in July 1962 after eight years of warfare and terrorism (progressed Sun sesquare Mars; MC opposition Uranus; progressed ASC conjunct Pluto).

France withdrew its troops from NATO in 1966 (progressed Sun trine Venus; progressed MC opposition Mars; progressed ASC sextile Uranus). The following year, NATO was expelled from Paris altogether and had to move its headquarters to Brussels (progressed Sun inconjunct Pluto; progressed ASC sextile Mars). Tighter immigration controls were instituted in 1993 and two years later, terrorist activities increased dramatically throughout France. General strikes broke out over government-mandated pay cuts and fury erupted over continued atomic bomb testing in the South Pacific (progressed Sun inconjunct Venus; MC inconjunct Mars). Military conscription ended at the end of 2001.

In October 2005, riots began in the northern suburbs of Paris as youths erupted into a frenzy of violence which soon spread to other cities in France (Sun opposition Mars; ASC square Mercury opposition Moon; MC square Uranus/Neptune).

# Paris

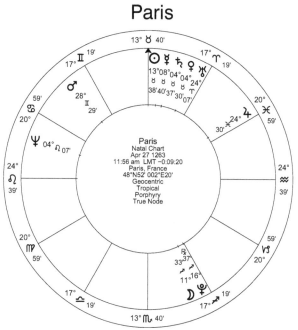

**April 27, 1263, 11:56 a.m. LMT**
**Source: Bibliotheque Nationale**

The capital and largest city in France was founded in the 5th century BC by the Parisii. Around 52 BC, the Romans founded a village called Lutetia but by the time the Merovingians ruled France in the 5th century, this place was known as Parisia, and within a few centuries, due to influence from the Counts of Paris and the Mayors of the Palace, it became the most powerful city in France. Monarchs made it their showplace, even though the city was situated mainly on the lies St. Louis and the lie de la Cite in the middle of the Seine River. Paris was the focal point of the French Revolution which began on July 14, 1789 when the Bastille was attacked. During the 19th century, Paris became a major hub due to the numerous rail lines entering the city and Baron Hausmann completely rebuilt parts of the city by creating broad, majestic boulevards for which this city is so famous.

Paris is an elegant, sophisticated and cultured city which has been the center of style, fashion, art, science and literature for generations. Its tourist attractions entrance visitors from around the world. Paris has many large green areas such as the Bois de Boulogne and the Bois de Vincennes on the edge of the city and the Jardin du Luxembourg and the Jardin des Tuileries offer respite from traffic and noise. The Champs Elysees, possibly the most attractive main street in the world, runs from the Place de la Concorde to the Arc de Triomphe where 12 avenues radiate to the poshest areas of Paris. Behind the Tuileries is the Louvre, the most famous art museum in the world. Nearby are the Cathedral of Notre Dame (1163), where monarchs have been crowned for centuries, and the famed Opera House, a fine example of Second Empire architecture. Across the river on the Left Bank, also known as the Latin Quarter, are the Hotel des Invalides where Napoleon is buried and the bohemian district of St. Germain.

Towering over Paris is the Eiffel Tower, fronting the Seine, the Champs de Mars and the Place du Chaillot. Paris has many museums besides the aforementioned from the Grand and Petit Palaces, the Musee de Cluny, Musee d'Orsay (housed in a former railway station) and the Centre Pompidou, built on the site of Paris' former market, Les Halles. Many famous Parisians and international figures are entombed in the Pere Lachaise cemetery. Paris has one of the oldest universities in Europe, called the Sorbonne. On a hill overlooking Paris is the district of Montmartre with its Church of Sacre Coeur and its 367 foot tower. Nearby is Place Pigalle home of entertainment for the adult-oriented. Outside of Paris are the villages of Chartres with its famous Cathedral and the royal enclave of Versailles which was rebuilt by Louis XIV from a hunting lodge into the largest royal palace on the continent.

# Bordeaux

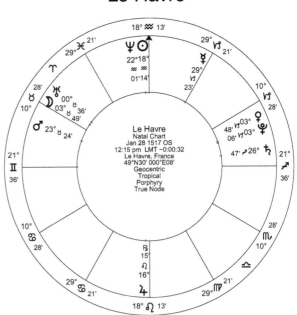

**July 1, 1199, 12:03 p.m. LMT**
**Source: Bibliotheque Municipale**

France's eighth-largest city lies on the Gironde River 60 miles from the Atlantic Ocean. From 1152 until 1453 it was part of England and capital of the Duchy of Guienne. Bordeaux is famous for its production of wine.

# Le Havre

**January 28, 1517, 12:15 p.m. LMT**
**Source: Bibliotheque du Havre**

Le Havre is France's second-largest port and its chief point of embarkation on the Atlantic. Located at the mouth of the Seine River, it was founded by Francis I as Havre de Grace. It was destroyed by bombs in 1944, but quickly rebuilt due to its maritime importance.

# Clermont Ferrand

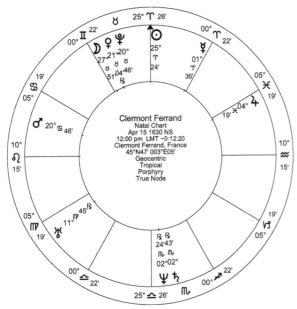

**April 15, 1630, noon LMT**
**Source: Bibliotheque Municipale**

Situated 85 miles west of Lyons, the towns of Clermont and Montferrand were united in 1731. This city is primarily industrial.

# Lyon

**June 21, 1320, 12:02 p.m. LMT**
**Source: Le Maire de Lyon**

France's third-largest city is located at the junction of the Rhone and Saone rivers. Founded in 43

B.C. by the Romans as Lugdunum, it was annexed to France in 1307. In 1595, the oldest Bourse in France opened here due to its silkworm cultivation. Today, Lyon is a gastronomic center with many five-star restaurants. Chief sights in town are the Fourviere Basili Musee des Tissus (silk), Institut Lumiere (films) and the Musee de la Marionette.

## Marseille

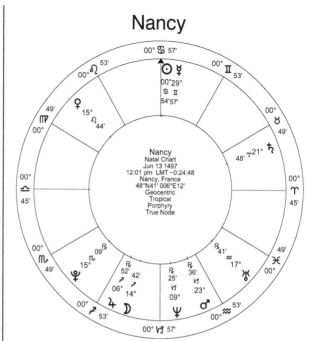

**January 1, 1767, 12:04 p.m. LMT**
**Source: Archives de la Ville**

Marseille is the second-largest city in France and its largest port. Situated on the Mediterranean Sea just east of the Rhone delta, it was founded in the 7th century B.C. by Greek traders and named Massalia. During the 11th century, it was the departure point for the Crusades but didn't become part of France until 1481. Marseille sprawls on slopes above the harbor with Notre Dame de la Garde standing watch over the city. Out in its harbor is the famed Chateau d'If made famous in many novels. During the French Revolution, soldiers from this city gave birth to a tune which is today the national anthem of France, "Le Marseillaise." Marseille is a cosmopolitan city with a large Arab quarter. Being on the Riviera enables this city to be more liberal and sophisticated than one would surmise, and definitely should not be missed by tourists racing towards Nice or Monte Carlo.

## Nancy

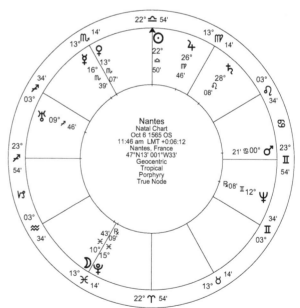

**June 13, 1797, 12:0l p.m. LMT**
**Source: Archives Municipale**

Nancy is the capital of the Duchy of Lorraine. The city has an elegance due to its redesign by King Stanislaus of Poland in the 18th century. The Place Stanislaus has the Musee des Beaux Arts, the Hotel de Ville and L'Opera.

## Nantes

**October 6, 1565, 11:46 a.m. LMT**
**Source: Bibliotheque Municipale**

Nantes is France's seventh-largest city, situated on the Loire River 30 miles from the Atlantic Ocean.

Its wealth increased during the 18th century due to trade with Africa and the Caribbean. In Medieval times, it was the capital of the Dukes of Brittany.

## Nice

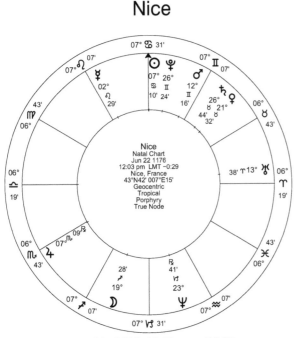

**June 22, 1176, 12:02 p.m. LMT**
**Source: Mairie de Nice and Bibliotheque de Cessole**

Nice is the fifth-largest city in France and capital of the Alpes-Maritimes. Situated on the Mediterranean Sea 15 miles from Italy, it was founded by Phoenicians in the 5th century B.C. and by the time the Romans came three centuries later, they named it Nicaea. From 1388 until 1860, Nice was a part of Savoy, a kingdom now based in Italy. Nice is a very popular tourist spot and is famed for Carnival during the beginning of Lent. Close to other resort cities like Cannes, St. Tropez, Monaco and San Remo, Nice can hold its own and has some of the most sumptuous hotels and restaurants in the country. The Promenade des Anglais along the beach is one of the most beautiful seashore drives in the world which overlooks the Bale des Anges. From the Colline de Chateau one can view the entire region, including the Old City. For museum and art lovers, there's the Musee Matisse, Marc Chagall and the Musee Massena.

## Rouen

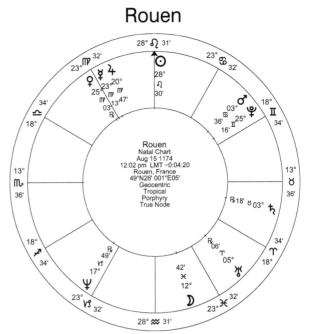

**August 15, 1174, 12:02 p.m. LMT**
**Source: Ville de Rouen**

Rouen is a port city on the Seine River 75 miles northwest of Paris. It was the medieval capital of Normandy and was founded by the Romans as Rotomagus. It was here in May 1431 that Joan of Arc was burned at the stake. Don't miss the Notre Dame Cathedral with the second tallest steeple in France. Rouen is famous for its churches and is known as the City of Spires.

# Strasbourg

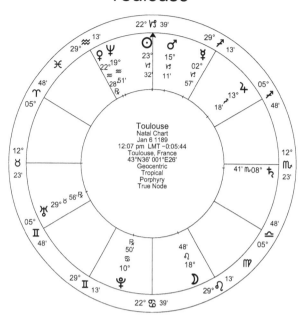

**April 21, 1263, 11:57 a.m. LMT**
**Source: Bibliotheque Municipale**

Strasbourg is located at the junction of the Ill and Rhine rivers and is the sixth-largest city in France. During Roman times it was known as Argentoratum and in 1262, Strasbourg was made an Imperial Town. Only in 1681 did it become part of France, but from 1870 until 1918, it was capital of Alsace-Lorraine and belonged to Germany.

This city is home to the EEC Council of Europe and the European Parliament. Due to its location between France and Germany, it has a mixed culture. Strasbourg is probably most famous for its Notre Dame Cathedral built in the Gothic style. Its spire towers 471 feet above the city and is the second-highest in Europe, after Cologne. The main museums are contained in the Palais Rohan.

# Toulouse

**January 6, 1189, 12:07 p.m. LMT**
**Source: Bibliotheque Municipale**

Toulouse is the fourth-largest city in France and situated on the Garonne River 55 miles from the Spanish border. It's called La Ville Rose for the numerous red-brick buildings that permeate the older part of town. The Romans knew it as Tolosa and from 419 to 508 A.D., Toulouse was a Visigoth capital. The main tourist sight is the Basilique St. Sermin, the largest Romanesque structure in France and Les Jacobins Gathedrale, built in the Gothic style. Toulouse's main industry is aircraft manufacture, for this is the home of the Concorde and home to Airbus.

# Georgia
## Sakartvelo Respublica

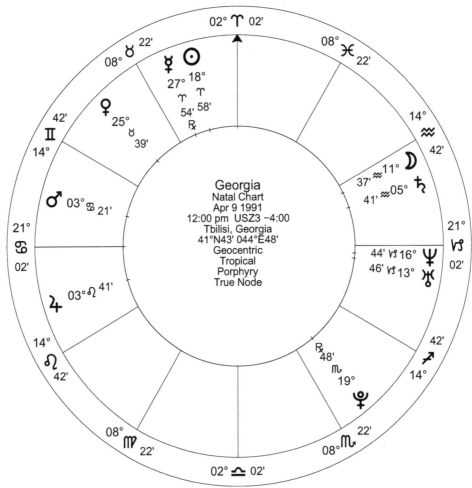

**April 9, 1991, noon BGDT, 8:00 a.m. GMT, Tbilisi**
**Source: Nicholas Campion's Book of World Horoscopes**

Georgia is situated in the Trans-Caucasus region, on the border "between Europe and Asia, on the eastern shores of the Black Sea. Europe's highest point, Mt. Elbrus, rises to a height of 18,510 feet on the border with Russia. Georgia is a land of turbulent rivers, dense forests, deep ravines and fertile valleys. The main rivers are the Kura and Rioni.

Population: 4,989,285; 70% Georgian, 8% Armenian, 6% Russian

Religion: 75% Orthodox, 11% Moslem

Area: 26,911 square miles (the size of the Netherlands and Belgium combined); 57% urban, 9% arable

Economy: Georgia mines most of the world's supply of manganese and exports huge amounts of citrus fruit, grapes and tea.

To the ancient Greeks this region was known as Colchis, the land of the Golden Fleece. Christianity arrived in the 5th century A.D., and Arabs invaded three centuries later. In 1236, Georgia was conquered by the Mongols.

In 1801, Georgia asked Russia for protection against the Turks and Persians, thus beginning almost two centuries of occupation. In May 1918, Georgia declared its independence from Russia but soon became a German protectorate until the end of World War I six months later. Britain then assumed a mandate until July 1920. Bolshevik occupation came in February 1921, and by the end of 1922, Georgia became a charter member of the Soviet Union in the Trans-Caucasian Republic. In December 1936, Georgia became its own republic, as did Armenia and Azerbaijan.

Independence was again declared from the Soviet Union on April 9, 1991, but it refused to join the Commonwealth of Independent States that December. The President of Georgia fled the country in January 1992 after trying to establish a dictatorship (transiting Jupiter trine Uranus); five months later the region of Abkhazia declared its independence from Georgia (progressed MC square Mars trine Jupiter; progressed Sun square ASC).

In August 1995, Shevardnadze was wounded by a car bomb en route to sign a new constitution (progressed MC sextile Saturn; transiting Jupiter sextile Saturn; transiting Uranus square Mercury). In February 1998, Shevardnadze again escaped an attempt to assassinate him (progressed MC semisquare Venus; transiting Jupiter trine Mars; transiting Saturn square Neptune).

## Tbilisi (Tiflis)

Tbilisi is built on the slopes of Mt. Mtatsminda and was founded in 455 A.D. as the new capital of Georgia. It was a center for trade between Europe and Asia. Captured many times over the centuries by Persians, Byzantines, Arabs, Mongols and Turks, it came under Russian control in 1801. This city is one of the world's oldest centers of Christendom and has a 6th century cathedral and 7th century basilica.

# Germany
## Bundesrepublik Deutschland

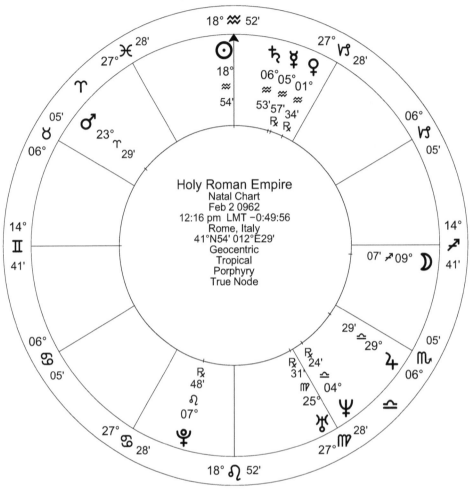

**Chart 1, Holy Roman Empire, February 2, 962 A.D., 12:16 p.m. LMT, Rome, Italy**
**Source: Encyclopedia Britannica; noontime presumed, when Otto I was crowned**

Germany lies in the heart of Europe. On its northern border lie the Baltic and North Seas; the coastline is 1,385 miles long. On the southern border are the Alps, including its highest point, Zugspitze (elev. 9,721 feet). Surrounded by Poland and the Czech Republic on the east, Austria and Switzerland on the south, by Denmark in the north and by the Netherlands, Belgium and Luxembourg on the west. Inside its boundaries lie the provinces of Bavaria, Franconia, Swabia, Baden and Wurttemburg in the south. Saxony, Thuringia, Brandenburg, Mecklenburg and Pomerania in the east, and Schleswig-Holstein, Hannover, Brunswick, Hesse, Westphalia and the Rhineland in the west.

The Harz Mountains occupy the center of Germany while in the south lie the largest lakes: Konstanz, Chiemsee and Starnberger. The main rivers are the Rhine, Main, Danube, Weser, Mosel, Oder and Neisse.

Population: 83,029,536; 32% German, 5% Turkish

Religion: 38% Protestant, 34% Catholic, 5% Moslem

Area: 137,803 square miles (the size of Poland or Montana); 87% urban, 33% arable

Economy: Germany is the industrial powerhouse of Europe. It produces half of its iron and steel and 60% of its coal. Main exports are machinery, automobiles, chemicals and electronics. And lets not forget the beer and schnapps.

During the first millenium BC, Germanic tribes settled northern and central Europe and by 500 B.C., barbarians arrived from central Asia. Roman troops were defeated by Marius, leader of the Allemanni, Burgundians, Franks, Lombards, Ostrogoths and Visigoths in 101 BC. Further Roman advances were halted at Teutoberg forest in 9 A.D. During the reign of Clovis (481-511 A.D.) a united state in what is now France and Germany was founded and by the reign of Charlemagne (768-814 A.D.) his Prankish kingdom expanded considerably.

Charlemagne was crowned Roman Emperor by the Pope at the Vatican on Christmas Day 800 A.D. When the Treaty of Verdun was signed in 843 A.D., Charlemagne's empire was divided among his grandsons. Louis received the eastern portion of what would eventually become the nation of Germany. During the reign of Otto I (936-973 A.D.), Germanic regions began to consolidate, especially after Otto was crowned Emperor of the Holy Roman Empire on February 2, 962 A.D. (chart 1). This date I deem very important to the birth of Germany. What constituted Germany was a loose confederation of numerous kingdom, duchies, principalities and baronies. The Pope had little real authority, but over the centuries, Germanic monarchs usually ruled this "Empire." Eventually, lordship over the Holy Roman Empire fell to the Hapsburgs of Austria.

In 1122, the Concordat of Worms settled the dispute between the Pope and Germanic leaders by giving the Pope the exclusive right to invest individuals with spiritual powers while the Holy Roman Emperor was given the right to all temporal powers (progressed MC sextile Uranus; progressed ASC trine Sun). During the reign of Frederick Barbarossa of the Hohenstaufen dynasty, Slavs in eastern Germany were Christianized by 1190 (progressed MC trine Mars). In 1241, towns in northern Germany organized for protection and trade (progressed ASC trine Uranus). After Barbarossa's death, his successors ruled the Empire from Sicily.

Between 1254 and 1273 was a period called the Interregnum, a time when there were no rulers at all (progressed MC sextile Neptune). In August 1273, Rudolf von Hapsburg was elected Emperor in Frankfurt and crowned two months later in Aachen (progressed MC trine Mars square Uranus). When the Golden Bull was signed in 1356, it regulated the succession of the Empire, usually to the Hapsburgs (progressed MC semisquare Venus; ASC inconjunct Moon).

On October 31, 1517, Martin Luther shook up Europe and the religious with the posting of his 95 Theses on the door of a church in Wittenberg (progressed MC semisquare Jupiter, ruler of religion). While Luther was in prison in 1521, he translated the Bible into German (progressed ASC sextile Venus) and by 1545, the Council of Trent attempted to codify Catholic beliefs and doctrine. A war broke out in 1546 between Protestant princes and the Emperor Charles V (progressed ASC sextile Sun), but the rebels were defeated. The Peace of Augsburg in 1555 demanded that subjects of a particular region adopt the religion of their ruler of move elsewhere (progressed ASC square Uranus). Due to this treaty, religious wars were temporarily halted.

The Thirty Years War began at Prague in early 1618 when heretics were thrown out windows (progressed MC trine Mars sesquare Pluto; progressed ASC semisquare Venus). This conflict was a combination of religious, political and dynastic differences. The northern part of Germany was largely Protestant, and allied itself with Sweden and France. The south which was mostly Catholic sided with Austria and the Pope. When the war ended with the signing of the Treaty of Westphalia in 1648, the power of the Holy Roman Emperor was restricted (progressed MC square Mars semisquare Moon). Germany had lost one-third of its population, more than eight million had died and Germany now had more than 1,700 separate political units. From 1648 until August 1806, the vision of a united Germany was only a pipe dream. Napoleon disbanded the Holy Roman Empire in 1806 and left Germany to its fate (progressed MC inconjunct Venus; progressed ASC trine Venus).

## Prussia

The Kingdom of Prussia grew out of the Electorate of Brandenburg and the Duchy of Prussia in the 16th century. The Kingdom of Prussia was founded on January 18, 1701 (chart 2), when its first ruler was crowned in the city of Konigsberg (now Kaliningrad, Russia). Prussia began to amass a powerful army so when Frederick the Great ascended the throne in 1740, he immediately involved himself in the Austrian Secession War. When a treaty was signed in 1748, Prussia won territory from Austria (progressed ASC inconjunct Venus). In 1756, Frederick again went to war against Austria, this time it was called the Seven Years War (progressed ASC sesquare Saturn).

During the first partition of Poland in 1773, Prussia gained land near the Baltic (progressed MC sextile Jupiter; progressed ASC trine Neptune). The Polish Partition of 1793 (progressed ASC inconjunct Mars) and 1795 (progressed MC semisquare Mars; progressed ASC trine Venus) took what was left of Poland surrounding East Prussia. After being defeated by Napoleon at Austerlitz, the Emperor of Austria was forced to relinquish the additional title of Holy Roman Emperor in August 1806 (progressed MC sextile Uranus square Pluto; progressed ASC inconjunct Sun semisquare Uranus). Prussia was

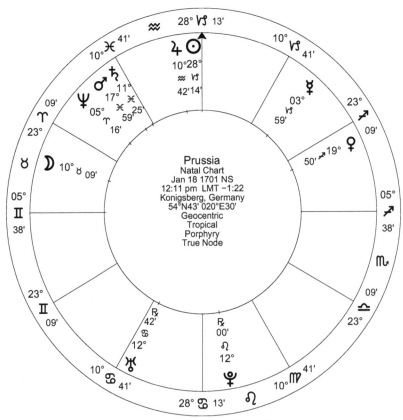

**Chart 2, Prussia, January 18, 1701, 12:11 a.m. LMT, Konigsberg (now Kaliningrad)**
**Source: Prussian Royal Archives; noontime presumed as most coronations take place at this time**

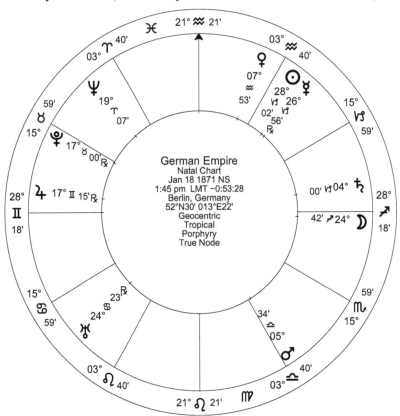

**Chart 3, German Empire, January 18, 1871, 1:45 p.m. LMT, Berlin**
**Source: *Mundane Astrology* by Baigent, Campion and Harvey; chart has been relocated from Versailles to Berlin**

again defeated by France in 1807 (progressed ASC inconjunct Sun) but by 1813, Prussia joined a coalition against Napoleon (progressed MC sextile Mars). With Napoleon's defeat at Waterloo in June 1815, the Treaty of Vienna restored old Prussian territories and a federation of German states, called the Confederation of the Rhine was established. Germany was now a region with 39 different political entities, each with its own rulers, laws and customs.

## German Empire

Revolutions broke out all across Europe in the spring of 1848 (progressed ASC sesquare Moon and Jupiter). A Constitution was drawn up in Frankfurt in 1848 but it was rejected by the Prussian King. Revolutionaries demanded a free press, juries, a national militia and a Parliament. Otto von Bismarck was appointed Chancellor in 1862 (progressed MC square Neptune; progressed ASC square Mercury) and he took Prussia into a war with Austria against Denmark to gain their provinces of Schleswig and Holstein that Bismarck deemed to be German (progressed ASC opposition Neptune). Austria and Prussia, however, were on opposite sides by 1866 and this time Prussia was the victor (progressed MC sextile Moon inconjunct Jupiter). Bismarck then took Prussia into a war with France in 1870 and Prussia was again the victor, and gained the regions of Alsace and Lorraine. France was ordered to pay an indemnity to Prussia (progressed ASC trine Jupiter inconjunct Moon).

Germany was united on January 1, 1871 (chart 3), but the true date for the birth of the German Empire was when King Wilhelm I was proclaimed Emperor of Germany in the Hall of Mirrors at the Palace of Versailles outside Paris on January 18, 1871, the 170th anniversary of the founding of Prussia (progressed ASC inconjunct Saturn sextile Pluto).

Bismarck was still Chancellor of the German Empire, but when Kaiser Wilhelm II became Emperor in late 1888, Bismarck's days were numbered as his vision for Germany differed radically from that of the Kaiser. Bismarck was dismissed in 1890 (progressed Sun trine Jupiter square Pluto). Over the next 25 years, Germany continued to build up its military in hopes of having a dominant place in European affairs. Many in Europe secretly feared German power and before long, they would be correct in their assumptions.

With the assassination of the Austrian Archduke Franz Ferdinand in Sarajevo in June 1914, the drumroll started. Germany wanted to get into the action and sided with Austria-Hungary against the powers of Britain, France, Italy and Russia and war was declared in early August. Germany had designs on more territory: it already had 208,000 square miles but was greedy for more (progressed Sun semisquare Sun and Mercury; progressed MC opposition Mars). Most of the Great War was fought on the battlefields of northern France, the front hardly moving from one year to the next in complete stagnation. Places like the Marne, the Somme and Verdun resulted in catastrophic losses of life for all sides. Until the Americans entered the fray in late 1917, Germany thought it might eventually win the conflict. Germany was forced to sign an Armistice on November 11, 1918, the Kaiser had already fled to neighboring Netherlands and a Republic had already been proclaimed in Berlin two days before (progressed ASC inconjunct Saturn semisquare Jupiter). Saturn was sextile the ASC of the German Empire, and it was conjunct that ASC when the war began; a bad omen, I think. When the war began, Neptune was opposing the Sun (inflated egos) but when the Armistice was signed, Pluto was squaring Mars.

## German Republic

The Republic began under inauspicious circumstances. More than 1.8 million Germans had lost their lives in the Great War and nearly 4.2 million had been wounded. The Treaty of Versailles, which was signed on June 28, 1919 (chart 4), placed heavy burdens on the fledgling nation (progressed ASC semisquare Mars; transiting Mars trine Uranus; Saturn opposition Uranus) including reparations to the Allies of $33 billion ($650 billion in 2000 dollars). To pay that massive sum, the German government just printed more cash which caused its currency to reach a value of 4,000 billion dollars to one U.S. dollar. It took a wheelbarrow of money just to buy a loaf of bread (progressed MC inconj Jupiter; progressed ASC conjunct Uranus). In November 1923, Hitler staged a putsch in an attempt to take over the government (transiting Mars trine ASC; Pluto trine Venus).

The worldwide financial depression that began in November 1929 hit Germany especially hard (progressed Sun square Saturn; progressed ASC trine Pluto; transiting Saturn conjunct Mars; Pluto opposition Moon). More than eight million Germans were unemployed, money was worthless and the Allies still had too much control over Germany's affairs. The Nazis, however, had a vision for Germany and to placate them, Hitler was appointed Chancellor and sworn in by Hindenburg on January 30, 1933 between 11:00 a.m. and 11:15 a.m. in Berlin (progressed Sun conjunct Mercury sesquare Jupiter; pro-

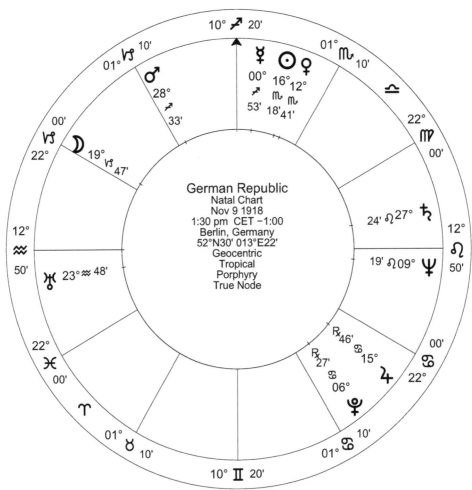

**Chart 4, German Republic, November 9, 1918, 1:30 p.m. MET, Berlin**
**Source:** *The New York Times* says 1:30 p.m.

gressed MC sesquare Neptune; progressed ASC trine Sun; transiting Uranus square Moon). Hitler had the Reichstag burned soon after and began to rid himself of his enemies. With Hindenburg's death in August 1934, Hitler now had complete power and control (transiting Neptune square MC; Pluto inconjunct Uranus). Democratic government in Germany came to an end and intimidation and coercion became the norm.

The first anti-Jewish laws were enacted in late 1934 and the Treaty of Versailles was repudiated. The Nuremburg Laws became effective in September 1935 (progressed MC semisquare Venus trine Saturn; progressed ASC sesquare Neptune; transiting Jupiter sextile Moon; Saturn sextile Pluto; Pluto inconjunct Uranus). Germany also got out of the League of Nations at this time. Hitler reoccupied the Rhineland in March 1936 (progressed Sun semisquare Moon; progressed ASC sesquare Venus inconjunct Saturn; transiting Jupiter trine Uranus; Saturn trine Jupiter).

Hitler annexed his homeland, Austria, in March

1938; it was called the Anschluss (progressed Sun inconjunct Pluto; progressed ASC trine Mercury semisquare Sun; transiting Saturn square Pluto). In September 1938, Hitler met with British Prime Minister Chamberlain in Munich to settle the Sudetenland crisis. Hitler wanted this largely-German region of Czechoslovakia for his Third Reich. Chamberlain was appeased and Europe looked the other way hoping Hitler would be satisfied (transiting Mars square MC; Jupiter conjunct Uranus; Saturn square Jupiter; Pluto trine Mercury). But Hitler wasn't satisfied and he soon gobbled up the; entire country of Czechoslovakia. With the U.S. in isolation and Europe still too weak from the previous war, Hitler seemed invincible when German troops invaded Poland on September 1, 1939 (progressed MC semisquare Sun; Jupiter square Pluto; Uranus inconjunct Mercury). Hitler had previously signed a Non-Aggression Pact with Stalin whereby they would divide Poland which both leaders detested and Hitler wouldn't interfere when the Soviet Union would invade the Baltic countries.

Hitler then set his sights on Scandinavia and invaded Norway and Denmark in late April 1940 (progressed ASC square Pluto). He then invaded the Netherlands, Belgium, Luxembourg and France in May 1940 (transiting Saturn sextile Pluto; Pluto trine Mercury). France quickly surrendered and a puppet government based at Vichy was established. Italy also entered the war on the Axis side with Hitler as Mussolini also wanted to carve up Europe.

Hitler betrayed Stalin when he invaded the Soviet Union in June 1941 (progressed Sun trine Neptune; progressed ASC trine Neptune semisquare Uranus; transiting Saturn square Uranus; Uranus square Saturn). Nazi troops laid siege to Moscow, Leningrad, Kiev and Stalingrad; the latter city had access to the oilfields of the Caspian vitally important to the war effort. Hitler's troops were not prepared for the Russian weather, which killed as many as died in battle. North Africa, however, was a more victorious arena for the Nazis until Allied troops landed in November 1942 and began to drive the Nazis into the sea (progressed ASC inconjunct Venus sesquare Saturn; transiting Saturn opposition MC). By February 1943, German troops were in defeat from Russia (transiting Jupiter conjunct Jupiter; Uranus opposition Mercury).

With the landing of the Allies on the beaches of Normandy in June 1944, Hitler was more and more backed into a corner from which there was no retreat (progressed MC opposition Pluto; progressed ASC inconjunct Sun; transiting Mars conj Neptune; Saturn opposition Mars; Uranus sextile Neptune). Soon, France was liberated and the march towards Germany began. The Germans put up a final last stand in the Ardennes during the winter of 1945. Then the Allies crossed the Rhine and headed for Berlin. Soviet troops were entering Germany from the east and it was a race to see which side would get to Berlin first. Hitler had retreated into his bunker where on April 30, 1945, he committed suicide with his wife of one day, Eva Braun (transiting Mars square Mars; Saturn conjunct Pluto; Uranus opposition MC). The Germans surrendered a week later and the war in Europe was over.

The Potsdam Conference of July 1945 was attended by U.S. President Truman, Joseph Stalin from the Soviet Union and Clement Attlee from Great Britain. It was decided to divide Germany (and Berlin) into four zones of occupation: Russian, British, French and American (transiting Saturn trine Sun; Mars square Uranus; Jupiter inconjunct Uranus; Uranus inconjunct Sun; Pluto conjunct Neptune). The old Germany of Hitler and his "1,000 Year Reich" was dead and four years of occupation began.

More than 14 million refugees were strewn across Europe: 9 million from Poland alone. Nearly 3 million Germans were in Allied prison camps and another 3 million persons were considered dead or missing. Germany had lost 3.2 million soldiers, and 7.3 million were wounded in Hitler's futile attempt to dominate the world. Berlin was decimated by 70,000 tons of bombs and 60 percent of its houses destroyed. Russians seized 80 percent of the industrial equipment in their sector as reparation for their suffering. The Russians also seized 75 percent of East Germany's food supply.

The Jewish population had been reduced by 90 percent and more than 6 million Jews were exterminated in the concentration camps. Germany lost all its land east of the Oder-Neisse rivers to Poland, including East Prussia. The black market was thriving and millions were either starving or homeless. Aid poured in from America under the Marshall Plan to resuscitate Germany. The eastern zone under the Soviet Union remained in ruins and disarray. The Soviets blockaded Berlin in June 1948 over a currency dispute, but the Allies formed an airlift to keep the city from starvation. The airlift lasted one year.

# West Germany

West Germany was developed and formed in many stages. On May 8, 1949 at 11:55 p.m. MEDT (chart 5), Konrad Adenauer signed the Basic Law, or Constitution (Source: *TIME* magazine). The Basic Law was in force as of May 23, 1949 at 12 midnight in Bonn (Source: *Collier's* magazine). The Peace Conference began on May 23, 1949 at 4:00 p.m. MET in Paris (Source: *The Times* of London) and the West German Parliament opened in Bonn on September 8, 1949 at 11:15 a.m. MEDT (Source: *Newsweek* magazine). Many astrologers use the May dates listed above in error, for the real moment of birth for the Bundesrepublik was when the Allied High Command handed over most of its powers to the new nation. That occurred in Bonn on September 21, 1949 at 11:15 a.m. MEDT (Source: *Newsweek* magazine).

West Germany gained complete sovreignty on May 15, 1955 (progressed MC semisquare Neptune; progressed ASC semisquare Sun; transiting Mars sextile MC; transiting Saturn square Pluto; transiting Pluto conjunct MC). Germany joined the European Union on January 1, 1958 as a charter member and West Germany finally joined the United Nations in 1973 (progressed Sun opposition Jupiter). The following year, a treaty was signed with East Germany which settled a border dispute.

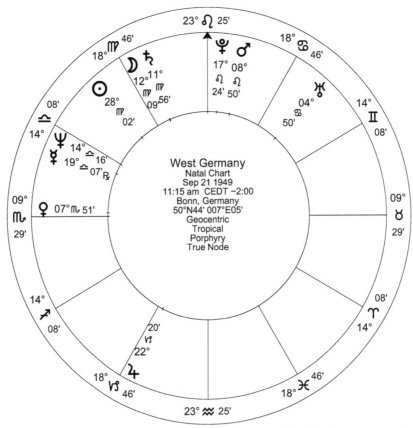

**Chart 5, West Germany, September 21, 1949, 11:15 a.m. MEDT, 9:15 a.m. GMT, Bonn**
**Source:** *Newsweek* **magazine says 11:15 a.m.**

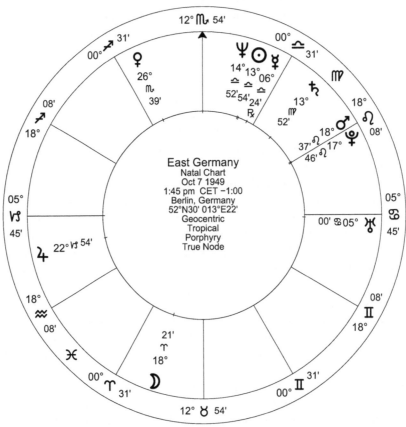

**Chart 6, East Germany, October 7, 1949, 1:45 p.m. MET, Berlin**
**Source: Reinhold Ebertin and AFA, November 1989, both state 1:45 p.m.**

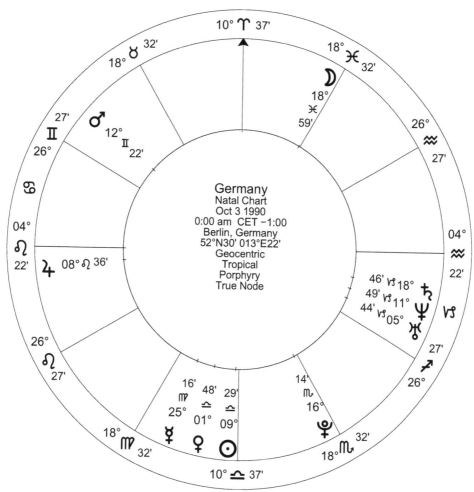

**Chart 7, Germany, October 3, 1990, 12:00 a.m. MET, Berlin**
**Source: CNN, shown live on TV**

With the fall of the Berlin Wall in November 1989, Helmut Kohl was at last able to unite Germany by October 3, 1990 (progressed Sun square Mars; progressed MC square Uranus; progressed ASC semisquare Jupiter; transiting Mars square Moon; transiting Jupiter conjunct Mars square Venus and ASC; transiting Uranus opposition and Pluto square their natal positions).

## East Germany

The Soviets formed the nation of East Germany (aka People's Republic) on October 7, 1949 (chart 6). A revolution broke out in East Berlin against Soviet occupation on June 17, 1953 (progressed Sun sextile Pluto; transiting Jupiter trine Mercury inconjunct ASC). To keep its citizens from fleeing to the western sector, the Soviets erected a wall around West Berlin in August 1961 and East Germany became more of a police state than it already was under the Stasi (progressed ASC square Moon inconjunct Mars; transiting Uranus square Venus). After a quar-

ter century, a border dispute with Poland was finally settled in November 1970 (progressed Sun trine Uranus; progressed MC sesquare Moon). The Berlin Wall was breached in November 1989 and Communism fell into oblivion, thus ending four decades of Soviet occupation. Less than a year later, Germany was reunited (progressed ASC opposition Saturn; transiting Saturn and Neptune semisquare Venus).

## Germany

Celebrations uniting East and West Germany took place in Berlin at midnight on October 3, 1990 (chart 7). The capital was to remain in Bonn for a while until Berlin could be fully-prepared to become the permanent capital by the close of the 20th century. Attacks by skinheads on foreigners rankled the government and reminded elders of horrors witnessed during the days of the Third Reich. But this was 1992 (progressed Sun square Neptune; progressed MC sextile Mars; progressed ASC inconjunct Uranus). By May 1993, Germany began to restrict its extremely liberal asylum laws (progressed Sun trine Mars; transiting Jupiter square Uranus). By the end of September 1994, American, British, French and Russian troops had finally left as German occupiers under the High Command were no longer required. The Church of Scientology was attacked on several grounds by the German government in 1997 (progressed MC inconjunct Pluto; progressed ASC conjunct Jupiter). The government wondered whether it was a real religion or just a way to avoid German taxation which would require an exemption from Berlin.

In late 2005, Angela Merkel became the first female Chancellor in German history (MC inconjunct Mercury). She grew up in East Germany and will lead Europe's largest economy, but one which is in the throes of high unemployment, low growth and the need to reform the welfare state.

## Berlin

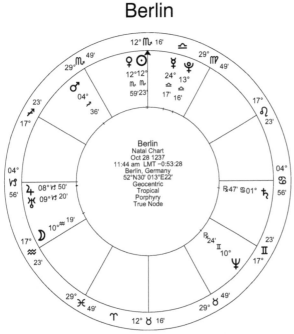

Berlin
Natal Chart
Oct 28 1237
11:44 am LMT −0:53:28
Berlin, Germany
52°N30' 013°E22'
Geocentric
Tropical
Porphyry
True Node

**October 28, 1237, 11:44 a.m. LMT**
**Source: Berliner Stadtsbibliotek**

The capital and largest city in Germany is composed of 23 districts which merged to form Greater Berlin on October 1, 1920. Founded in the 13th century on marshes along the River Spree, it was originally two towns, Berlin and Kolin, which merged on January 1, 1710, one year after its medieval walls were torn down. Berlin has been ruled by the Hohenzollerns since the 15th century and their dynasty founded the German Empire in 1871. At that time Berlin had only 800,000 residents, but by World War I, more than 4.5 million lived there; it was the second-largest city in Europe after London. During the 1920s, Berlin was a fulcrum of artistic freedom of

expression and had the reputation of being avant garde and risque.

After Hitler took over in 1933, Berlin took on a more somber, serious tone. Heavily bombed by the Allies in the Second World War, over 60 percent of the city lay in ruins by the time the Soviets entered in April 1945 and occupied the eastern half of the city. The western districts were jointly ruled by the British, French and Americans. To keep its citizens alive when the Soviets cut off supplies in 1948, the Allies formed an airlift for a year. The Berlin Wall was erected in August 1961 to permanently keep the East Germans from fleeing to the West, but by November 1989, Communism was in its death throes and the wall came crashing down piece by piece. East and West Germany were united here in October 1990, and the capital of Germany was relocated here at the beginning of the millenium.

Through extensive restoration, much of pre-war Berlin still survives. In Potsdam is Frederick the Great's palace of Sans Souci and the Charlottenburg Palace still reminds one of former German imperialism. The western boundary of Berlin has a series of lakes, called the Havel, and its largest park, the Grunewald. In nearby Dahlem are the world-famous zoo and eight museums. The main street of Berlin is the Kurfurstendamm which extends from the bombed Kaiser Wilhelm Church to the southwest. The symbol of Berlin is the Brandenburg Gate and to the east the Unter den Linden, once the premier shopping street of Berlin. Near the gate is the infamous Reichstag, or Parliament, which was torched shortly after Hitler came to power, shelled by the Soviets during World War II and recently restored to its former glory with the addition of a glass dome. Nearby is the Tiergarten and the Victory monument. The heart of old Berlin lies on an island in the River Spree: the massive Dom (cathedral) is constructed in the Baroque style and the Pergamon Museum has one of the largest collections of Egyptian artifacts.

# Bonn

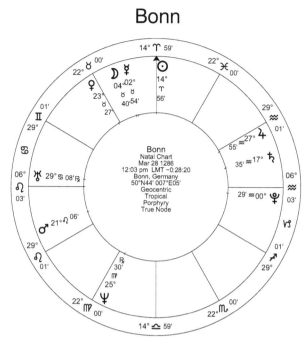

**March 28, 1286, 12:03 p.m. LMT**
**Source: Der Stadt Bonn**

Bonn was the capital of West Germany from 1949 until 1990, when East and West Germany were united. Most government offices were moved to Berlin by the end of the 20th century. Founded by the Bishop of Cologne in 1243, it was a quiet and sleepy university town until the end of World War II. Its chief claim to fame had been that it was the birthplace of Ludwig von Beethoven. Situated on the picturesque Rhine river 20 miles south of Cologne, only time will tell what its role will be after the Bundestag (Parliament) and Bundesrat (lower house) move away.

## Bremen

Bremen is Germany's second-largest port, located on the Weser river 60 miles SW of Hamburg. A bishopric was established here in 788 and by 1358, Bremen had become a Hanseatic city. It was created an Imperial Town in 1646. The tenth-largest city in Germany is a major shipbuilding center and oil refiner.

## Chemnitz

Chemnitz is located on the Ghem River 45 miles southeast of Leipzig. During the l4th century it was a major textile center and a major industrial center five centuries later. Chemnitz was heavily bombed during World War II, but after the Soviets took over its name was changed to Karl Marx Stadt. It reverted to its old name after the fall of Communism.

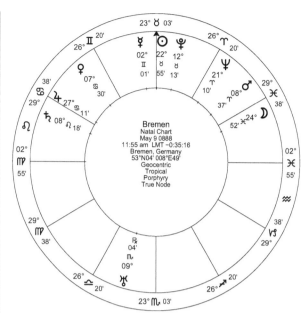

**May 9, 888, 11:55 a.m. LMT**
**Source: Staatsbibliothek**

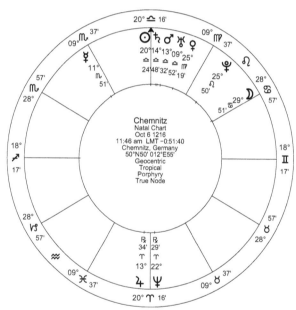

**October 6, 1216, 11:46 a.m. LMT**
**Source: Stadtarchiv**

## Cologne (Koln)

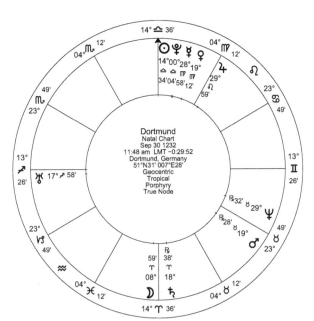

**June 5, 1288, 11:59 a.m. LMT**
**Source: Stadt Koln**

Situated on the Rhine River 20 miles north of Bonn, it was founded by the Romans in 50 A.D. and called Colonia. An archbishopric was founded here in 785 and the famed Cathedral was begun in the late 13th century. Completed only in 1880, its 515 foot spires are the tallest in Europe and the Cathedral was fortunately left untouched by Allied bombers during the war. Cologne's university was founded in 1388 and the city was proclaimed a Free City in 1475. Cologne is famous for its Carnival which begins in mid-November. The Romisch-Germanisches museum is a storehouse of Roman life in ancient Germany. Cologne is the fourth-largest city in Germany and is also a major industrial center.

## Dortmund

Germany's seventh-largest city and second-largest city in the Ruhr is located 20 miles east of Essen. It's Europe's biggest maker of beer and a major steel center.

## Dresden

Germany's center for Baroque architecture, the "Florence of the North" and one of Europe's most beautiful cities is situated on the Elbe River 90 miles southeast of Berlin. This capital of Saxony was founded by the Slavs and called Drezhdane. After 1270 it was home to the Margraves of Meissen. Almost obliterated during the Allied firebombing of February 1945, most of the old city has been restored

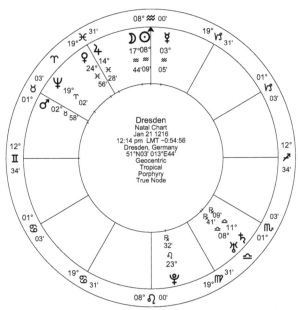

**September 30, 1232, 11:48 a.m. LMT**
**Source: Stadt Dortmund**

**January 21, 1216, 12:14 p.m. LMT**
**Source: Staatsarchiv**

to its former glory.

Dresden is famous for its porcelain china, Dresden and Meissen; it's also famous for its nuclear research, medical centers and numerous plants which make precision tools, aircraft, electronics and office equipment. Dresden is also famous for its Neumarkt and the Frauenkirche. The Kreuzkirche on Altmarkt is also popular with tourists. The most noted art museum in the city is the Albertina and the Zwinger Palace complex is an architectural favorite.

# Duisburg

Situated at the junction of the Rhine and Ruhr Rivers 10 miles west of Essen, it's the largest inland port in Europe. A heavily-industrial city, Duisburg is a steel center with vast shipbuilding yards.

# Dusseldorf

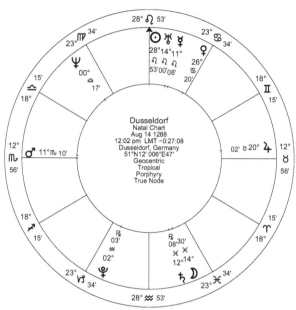

**August l4, 1288, 12:02 p.m. LMT**
**Source: Stadtarchiv**

Situated on the Rhine River 20 miles north of Cologne, Dusseldorf is the commercial heart of the Ruhr. It has Northern Germany's main Stock Exchange and the Rheinturm which towers over the city at 770 ft. Dusseldorf is the center for the German film industry and a center of avant garde art. It's a city of many wealthy people and is quite modern in appearance as most of it was bombed during the war. It's the ninth-largest city in Germany.

# Essen

Germany's sixth-largest city and the largest metropolis in the Ruhr lies 35 miles north of Cologne. Founded in 873 by the sister of Henry the Fowler, it was chartered sometime during the 10th century. Essen is home to the massive Krupp Works, the largest steel mills on the continent. Essen is also in the heart of the biggest coal-mining area in Europe. It makes machinery, electronics and is a commercial and financial center.

# Frankfurt Am Main

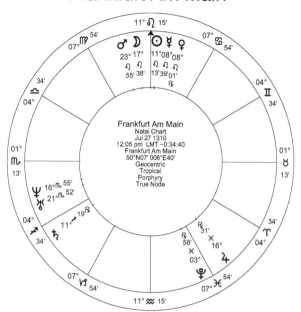

**July 27, 1310, 12:05 p.m. LMT**
**Source: University of Frankfurt**

Germany's fifth-largest city is located on the Main River 95 miles southeast of Cologne. Founded June 12, 794 A.D. (per CBS), its name means "ford of the Franks." In 1372 it was made a Free City and after 1562, Emperors were crowned here. Its ancient walls were torn down in 1806 and in 1815, Frankfurt was made capital of the German Confederation. Most of the old town was bombed in 1944, thus contributing to the overwhelmingly-modern look of the city.

Frankfurt is a major commercial and financial center, housing Germany's main Stock Exchange, Germany's largest bank (Deutsche Bank) and the headquarters for the vast Rothschild financial empire. Frankfurt hosts numerous trade shows including the world's biggest book fair. It has Germany's largest international airport and is the focal point for the country's autobahn and railroad networks.

Frankfurt is also a major cultural center. Goethe's house is quite popular, as is the Romer (City Hall) which fronts the Romerbergplatz. Its Dom (cathedral) has a 300 foot tower and the city has seven museums on the south side of the river. Frankfurt also has the Museum Judengasse near to the old ghetto that was obliterated during the war.

# Halle

Halle is located on the Saale River 20 miles northwest of Leipzig. Founded in 806 A.D., it was a member of the Hanseatic League in the 13th and l4th centuries. Halle is famous for its printing firms and is a major salt-mining center.

# Hamburg

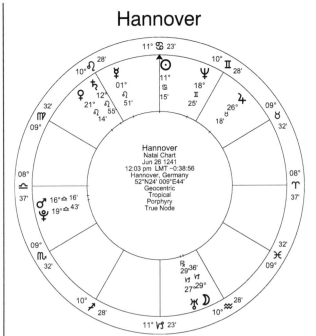

**May 7, 1189, 11:55 a.m. LMT**
**Source: Staatsbibliothek**

Germany's second-largest city and largest port (third biggest in Europe) sits on the Elbe River 70 miles from the North Sea. It has 39 square miles of docks and is a favorite spot for tourists and sailors alike due to its St. Pauli district and the Reeperbahn with its numerous sex venues and Museum of Erotica. Founded by Charlemagne in 810 A.D., the Hanseatic League was founded here in 1241. An Imperial town after 1510, the port was enlarged in 1783. Heavily bombed by the Allies in 1943, it was made an independent city when West Germany was created six years later.

Hamburg's inner city is surrounded by the Innen and Binnen Alsters, two small lakes which offer respite from the turmoils of modern life. The Rathaus (City Hall) is one of the largest municipal buildings on earth and Michaelskirche with its spire is the most elaborate place of worship in town.

# Hannover

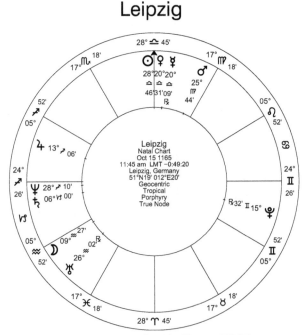

**June 26, 1241, 12:03 p.m. LMT**
**Source: Stadtbibliothek**

Capital of Lower Saxony, this city lies 60 miles southeast of Bremen. Founded as a burgh in 1169, it became residence of the Electors of Hanover after 1636. The Hanovers went on to rule England after 1714. Hannover is a cultural and educational center and hosts a huge trade fair in the spring.

# Leipzig

**October 15, 1165, 11:45 a.m. LMT**
**Source: Stadt Geschichtliches Museum**

Leipzig has been called "Paris in Miniature," and is the home of Luther, Schiller, Goethe, Bach and

Wagner. It's located 110 miles southwest of Berlin and since the 13th century has hosted a trade fair. Leipzig is a huge printing and publishing center as well as a large paper manufacturer. Leipzig's main tourist attractions are the Altes Rathaus with its off-center tower, the Augustusplatz and University tower (510 feet), the Nikolaikirche and the Tomaskirche where Bach reigned as Choirmaster during the early 18th century.

## Magdeburg

Located on the Elbe River 75 miles southwest of Berlin, Magdeburg was founded in the 9th century and became a Hanseatic town in the 13th century. Its main industries are machinery, chemicals and precision instruments.

## Mainz

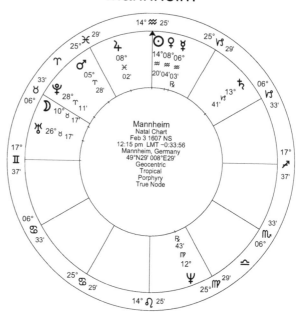

**November 13, 1244, 11:47 a.m. LMT**
**Source: Stadtarchiv**

Situated at the junction of the Rhine and Main Rivers 20 miles southwest of Frankfurt, it was founded in 13 B.C. by Drusus as Maguntiacum. In 747 it became an Archbishopric and in 1254 the Chief of the Rhine League. Mainz is famous for being the place where Johannes Gutenberg printed the Bible in 1452. The museum devoted to him is the main tourist spot in this city along with the 10th century Romanesque Martinsdom cathedral. Mainz is also famous for its annual Carnival and is a major wine center.

## Mannheim

**February 3, 1607 (NS), 12:15 p.m. LMT**
**Source: Stadtarchiv**

Mannheim is located at the junction of the Rhine and Neckar Rivers 45 miles south of Frankfurt. Founded on January 24, 1607 (OS) by Frederick IV, Elector of the Palatinate, it was laid out in a fan shape with major avenues radiating from the palace. Mannheim is famous for being the home of Mercedes Benz, which built its first automobile in 1885.

# Munich (Munchen)

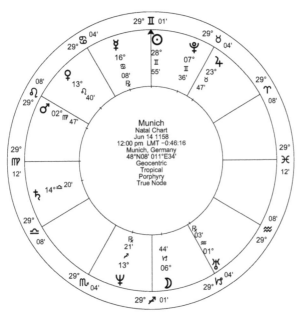

**June 14, 1158, noon LMT**
**Source: Staatsarchiv**

# Nuremberg (Nurnberg)

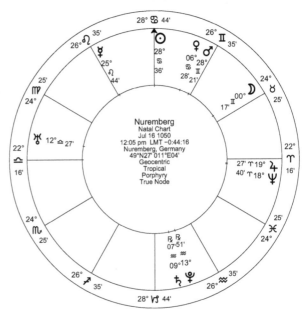

**July 16, 1050, 12:05 p.m. LMT**
**Source: Stadtarchiv**

Munich is Germany's third-largest city and capital of Bavaria. Situated 35 miles from the Austrian border, it was founded:by Henry the Lion and ruled by the Wittelsbachs until 1918. Capital of Bavaria since 1255, Munich was made a Free City in 1294. It was here in a beer hall that Hitler's putsch took place in November 1923. Two decades later, this city was bombed by the Allies. Munich hosted the Summer Olympics in 1972.

Munich is famous for the Oktoberfest in the autumn and for Fasching (Carnival) in the spring. Its famed Hofbrauhaus was founded in 1589. The tourist attractions are numerous. In the center city is the Marienplatz which borders the Neues Rathaus (City Hall) with its famous Glockenspiel. The Frauenkirche and Peterskirche (with its 300 foot tower) are the most famous churches in town, the Pinakothek (art museum), Deutschesmuseum (world's largest science and technology museum) and the Haus der Kunst are quite popular. Munich has many royal palaces in its vicinity: the Residenz, palace of the Wittelsbachs, and Nymphenburg, the summer palace located in a 500-acre park, the largest Baroque palace in Germany today. Outside of Munich is a much more somber place called Dachau where so many died to keep the Third Reich pure and aryan.

Munich makes automobiles (BMW), cigarettes and beer, as well as machinery, chemicals and pharmaceuticals.

The second-largest city in Bavaria is located 95 miles north of Munich. A castle was erected here in the 10th century and Nuremberg is famous for its medieval walls and 14th century churches and houses. It was made an Imperial town in 1219 but achieved notoriety in the 1930s with the huge rallies for Hitler. This was the place where the war crimes trials took place after World War II in 1945.

The most popular sites in town are the Hauptmarkt (open-air square), Albrecht Durer's house and the German National Museum of Art and Culture. The Nazi stadium still stands (Reichsparteitagsgelande) as a reminder to the ignomy of the past. Nuremberg is a major printing and publishing center and is also a major automobile and toy manufacturer.

## Stuttgart

Germany's eighth-largest city is situated on the Neckar River 95 miles south of Frankfurt. Founded as a stutgarten (stud farm) in the 10th century, it was chartered around 1229. It became the capital of Wurttemberg in 1482. An attractive city, half of the downtown area is wooded or parklands. Stuttgart is the home to more than 100 publishers as well as the home of Daimler-Benz and Porsche.

# Greece
## Elliniki Dimokratia

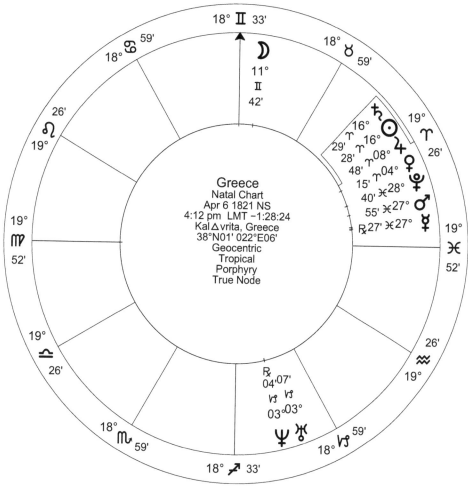

Greece
Natal Chart
Apr 6 1821 NS
4:12 pm LMT −1:28:24
Kal∆vrita, Greece
38°N01' 022°E06'
Geocentric
Tropical
Porphyry
True Node

**Chart 1, April 6, 1821 (NS), 4:12 p.m. LMT, Kalavryta**
Source: Finley's History of the Greek Revolution says 4:00 p.m.; time has been rectified slightly.
The date has been corrected from most sources which state March 25, which was Old Style (OS) as
Greece didn't change to the New Style (NS) calendar until 1916.

Situated at the southern tip of the Balkan peninsula, Greece is bordered on the west by the Ionian Sea, on the east by the Aegean Sea and on the south by the Mediterranean Sea. About 75 percent of the country is mountainous: the Pindus Mountains divide Macedonia from Epirus and contain Mount Olympus (elev. 9570 feet). The coastline of Greece is 8,500 miles long and no point is more than 45 miles from the sea. Greece also has more than 4,000 islands, but only 170 are inhabited, the largest being Crete, Rhodes, Corfu, Chios, Lesbos, Samos. Euboea, Delos and Mykonos. The main island chains are the Cyclades and Dodecanese. The southern part of Greece is called the Peloponnese.

Population: 10,623,835; 95% Greek
Religion: 95% Orthodox, 4% Moslem

Area: 50,942 square miles (the size of England or Alabama); 18% arable, 60% urban

Economy: Main exports are tobacco, cotton and citrus. Tourism is the chief source of income along with olive oil. Main resources are iron, nickel, bauxite, lignite and marble.

About 3500 B.C. the Hellenes invaded this region which was already occupied by the Aegeans. By 3000 B.C., the Minoan civilization had begun on Crete. In 1400 B.C., the Trojan Empire collapsed to the Mycenaens during the famous Trojan War mentioned by Homer. About 1000 B.C., the Greek city-states reached their greatest power, and the first Olympics were held in 776 BC.

Solon gave birth to the idea of democracy in 594 B.C. shortly before the Persians conquered Greece in

546 B.C. Greece was a land that gave the world architecture, mathematics, science, philosophy, drama and literature. The Greeks finally ousted the Persians in 479 B.C. at Marathon, giving rise to the Age of Pericles which lasted until 431 B.C. This was the Golden Age of Greece when the Parthenon was built, but it ended when Athens was defeated by Sparta in the Peloponnesian War of 404 B.C.

Greece was conquered by Alexander of Macedon in 336 B.C. and with the establishment of the Library at Alexandria, Greek culture flourished throughout the ancient world. Rome invaded Greece in 146 B.C. and made it a Roman colony. Greek culture ascended dramatically again after the Emperor Constantine dedicated his new capital at Byzantium (aka Constantinople) in May 330 A.D. For the next eleven centuries, Greece was ruled from that city. Constantinople, however, fell to the Ottoman Turks in May 1453, and seven years later, Greece fell to the Ottomans as well. It then became a neglected step-child.

Independence from Ottoman domination took place at the Abbey of Agia Lavra in the region of Kalavryta, near Patras on the afternoon of April 6, 1821 (NS) (chart 1). The rebellion which followed lasted until 1827 when the British, French and Russian forces won the Battle of Navarino for Greece. A treaty in February 1830 recognized their sovereignty (progressed MC square Mercury/Mars; progressed ASC opposition Mercury/Mars). Two years later, Greece became a monarchy and Otto of Bavaria was chosen to be its first King, (progressed Sun semisquare Moon; progressed MC square Pluto; progressed ASC opposition Pluto). Otto was forced to grant a Constitution in 1843 by the military (progressed ASC opposition Jupiter) but was himself deposed in 1863. Prince George of Denmark was asked to replace Otto (progressed Sun sextile Mercury/Mars; progressed MC trine Pluto; progressed ASC sesquare Moon). Greece prospered under George I's reign of 50 years; he was assassinated in 1913 during the Balkan wars (progressed MC inconj Sun/Saturn; progressed ASC sesquare Sun/Saturn).

The first Balkan War erupted in October 1912 against Turkey and Greece won Crete, Thrace, Macedonia and Epirus (transiting Saturn sextile Venus) and during the Second Balkan War, which began in June 1913, Greece won islands in the Aegean (transiting Jupiter square Sun and Saturn; transiting Pluto square Pluto) When World War I broke out in August 1914, Greece's King and the Prime Minister Venizelos were on opposing sides. The King was married to a German but Venizelos wanted to join the Allies. King Constantine prevailed until 1917 when he was deposed and then exiled. Greece then joined the Allies for the duration of the war

With the signing of the Armistice by the Germans in November 1918, Venizelos realized that 20 percent of all Greeks lived in Asia Minor (aka Turkey) under Ottoman rule. Venizelos wanted to bring them home so Greek troops landed at Smyrna and suffered a humiliating defeat from the Turks. Meanwhile, King Alexander died and his father, former King Constantine, was recalled to take the throne in 1920 (progressed ASC trine Jupiter). When a treaty was signed between Greece and Turkey in 1923, there was an exchange of Greeks and Turks from one country to their homelands. Meanwhile, Constantine had been replaced by his son, George II, who ruled until April 1924. The Greeks had tired of monarchs and thus proclaimed a Republic (progressed Sun semisquare Moon; progressed MC opposition Mercury/Mars; progressed ASC opposition Moon; transiting Jupiter square ASC; transiting Uranus square MC).

The Republic was dissolved in November 1935, a dictatorship under Metaxas was instituted and King George II again took the throne (progressed MC square Jupiter). During the period from 1913 to 1936, Greece yo-yoed back and forth from one monarch to another and flirted with the idea of republicanism. Ironically, in 1936 transiting Saturn sextiled Uranus and Neptune and Pluto sextiled Mercury and Mars.

In June 1940, the Italians invaded Albania and by late October, they set foot on Greek soil (progressed Sun sextile Moon; transiting Jupiter/Saturn semisquare Mercury/Mars). Metaxas died in January 1941 and guerilla warfare against the Nazis lasted until October 1944. The Nazis left but the Soviets stepped in and tried to occupy the country (progressed MC opposition Sun/Saturn; progressed ASC square Mercury; transiting Jupiter opposition Mercury/Mars). A civil war broke out after elections were held in March 1946 (progressed Sun sextile Sun/Saturn; progressed ASC square Mars/Pluto). The U.S. voted aid to Greece in its fight against Communism in 1947, the same year King George II died and his brother Paul became king. The Communists were defeated in 1949 (progressed Sun sesquare Venus). In 1954, demands for union with Greece (called Enosis) rose throughout Cyprus (progressed Sun sesquare Jupiter; progressed MC inconjunct Mercury/Mars; progressed ASC opposition Venus conjunct Uranus and Neptune). Cyprus was 80 percent Greek and by 1959, independence for Cyprus was agreed upon by Greece, Turkey and Britain (progressed Sun inconjunct Pluto; progressed ASC square Jupiter).

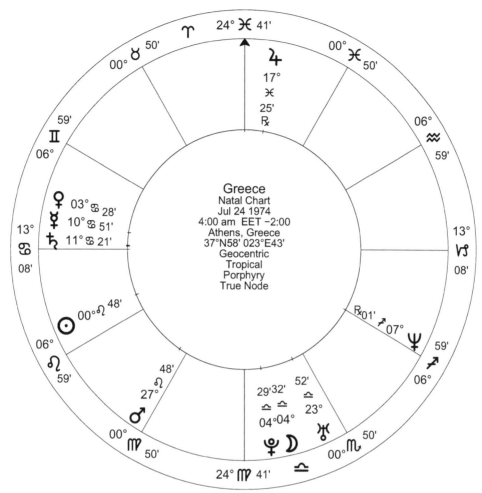

**Chart 2, Second Greek Republic, July 24, 1974, 4:00 a.m. EET, Athens**
**Source:** *The Times* **of London and** *The Guardian* **both state 4:00 a.m.**

A military coup took place in April 1967, and King Constantine had been deposed by the end of the year; he fled to Spain (progressed MC inconjunct Jupiter; progressed ASC square Sun/Saturn; transiting Uranus opposition Pluto). A Republic was proclaimed in July 1974 and the monarchy abolished (progressed MC inconjunct Sun/Saturn; transiting Pluto opposition Venus).

## Second Greek Republic

The Second Greek Republic came into being on July 24, 1974 (chart 2). Greece joined the European Union in January 1981 (progressed Sun trine Neptune; progressed MC trine Sun; progressed ASC trine Jupiter; transiting Jupiter and Saturn square Mercury, ruler of trade). The following year, disputes between Turkey over petroleum rights led to a cessation of further exploration for oil in the Aegean. Problems with the former province of Macedonia, now an independent nation, finally ended in September 1995. Greece had complained that Macedonia had stolen the name of one of its own regions, the land of Alexander the Great. In April 2001, massive Constitutional revisions were passed by Parliament.

## Athens (Athenai)

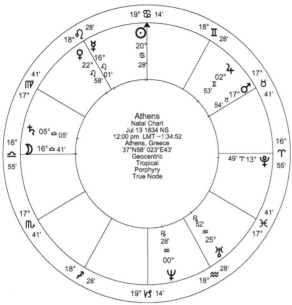

**July 13, 1834, noon LMT**
**Source: Mayor's Office**

Athens is the largest city in Greece and its capital since 1834. Situated on the Attic plain near the Gulf of Saronia, it's the fountainhead of western civilization and the fulcrum of Hellenic culture since the 8th century B.C. The center of Athens.is the Acropolis which rises 500 feet above the city. Here lies the Parthenon, dedicated to the goddess Athena, for whom this city is named. Nearby are the Propylaia, Temple of Athena, Erechtheion, Theatre of Dionysus and the temples of Theseion and Olympeion. Athens' Golden Age was in the time of Pericles during the 5th century B.C. when it had a population of 50,000, a place where men like Plato, Aristotle and Socrates roamed the streets. The downfall of Athens began in 146 B.C. with Roman occupation, and in 86 B.C. it was sacked by Sulla. From 1460 until 1830, Athens was occupied by the Ottomans who once used the Parthenon as a magazine for ammunition and who accidentally blew it up in the late 17th century.

Athens today is a crowded, bustling, noisy and very polluted city stretching all the way to the port city of Piraeus. Besides the Acropolis, the main sights are the Agora (ancient marketplace), Archaeological museum. National Library, Royal Palace and the Roman Forum built by Augustus and Hadrian.

## Thessalonika (Salonika)

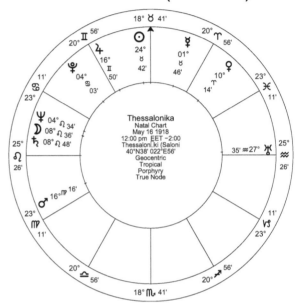

**May 16, 1918, noon EET**
**Source: Mayor's Office**

Salonika is the second-largest city in Greece and the chief port for Thrace and the country of Macedonia. Situated on Thermaic Bay, an arm of the Aegean, it was founded in 315 B.C. and is where Aristotle taught Alexander and where Paul wrote his Epistles. Jews fleeing Spanish persecution in the 16th century were granted asylum here by the Turks. Ottomans captured Salonika in 1430 and didn't cede it back to Greece until 1912. The main sites in town are the Archaeological Museum, which has the tomb of Philip of Macedon, and the White Tower, which is an excellent place from which to view the city and its harbor.

# Hungary
# Magyar Koztarsasag

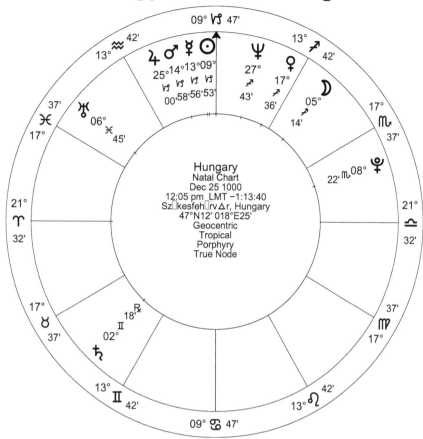

**Chart 1, December 25, 1000, 12:05 p.m. LMT, Szekesfehervar**
**Source:** *Encyclopedia Britannica* **for the date; noon assumed**

Hungary lies in the heart of Europe. Divided by the Danube River, its eastern plain, called the Alfold, is one of the largest agricultural regions in Europe. Its western region has the Bakony Mountains and Lake Balaton, the largest body of water in central Europe. The northeast has the Carpathian Alps. The highest point is Kekes (elev. 3330 feet).

Population: 10,106,010; 30% Magyar, 3% German, 4% Gypsy

Religion: 68% Catholic, 25% Protestant, 3% Orthodox

Area: 35,918 square miles (the size of Portugal or Indiana); 51% arable, 64% urban

Economy: Main exports are transportation equipment, precision instruments, pharmaceuticals, chemicals and textiles. Hungary also grows tons of fruits, vegetables and wine.

Romans called the region Pannonia and occupied it until the 5th century when Huns, under Attila, settled the area. In 896 A.D., Arpad, leader of the Magyars, founded a dynasty and by 973 A.D., King

Geza had accepted Christianity.

Modern Hungary began with the coronation of Stephen by the Pope on Christmas Day 1000 A.D. (chart 1). In 1222, the Golden Bull, Hungary's Magna Carta, was signed (progressed MC inconjunct Mars trine Venus; progressed ASC trine Uranus). Mongols invaded in 1242 (progressed MC opposition Uranus) but didn't stay long. The Golden Age of Hungary began in 1301 when the House of Anjou took over after the Arpad Dynasty ended (progressed ASC inconjunct Saturn).

Hungary fought its first war against the Ottomans in 1389, shortly after the Serbian defeat in Kosovo (progressed Sun trine Saturn inconjunct Venus; progressed ASC conjunct Saturn). Further peasant revolts against the Turks erupted in 1514 (progressed MC opposition Pluto). Turkish troops finally conquered Hungary under Suleiman the Magnificent in the summer of 1526, but Austria still controlled the northern and western parts of the country (progressed ASC trine Neptune). The Turks, however,

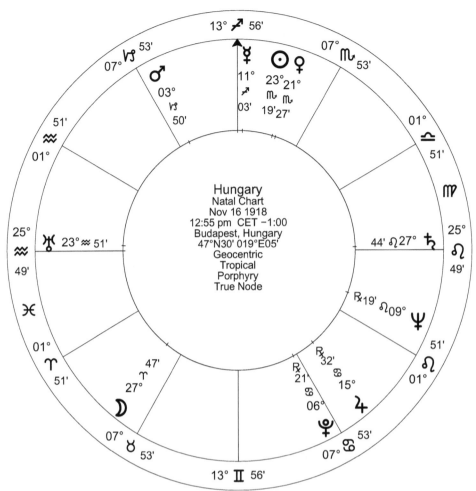

**Chart 2, Republic of Hungary, November 16, 1918, 12:55 p.m. MET, Budapest**
**Source: Fovaros Leveltara alludes to a time of "early afternoon"; chart rectified**

suffered a defeat in 1683 when they were turned back for the second time from the gates of Vienna (progressed ASC sextile Sun semisquare Jupiter). The Turks finally left Hungary in 1699 (progressed MC sextile Uranus and Pluto).

Beginning in 1740, the reign of Maria Theresa of Austria brought an era of peace and by 1843 Magyar had become the official language. In April 1848, a patriot named Kossuth led a revolt against the Hapsburgs which had in effect ruled Hungary since 1526 (progressed MC opposition Moon; progressed ASC trine Sun). A wave of nationalism swept all across Europe, but by 1849 the revolt was over, put down by the Russians (progressed MC square Uranus). To assuage the Hungarians, a dual monarchy was formed with Austria in February 1867 after Austria had lost a war with Prussia and the German Confederation had collapsed (progressed MC sesquare Pluto; progressed ASC trine Jupiter). Peasants again revolted in 1897 and more than one million decided to emigrate, most of them to America (progressed MC sesquare Uranus; progressed ASC sesquare Sat-

urn).

World War I began in August 1914 with Austria-Hungary on the Axis side with Germany (progressed MC square Pluto; transiting Saturn opposition Neptune; transiting Uranus square Pluto). The signing of the Armistice in November 1918 ended the dual monarchy and the Hapsburg dynasty was finished. Hungary tried for a separate peace with the Allies but failed (progressed MC sesquare Neptune; progressed ASC inconjunct Saturn semisquare Venus; transiting Jupiter opposition Mars; Saturn trine Neptune; transiting Pluto trine Uranus). Hungary decided to become a republic instead.

## Republic of Hungary

Hungary was proclaimed a Republic on November 16, 1918 (chart 2), three days after Emperor Charles abdicated the Hapsburg throne. Democracy lasted only a few months, however, as Bela Kun formed a Communist dictatorship in March 1919 (progressed Sun square Uranus; transiting Jupiter

76

conjunct Pluto; transiting Pluto opposition Mars). The Romanians arrived in August 1919 and ousted Kun, who had failed to gain support from the Russians. In March 1920, Hungary officially became a monarchy with no king as Admiral Horthy took the reins of power (progressed MC inconjunct Jupiter; progressed ASC opposition Saturn; transiting Mars square Neptune; transiting Jupiter conjunct Neptune). In June 1920, Hungary signed the Treaty of Trianon, which cost Hungary 70 percent of its territory (transiting Jupiter trine MC; transiting Uranus trine Pluto).

In 1921, former Emperor Charles and his wife, Zita, tried to claim the throne of Hungary but were rebuffed (progressed Sun conjunct Saturn/Uranus midpoint; progressed ASC sesquare Jupiter). During the 1930s, Hungary made many concessions to the Nazis, but when World War II erupted, Hungary decided to remain neutral in May 1940, allowing the Germans carte blanche (progressed Sun inconjunct Jupiter; progressed MC opposition Pluto; progressed ASC sesquare Saturn; transiting Mars trine ASC; transiting Jupiter conjunct Moon trine Saturn). Hungary allowed Hitler's troops to march through its territory in June 1941 on their way to the Soviet Union, but when the Russians were attacked, Hungary entered the war on Germany's side (progressed MC semisquare Venus; progressed ASC square Jupiter; transiting Saturn square Uranus opposition Sun; transiting Uranus square Saturn). Until October 1944, Hungary was pretty well left out of the war until the Nazis began to throw their weight around and a reign of terror ensued (progressed MC inconjunct Neptune; progressed ASC inconjunct Venus).

Soviet troops landed in Budapest in January 1945 (progressed ASC inconjunct Sun; transiting Saturn conjunct Pluto; transiting Uranus sextile Neptune; transiting Neptune square Pluto; transiting Pluto conjunct Neptune). When the war ended four months later, Budapest was 75 percent in ruins and more than 500,000 had lost their lives. Hungary was asked to pay an indemnity of $300 million. About 150,000 soldiers died in battle and 89,000 were on the casualty list (transiting Mars square Mars; transiting Neptune square Mars). Communists won elections in late 1945 and the Hungarian People's Republic was proclaimed on February 1, 1946 (progressed ASC sesquare Mercury; Uranus opposition MC). Ironically, a non-Communist was asked to lead the government.

Cardinal Midszenty was tried in February 1949 and sentenced to life imprisonment (progressed Sun sextile Uranus sesquare Neptune; progressed MC opposition Jupiter; Saturn trine Mars; Uranus trine ASC; Neptune square Jupiter). In late October 1956, the Hungarian Revolution began but was quickly put down by the Soviets. More than 200,000 Hungarians fled across the border to Austria and 4,000 were killed (progressed MC sextile Sun and Venus; progressed ASC sextile Jupiter; transiting Mars trine Jupiter; Jupiter sextile Sun). By 1965, Janos Kadar had eased travel restrictions, reformed the secret police and freed many prisoners (progressed ASC semisquare Jupiter). Hungary began to make economic reforms in 1968 but went easy after the Soviets invaded neighboring Czechoslovakia in late August 1968 (progressed ASC inconjunct Mars; transiting Saturn sextile Uranus; transiting Neptune square Uranus).

With the fall of Communism in eastern Europe, a new Republic was formed on October 23, 1989, two weeks before the Berlin Wall fell (progressed Sun inconjunct Pluto; progressed MC opposition Saturn; transiting Jupiter conjunct Jupiter/Pluto; transiting Pluto trine Jupiter). Soviet troops were finally gone by June 1991 (progressed MC and ASC sextile the Moon). In March 1999, Hungary became a member of NATO. Hungary joined the European Union in May 2004 (progressed Sun trine Mercury and Neptune; progressed MC inconjunct Mercury; progressed ASC semisquare Pluto square Sun opposition Uranus).

# Budapest

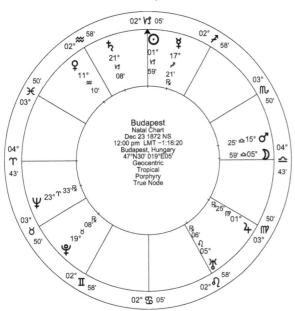

**December 23, 1872, noon LMT**
**Source: Fovaros Leveltara**

The capital and largest city of Hungary lies on the banks of the Danube. Budapest is actually three cities—Buda, Pest and Obuda—and they merged in 1872 to form one metropolis. Buda is on the west bank of the river and was founded on the ruins of the Roman city of Aquincum. It was burned by the Mongols in 1241, conquered by the Turks in 1568 and came under Hapsburg rule in 1699. It had been chartered back in 1242, but it became the second city of the Austro-Hungarian empire when that union was formed in 1867. Buda has Castle Hill with the Royal Palace and St. Matthias church. South of Castle Hill is Gellert Hill with the Citadel built in 1849 and the Liberation Monument.

Pest lies on the east bank of the Danube and has the ornate and Gothic Parliament Building which was completed in 1902; it has nearly 700 rooms with dozens of statues outside. While Buda is hilly, Pest is flat, the commercial and industrial part of the city. Pest opened the first subway in Europe in 1895 and the Chain Bridge connecting the two cities was completed in 1839. It was blown up by the Nazis during the last war. The Nagy Synagogue is the most famous temple in Budapest and is recognizable for miles around due to its onion dome. Inside is a Holocaust memorial. Stroll through Szobor Park, which has one of the largest bathhouses on the continent. In the middle of the Danube lies Margaret Island, a natural preserve with numerous hot springs for which this city is so famous. The district of Obuda once belonged to the Crown, and became a market town in 1840.

## Debrechen

Hungary's second-largest city is situated in the middle of the Alfold, 120 miles east of Budapest. It's the center of the richest crop land and stock raising area in Europe. Chartered in 1360, it survived Turkish occupation to become Calvinist and a center for Protestantism. In 1715, it was made a free royal town and it was here in 1849 that Kossuth declared independence from Austria. The most popular sites in town are the thermal baths (indoor and outdoor) located in a park called the Great Forest.

## Miskolc

Hungary's third-largest city is located on the Sajo River 85 miles northeast of Budapest. It's primarily an industrial city.

## Pecs

Hungary's fifth-largest city lies 105 miles southwest of Budapest in Transdanubia. Founded in the 9th century A.D., it was called Ad Quinque Basilicas, or five churches, in Latin. Pecs has catacombs beneath the old sections of the city. Pecs is also famous for its churches, Christian as well as two mosques and a synagogue. Under Turkish domination from 1543 until 1686, its most famous site is the City Parish Church, the finest example of Turkish architecture in the country. Its dome shares a cross with a crescent moon. The four-towered cathedral looks austere from the exterior but the interior is a riot of colors.

## Szeged

Hungary's fourth-largest city lies on the Tisza River. Founded in the 13th century, it became a royal town in 1498. A massive flood in 1879 nearly wiped this town off the map. Its main attraction is the neo-Romanesque cathedral built in 1912. Szeged also has 15 universities, which makes it a major cultural and artistic center with lively cafes.

# Iceland
## Lydhveldidh Island

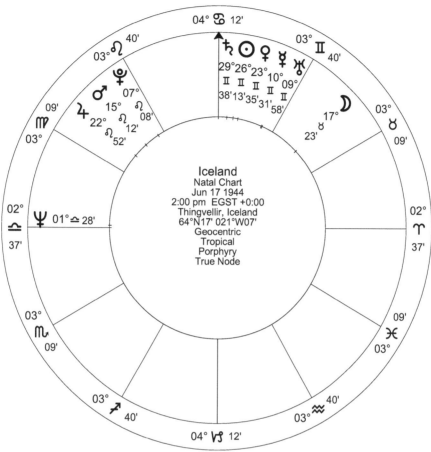

**June 17, 1944, 2:00 p.m. WADT, 2:00 p.m. GMT, Thingvellir**
**Source: *The Times* of London says 2:00 p.m.**

Situated in the North Atlantic Ocean just south of the Arctic Circle, Iceland lies only 190 miles from the world's largest island, Greenland. Over 75 percent of the nation is wasteland with no arable land, more than 200 volcanoes dot the region and 80 percent of Iceland is frozen for most of the year. The coastline is 3,100 miles long. Known as the land of fire and ice, 700 hot springs and geysers keep water bills low and the natives warm during the winter. The highest point is Oraefajokull (elevation 6,992 feet).

Population: 277,906; 96% Icelandic

Religion: 96% Protestant (Lutheran)

Area: 39,768 square miles (the size of Yugoslavia or West Virginia); 92.% urban

Economy: Over 75% of Iceland's income is from fishing.

Iceland was first settled in 870 A.D. by Vikings. The world's oldest Parliament, the Althing, was founded in 930 A.D. It was from Iceland that Eric the Red founded settlements in Greenland by 986 A.D. and where Leif Ericson left on his voyage to America around 1000 A.D. Iceland became part of Norway in 1262 but was ceded to Denmark in 1380. In 1874, limited self-government was granted along with a constitution.

On December 1, 1918, Iceland became part of Denmark, but after the invasion of Denmark by the Nazis in June 1940, Iceland was occupied by British troops to protect North Atlantic shipping lanes. On June 17, 1944 Iceland was granted complete independence by Denmark. In 1972, the Cod War broke out when Iceland expanded its territorial waters 50 miles from shore (progressed MC sextile Neptune). In 1980, Iceland became the first nation in Europe to elect a female head of state (progressed Sun sextile Neptune; progressed ASC trine Venus sextlle Jupiter).

To date, Iceland has decided not to join the European Union.

# Reykjavik

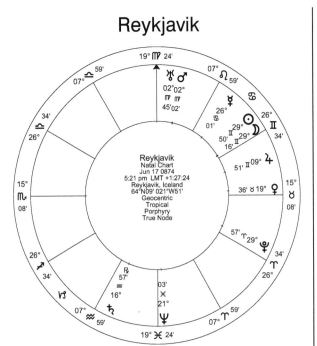

**June 17, 874 A.D., 5:21 p.m.  LMT**
**Source: Borgarbokosafn**

The capital and largest city of Iceland, which is the world's northernmost capital, is situated on Faxafloi Bay on the southwest part of the island. Founded in 874 by Ingolfr Arnarsson, its name means "smoking bay," an apt name considering the number of geysers and volcanoes in the vicinity. Buildings are heated by water pumped from hot springs and Reykjavik has a year-round swimming pool. Capital of Iceland only since 1843, its university was founded in 1911. The main point of interest is the Althing, constructed in 1843. Reykjavik was chartered August 18, 1786.

# Ireland
# Eire

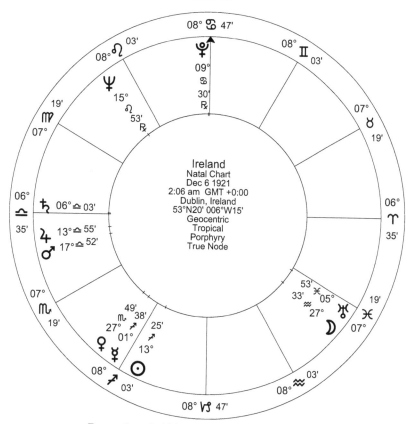

Ireland
Natal Chart
Dec 6 1921
2:06 am GMT +0:00
Dublin, Ireland
53°N20' 006°W15'
Geocentric
Tropical
Porphyry
True Node

**December 6, 1921, 2:06 a.m. GMT, Dublin**
**Source:** *The New York Times* says 2:06 a.m. in London

Ireland is an island in the North Atlantic, separated from Great Britain by the Irish Sea. Its center is a plateau ringed by low hills and mountains, the highest point, Carrauntoohill (near Killarney) being 3,415 feet. No place is more than 70 miles from the sea and the coastline is 900 miles long. The political divisions are called Munster, Leinster and Connacht. The Shannon is the longest river.

Population: 3,840,838; 95% Irish

Religion: 93% Catholic

Area: 27,135 square miles (the size of West Virginia or the Czech Republic); 13% arable, 59% urban

Economy: Main exports are meat, livestock, wool, dairy products, textiles and machinery. Ireland is also famous for its whiskey, ale and lace.

Ireland was conquered by the Celts about 350 B.C. but never colonized by the Romans. In 380 A.D., Niall founded a dynasty that lasted until 1603. By 432 A.D., St. Patrick had brought Christianity to this emerald isle, then called Hibernia, and before long it became a center of monastic culture. Vikings began to raid coastal settlements in 795 A.D. and in

1014, Brian Boru was killed trying to oust the Norsemen.

King Henry II of England forced Irish nobles to submit to his authority in 1171, thus beginning centuries of conflict with the English. The Statutes of Kilkenny favored anything British and intermarriage with anyone Irish was forbidden, including speaking Gaelic, the national language. Poyning's Law in 1495 demanded English approval of all legislation.

King Henry VIII of England destroyed Catholic abbeys and churches in 1541. Fifteen years later the English began to settle the counties of Loix and Offaly. Revolts against English rule erupted at Munster in 1579 and in Ulster in 1594. Ireland sided with Spain in 1601 in an abortive fight for its freedom. About that same time Catholics in Ulster lost their land to Protestants emigrating from Scotland.

Oliver Cromwell began to lay waste to Ireland in August 1649, the most famous massacre occurred at Drogheda. The counties of Meath and Kildare were given to the Protestants, and after the war ended in 1652, the population had decreased by 55 percent and landowners east of the Shannon were forced to move west to Connaught. Catholics now held only 25 percent of the land in Ireland. Ireland supported King James II of England, a Catholic who tried to regain his throne at the Battle of the Boyne in 1690, but James II lost and was forced into exile.

In 1695, Irish penal laws assumed that all Irish Catholics were enemies and were due only poverty. They were denied citizenship, forbidden to vote and barred from military and government service as well as the legal profession. The teaching of religion was restricted and large estates were broken up. The penal laws were finally outlawed in 1829. By 1783, legislative autonomy for the Irish Parliament was granted by King George III, a man who had just lost America.

In 1798, Ireland gained support from Napoleon in its fight for freedom, two years later, British Prime Minister William Pitt bribed Parliament by creating peerages and allowing Catholics to sit in the House of Lords and Commons. On January 1, 1801 Ireland became part of Great Britain and its Parliament was dissolved. By 1843, partial civil rights were granted at last.

Beginning in 1845, a fungus emerged which began to decimate the potato, Ireland's chief crop and mainstay of the peasant economy. During the following six years the famine killed 1.5 million peasants and more than 1 million emigrated, mainly to America. The British did little to alleviate Ireland's suffering and most aid was too little too late. Before the famine, Ireland was a nation of 8 million; when the famine ended, it had only half that number. In 1870, Prime Minister Gladstone introduced land reform but also eliminated the Church of Ireland. Parnell succeeded in reducing rents 20 percent for farmers by 1881. In 1899, the Sinn Fein, an arm of the IRA, was formed.

During World War I, which began in August 1914, Ireland sided with Great Britain, four years after Home Rule was offered. On Easter Monday, April 24, 1916, the Irish Rebellion began at noon in Dublin. Ireland was proclaimed a republic and the revolt lasted five days and more than 2,500 were jailed. By April 1918, conscription protests had erupted across Ireland. In January 1919, Michael Collins began his terrorist war against British occupation and Sinn Fein proclaimed independence.

Negotiations dragged on through most of 1921 and finally on the morning of December 6, 1921, Ireland agreed to partition. The southern part was to become the Irish Free State while the six northern counties of Ulster were to remain with Britain. Ireland would remain inside the British Commonwealth.

The treaty was ratified in January 1922, but five months later a civil war broke out between forces loyal to Collins and those of Eamon de Valera, who was to become the first leader of the newly-formed nation. On December 6, 1922 (one year after the treaty was promulgated), King George V of Britain signed a document granting Ireland's freedom (progressed Sun sextile Jupiter; progressed MC conjunct Pluto; transiting Jupiter trine Pluto and MC; Uranus trine MC and Pluto). The civil war dragged on until April 1923 (transiting Jupiter square Neptune; Saturn sextile Neptune). When De Valera was released from prison in 1924, he had problems with swearing to the Oath of Allegiance to the Crown. During the 1930s, Ireland fought against high tariffs imposed by the British. A Constitution of 1937 declared Irish sovreignty and the position of Governor General was abolished.

When World War II broke out in September 1939, Ireland decided to remain neutral (progressed Sun sesquare Neptune; transiting Jupiter opposition Saturn). Ireland finally separated from the British Commonwealth by becoming a Republic on April 18, 1949 (progressed Sun square Pluto; progressed MC sextile Saturn inconjunct Uranus; transiting Pluto sextile Jupiter trine Sun).

Riots broke out in Ulster, fomented by the IRA, in August 1969 (progressed MC opposition Moon square Venus semisquare Pluto; progressed ASC trine Pluto; transiting Jupiter square Saturn). In January 1973, Ireland joined the European Union (progressed MC square Mercury; progressed ASC = Sun/Jupiter). In July 1979, Lord Mountbatten, the last Viceroy of India, was assassinated by the IRA (progressed MC opposition Uranus). A cease-fire was arranged in August 1994 which attempted to end the troubles in Northern Ireland (progressed Sun conjunct Moon; progressed ASC conjunct Venus square Moon).

## Dublin (Baile Atha Cliath)

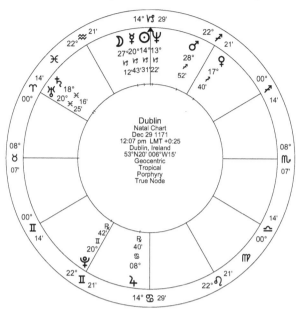

**December 29, 1171, 12:07 p.m. LMT**
**Source: Lord Mayor's Office**

## Cork

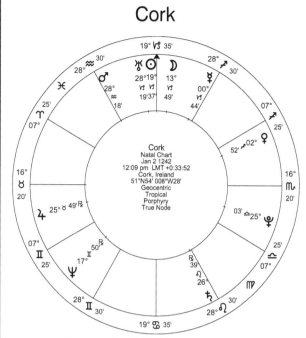

**January 2, 1242, 12:09 p.m. LMT**
**Source: Cork Library**

Dublin was first settled by the Celts in the 2nd century A.D. Situated on the River Liffey a few miles from where it empties into the Irish Sea. The Vikings arrived in the 8th century and were ousted by Brian Boru in 1014. The English, however, also had designs on Ireland and King Henry I arrived in late December 1171 to stake his claim. Dublin's Celtic name means "city of hurdles," while Dublin comes from Dubhlin, which means "black water."

Trinity College was founded in 1591, one of Ireland's most famous schools. Numerous structures are built in the Georgian style of the 18th century. The most popular site in town is the Guiness Brewery, and Ireland's most famous landmark is St. Patrick's Cathedral. Downtown along the river are the famous Customs House, Mansion House, Leinster House (from which the White House was copied) and the Four Courts. The main area for recreation is Phoenix Park.

Ireland's second-largest city is situated on the River Lee 140 miles southwest of Dublin near the Atlantic Ocean. The Vikings founded the city on an island and in 1172 it was attacked by the Normans. Cork is famous for its Protestant and Catholic cathedrals as well as being the home to the University of Ireland. Despite being considered provincial, its rural charm is more inherently Irish than is the capital of Dublin to the north.

# Italy
## Repubblica Italiana

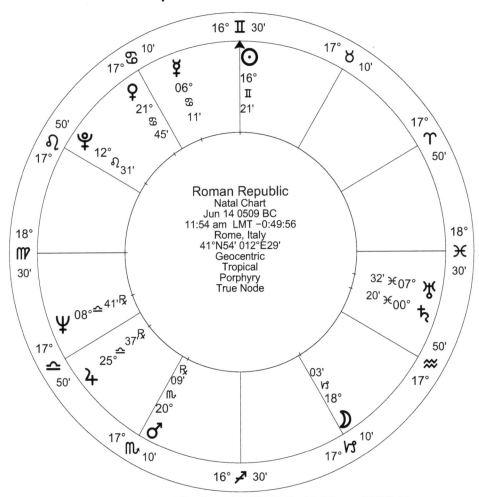

16° ♊ 30'

17° ♋ 10'

☿ 06° ♋ 11'

⊙ 16° ♊ 21'

17° ♉ 10'

♀ 21° 45'

17° ♈ 50'

♇ 12° ♌ 31'

17° ♌ 50'

Roman Republic
Natal Chart
Jun 14 0509 BC
11:54 am  LMT −0:49:56
Rome, Italy
41°N54' 012°E29'
Geocentric
Tropical
Porphyry
True Node

18° ♍ 30'

18° ♓ 30'

32' ♓ 07' ♅
20' ♓ 00' ♄

♆ 08° ♎ 41' ℞

50'

17° ♎ 50'

25° ℞ 37'

17° ♒

♃

℞ 09°

03' ♑ 18'

♂ 20° ♏

17° ♑ 10'

17° ♏ 10'

16° ♐ 30'

**Chart 1, Roman Republic, June 14, 509 B.C., 11:54 a.m. LMT, Rome**
**Source: Encyclopedia Britannica for the date; noontime assumed**

Situated on a peninsula between the Tyrrhenian and Adriatic Seas, Italy's shape makes it the most easily-recognized country on earth. Bordered on the north by the Alps, the Appenine Mountains run down the spine of Italy. Most of its flat land lies in the north along the Po River. The coastline is 4,723 miles long.

The main provinces are Piedmont, Lombardy, Venezia and Liguria in the north; Emilia Romagna, Marchese, Tuscany, Umbria and Latium in the center; Abruzzi e Molise, Campania, Apulia, Basilicata and Calabria in the south. Offshore lie the Islands of Sicily (9,926 square miles), Sardinia (9,301 square miles) and the smaller isles of Ischia, Capri and Elba. Italy's largest lakes are in the north: Como, Garda and Maggiore. Italy also has Europe's two most famous volcanoes: Mt. Etna and Mt. Vesuvius. The highest point is Monte Bianco (elevation 15,616 feet).

Population: 57,679,825; 98% Italian

Religion: 39% Catholic, 2% Moslem

Area: 116,305 square miles (the size of Poland or Arizona); 35% arable, 67% urban

Economy: Main exports are machinery, automobiles, motor scooters, office machines, textiles and footwear. Italy is the second-largest producer of wine and olives, and also the number-one tourist destination in Europe. Main resources are mercury, potash, sulfur and marble.

During the 10th century B.C., Greeks began to colonize the Italian peninsula and Sicily. Two centuries later, the Etruscans began to occupy central Italy and founded the city of Rome in 753 B.C.

## Roman Republic

The Roman Republic was founded on June 14, 509 B.C. (chart 1) after the Etruscans were defeated.

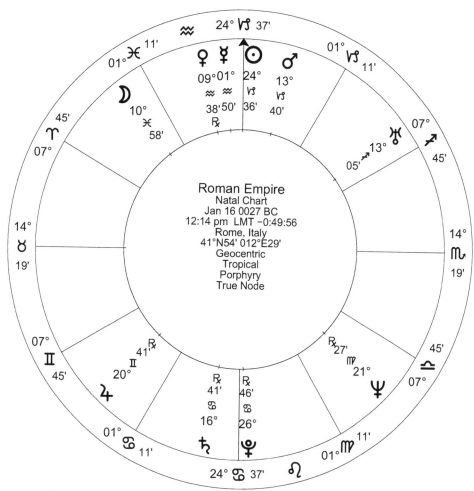

**Chart 2, Roman Empire, January 16, 27 B.C., 12:14 p.m. LMT, Rome**
Source: *Encyclopedia Britannica* for the date; noontime assumed

The first Punic War erupted against Carthage in 264 B.C. (progressed Sun square Mars; progressed ASC conjunct Sun). Hannibal was defeated by Scipio Africanus in 202 B.C. when he tried to conquer Rome by crossing the Alps with a herd of elephants (progressed MC inconjunct Mars). Greece was annexed to Rome two years later (progressed ASC trine Moon). Spartacus led a slave revolt against Rome in 73 B.C. (progressed ASC square Pluto).

Julius Caesar began his conquest of Gaul and visited Britain in 58 B.C. (progressed Sun opposition Uranus; progressed ASC semisquare Neptune). By 49 B.C., Caesar had become Head of State (progressed Sun trine Moon; progressed ASC square Saturn) but many senators felt he had achieved too much power after he had been declared dictator for life. A group of conspirators, led by Brutus, slew Caesar in the Forum of Rome on March 15, 44 B.C. (progressed Sun sextile Venus; progressed ASC semisquare Moon).

A Triumverate between Marc Antony, Octavian and Lepidus was formed to rule Rome. In the summer of 30 B.C., Marc Antony who wanted to run Rome by himself was defeated by Octavian's forces at the Battle of Actium. He committed suicide along with his mistress, Queen Cleopatra of Egypt (progressed Sun conjunct Neptune). Egypt then became part of the Roman Empire.

## Roman Empire

The Roman Empire was formally founded on January 16, 27 B.C. (chart 2) with Octavian, now known as Augustus Caesar, as Emperor. Sometime around September 7 B.C. an event which would eventually transform Europe took place in a small village in Palestine, the man we know as Jesus Christ was born (progressed ASC square Moon semisquare Pluto). Augustus died in 14 A.D. and was succeeded by his stepson, Tiberius, and then Caligula. Claudius began the conquest of Britain in 43 A.D. (progressed ASC sextile Neptune) and a decade later, Nero began persecuting the Christians (progressed MC square Mars and Saturn; progressed ASC opposition Mercury).

Nero set Rome ablaze in 64 A.D. and then blamed the Christians (progressed MC square Sun; progressed ASC semisquare Neptune).

The height of the Roman Empire was during the 2nd century under Trajan, Hadrian and Marcus Aurelius. Constantine accepted Christianity and by 313 A.D. had stopped persecuting Christians (progressed MC inconjunct Pluto; progressed ASC trine Pluto). Constantine convened the Council of Nicaea in 325 A.D. to establish Christian ritual and dogma (progressed MC sextile Moon; progressed ASC sextile Jupiter). Constantine then moved the capital from Rome to Byzantium in May 330 A.D., which he had renamed after himself (progressed ASC sesquare Uranus).

In January 395 A.D. the Roman Empire was formally divided East and West (progressed MC square Jupiter opposition Neptune; progressed ASC opposition Mars inconjunct Uranus). Barbarian invasions increased after 410 A.D. when the Goths invaded Rome (progressed ASC opposition Sun). Attila the Hun was stopped at the last moment from sacking Rome by the Pope in 451 A.D. (progressed MC sextile Saturn; progressed ASC inconjunct Sun).

Weak emperors and petty internal squabbling dissolved the Western Roman Empire by September 476 A.D. and the Dark Ages of Europe began (progressed MC trine Venus sesquare Sun; progressed ASC trine Mars square Uranus). The Eastern Roman Empire located in Constantinople would rule for another thousand years until the Moslems took over.

Over the next 14 centuries, Italy was a conglomeration of small principalities with no central authority or government. Lombard tribes conquered around Milan in 568 A.D. and the Franks founded the Papal States in 756 A.D. To regenerate the glory of the Roman Empire, the Pope crowned Charlemagne on Christmas Day 800 A.D., but the experiment essentially failed. When Charlemagne died in 814 AD, he divided the empire amongst his grandsons at the Treaty of Verdun in 843 A.D. The Holy Roman Empire was founded in 962 A.D. and had more success, but not in Italy. Its major realm of influence was up north in Austria and Germany.

Moslems invaded southern Italy and Sicily in 840 A.D., but were ousted by the Normans in 1016. Anti-papist factions were subdued by 1152 when Barbarrosa quieted the Guelphs, major agitators during Medieval Italy. During this era, Italy was a collection of more than 200 city-states. The French became rulers of Naples and Sicily in 1268 and Aragon annexed Sicily 15 years later. Because of internal unrest, the Papacy moved to Avignon, France in 1309 and stayed there until 1377.

Dante died in 1321, a date some historians consider to be the birth of the Italian Renaissance. Six decades later, Venice defeated Genoa and became the chief maritime power in the Mediterranean. The Medici family began their rule of Florence in 1454, the Visconti family ruled Milan, the Gonzagas held sway in Mantua and the d'Este family governed Ferrara. The Borgia family was also rising to prominence and Calixtus was elected Pope. With the death of Lorenzo de Medici in 1494, the Golden Age was over when France invaded "La Bella Italia." In 1533, the Pope began the Counter Reformation to counteract the rising influence of Protestantism throughout northern Europe.

At the end of the War of Spanish Succession in 1713, Savoy obtained Sicily and Austria received Naples, Milan and Sardinia. The Papal States were neutral ground between the Hapsburgs in the north and the Bourbons in the south. The King of Savoy traded Sicily for Sardinia in 1720 and Lombardy and Venezia became Austrian in 1748. France annexed Nice and Savoy in 1791 and six years later Napoleon invaded and ousted the Austrians. In 1798, Napoleon founded the Cisalpine Republic in northern Italy. Napoleon then proclaimed himself King of Italy in 1805, and four years later he annexed the Papal States. With Napoleon's defeat in June 1815, the Treaty of Vienna restored the old boundaries. The King of Sardinia got the Piedmont, the eventual birthplace of modern Italy.

Italy in the early 19th century consisted of the Kingdom of Naples, the Grand Duchy of Tuscany, the Duchies of Parma, Modena and Lucca, the Papal States, Venetia and Lombardy. Revolutions erupted in Naples and the Piedmont in 1820 and by 1831, Mazzini established the Risorgimento and riots began in the Papal States. During 1848, residents in Lombardy and Venetia rose up against the Austrians.

Steps towards unification began in 1852 when Count Cavour became Prime Minister of the Piedmont. When the Sardinians took Lombardy from the Austrians in 1859, the die had been cast and before long Giuseppe Garibaldi invaded Sicily and conquered southern Italy by October 1860, thus uniting Italy for the first time in centuries. Sardinia also invaded the Papal States and took Romagna, Parma, Naples, Modena and Tuseany.

## Italy

The Italian Parliament opened its first session February 18, 1861 (chart 3). The agreement to unite Italy passed the Senate on February 26 and passed the Chamber on March 14. Three days later, on March

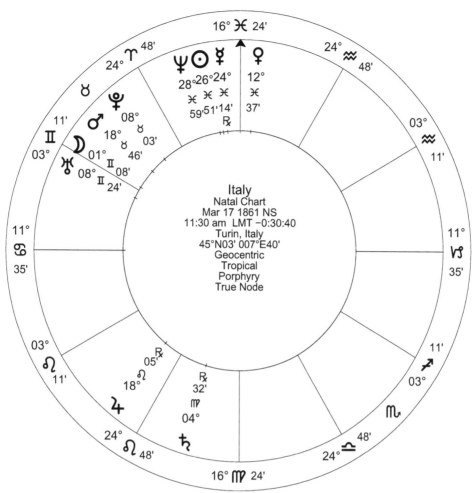

**Chart 3, Italy, March 17, 1861, 11:30 a.m. LMT, Turin**
**Source: Biblioteca Nazionale for the date; time approximate; chart rectified**

17, 1861, Victor Emanuel II was proclaimed King of Italy. The new country then proceeded to conquer and absorb the rest of the peninsula. Venetia and Mantua were ceded by Austria in 1866 (progressed Sun sesquare Jupiter; progressed ASC semisquare Moon) and the Papal States were annexed in September 1870 and the Pope became a prisoner in the Vatican by his own choice (progressed ASC sextile Mars). In July 1871, the King entered Rome and made it the capital of a united Italy (progressed MC conjunct Sun; progressed ASC semisquare Saturn).

Italy began its quest for an empire by trying to annex Libya, Eritrea and Somalia. The fateful Triple Alliance with Germany and Austria was signed in 1882 (progressed Sun trine Jupiter; progressed ASC trine Sun sesquare Venus). In 1900, King Umberto was assassinated (progressed Sun trine Saturn; progressed MC semisquare Uranus; progressed ASC square Pluto sextile Uranus). In 1911, Libya became part of Italy after the Turks were ousted (progressed ASC conjunct Jupiter).

With Jupiter opposing itself, Uranus and Neptune trining themselves, World War I broke out in August 1914 but Italy at first decided to remain neutral (progressed Sun square Jupiter; progressed MC conjunct Pluto; progressed ASC square Mars). The Allies, however, managed to coax Italy onto their side by May 1915, but the Italians were unprepared for a modern war (progressed Sun conjunct Mars; transiting Jupiter conjunct Mercury).

When the Armistice was signed in November 1918, more than 650,000 soldiers had died and nearly 1 million were placed on the casualty list (progressed Sun sextile Mercury; progressed MC semisquare Sun sextile Venus; transiting Jupiter trine MC; transiting Neptune sextile Uranus square Pluto). With the end of war came massive unemployment and inflation, just like Germany, Italians wanted a return to order and Benito Mussolini promised them that. On October 30, 1922, "Il Duce" and his brown shirts marched on Rome and took over the government. At that time, Mars was sextile natal Neptune, Uranus was squaring itself, Neptune was sitting on Jupiter squaring Mars and Pluto was crossing the ASC.

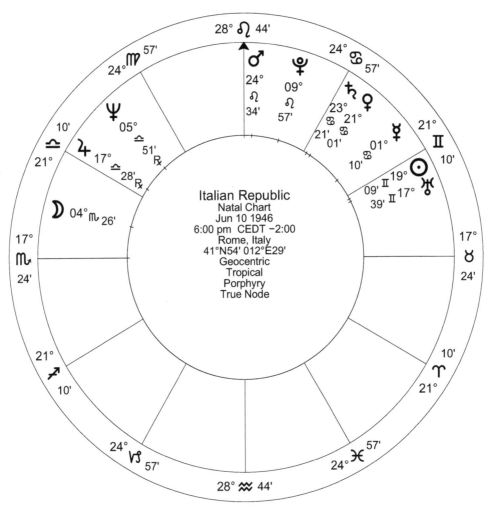

**Chart 4, Italian Republic, June 10, 1946, 6:00 p.m. MEDT, Rome**
**Source: The New York Times says 6:00 p.m.**

Mussolini finally managed to placate the Pope by creating the Lateran Treaty, which gave the Pope authority over a new nation called the Holy See, or Vatican City on February 11, 1929 (progressed ASC square Moon inconjunct Neptune). Before the end of that year, however, the Great Depression had begun all across Europe, throwing millions out of work (progressed Sun square Saturn; progressed ASC square Moon; transiting Saturn square Sun; transiting Pluto trine MC).

Italy attempted to conquer the African nation of Abyssinia (Ethiopia) in October 1935, a wildly unpopular move, especially after the heartfelt plea by Haile Selassie in front of the League of Nations (progressed Sun conjunct Uranus; progressed MC sextile Neptune; progressed ASC conjunct Saturn; transiting Saturn opposition Saturn; transiting Neptune opposition MC; transiting Pluto trine Sun). Mussolini then involved himself helping Franco during the Spanish Civil War (progressed MC square Moon). The war was costly to the Italians who also invaded neighboring Albania in late 1939 (pro-

gressed Sun square Venus; progressed ASC trine Pluto). Mussolini brought Italy into World War II on the Axis side in June 1940 (progressed MC square Saturn; progressed ASC square Uranus).

The Allies landed in southern Italy in July 1943 and pushed their way up the peninsula (transiting Mars semisquare MC; Neptune opposition Neptune). Mussolini fled Rome for the north but was hanged by his own countrymen, along with his mistress, Clara Petaeci, upside down at a gas station outside Milan in late April 1945 (progressed Sun sextile Jupiter; progressed MC conjunct Uranus; progressed ASC opposition Venus; transiting Mars opposition Sun; transiting Pluto square Pluto). Being on the wrong side during the war cost Italy more than 150,000 lives with 66,000 wounded. Italy had declared war on Nazi Germany in October 1944, but by then most of the damage had already occurred. A vote was held in June 1946 whereby the Italians voted to become a republic, thus abolishing the monarchy altogether (transiting Jupiter sextile Jupiter; Saturn trine Mercury; Uranus sextile Jupiter square MC).

## Italian Republic

The Italian Republic was proclaimed in Rome on June 10, 1946 (chart 4). The region of Istria was ceded to Yugoslavia in 1947 and Trieste was returned back to Italy in 1954 (progressed MC semisquare Venus; progressed ASC trine Saturn). Italy joined the European Union as a charter member in January 1958 (progressed Sun conjunct Mercury; progressed ASC square Mars; transiting Jupiter sextile MC; Saturn opposition Sun; Uranus conjunct Pluto; Neptune conjunct Moon and Pluto sextile Mercury). Later that year, all state-run brothels were closed and the venereal disease rate skyrocketed, traffic jams increased as the girls now had to walk the streets.

Premier Aldo Moro was assassinated by the Red Brigade in May 1978 (progressed MC square Mercury; progressed ASC trine Pluto; transiting Jupiter square Neptune; Saturn conjunct Mars). Italy has had one of the world's most unstable governments; by 1991, its 50th postwar government was formed (progressed ASC opposition Sun semisquare Moon). Huge corruption scandals emerged in 1993 that completely engulfed the government due to implication of its ties to the Mafia (progressed Sun semisquare Sun square Moon; progressed ASC inconjunct Venus; transiting Saturn opposition MC and Pluto opposition Mars).

## Rome

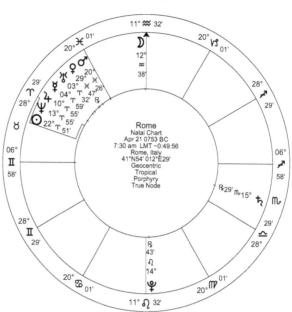

**April 21, 753 B.C., 7:30 a.m.**
**Source: Biblioteca Nazionale for date; time from Roman astrologer Lucius Tarrutius**

Rome is the capital and largest city of Italy. Located on the Tiber River 15 miles from the coast, this Eternal City was founded by Romulus and Remus on April 21, 753 B.C. according to legend. Built on seven hills and surrounded by walls, it had more than 1 million residents during the early days of the Roman Empire and was the largest city in the world. Capital of Italy only since 1871, it has more than 500 churches, including the largest place of worship on earth, St. Peter's Basilica inside the Vatican City built in 1626.

Rome has more monuments of the ancient world than one can imagine. The Roman Forums sit in the center of town along with the famous Colloseum, Pantheon, Baths of Caracalla (where opera are performed outdoors) and the Arches of Titus and Constantine. Hadrian's Tomb (aka the Castel Sant'Angelo) sits astride the Tiber next to the Vatican. Under the city lie the Catacombs where Christians worshiped during the days of the early Caesars.

Rome has numerous museums as well. The Capitoline is famed for its sculpture, the Villa Borghese has three museums inside a park-like setting and the Vatican has numerous galleries including the Sistine Chapel, painted by Michelangelo. Rome is also famous for its open-air plazas and squares like the Piazza de Popoli, Navona and Venezia at the foot of the Spanish steps. The Trevi fountain is where tourists throw coins into its waters. The Tivoli (Villa d'Este) was designed by Hadrian and is the finest example of Roman domestic architecture in the region. The Campidoglio, designed by Michelangelo in 1536, is a masterpiece of early Rococo, while the massive Victor Emanuele II Monument is built in the wedding-cake style of the early 20th century. Rome is a crowded city with a density of more than 100,000 per square mile. If one desires to see the more prosaic side of Rome, go to the Trastevere on the west side of the river just south of the Vatican. The pace is slower, the prices cheaper and the ambience more Italian and less touristy. Outside of Rome is Cinecitta, the huge movie complex which rivals anything Hollywood can produce. The most famous street in Rome is the Via Veneto which is lined with expensive shops, hotels and outdoor cafes.

# Bari

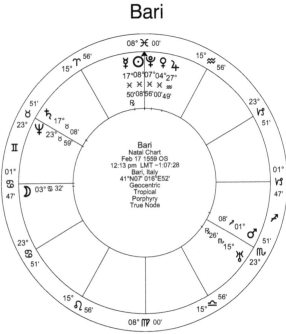

**February 17, 1559, 12:3 p.m. LMT**
**Source: Biblioteca Nazionale**

Bari is situated on the Adriatic coast 150 miles east of Naples. Founded by the Romans and named Barium, it was the chief seaport of Apulia in ancient times. Over the centuries it has been conquered by the Lombards, Saracens, Normans, Byzantines and Venetians. Today it's a major oil refining center.

# Bologna

Situated 50 miles north of Florence, it was founded by the Etruscans as Felsina and after 190 B.C. it was known to the Romans as Bononia. From the 11th century until 1506 it was an independent city-state; it's now the capital of Emilia Romagna and the 7th-largest city in Italy. Built in a Ro-

man-style grid it has the oldest university in Europe, founded in the 11th century. Known as "Fat City" because of its pasta lovers, it's also a city of towers and domes. The main sights are the church of San Petronio, a huge Gothic edifice and the Pinacoteca Nazionale with its art collections.

## Catania

Catania is Sicily's second-largest city, situated on the east coast of the island near Mt. Etna. Founded by the Greeks in the 8th century B.C., it was destroyed by earthquakes in 1169 and 1693 and was buried by lava in 1669. It was then rebuilt using a grid plan after 1700.

# Florence (Firenze)

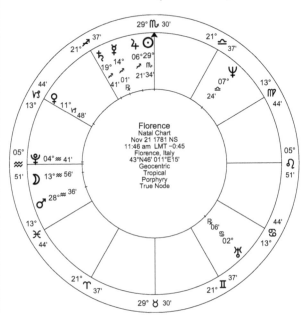

**November 21, 1781, 11:46 a.m. LMT**
**Source: Il Sindaco de Firenze**

Florence is the capital of Tuscany and located 145 miles northwest of Rome on the Arno River. Founded in 200 B.C. by the Etruscans as a military camp and called Florentia, its rise to power began in the 12th century due to its wool and silk industries. Florence reached its cultural peak in the 15th century when the Medici family ruled this city-state at the height of the Italian Renaissance. Florence was then home to people like Giotto, Donatello, Brunelleschi, Botticelli, Michelangelo and Leonardo da Vinci. From 1865 until 1871, Florence was the capital of Italy and in the autumn of 1966 was severely damaged by floodwaters when the Arno overflowed.

Florence has so many cultural attractions in a small area that it's often overwhelming to the tourist. Works of art and sculpture and architecture are a feast for the eyes. The center of town is the huge, domed Duomo (Santa Maria del Fiore) with its Baptistry. The church of Santa Croce has the tombs of Michelangelo, Macchiavelli and Galileo, while the tombs of the Medici lie inside the Church of San Lorenzo. For art lovers there's the Uffizi and Pitti Palaces, the Museo Bargello and San Marco. The Palazzo Vecchio was the headquarters for the Florentine Republic while the bridge of the same name is the most famous span in the region. Overlooking Florence are the Boboli Gardens near the Belvedere.

Florence today is not only a major tourist destination but is also a major banking, publishing and fashion center. It's famous for its leather-working, jewelry and furniture.

## Genoa (Genova)

Located on the Ligurian Sea, an arm of the Mediterranean 75 miles southwest of Turin, Genoa is Italy's leading port and sixth-largest city. During the Middle Ages it was a wealthy and powerful city-state that was rivaled only by Venice. Today it's a major trading center and naval base with steel mills and shipbuilding yards. During the 12th century, Genoa was part of the Republic of St. George, and in the early 19th century, it was headquarters for the Risorgimento, the organization dedicated to the unification of Italy. The main sights in town are the Casa Columbo (home of Christopher Columbus who was born here in 1451), the Cathedral of San Lorenzo and the Via Garibaldi with its palaces.

## Milan (Milano)

Milan is Italy's second-largest city and leading industrial, commercial and banking center. Founded in the 4th century B.C., by the 4th century A.D. it was the capital of the western Roman Empire and known as Mediolanum. From the 11th to the 13th centuries, Milan was a city-state under the rule of the Sforzas, a center for art, culture and politics. By the 19th century, Milan was the most prosperous city in Italy, and the capital of Lombardy from 1814 to 1859.

The most famous sight in Milan is the Duomo, the huge 14th century Gothic cathedral which sits in the center of the city. It's the third-largest church in the world and fronts the massive Piazza del Duomo with its neon signs that light up the night sky. Next door is the Galleria Victor Emanuele, a magnificent arcade of shops and cafes. Milan is also home to the most famous opera house on earth, La Scala. Inside the church of Santa Maria delle Grazie is Da Vinci's painting, "The Last Supper," which has just recently been restored to its former glory. Milan has many art museums like La Pinacoteca, the Brera, and the

Castel Sforzecco.

Milan has three universities, numerous publishing houses, a Stock Exchange and is fully-integrated into Europe's cultural, industrial and financial communities. It's the home to Fiat and Olivetti and is also a major center for fashion.

# Naples (Napoli)

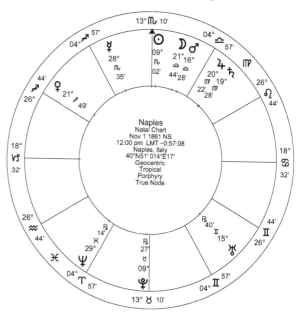

**November 1, 1861, noon LMT**
**Source: Biblioteca Universitaria**

Naples is Italy's third-largest city and the capital of Campania. Located on the Bay of Naples, an arm of the Tyrrhenian Sea, 115 miles southeast of Rome, it sits in the shadow of Mt. Vesuvius which buried Pompeii and Herculaneum in August 79 A.D. Founded by the Greeks in the 6th century B.C. and known as Neapolis, it's been under Roman, Byzantine, Norman and Spanish rule until it was united with Italy in 1860. A major earthquake in November 1980 caused extensive damage. Naples is often a city of horrible slums and high crime, part of it due to the Camorra who run certain parts of the city.

The most famous sights in town are the 13th century Castel Nuovo and the opera house, Teatro de San Carlo. The Palazzo Reale, the Castel Sant'Elmo and the Museo Capodimonte are also popular. The Duomo is called the Cathedral of San Gennaro.

Naples is a major industrial center making steel, chemicals and refining oil and processing food. Nearby are the islands of Capri and Ischia and the picturesque towns of Sorrento and Amalfi down the coast.

## Palermo

Palermo is Sicily's largest city and capital and Italy's fifth-largest city. Founded by the Phoenicians in the 8th century B.C., it was known to the Greeks as Panormos. Under Arab rule from 831 until the Normans ousted them in 1072, Spain ruled the island during the 17th and 18th centuries. Palermo is a noisy, chaotic and often dangerous place with large pockets of poverty. The main sights in town are the National Gallery of Sicily, Museo delle Marionette, the Palazzo Normanni (built in the 11th century), and the churches of San Giovanni and the 12th century Duomo.

## Trieste

Located at the northern end of the Adriatic Sea, it was founded as Tergeste by the Romans in the 2nd century B.C. From 1383 until 1797 it was part of Austria when Napoleon took over; it didn't become part of Italy until 1919 after the Treaty of Versailles put an end to World War I. Trieste was occupied by American and British military forces from 1946 until 1954. Trieste is primarily an industrial town that makes steel and refines oil.

## Turin (Torino)

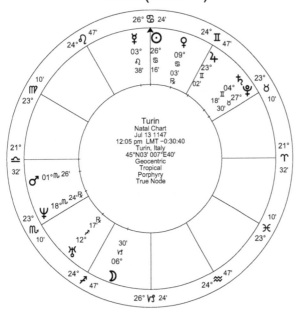

**July 13, 1147, 12:05 p.m. LMT**
**Source: Citta del Torino**

Turin is the fourth-largest city in Italy and is located on the Po River 80 miles west of Milano. The capital of Savoy (French) from 1060 until 1814 when it became property of the King of Sardinia. This was where the unification of Italy took place in March 1861 and Turin was its first capital until 1865.

Founded by the Romans, it was built in a grid pattern with numerous squares and broad tree-shaded boulevards. Its name comes from the tribe of the Taurini.

The most famous sight in Turin is its Romanesque Cathedral which houses the Holy Shroud, the cloth which supposedly wrapped the body of Christ after his crucifixion. Turin is the second-largest manufacturing city in Italy and makes cars, TV and radio sets, chemicals, rubber, plastic and pharmaceuticals. Turin is also a major publishing center with a growing art and fashion community.

## Venice (Venezia)

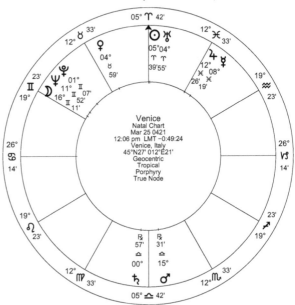

**March 25, 421 A.D., 12:05 p.m. LMT**
**Sources: *Venice* by Peter Lauritzen and *La Vita dei Dogi* by Marin Sanudo**

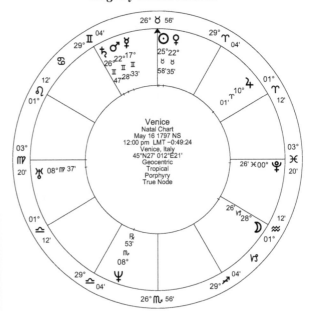

**May 16, 1797, noon LMT**
**Source: *Venice* by Hibbert**

Venice is the world's greatest cultural and architectural storehouse built on wooden piles which were driven into a lagoon at the north end of the Adriatic Sea. Founded March 25, 421 A.D., most history books give the year as 452 when mainlanders founded the city to protect themselves from invading barbarians. By the 9th century, Venice had become a city-state under the rule of a Doge who had been first elected in 697. The Republic of Venice was a maritime power and ruled the Mediterranean for five centuries. Venice has more than 100 islands and 400 bridges and was connected by a railroad causeway in 1846 to the mainland. Venice is famous for its gondolas which weave their way through the maze of canals that interlace this beautiful city. Currently, Venice is sinking and flooding from the lagoon in the fall is becoming more and more prevalent. Tourists often have to walk on boards through the center of Venice, and water marks on buildings lining the canals are reminders that residents live in a precarious state of grace.

The most famous square in Italy, if not the world, is the Piazza de San Marco which fronts the 11th-century Cathedral of St. Marks and the 14th-century Doges Palace. The highest point in Venice is the Campanile which was rebuilt in 1912. The church of Santa Maria della Salute is probably the finest example of Rococo church architecture in Italy sitting astride the Grand Canal. The Bridge of Sighs and the Rialto Bridge are also world-famous. Venice was home to Canaletto, Bellini, Titian, Tintoretto, Veronese and Tiepolo during the height of the Renaissance. The islands of Burano, Murano and Torcello are also popular tourist sights while the rich sunbathe on the shores of the Lido. At Mestre, which is on the mainland, Venice makes textiles, lace and glass. The Jewish quarter, called Ghetto, is also a must-see for it was here in Venice that Jews became financiers back in the Middle Ages when other professions were closed to them.

# Latvia
## Latvijas Republika

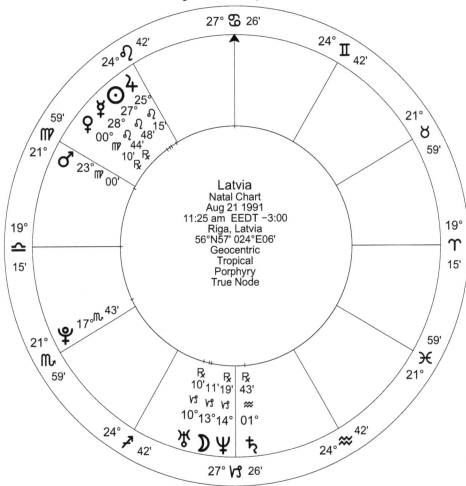

**August 21, 1991, 11:25 a.m. EEDT, 8:25 a.m. GMT, Riga**
**Source:** *Book of World Horoscopes* by Nicholas Campion; CNN says 8:45 a.m. GMT

Situated on the eastern shore of the Baltic Sea on the Gulf of Riga, Latvia is a fertile lowland with more than 3,000 lakes. The highest point is 1,020 feet above sea level.

Population: 2,385,231; 57% Latvian, 30% Russian

Religion: 55% Lutheran; 25% Orthodox

Area: 24, 748 square miles (the size of Lithuania or West Virginia); 30% arable, 69% urban

Economy: Main exports are electrical equipment, chemicals and textiles. Chief resources are peat, amber and limestone.

This region was first settled in the 9th century AD by the Letts and was conquered by the Teutonic Knights during the 13th century. In 1562, this area, then called Livonia and Courland, was taken by Poland until 1629 when it was ceded to Sweden. Peter the Great made Livonia part of his newly-formed Russian Empire in 1721 and Courland fell to the Russians in 1795.

In November 1918, Latvia declared its independence from Russia but the Soviet Union annexed this region in July 1940. Latvia was then occupied by the Germans from 1941 to 1944. Latvia again declared its independence on August 21, 1991. Soviet troops finally left three years later. By October 1998, Latvia eased citizenship laws against native Russians (transiting Saturn trine Venus). Latvia joined the European Union in May 2004 (progressed Sun trine Uranus; progressed MC inconjunct Uranus; progressed ASC sextile Sun).

# Riga

Capital and largest city of Latvia is situated on the Baltic where the Dvina River empties into the Bay of Riga. Founded by Bishop Albert and the Teutonic Knights in 1190, it was granted town rights (or chartered) around 1225. Sweden occupied the city from 1621 to 1710, when the Russians took over. Independence was brief from 1918 until 1940, when the Soviets illegally incorporated the country into the Soviet Union. Riga was occupied by the Germans during World War II. Riga is a major shipbuilding and textile center.

# Liechtenstein
# Furstentum Liechtenstein

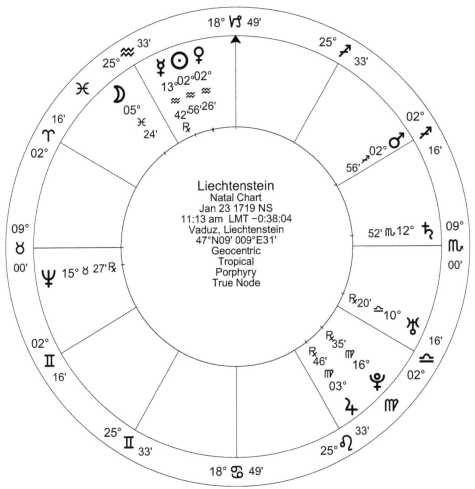

**January 23, 1719, 11:13 a.m. LMT, Vaduz**
**Source: *Encyclopedia Britannica* for the date; time rectified**

This tiny country is situated in the Alps between Switzerland and Austria on the east bank of the Rhine River.

Population: 32,528; 99% Germanic

Religion: 80% Catholic, 7% Protestant

Area: 61 square miles (the size of Washington, DC)

Economy: Main exports are precision instruments, specialized machinery, artificial teeth and pharmaceuticals. Liechtenstein is also a major banking center and thus is a headquarters for many international corporations.

The Barony of Vaduz was founded in 814 A.D., nine centuries before Liechtenstein became the last principality created by the Holy Roman Empire on January 23, 1719. Napoleon disbanded that "empire" in August 1806 (progressed Sun square Venus; progressed MC semisquare Mars sesquare Jupiter

inconjunct Pluto; progressed ASC inconjunct Moon). After the Treaty of Vienna of June 1815 and the defeat of Napoleon, Liechtenstein became part of the German Confederation (progressed Sun inconjunct Uranus; progressed ASC sextile Uranus square Saturn). It seceded from that union on October 3, 1866 and two years later disbanded its armed forces (progressed Sun semisquare Neptune; progressed MC square Pluto; progressed ASC sesquare Sun and Venus).

When World War I broke out in August 1914, Liechtenstein decided to remain neutral (progressed Sun square Neptune; progressed MC opposition Venus semisquare Pluto). Liechtenstein remained neutral in May 1940 during World War II (progressed MC semisquare Uranus; progressed ASC conjunct Saturn square Mercury). Women were finally given the vote in July 1984 (progressed MC conjunct Uranus; progressed ASC sextile Mercury).

Liechtenstein was put on a blacklist for failure to cooperate in the fight against money-laundering in 2001 (progressed Sun opposition ASC). In March 2003, the Constitution was overhauled to give its monarch vaster powers (progressed Sun conjunct Saturn; progressed ASC semisquare Saturn).

## Vaduz

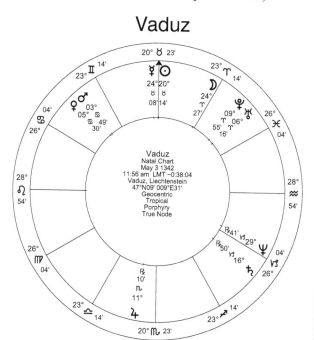

**May 3, 1342, 11:56 a.m. LMT**
**Source: Burgomeister of Vaduz**

The capital of Liechtenstein sits on a hill about 50 miles east of Zurich. Its famous castle was built in the 18th century and today is the residence of the royal family. Despite its small population (5,000), Vaduz appears much more cosmopolitan due to its liberal tax laws which encourage international banking.

# Lithuania
## Lietuvos Respublika

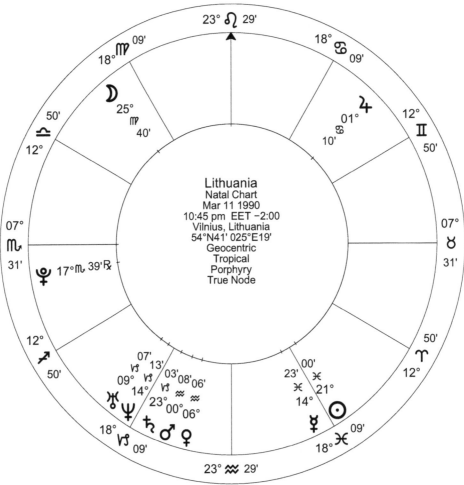

Lithuania
Natal Chart
Mar 11 1990
10:45 pm EET −2:00
Vilnius, Lithuania
54°N41' 025°E19'
Geocentric
Tropical
Porphyry
True Node

**March 11, 1990, 10:45 p.m. EET, 8:45 p.m. GMT, Vilnius**
**Source:** *International Herald Tribune* **says 10:45 p.m.**

Situated on the eastern shore of the Baltic Sea, Lithuania is a region of gentle, rolling hills and numerous forests. The highest point is 965 feet above sea level.

Population: 3,610,535; 80% Lithuanian, 8% Russian, 7% Polish

Religion: 85% Catholic

Area: 25,174 square miles (the size of Latvia or West Virginia); 35% arable, 68% urban

Economy: Main exports are electrical motors, machinery and linen. The main resource is peat

During the 14th century, the Duchy of Lithuania conquered White Russia (Belarus) and the Ukraine. Lithuania's territory ranged from the Baltic to the Black Sea. In 1386, Prince Jagiello of Lithuania married Princess Jadwiga of Poland was crowned King and united both countries. The following year, pagan Lithuanians were forced to adopt Christianity. Polish and Lithuanian forces defeated the Teutonic Knights at the battle of Grunwald (Tannenbaum) in 1410.

After the third and final partition of Poland in 1795, Lithuania was given to Russia. Russians then required Lithuanians to adopt the Cyrillic alphabet and other strict measures forced thousands to emigrate, most of them to America. Lithuania first declared its independence from Russia in February 1918 but its capital was occupied by Polish troops soon afterwards. The government then moved to Kaunas.

In July 1940, the Soviet Union illegally annexed Lithuania as part of a pre-arranged pact between Hitler and Stalin. Beginning in June 1941, the country was occupied by the Germans until the Soviets finally drove them out in 1944.

Lithuania again declared its independence on March 11, 1990. Russians then imposed severe economic sanctions which lasted until the Soviet Union itself fell into oblivion at the end of 1991 (progressed Sun sesquare ASC). Soviet troops finally left in August 1993 (progressed MC sesquare Uranus; transiting Pluto square MC). Lithuania joined the European Union in May 2004 (progressed Sun sextile Venus; progressed MC sesquare Saturn; progressed ASC conjunct Pluto sesquare Jupiter).

## Vilnius

The capital and largest city of Lithuania is situated 95 miles east of Kaunas. Founded in the 10th century, it was the heart of the vast Lithuanian Empire from 1323 until 1795 when it became part of Russia. Chartered in 1387, it has the oldest university in the Baltic states which was founded in 1579. Vilnius was ruled by Poland from 1919 to 1939 and by the Soviets from 1940 until 1991. Source: Vilnius University Library

# Luxembourg
## Grossherzogtum Letzeburg
## Le Grand Duche de Luxembourg

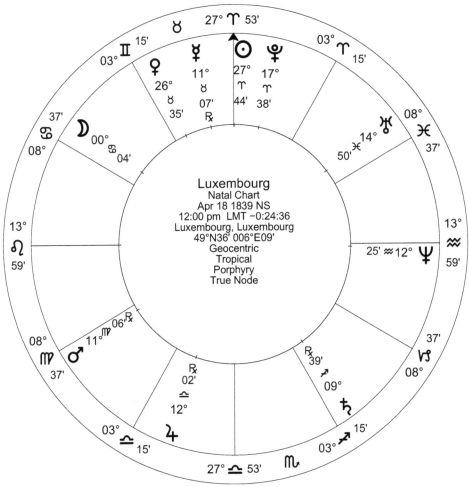

**April 18, 1839, noon LMT, Ville de Luxembourg**
**Source: Embassy of Luxembourg for the date; noon presumed; per astrologer Grietje Versatel**

Luxembourg is situated between Belgium, France and Germany in the Ardennes. The highest point is 1,855 feet above sea level.

Population: 442,972; 49% German, 48% French
Religion: 97% Catholic, 1% Moslem
Area: 999 square miles (the size of Rhode Island); 91% urban, 25% arable
Economy: Main exports are iron ore, steel, machinery, plastics and chemicals.

The feudal domain of Luxembourg was founded in 963 A.D. and a century later, the notable House of Luxembourg had been established. Created a Grand Duchy in 1354, it was alternately ruled by the Hapsburgs from the Netherlands, Spain, Burgundy or Austria from 1443 until 1795. Then Napoleon made this region part of his emerging empire.

After Napoleon's downfall, the Treaty of Vienna in June 1815 granted Luxembourg to the Netherlands. After the Netherlands' southern provinces revolted in October 1830 and formed the nation of Belgium, Luxembourg's political situation was in flux. The western part of this nation remained with Belgium until April 18, 1839, the date when the problems with Belgium ceased and modern Luxembourg was born.

Luxembourg then decided to become part of the German Confederation until 1866 when it seceded. In May 1867, the Treaty of London recognized the independence and sovereignty of Luxembourg (progressed ASC sesquare Pluto). There was only one problem: the ruler of this country was still the king of the Netherlands. Due to the fact that Luxembourg followed Salic Law which forbade a woman from sitting on the throne, when the King of the Netherlands died in November 1890, his daughter, Wilhelmina, became ruler of Luxembourg. It was decided to sever all ties to the Netherlands and it chose its own ruler (progressed Sun sextile Pluto).

When World War I began in August 1914, Germans occupied the region (progressed Sun sextile Mars inconjunct Saturn; transiting Pluto conjunct Moon). The Germans left shortly after the Armistice was signed in November 1918 (progressed Sun trine Uranus; progressed ASC conjunct Jupiter trine Neptune; transiting Jupiter trine Uranus; transiting Saturn trine Sun).

Germans invaded again in May 1940 on their way to occupying the Low Countries (progressed ASC inconjunct Venus semisquare Mars; transiting Mars conjunct Moon; transiting Jupiter semisquare Uranus; transiting Pluto sesquare Uranus). After the war, Luxembourg formed a trade pact with neighboring Belgium and the Netherlands in January 1948 (progressed Sun sextile Jupiter; transiting Jupiter square Uranus; Neptune conjunct Jupiter trine Neptune). Ten years later, Luxembourg became a charter member of the European Union (progressed Sun trine Sun/Pluto; transiting Jupiter opposition Sun; Uranus trine Saturn).

# Luxembourg Ville

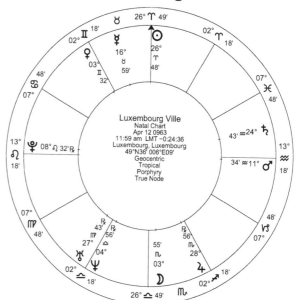

**April 12, 963, 11:59 a.m. LMT**
**Source: Burgomeister**

Founded on Palm Sunday 963 by Count Sigefroi, the fortress known as Lucilinburhuc rose on a cliff above the Alzette River. A new city was founded in the 19th century and in 1890 became the capital of the Grand Duchy of Luxembourg. The old and new parts of the city are now connected by viaducts over the deep ravine. The city was chartered in 1244.

This city is home to the European Court of Justice and the European Investment Bank. It also has Europe's oldest radio station, but the main attraction in the city are the Bock Casements, a series of tunnels and fortresses built by the Austrians and used extensively during both World Wars.

# Macedonia
# Respublika Makedonija

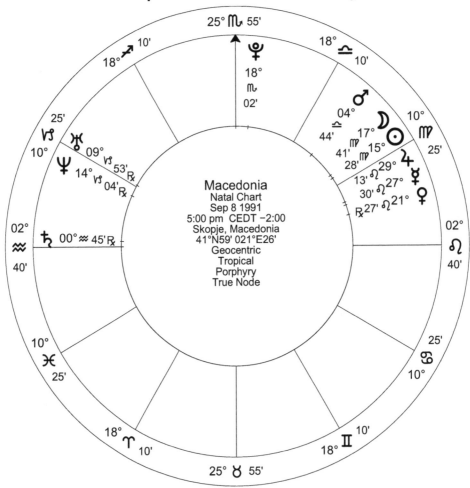

Macedonia
Natal Chart
Sep 8 1991
5:00 pm CEDT −2:00
Skopje, Macedonia
41°N59' 021°E26'
Geocentric
Tropical
Porphyry
True Node

**September 8, 1991, 5:00 p.m. MEDT, 3:00 p.m. GMT, Skopje**
**Source: Astrologer Simeon Atanasoski**

Macedonia is a landlocked country between Serbia, Albania, Greece and Bulgaria on the Balkan peninsula. Most of the country is very mountainous with extremely rugged terrain. The main river is the Vardar and the highest point. Mt. Korab (elevation 9,068 feet) sits on the Albanian border.

Population: 2,046,209; 66% Macedonian, 23% Albanian

Religion: 67% Orthodox, 30% Moslem

Area: 9,781 square miles (the size of Albania or Maryland); 5% arable, 62% urban

Economy: Main exports are tobacco, chemicals and cereal. Chief resources are chromium, lead, zinc and marble

Macedonia was conquered by the Romans in 146 B.C. when they took over the rest of Greece. In 395 A.D., this region became part of the vast Byzantine Empire which ruled it for the next 10 centuries. The Ottomans came in 1389 and stayed for five centuries. The Treaty of Berlin in July 1878 gave most of Macedonia to Bulgaria, but during the Second Balkan War of June 1913, it was transferred to Serbia with the southern part remaining in Greece.

On December 1, 1918, Macedonia became part of the new nation which would later be known as Yugoslavia. During World War II, Macedonia was occupied by Bulgarian forces which had sided with the Nazis.

In January 1991, Macedonia declared its independence from Yugoslavia but the European Union demanded that a referendum be held before independence could become official. That vote was taken and on September 8, 1991, the results were proclaimed. Conflict erupted over the choice of its name as Greece felt it had title to the name Macedonia, birthplace of Alexander the Great.

In 1994, Greece closed the main trade route to Salonika over the use of Macedonia's name as well as its national flag (progressed MC square Mercury; progressed ASC trine Mars). Normal relations with Greece ensued after September 1995 (progressed MC square Jupiter sextile Saturn). Macedonia became a haven for ethnic Albanians fleeing the Serbian region of Kosovo in March 1999 when the Serbian army began another round of "ethnic cleansing" (transiting Neptune conjunct ASC).

## Skopje

The capital and largest city of Macedonia is situated on the Vardar River, one of the most important trade routes of the Balkans. Turks occupied the city after 1392, and a massive earthquake in 1963 leveled much of Skopje, leaving 70 percent of its people homeless.

# Malta
# Repubblika Ta Malta

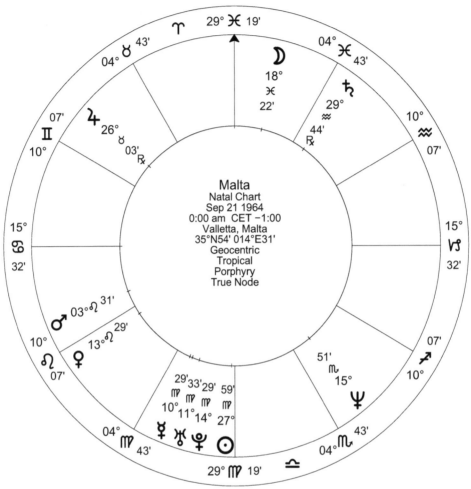

**September 21, 1964, 12:00 a.m. MET, Valletta**
**Source:** *The Times* **of London says midnight**

Malta is a group of five islands about 60 miles south of Sicily in the Mediterranean Sea. Its coastline is 87 miles long and the highest point is 835 feet above sea level. The terrain is quite rocky and the climate hot and dry.

Population: 394,583; 96% Maltese, 2% British
Religion: 98% Catholic

Area: 124 square miles (the size of Philadelphia, Pennsylvania); 38 arable, 90% urban

Economy: Main exports are textiles and flowers. Shipbuilding is a major industry.

During the 10th century B.C., Malta was colonized by the Phoenicians. Four centuries later, it was occupied by the Carthaginians. Roman legions arrived in 146 B.C. to be replaced by the Moslems in the 7th century A.D.

In 1091, Malta was invaded from Sicily by the Normans and from 1530 to 1798, it was the property of the Knights of St. John (aka Knights of Malta). Napoleon captured Malta in 1798 on his way to conquering Egypt, but two years later the British wrested control from the French.

The British granted independence to Malta on September 21, 1964 and on December 13, 1974, Malta became a republic (progressed MC inconjunct Mercury). Malta joined the European Union in May 2004 (progressed MC trine Mercury; progressed ASC square Neptune).

# Moldova
## Republica Moldoveneasea

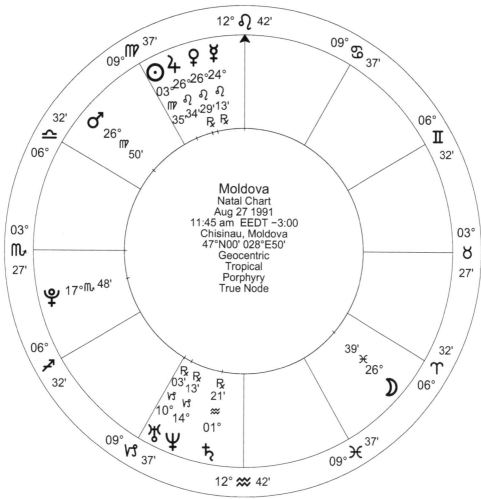

Moldova
Natal Chart
Aug 27 1991
11:45 am  EEDT -3:00
Chisinau, Moldova
47°N00' 028°E50'
Geocentric
Tropical
Porphyry
True Node

**August 27, 1991, 11:45 a.m. EEDST, 8:45 a.m. GMT, Chisinau (Kishinev)**
**Source: Astrologer Ludmilla Gagara**

Moldova is sandwiched between Romania and the Ukraine, a region of hilly plains between the Dniester and Prut Rivers. Over 75% of its soil is chernozem, the richest on earth. Even though this country is landlocked, it does have an outlet to the Black Sea along the Danube River of about one kilometer, or half a mile. The highest point is 1,407 feet above sea level.

Population: 4,431,750; 65% Moldavian, 14% Ukrainian, 13% Russian

Religion: 98% Orthodox

Area: 13,012 square miles (the size of Belgium or Maryland); 53% arable, 46% urban

Economy: Main exports are corn, fruit, vegetables, wine and tobacco.

Moldavia was settled by the Romans in the 1st century A.D. and by Slavs eight centuries later. Mongols overran the region in 1241 and laid waste to this fertile land. Lithuanians took over from 1389 to 1456 when the Ottomans gained ascendancy. Russians began to infiltrate Moldavia in 1791. Bessarabia, once a part of Romania, was ceded to Russia in 1812. Beginning in 1822, Moldavia bounced like a ping-pong ball between Turkey and Romania. Finally in 1919, all of Bessarabia was incorporated into Romania from the defunct Ottoman Empire.

The Soviet Union annexed Moldavia in June 1940, but from 1941 to 1944, German and Romanian troops occupied the region. In 1989, Moldavia switched from using the Cyrillic alphabet to the more westernized Roman alphabet.

On August 27, 1991, Moldavia declared its independence from the Soviet Union. Conflicts arose between the Russians and Romanians, the latter which felt that ethnically this region was part of their own country (progressed MC square Moon). A plebiscite in March 1994 voted against reunion with Romania (transiting Saturn opposition Sun trine ASC; Uranus sextile Moon trine Mars). Russians in the Dniester region desired reunion with the Ukraine, shortly before Russia cut oil exports by 20 percent (transiting Jupiter square Moon and Mars; transiting Saturn trine Pluto). In February 2001, attempts to make Russian the second language drew numerous protests.

## Chisinau (Kishinev)

The capital and largest city of Moldova was first mentioned in the 14th century. Ceded to Russia in 1812 during the Napoleonic wars, Chisinau became capital of Bessarabia in 1873 and was ceded again to Russia in 1940 as capital of the Moldavian SSR.

# Monaco
## Principaute de Monaco

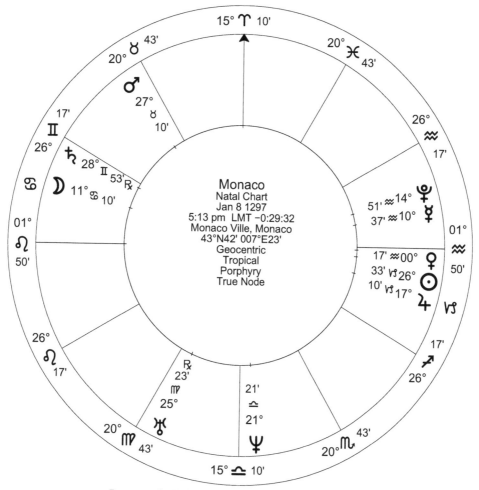

**January 8, 1297, 5:13 p.m. LMT, Monaco Ville**
Source: *Grimaldis of Monaco* by Paolo Lingua and *Princes of Monaco* by Francoise de Bernardy
both state "sundown"; chart rectified

Monaco is located along the Mediterranean Sea between Nice and San Remo on the French Riviera. Surrounded by France, its coastline is 2.5 miles long. It's the third-smallest country in Europe after the Vatican and the Sovereign Military Order of Malta.

Population: 31,842; 47% French, 16% Italian, 16% Monegasque

Religion: 95% Catholic

Area: 465 acres (about half the size of New York's Central Park); 100% urban

Economy: Tourism and gambling are the main sources of income. Due to its liberal tax laws, many foreigners reside in Monaco. Native Monegasques pay no taxes but cannot gamble in the casinos.

During the 10th century B.C., this region was colonized by the Phoenicians and Greeks who gave it the name Monikos. The Principality of Monaco was established in 968 A.D. and it was ceded to Genoa in 1162.

On January 8, 1297, Francesco Grimaldi, a Genoan, seized the fortress while masquerading as an itinerant monk. The Grimaldis increased their wealth over the centuries by exacting tolls to anyone who desired to pass through the region. Monaco became a Spanish protectorate in 1524 (progressed MC sextile Sun opposition Mars) but in 1641 it passed into the hands of the French (progressed ASC opposition Jupiter inconjunct Pluto).

Before the French Revolution, Monaco was 10 times its size today: the cities of Menton and Rocquebrune declared their independence. Napoleon annexed Monaco into France in 1793 (progressed Sun sesquare Neptune; progressed ASC sesquare Saturn). After Napoleon's defeat in 1814,

Monaco became a Sardinian protectorate (progressed Sun inconjunct Sun; progressed MC sesquare Venus inconjunct Pluto; progressed ASC inconjunct Saturn).

In February 1861, Monaco signed a pact with Napoleon III which insured its sovereignty under French protection (progressed Sun semisquare Uranus; progressed MC trine Saturn). About this time, the ruling Prince established gambling and before long Monaco was the darling of the rich and famous. You see, gambling was illegal in France and Italy.

Universal suffrage was granted in May 1910 and eight months later, Monaco's first Constitution was framed (progressed Sun square Saturn; transiting Saturn sextile Saturn; Uranus trine Uranus; Pluto square Uranus).

The most glamorous occasion in Monaco's history took place April 18, 1956 when Prince Rainier married Grace Kelly, an American film star (progressed ASC trine Sun conjunct Mars; transiting Jupiter sextile Neptune; Saturn trine ASC; Uranus opposition Sun/Venus; Neptune trine Saturn square Venus). Women were finally given the vote in 1962 and five years later Prince Rainier took over the Societe de Bains de Mer which ran the world-famous casino (progressed Sun sextile Uranus; progressed MC sesquare Saturn).

Tragedy, however, came to Monaco and the world in September 1982 when Princess Grace was accidentally killed in a car crash on a winding road above Monaco (progressed Sun inconjunct Moon; progressed ASC square Uranus inconjunct Sun). Transiting Pluto was also square the natal Sun. In 2000, France accused Monaco of being a money-laundering paradise with lax banking laws (progressed Sun opposition Saturn; progressed MC sextile Jupiter; progressed ASC conjunct Moon semisquare Mars).

In July 2005, Prince Albert took over after the death of his father, Prince Rainier, and quickly began to clean up Monaco of its more undesirable characters (progressed Midheaven inconjunct Neptune; progressed Ascendant inconjunct Pluto).

# Montenegro

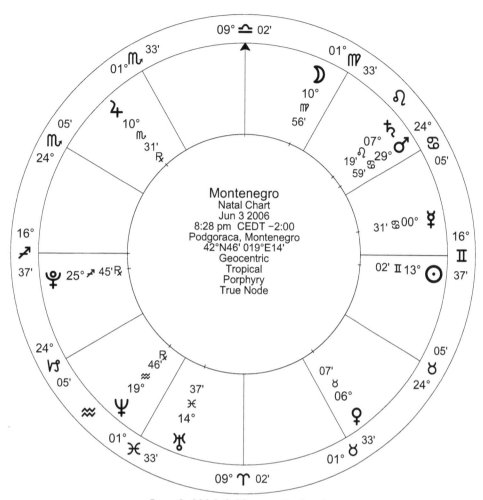

**June 3, 2006, 8:28 p.m., Podgorica**
**Source: Branka Stamenkovic, from Serbian TV**

This smallest republic of the former Yugoslavia was known in ancient times as part of the Roman province of Illyria. After the Battle of Kosovo in June 1389, Montenegro gained its independence from Serbia as that region was swallowed-up by the Ottoman Empire. The Ottomans formally recognized the independence of Montenegro in 1799. In 1860, the Petrovich dynasty was formed, which ruled until Montenegro joined the new nation of Yugoslavia in December 1918.

After the secession of Slovenia, Croatia, Bosnia and Macedonia from Yugoslavia in 1991, what was left of Yugoslavia was renamed Serbia and Montenegro in 1992. Its union was fractious at best, and after 1997, Montenegro became more and more independent of Serbia. It adopted the Euro as its cur-

rency, formed its own customs union and tax system and created its own paramilitary police.

A referendum was held May 21, 2006 on independence and the vote was 55 percent in favor of separation from Serbia. Members of Parliament issued a formal declaration of independence June 3, 2006.

Population: 650,000; 40% Montenegrin, 30% Serbian, 10% Albanian

Religion: Orthodox Christian and Moslem

Area: 5,531 square miles (the size of Connecticut, or half the size of Albania or Macedonia)

Geography: Very mountainous with a 124-mile coastline on the eastern shore of the Adriatic Sea. It shares Lake Scutari with neighboring Albania. The highest point is Durmitor (elevation 8,322 feet).

# Netherlands
## Koninkrijk Der Nederlanden

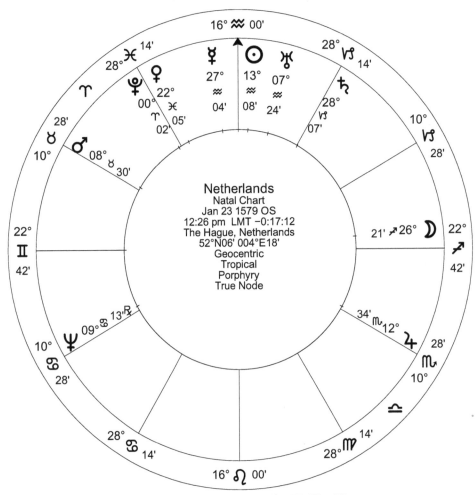

**January 23, 1579, 12:26 p.m. LMT, The Hague**
**Source: Rijksarchief for the correct date (some sources stated January 29); time is speculative**

Situated at the northwest corner of Europe along the North Sea, about 20 percent of the country lies below sea level and is protected by 1,500 miles of dikes and levees. Over 40 percent of its territory has been reclaimed from the sea, and thus it is the only country in Europe which is continually growing in area. Holland in fact is the name of a southwest province on the border with Belgium. The highest point, Vaalserberg (elevation 1,058 feet), lies in the province of Limburg. The Netherlands coastline is 280 miles long and the main rivers are the Rhine, Maas and Schelde.

Population: 15,981,472; 94% Dutch, 5% Indonesian

Religion: 34% Catholic, 25% Protestant, 5% Moslem

Area: 16,033 square miles (the size of Switzerland or New Hampshire); 89% urban, 25% arable

Economy: Main exports are meat, chemicals, petroleum, textiles, machinery, electrical equipment and dairy products. The Netherlands is also a major producer of flowers and leads the world in diamond cutting and polishing. Fishing and shipbuilding are major industries and Rotterdam is Europe's leading port and handles over 25 percent of its freight.

Julius Caesar conquered the Frisians and Batavians in 55 B.C. and three centuries later the Franks arrived from the east. The Zuider Zee was formed in 776 A.D. when the first levees were constructed against the sea. At the Treaty of Verdun in 843 A.D., Holland was given to Lothair, grandson of Charlemagne. Soon the Vikings were raiding settlements along the coast. From 1384 to 1455 the Netherlands was occupied by the Burgundians, but in 1477 the region passed into Hapsburg hands. The Inquisition arrived in 1525 and even harsher rule came when Philip II of Spain imposed a reign of terror in the 16th century. William the Silent began a revolt against Spanish rule in 1568 which resulted in the northern provinces of the Netherlands uniting on January 23, 1579. This pact was called the Union of Utrecht, even though it was signed in the Hague. I consider this the birth of the Netherlands.

Two years later, on July 26, 1581, the Dutch Republic was formed (progressed Sun semisquare Pluto; progressed ASC opposition Moon). William the Silent, the first leader of the nation, was assassinated in 1584 (progressed ASC sesquare Sun and Jupiter). The Golden Age of the Netherlands began in 1596 when ships were sent to Java in the East Indies (progressed ASC sextile Mars conjunct Neptune). Six years later, the Dutch East India Company was chartered for the purposes of trade, not colonization (progressed MC trine Neptune; progressed ASC trine Jupiter).

Spain recognized the independence of the Netherlands in 1609 (progressed Sun trine Jupiter semisquare Saturn) but peace didn't last long and by 1621, the Netherlands was again at war with Spain (progressed Sun square Moon; progressed MC semisquare Sun sesquare Jupiter; progressed ASC inconjunct Moon). The Treaty of Westphalia in 1648 made the Netherlands completely independent of Spain as well as ending the Thirty Years War over religious differences (progressed ASC opposition Sun square Jupiter). The Netherlands was now the largest trading nation in Europe, its fleet was twice the size of England and France combined.

In April 1652, the Dutch established a refueling and refreshment station on the southern tip of Africa and named it Cape Town (progressed Sun trine Moon; progressed MC square Saturn; progressed ASC sesquare Pluto). In 1672 the Netherlands was attacked by British and French forces (progressed ASC inconjunct Pluto) who were obviously jealous of its wealth. However, in November 1689, William of Orange, Stadtholder of the Netherlands, became King of England; his wife, Mary, was daughter of the deposed Catholic King James II who was forced into exile (progressed ASC sextile Jupiter). The Treaty of Rijswijk in 1697 opened up trade and granted larger commercial privileges to the Netherlands (progressed MC trine Sun inconjunct Jupiter). By 1715 the Golden Age began to wane due to a decline in world trade (progressed Sun opposition Moon; progressed MC sesquare Sun; progressed ASC opposition Pluto). Between 1780 and 1784, the Netherlands went to war against England (progressed ASC square Sun).

In 1795, the Batavian Republic was formed under French guidelines (progressed Sun inconjunct Sun square Jupiter sesquare Saturn). The government took over control of the East India Company in 1798. In 1806, Napoleon put his brother, Louis, on the throne of Holland (progressed Sun sesquare Mars; progressed MC square Moon; progressed ASC trine Pluto). Four years later, the Netherlands became part of the emerging French Empire (progressed Sun trine Saturn; progressed MC opposition Pluto). The French were booted out in 1813 (progressed Sun opposition Pluto).

On March 16, 1815, the Kingdom of the Netherlands was founded in the city of The Hague. It comprised the southern provinces of Belgium and a good part of Luxembourg. The Belgians revolted on October 4, 1830 and declared their independence (progressed MC inconjunct Venus). A liberal Constitution was framed in 1848 (progressed MC opposition Mars trine Neptune). Slavery was finally abolished in the Far East in 1860.

When World War I began in August 1914 the Netherlands decided to remain neutral (progressed Sun sextile Jupiter; progressed ASC conjunct Mars sextile Neptune; transiting Jupiter conjunct MC; Uranus square Mars; Pluto square Pluto). Beginning in 1920, the Zuider Zee was drained bit by bit and in 1932, the Ijsselmeer Dam was completed to block the sea from the newly-drained land (progressed ASC trine Uranus).

Nazi Germany invaded the Netherlands in May 1940, completely disregarding the fact that the Netherlands was a neutral country. Queen Wilhelmina fled to England (progressed Sun square Mars inconjunct Neptune; progressed MC square Jupiter semisquare Moon; transiting Mars opposition Moon; Jupiter square Saturn; Saturn square Uranus; Pluto trine Pluto). In early 1945 when the Germans were in retreat, they blew up numerous dikes, thus flooding the countryside. More than 20,000 Dutch died in the war which ended in May 1945 (progressed ASC square Venus semisquare Mars). Three months later, Sukarno declared the independence of Indonesia just as the Japanese were surrendering to the Allies (tr Uranus trine Sun/Uranus; Pluto square Mars).

Queen Wilhelmina abdicated in favor of her daughter, Juliana, in 1948 (progressed ASC trine Mercury square Moon). After years of fighting the Indonesians, independence was granted on December 27, 1949 (progressed ASC sesquare Sun inconjunct Saturn; transiting Mars opposition Pluto; Neptune trine MC).

Torrential rains and extremely high winds caused extensive flooding in the province of Zealand in February 1953. Over 375,000 acres were underwater,

70,000 had to be evacuated, 47,000 homes were destroyed, 200,000 cattle drowned and nearly 2000 Dutch lives were lost (progressed MC sesquare Neptune; progressed ASC square Pluto; transiting Jupiter square Sun semisquare Pluto opposition Jupiter). In January 1958, the Netherlands joined the European Union (progressed Sun conjunct Mercury sextile Moon; transiting Jupiter trine Mercury).

In 1963 the western half of the island of New Guinea (Irian) was ceded to Indonesia (progressed ASC conjunct Neptune sextile Mars). Dutch Guiana received its independence in November 1975 as the new nation of Surinam. The Netherlands still have the islands of Aruba, Bonaire, Curacao and Saba in the Caribbean. In April 1960, Queen Juliana abdicated in favor of her daughter, Beatrix (progressed MC conjunct Venus; progressed ASC trine Venus).

In 1986, a giant barrier against the North Sea on the Scheldt estuary was completed, thus curbing future inundations in this part of the country (progressed Sun square Moon; progressed MC sextile Saturn; progressed ASC inconjunct Moon). Severe flooding in 1995 along the Rhine and Maas rivers required evacuation of 250,000 in the provinces of Limburg and Gelderland (progressed MC sextile Uranus; progressed ASC trine Pluto). In 2000 the Netherlands legalized mercy killing and assisted suicide as well as marriage for same-sex couples who could also adopt children.

# Amsterdam

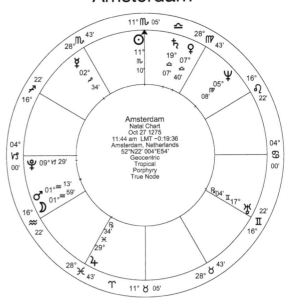

**October 27, 1275, 11:44 a.m. LMT**
**Source: Gemeentelijke Archiefdienst**

Amsterdam is the capital and largest city of the Netherlands. It was founded in 1270 when a dam was constructed on the Amstel river, hence its name. Built on piles, walls were constructed in 1482 and moats built in 1612. Most of the city's grand buildings were built during the Golden Age of the late 17th century and a series of grand canals, for which this city is so famous, were erected in the mid-19th century. The French occupied Amsterdam in 1795 and the Germans during World War II. The liberal philosophy and tolerance has made this city a haven for refugees over the years, be they Hugenots from France, Jews from Iberia or hippies trying to keep a lifestyle that faded a generation ago.

Amsterdam has a somewhat schizophrenic personality, for right in front of the City Hall lies the red-light district with women sitting in windows displaying their wares. Free-thinking but conservative, Amsterdam has for many become a place for hedonists to relish all that life has to offer, Marijuana is readily available but hard drugs are more difficult to obtain. The gay and lesbian community is extensive and accepted into the mainstream.

The most popular sights include the Royal Palace on Dam Square with the Nieuwe Kerk next door. The Sexmuseum is up the street towards the huge train station while at the other end of town is the Rijksmuseum which has Rembrandt's famous "Night Watch" and the Van Gogh museum. And don't forget the Anne Frank House on one of those picturesque canals that wind their was through the central heart of Amsterdam.

# The Hague
## (Den Haag—s'Gravenhage)

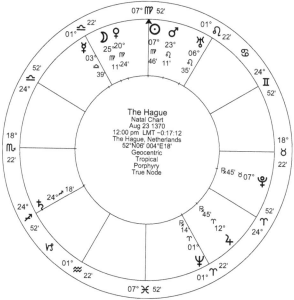

**August 23, 1370, noon LMT**
**Source: Algemeen Rijksarchief**

# Rotterdam

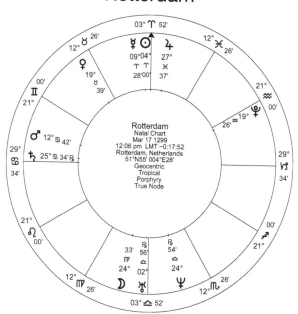

**March 17, 1299, noon LAT, 12:06 p.m. LMT**
**Source: Gemeente Rotterdam**

The Hague is Netherland's third-largest city and the seat of government. Located 35 miles southwest of Amsterdam, its western suburb, Scheveningen, fronts the North Sea. Founded in 1250 when a castle was erected, it became the Binnenhof, a royal palace. Since 1815, the Hague has been the seat for the Kings of the Netherlands. Its main attraction is the International Court of Justice and the International Peace Palace. Nearby is Huis ten Bosch, the summer residence of the monarch. Its museum, the Mauritshuts, is well worth the time as is the historical museum. Three royal palaces lie within its borders: Noordeinde, Kneuterdijk and Lange Voorhout.

The second-largest city in the Netherlands is also the world's busiest port, located as it is on the deltas of the Rhine and Maas Rivers. Founded as a fishing village at the end of the 13th century, it was burned in 1563 and then occupied by the Spanish a decade later. Hugenots arrived after 1685 when King Louis XIV of France revoked the Edict of Nantes. The French came in 1795 but didn't stay long. Rotterdam gained access to the North Sea in 1872 and its mass of docks and shipyards is today known as Europoort. Heavily bombed by the Germans in May 1940, Rotterdam has more miles of docks and warehouses than any port in Europe and it's also a major oil refining center.

The entire center of town was destroyed by the Nazis with the exception of the Stadhuis (Town Hall), the last remaining old building in a sea of modern-looking steel and glass buildings. The Maritime museum is popular where you can watch the workings of the port as is the Boymans museum across from the Architecture Institute.

# Utrecht

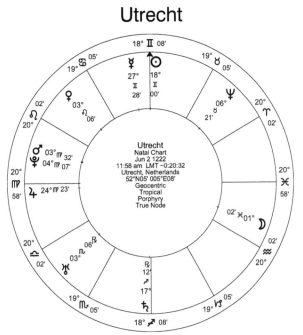

**June 2, 1222, 11:58 a.m. LAT**
**Source: Staatsarchiv**

The fourth-largest city in the Netherlands is located 25 miles east of Amsterdam. During Roman times, it was called Trajectum ad Rhenum, and during the Middle Ages it became famous for its cloth and textiles. Its University was founded in 1636 and this city houses the National Mint. Its main attraction is St. Martin's Cathedral whose spire (370 feet) is the tallest in the country. The Railway museum and the Museum of Christianity, which has the largest collection of medieval art in the country, are worth visiting.

# Norway
## Kongeriket Norge

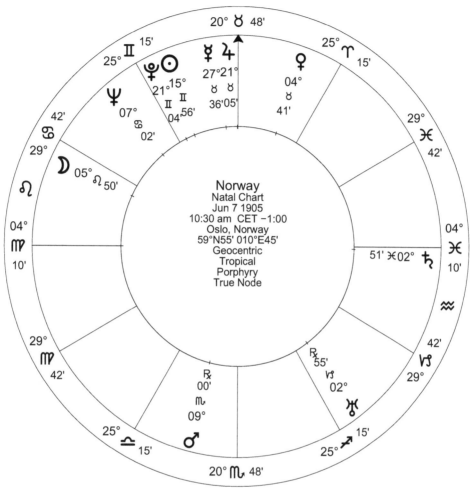

Norway
Natal Chart
Jun 7 1905
10:30 am CET −1:00
Oslo, Norway
59°N55' 010°E45'
Geocentric
Tropical
Porphyry
True Node

**June 7, 1905, 10:30 a.m. MET, Oslo**
**Source: *The Times* of London says 10:30 a.m.**

Norway occupies the western half of the Scandinavian peninsula. Its coastline is 13,626 miles long along the North Sea and Arctic Ocean and the shore is highly-indented by numerous fjords and over 150,000 islands. Over 70 percent of Norway is mountainous with glaciers, moors and plateaus. One-third of the country lies above the Arctic Circle. Norway is 1,100 miles long with the Langfjellene Mountains running north and south and the Dovre Mountains running east and west. Norway also has dominion over Svalbard and Spitzbergen, 360 miles north in the ocean and only 700 miles from the North Pole. The highest point is Galdhopiggen (elevation 8,147 feet).

Population: 4,530,440; 97% Norwegian

Religion: 88% Lutheran

Area: 125,183 square miles (the size of Poland or New Mexico); 3% arable, 75% urban

Economy: Main exports are petroleum, natural gas, paper and fish. Shipbuilding is a major industry and Norway has the world's fourth-largest fleet. Main resources are copper, nickel and aluminum.

By the 9th century, Norway was home to the Vikings, or Norsemen, whose range of influence extended to Britain, Ireland, France, Spain and Sicily. By the middle of the 11th century, the Viking Age was coming to a close. Norway was united under one crown by Harald Haarfagre in 872 A.D. Vikings also settled Greenland, Iceland and the eastern coast of North America.

In 1381, Norway became part of Denmark and it was united with Sweden in June 1397 at the Union of Kalmar. In January 1814, Norway was given to Sweden as punishment to the Danes who had sided with Napoleon. Norway's Constitution was also framed that year.

115

On June 7, 1905, Norway separated from Sweden and declared its independence. Prince Carl of Denmark became its first monarch, Haakon VII. In August 1914 when World War I broke out, Norway decided to remain neutral (progressed Sun sesquare Mars; progressed ASC sextile Mars; transiting Jupiter trine Sun/Pluto; Uranus square Mars; Neptune sextile Mercury). In 1936, old age pensions and unemployment compensation insurance were instituted (progressed MC conjunct Pluto semisquare Moon).

On April 9, 1940, Norway was invaded by Nazi Germany, which coveted its natural resources (progressed MC sesquare Mars; progressed ASC trine Mercury; transiting Mars square ASC; Saturn sextile Saturn trine Uranus; Uranus conjunct MC). A puppet government was set up under Quisling, a name which has since become synonymous with treason. The Germans were using Norwegian resources to build their atomic bomb but were fortunately thwarted before the "heavy water" could reach the Nazis who could have bombed most of Europe. Allied liberation came in May 1945 (transiting Saturn conjunct Neptune; Pluto square Mars).

Oil was discovered in the North Sea in 1968 (progressed Sun sextile Sun; progressed MC sextile Jupiter). Preferring to remain neutral from the rest of Europe, Norway voted against joining the European Union in November 1994 (progressed MC sextile Sun; progressed ASC sesquare Sun; transiting Jupiter opposition Mercury/Jupiter; Neptune trine Jupiter/MC; Pluto opposition Mercury).

# Bergen

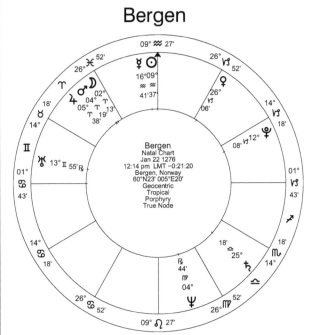

**January 22, 1276, 12:14 p.m. LMT**
**Source: Offentlige Bibliotek**

Bergen is the second-largest city in Norway and was founded by King Olaf III in 1070 and remained Norway's capital until 1300. Soon after, Bergen became a major Hanseatic League port for the next two centuries. Located on a fjord, it was largely isolated from the rest of the country until the Germans built a highway during World War II. Bergen is the center of the petroleum industry and a major shipbuilding center. Built largely of wood, in its infancy it endured numerous fires: those of 1702, 1855 and 1916 were quite devastating. Bergen is also the hometown of Edvard Grieg.

## Hammerfest

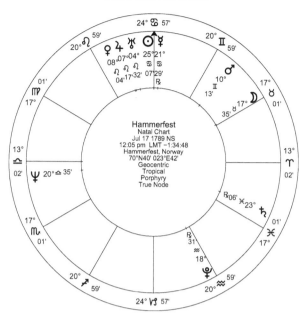

**July 17, 1789, 12:05 p.m. LMT**
**Source: City Hall**

## Oslo

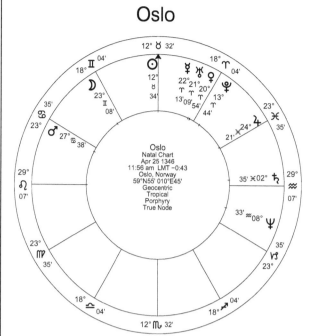

**April 25, 1346, 11:56 a.m. LMT**
**Sources: Riksarkivet**

Hammerfest is located 285 miles north of the Arctic Circle and 60 miles south of North Cape at the top of Norway. It's the northernmost town in Europe and from mid-May until the end of July, it's bathed in perpetual sunlight as this is truly the land of the "midnight sun." Conversely, from mid-November until the end of January, the sun never rises above the horizon. Thus, when one erects a horoscope for those times of year, the house cusps will be completely skewed and often read in reverse. The Germans wrecked the place in World War II. The main industries are fishing, fur trading and processing of cod liver oil.

## Trondheim

Norway's third-largest city was founded as Nidaros by the Viking king, Olav Tryggvason in 997. It was Norway's first capital and coronation site for Norway's monarchs until 1906. Trondheim has Norway's largest wooden building, the Stiftsgarden, an edifice of 13,000 square feet and now a royal residence. The city is dominated by the Nidaros Domen, a cathedral which is Scandinavia's largest medieval structure. It stands over the grave of St. Olav who brought Christianity to Scandinavia.

Oslo is the capital and largest city of Norway and lies at the northern end of the Oslofjord at the junction of the Aker River. Founded by King Hardrade III in 1048, it became capital of Norway in 1300. A massive fire in 1624 created the necessity to build a new city which was called Christiania after King Christian IV of Denmark. Its university was founded in 1811 and in 1814 after Sweden took over from Denmark, Oslo again became capital of Norway. Oslo reverted to its original name in 1925.

Oslo is a city of spectacular beauty, taking true advantage of its natural surroundings and wilderness areas. Popular sights include the Storting (Parliament), the Royal Palace and the old City Hall. On the Bygdoy peninsula is the Norsk Folkemuseum and the Kon-Tiki museum and the Viking ship museum, three musts for any seafarer or adventurer. The most famous art works in Oslo, however, are the 212 statues by Vigeland in Frogner Park.

# Poland
## Rceczpospolita Polska

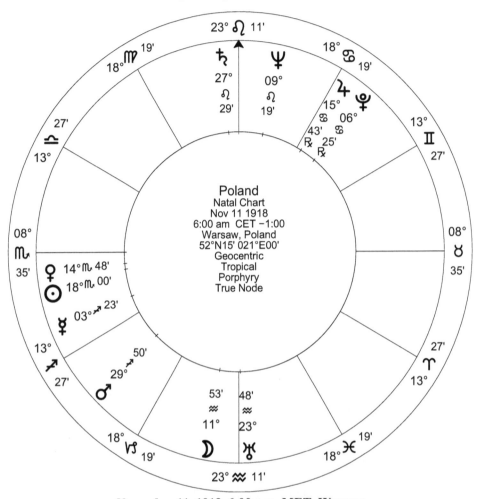

Poland
Natal Chart
Nov 11 1918
6:00 am CET −1:00
Warsaw, Poland
52°N15' 021°E00'
Geocentric
Tropical
Porphyry
True Node

**November 11, 1918, 6:00 a.m. MET, Warsaw**
**Source:** *Chronicles of the 20th Century* states that Polish independence would commence when the Germans signed the Armistice which was at 5:00 a.m. It became effective at 11:00 a.m., November 11, 1918. *Bitter Glory* by Watt gives the time of 8:00 a.m., while other astrology books give the date of November 14, 1918, when Pilsudski became its first leader.

Poland lies in north-central Europe between Germany and Belarus on a vast plain containing the provinces of Pomerania, Silesia and Galicia. In the south are the Tatra Mountains, Sudetes Mountains and the Carpathian Alps. Poland's coastline along the Baltic Sea is 305 miles long, the main rivers are the Vistula, Oder and Neisse. The highest point is Rysy (elevation 8,245 feet) on the Slovakian border.

Population: 38,633,912; 98% Polish

Religion: 35% Catholic

Area: 120,726 square miles (the size of Norway or New Mexico); 65% urban, 47% arable

Economy: Poland is Europe's largest coal exporter and the world's second-largest producer of rye and potatoes. Other exports are copper, sulphur, textiles, iron and steel, cement, chemicals and ships. Main resources lead and zinc.

During Roman times, this region was known as Sarmatia. In 965 A.D., Mieszko I, founder of the Piast Dynasty, accepted Christianity. He ruled an area from the Oder to the Vistula which included Bohemia, Moravia and Saxony. In 1240, Mongols from central Asia invaded the region.

The reign of Casimir the Great (1333-70) ushered in the Golden Age for Poland; in 1386, Poland and the Grand Duchy of Lithuania were united by the marriage of Princess Jadwiga of Poland to Prince Jagiello of Lithuania. Poland now extended from the Baltic to the Black Sea. In 1410, the infamous Teutonic Knights were defeated at the battle of

Grunwald (Tanenbaum) thus opening up the region to outside trade. Poland received its first Parliament, the Sejm, in 1454. The reign of Sigismund I (1506-48) brought Italian culture to his court at Krakow.

In 1648 at the end of the disastrous Thirty Years War, Poland went to war against Russia and 19 years later it lost the Ukraine to the Russians. In 1683, the Ottomans were turned back at the gates of Vienna with the support of troops led by King Jan Sobieski of Poland. But when Sobieski died in 1696, Russia and Prussia imposed their rulers on Poland, thus weakening the strength of the monarchy. In 1733, the War of the Polish Succession took place and 30 years later, Stanislaus Poniatowski became the last King of Poland.

Russia and Prussia then proceeded to divide Poland between themselves. The first partition of 1772 allowed Russia to take Byelorussia while Prussia grabbed Pomerania and Austria took Galicia. In January 1793, the second partition reduced Poland by another 50 percent as Russia took what was left of the Ukraine and the rest of Byelorussia, and Prussia absorbed Silesia. In October 1795, the third and final partition of Poland gave the remainder of the country east of Warsaw to the Russians, Austria took what was left in the southwest and Prussia got what was left. Poland was thus wiped off the map of Europe. Poland went from a nation of 280,000 square miles which extended from the Dnieper in the east to the Dvina in the north and the Oder in the west to nothing.

In July 1807, Napoleon created the Duchy of Warsaw, and the Treaty of Vienna in June 1815 created the Kingdom of Poland but it was literally under Russian domination. In November 1830, an uprising in Warsaw was crushed by Russian troops and Poles began to emigrate. In 1846, a revolt against the Austrians erupted in Krakow and two years later, riots broke out in Poznan against the Prussians. Draft riots in 1863 against conscription into the Russian army resulted in more military control and economic strictures. Workers in Lodz rose up against the Russians in 1905 during the first Russian Revolution.

When World War I broke out in August 1914, Poland was invaded by Germany and Austria; the Russians retreated east, burning everything in sight, so typical of their "scorched earth" policy familiar to Napoleon. Germans dismantled factories and shipped materials back to the Vaterland and relocated thousands of workers. In November 1916, the Emperors of Germany and Austria agreed in theory to establish a separate Polish state, but four months later the Russians declared their intent as well. Once the Germans and Austrians had gone by October 1917, Poland was administered by a regency council on behalf of the Germans. With the war winding down, a Polish Republic was declared prematurely on November 3, 1918.

With the signing of the Armistice which ended World War I (aka the Great War) at 5:00 a.m. on November 11, 1918, Poland was freed from all outside control. The Armistice became effective at 11:00 a.m. that day, but in the agreement, it was when the document was *signed* that Poland became a new nation. Three days later, Pilsudski became Chief of State. Poland was in ruins with over 12 percent of its villages destroyed, typhus was rampant and unemployment was endemic.

In July 1920, Poland went to war against Russia over the Ukraine (progressed MC opposition Uranus; progressed ASC trine Neptune; transiting Jupiter conjunct MC; Saturn sextile ASC). In March 1921, the border with Russia was settled (progressed Sun sesquare Pluto). Pilsudski became dictator of Poland in November 1926 (progressed MC semisquare Jupiter; progressed ASC conjunct Venus semisquare Mars; transiting Jupiter square Sun; Saturn square Saturn; Pluto conjunct Jupiter). Pilsudski died in May 1935 and the military took over the government (transiting Mars square Pluto; Jupiter square Sun; Saturn trine ASC).

Hitler had for a long time hated the Slavic people, especially the Poles. He vowed to wipe them off the face of the earth when Nazi troops invaded Poland September 1, 1939, beginning World War II (progressed Sun trine Neptune; progressed MC sextile Venus; progressed ASC sesquare Pluto). The Poles surrendered 27 days later, 10 days after the Russians invaded. The Germans took 700,000 prisoners and the Russians 190,000. The Soviets annexed eastern Poland and deported more than 1 million to Siberia. Jews inside the Warsaw Ghetto rose up against their Nazi overlords in January 1943. The ghetto contained 1,700 buildings and housed more than 500,000 Jews but had only two exits. Typhus and tuberculosis were rampant. When the ghetto surrendered in May 1943, only 200 survivors remained (progressed Sun sextile Moon; progressed MC sextile Sun; progressed ASC square Saturn/Uranus; transiting Neptune square Mars).

In July 1944, the Soviets formed a puppet government in Lublin while in Warsaw the Russians waited until the Nazis wiped out the Polish army before the Reds took over the city. In April 1945, Poland was liberated from the Nazis by the Soviets (progressed Sun inconjunct Jupiter; transiting Jupiter sextile Sun; Saturn conjunct Pluto; Pluto square Sun). Civilian casualties numbered 530,000 with 655,000 soldiers dead. More than 6 million Poles were killed, including 3 million Jews. This was 17 percent of Poland's pre-war population. Poland's borders were shifted west thus causing Poland to lose 70,000 square miles to the Russians along with 11 million people. Poland gained 39,000 square miles from Germany along with 8.5 million people. Refugees were on the move from one end of Poland to the other. Warsaw, the capital, was 87 percent in ruins. Poland's population went from 36 million in 1939 to only 24 million in 1945.

Communists won elections throughout Poland in early 1947 and on January 19, 1947 a People's Republic was proclaimed (progressed ASC square Saturn; transiting Jupiter square Uranus and MC; Pluto opposition Moon). Strikes across Poland in June 1956 forced Gomulka to abandon collective farming as well as grant more religious freedom as long as the Church would stay out of politics (progressed MC square Mars; progressed ASC conjunct Mercury; transiting Jupiter opposition Uranus conjunct Saturn; Saturn square Saturn). Strikes broke out in 1970 over the price of food (progressed MC square Jupiter).

A Polish Cardinal named Karol Wojtyla was named Supreme Pontiff of the Roman Catholic Church by the College of Cardinals in the Vatican in October 1978, the first non-Italian Pope in centuries (progressed Sun sextile Sun; progressed MC trine Uranus). Two years later, in August 1980, a labor union called Solidarity was founded at the Gdansk shipyard by Lech Walesa (transiting Jupiter sextile Venus and Jupiter). Martial law was declared in December 1981 and Walesa was arrested (progressed MC sextile Saturn; transiting Uranus square Jupiter; Neptune sextile Uranus). Martial law was lifted a year later (progressed ASC sextile Uranus sesquare Neptune).

In April 1989, the government promised political and economic reforms along with free elections. With the fall of the Berlin Wall in November 1989, those were no longer empty promises. In December 1990, Lech Walesa became the leader of Poland (progressed MC trine Pluto; progressed ASC conjunct Mars semisquare Venus; transiting Uranus sextile ASC; Pluto conjunct Sun). Poland became a member of NATO in March 1999. Poland became a member of the European Union in May 2004 (progressed Sun inconjunct Jupiter semisquare Mars; progressed MC sesquare Pluto; progressed ASC sextile Venus opposition Jupiter).

# Gdansk (Danzig)

Poland's sixth-largest city and largest port lies on the Gulf of Gdansk on the Motlawa River. From 1343, it was a Hanseatic port largely German in appearance. From 1793 until 1918 when Poland regained its independence, Gdansk was ruled by Prussia and was capital of East Prussia. From 1919 to 1939 when Hitler invaded Poland, Gdansk was a free city at the top end of the Polish corridor which Hitler vowed to obliterate.

It was here in the Lenin shipyard that the Solidarity movement began in the summer of 1980. Its leader, Lech Walesa, eventually became leader of Poland a decade later. Most of the medieval town still survives even though much of the city was in ruins after the Nazis departed. The 14th-century Church of Our Lady can seat more than 25,000 parishioners and is the largest brick church in the world and the largest cathedral in Poland. Its 500-year-old clock features the signs of the zodiac and traces phases of the Sun and Moon.

# Krakow (Cracow)

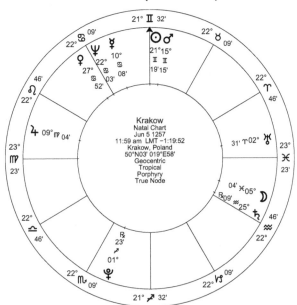

**June 5, 1257, 11:59 a.m. LMT**
**Source: Biblioteka Jagiellonska**

Poland's third-largest city is located on the Vistula river 155 miles southwest of Warsaw. Founded by Krak, it was the capital of Poland from 1320 until 1590. Its university was founded in 1364 and is the second-oldest in Europe. Occupied by the Germans during World War II, it was left untouched by bombing raids so much of its medieval and baroque structures survive intact.

Krakow's main attractions are the Kazimierz, the

center of Jewish life after 1494; by the time Hitler's troops arrived in 1939, over 25 percent of the city was Jewish, but most of them were deported to the death camps. Krakow also has Europe's largest medieval marketplace. Walking along through St. Florian's Gate to Wawel Hill one takes the procession route for all Polish kings to the Katedra Wawelska, a mixture of Gothic, Renaissance and Baroque styles. Nearby Wawel Castle was constructed in the 10th century but added onto in the 16th century. Some 35 miles east of Krakow lies Auschwitz, the infamous concentration camp, where more than 1.5 million people died under Nazi extermination orders. Krakow's Stare Miasto (Old Town) still has more than 300 houses, five dozen churches and palaces with millions of pieces of precious art, all of which survived the Nazi occupation.

## Poznan (Posen)

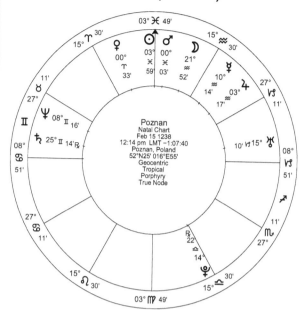

**February 15, 1238, 12:14 p.m. LMT**
**Source: Biblioteka Universtycka**

Poland's fifth-largest city is situated on the Warta River 165 miles west of Warsaw. Founded in the 10th century equidistant between Gdansk and Prague, it became a market and crafts center during the Middle Ages as it was also equidistant from Berlin to Warsaw. Poznan is literally the birth place of Poland where the Polanie tribe made their first settlement more than 1,000 years ago. Its main tourist attractions are its Old Town and famed Town Hall built during the Renaissance. Its Cathedral was built in the 9th century and rebuilt after the last war.

## Lodz

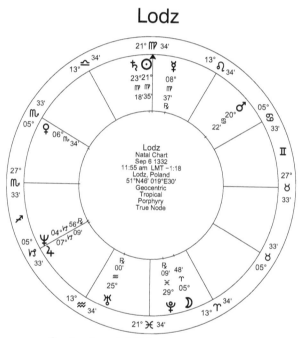

**September 6, 1332, 11:55 a.m. LMT**
**Source: Biblioteka Universytecka**

Poland's second-largest city is situated 75 miles southwest of Warsaw. After 1815 it became a spinning and weaving center where textiles were dyed before clothing was manufactured.

# Szczecin (Stettin)

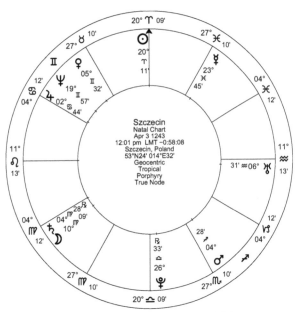

**April 3, 1243, 12:01 p.m. LMT**
**Source: Archiwum Panstwowe**

Poland's seventh-largest city lies 35 miles from the Baltic Sea on the Oder river in Pomerania. It rivals Gdansk as the main port of Poland. During the Middle Ages it was a Hanseatic town and from 1720 until 1945, it was under Prussian domination. By the end of World War II, over 65 percent of the city was in ruins.

# Warsaw (Warszawa)

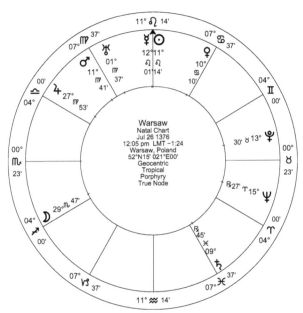

**July 26, 1376, 12:05 p.m.**
**Source: Polska Akademia Nauk**

The capital and largest city in Poland is situated on the Vistula River. Capital only from 1596 until the entire country was absorbed by the Russians, Prussians and Austrians in 1795. A massive fire burned most of the Old Town in 1656 and revolts in 1830 and 1863 caused extensive damage. But it was nothing compared to the devastation inflicted by the Nazis during World War II. Before the Germans arrived in 1939. Warsaw had 1.3 million people of which 35 percent were Jewish. When the guns were silenced in 1945, nearly 90 percent of the city had been leveled and most of its population dead or deported. Its population was only 160,000, only 12 percent of its pre-war total. The most horrific event during that war surrounded the Jewish Ghetto. Sealed off by the Nazis in November 1940, before the uprising more than 500,000 more were crammed inside this small area. Over time many of them died of starvation before the extermination squad arrived in July 1942. More than 300,000 Jews were deported to Treblinka. The ghetto uprising began in April 1943 and lasted for three weeks. Only one synagogue survived and only 200 survivors walked away from the horror alive.

Despite the massive devastation of World War II, much of the Stare Miasto (Old Town) has been restored to its former glory. The best example of its former eminence is Wilanow, the royal palace often compared to Versailles. Towering over the city is the Palace of Culture built in the Stalinist wedding-cake style from whose observation deck one may obtain an excellent view of the present city. Inside the Old

Town is the Royal Palace, built in the 14th century and blown up by the Nazis. The Old Town Square is now the central marketplace and is closed to automobiles. The Cathedral of St. John is the coronation sight for many Polish kings. Lazienski Park and the gardens around the Royal Palace are pleasant spots for relaxing. Don't miss the National Museum where old drawings of Warsaw enabled architects to reconstruct the city after the Nazis departed.

# Wroclaw (Breslau)

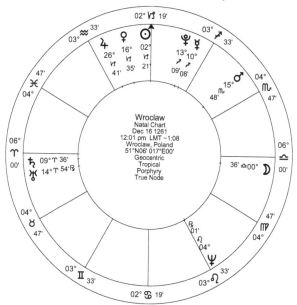

**December 16, 1261, 12:01 p.m. LMT**
**Source: Biblioteka Narodowa**

Poland's fourth-largest city is situated on the Oder River 190 miles southwest of Warsaw. Founded in the 10th century as a trading center, it was under Austrian rule from 1526 until 1741, when the Prussians took over until the end of World War II in 1945 when Poland's borders were shifted westward. Beginning in the 17th century, Wroclaw became a textile center with more than 100 bridges spanning its numerous canals. Wroclaw is one of the largest manufacturing centers in eastern Europe.

# Portugal
## Republica Portuguesa

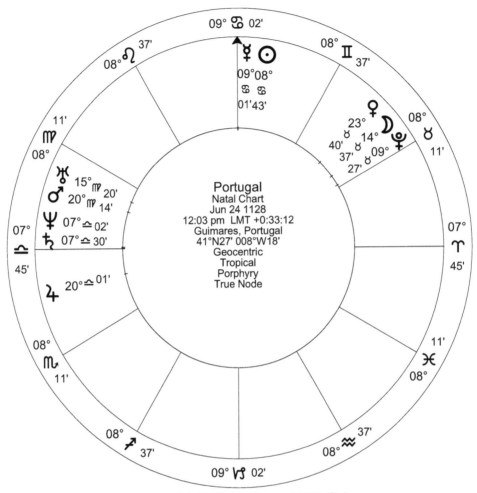

**Chart 1, June 24, 1128, 12:03 p.m. LMT, Guimares**
Source: Astrologers Helena Alvear and Luis Ribeiro; noontime presumed; Pinto de Moreira
prefers the date of October 5, 1143.

Portugal occupies the western part of the Iberian peninsula. Its coastline along the Atlantic Ocean is 1,114 miles long. The country is divided by the Rio Tejo (Tagus): Beira and Minho occupy the north while the south has the Alentejo and Algarve. Other main rivers are the Douro and Minho. The highest point is Serra de Estrela (elevation 6,532 feet). Portugal also has dominion over the Azores, a group of nine islands 740 miles west of Lisbon, as well as the Madeiras, two islands 350 miles southwest of the capital city.

Population: 10,066,253; 99% Portuguese

Religion: 97% Catholic

Area: 35,672 square miles (the size of Hungary or Indiana); 63% urban, 34% arable

Economy: Main exports are cork (50% of the world's total), sardines, wine, olive oil and textiles.

During the 3rd century B.C., Greeks began colonizing the region along the Tagus already inhabited by Iberians and Celts. Romans conquered the region in 138 B.C. and called it Lusitania. Swabian tribes invaded in 410 A.D. and in 585 A.D. the Visigoths ousted the Suevi. Moslem armies from North Africa took over in 711 A.D., the same year they conquered southern Spain. By 1097, the Moors had been driven south of the Duoro river and Portugal was given to Henry of Burgundy by King Alfonso VI of Leon and Castile.

On June 24, 1128 (chart 1), Alfonso Henriques declared war on his mother, Teresa, widow of Henry of Burgundy who had proclaimed herself Queen of Portugal. After getting rid of his mother, he then proceeded to act as monarch. By July 1139, Henriques had also driven the Moors out of Portugal (pro-

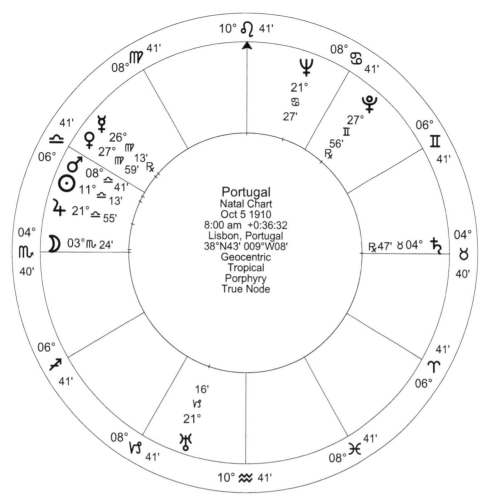

**Chart 2, Portugal, October 5, 1910, 8:00 a.m. LMT, Lisbon**
**Source:** *The Times* **of London. Astrologer Pinto de Moreira prefers the time of 9:50 a.m.**
**when the flag was raised.**

gressed MC sextile Mars square Jupiter). The Treaty of Zamora was signed with Spain in October 1143 which recognized the independence of Portugal (MC sextile Venus; ASC conjunct Jupiter). Lisbon was recaptured in 1147.

Portugal's first Parliament opened in 1211 at Coimbra (progressed MC sesquare Moon; progressed Ascendant inconjunct Mercury and Pluto). Burgundian rule ended in 1385 and the Avis dynasty began under Joao I. His son, Henry the Navigator, began to explore the west coast of Africa soon afterwards (progressed MC sextile Venus semisquare Pluto; progressed ASC sextile Moon). In 1488, Bartolomeo Dias rounded the Cape of Good Hope on his way to India; 10 years later, Vasco da Gama actually reached India.

In 1494, the Treaty of Tordesillas, arranged by the Pope, gave Spain all lands more than 370 leagues west of the Azores while Portugal had dominion over all lands east of that line. Thus did Portugal gain Brasil and Africa (progressed MC conjunct Mercury sextile Pluto; progressed ASC sesquare Venus

square Sun conjunct Saturn). After the Avis dynasty ended in 1580, Portugal was forced into a dual monarchy with Spain. Over the next six decades, Portugal's fortunes began to wane with competition from the Dutch, English and French. Portugal regained its independence in 1640.

In 1701, Portugal sided with England and France in the War for the Spanish Succession (MC sesquare Mars). When the conflict ended in 1713, nothing had changed inside Portugal (progressed MC inconjunct Mars/Uranus). The greatest natural disaster ever to befall Portugal occurred November 1, 1755 when Lisbon was rocked by a massive earthquake that virtually leveled the city. More than 40,000 died, a tsunami occurred and the city was reduced to rubble (progressed MC trine Mars inconjunct Jupiter).

In 1792, Portugal and Spain declared war on France during the early days of the French Revolution (progressed ASC square Moon). Spain, however, invaded the Alentejo region of southern Portugal in 1801 (progressed ASC semisquare Saturn and Neptune). Napoleon then invaded Portugal and King

Pedro I fled the country and moved his court to Rio de Janeiro (progressed MC trine Mars inconjunct Jupiter). Wellington defeated the French the following year.

King Pedro I returned from Brasil in 1821 and framed a Constitution. One year later, in September 1822, he proclaimed the independence of Brasil near Sao Paulo (progressed MC sesquare Jupiter; progressed ASC sextile Sun). Dom Pedro I again returned to Portugal in 1831 to fight against his brother who had abolished the Constitution (progressed ASC trine Moon conjunct Uranus). Brasil became a Republic in November 1889 ending their brief monarchy (progressed MC square Moon/Pluto; progressed ASC semisquare Mars).

In 1908, King Carlos and his heir, Luis, were both assassinated (progressed ASC sextile Uranus). Two years later, in October 1910, a revolution began which resulted in King Manoel II being sent into exile as a republic was proclaimed, ending the monarchy (chart 2).

When World War I began in August 1914, Portugal sided with the Allies but saw little real action on the battlefield (progressed Midheaven square Venus and Pluto; transiting Saturn conjunct Pluto square Venus; Uranus trine Mars; Neptune sextile Venus). By 1928, Portugal's finances were in a total mess, so Antonio Salazar was hired to clean up the books (progressed Sun trine Pluto; progressed MC sextile Pluto). Four years later in 1932, Salazar took over the reins of government and proclaimed himself Dictator (progressed Sun conjunct Moon; progressed ASC sextile Uranus trine Neptune).

Portugal decided to remain neutral when World War II broke out in September 1939 (progressed ASC sextile Mercury; transiting Uranus sextile Neptune; Pluto square Moon).

Portugal lost its possessions in India in 1961, and Salazar was ousted from power in September 1968 (progressed Sun sextile Mars; progressed MC conjunct Mars; transiting Pluto trine Neptune sextile Uranus). A military coup in April 1974 ousted Caetano and Guinea-Bissau was granted independence. Portugal gave Mozambique and Angola their walking papers in 1975 (progressed MC square Sun/Jupiter). Portugal joined the European Union in January 1986 (progressed Sun square Venus opposition Pluto; progressed MC trine Pluto; progressed ASC trine Saturn). Portugal lost Macao to China in December 1999 (progressed Sun square Sun; progressed MC semisquare Mercury; transiting Saturn square MC; Neptune square Moon; Pluto sextile Sun trine MC).

# Lisbon (Lisboa)

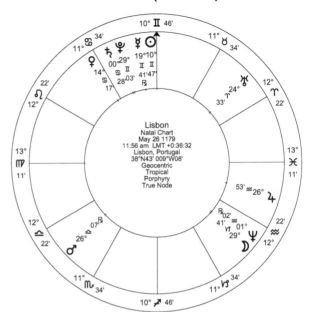

**May 26, 1179, 11:56 a.m. LMT**
**Source: Camara Municipal**

Capital and largest city of Portugal is situated on the Tagus river ten miles from the Atlantic Ocean. Founded by the Phoenicians in the 12th century BC, it was conquered by the Greeks, Carthaginians, Romans and Visigoths. It takes its name from Olispo of Lusitania, the ancient name for Portugal. In 714, Lisbon was conquered by the Moors and Alfonso Henriques drove them out in 1147. Capital of Portugal since 1255, it became a very wealthy port during the 11th and 15th centuries. The massive earthquake of November 1755 caused a tsunami and when the damage was viewed, most of Lisbon lay in ruins and more than 40,000 had perished. The Marquis de Pombal was hired to completely rebuild the central city known as the Baixa. A suspension bridge across the Tagus was completed in 1966 and a fire in 1988 destroyed much of the city.

Chief sites are the Alfama, the old Moorish settlement with its Citadel, Praca Dom Pedro IV, the Se (a 12th century church built atop a mosque), Monastery of Jeronimos, the Castelo de Sao Jorge and the Tower of Belem. Nearby are the resort communities of Sintra, Cascais and Estoril.

# Oporto (Porto)

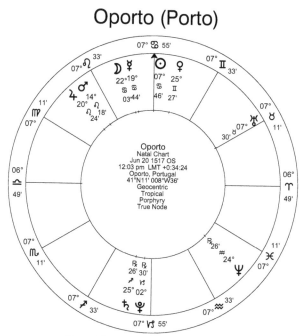

**June 20, 1517, 12:03 p.m. LMT**
**Source: Camara Municipal**

Portugal's second-largest city is situated on the Duoro river 270 miles north of Lisbon. In Roman times it was known as Portus Gale (Portucalia) from which Portugal takes its name. Oporto is world-famous for its port wine and achieved prominence after the 1730s. The main sites in Oporto are the Se, a 12th century cathedral and Sao Francisco church in the Gothic style.

# Romania
## Republica Romania

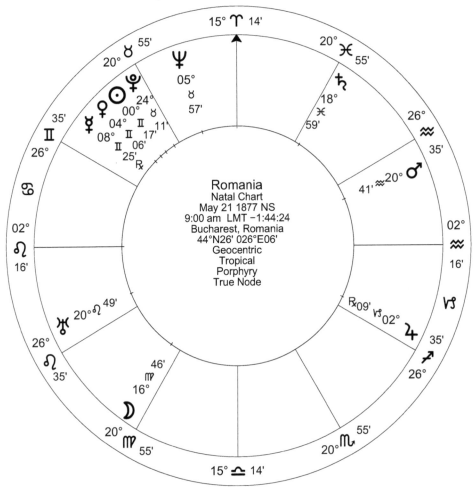

**Chart 1 May 21, 1877, 9:00 a.m. LMT, Bucharest**
**Source: Romanian Embassy for the date; time is speculative and rectified**

Situated in southeastern Europe on the Balkan peninsula, Romania has a 140-mile coastline along the Black Sea. The province of Moldavia is hilly while Wallachia is part of the Danube river plain. Bukovina in the north is heavily forested while the Banat in the southwest is a broad plain. The marshy area along the Black Sea is called the Dobruja. The Carpathian Mountains surround the Transylvanian plateau and the Transylvanian Alps arc towards the southwest. The highest point is Moldoveanu (elevation 8,381 feet) in the Alps.

Population: 22,364,022; 89% Romanian, 9% Hungarian

Religion: 70% Orthodox, 6% Catholic, 6% Protestant

Area: 91,699 square miles (the size of the United Kingdom or Oregon); 56% urban, 46% arable

Economy: The main export is petroleum (#2 in Europe), oil field equipment, farm machinery, timber and textiles. Main resources are coal, iron ore, lead, zinc, gold and bauxite.

Roman armies conquered this region in 106 A.D.; they called it Dacia. Roman occupation ended in 275 A.D. just as the barbarians began their numerous invasions. Christianity was introduced from Bulgaria in the 7th century. Transylvania was taken by the Magyars in the 10th century, but in 1330 the Wallachians defeated the Magyars. The Ottomans were defeated in 1396 but the fight against Turkish occupation lasted until 1476 when Vlad Tepes (aka Vlad Dracul aka Dracula) was killed in battle. Wallachia was then ceded to the Ottomans and Moldavia surrendered to the Turks in 1504. Transylvania also fell by 1526, the year the Turks advanced on Vienna.

In 1601, Wallachia, Moldavia and Transylvania

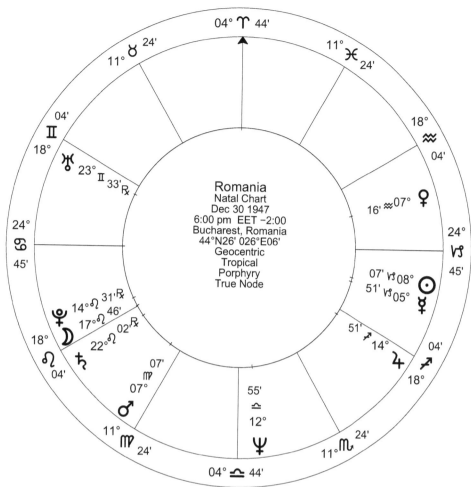

**Chart 2, December 30, 1947, 6:00 p.m. EET, Bucharest**
**Source:** *The New York Times* **says 6:00 p.m.**

were briefly united but Turkey regained supremacy in 1618. In 1829, Moldavia and Wallachia became autonomous Russian protectorates and in 1856 independent principalities. Moldavia voted for union with Wallachia on January 17, 1859 and on February 5, 1859, Wallachia agreed and the nation of Romania was born. According to the diary of its first King, Alexander Cuza, the time was 6:25 p.m. LMT in Bucharest.

Romania was proclaimed a kingdom in December 1861, but by February 1866, King Cuza was deposed. Independence from Turkey was finally proclaimed May 21, 1877 (chart 1) and was recognized by the Treaty of Berlin in July 1878 (progressed Sun inconjunct Jupiter; progressed MC inconjunct Moon; progressed ASC sextile Venus inconjunct Jupiter sesquare Saturn).

The first Balkan War broke out in October 1912 against the Turks (progressed MC sextile Saturn; transiting Saturn conjunct Venus; Uranus trine Sun). The second Balkan War erupted in June 1913 (progressed Sun sesquare Mars semisquare Uranus; pro-

gressed MC square Mars and Uranus; transiting Jupiter square MC; Saturn conjunct Mercury). When World War I engulfed Europe in August 1914, Romania decided to remain neutral as it had just fought two wars. Romania finally agreed to enter the war on the Allied side in August 1916 (progressed MC conjunct Pluto; progressed ASC square Sun; transiting Jupiter conjunct Neptune; Saturn sextile Pluto; Neptune conjunct ASC). When the Armistice was signed in November 1918, Romania gained Transylvania from Hungary along with the Banat, Bukovina and Bessarabia (transiting Mars inconjunct Sun; Jupiter square MC; Uranus square Pluto; Pluto semisquare Uranus sesquare Mars). More than 335,000 soldiers died in battle and 120,000 were placed on the casualty list.

In 1938, King Carol disbanded the fascist military group called the Iron Guard and then proclaimed himself dictator (progressed ASC square Moon). In June 1940, Romania was forced to cede Bukovina and Bessarabia to the Soviet Union and southern Dobruja to neighboring Bulgaria (progressed MC square Moon; progressed ASC opposition Saturn; transiting Uranus conjunct Pluto). Due to its animosity against the Russians, Romania entered World War 11^on the German side against the Soviets in June 1941 (progressed Sun semisquare Moon inconjunct Jupiter; progressed ASC sesquare Neptune; transiting Saturn conjunct Pluto; Pluto conjunct ASC). Romania again lost Transylvania to Hungary until September 1944 when the Soviet occupation began (progressed Sun sextile Venus sesquare Saturn; progressed MC trine Mars sextile Uranus semisquare Neptune; transiting Jupiter trine Neptune; Neptune square Jupiter; Pluto sextile Mercury). Romania had lost more than 350,000 in the war.

Communists won major elections in 1946 so it came as no surprise when King Michael was forced to abdicate on December 30, 1947 (chart 2) and a People's Republic was proclaimed (progressed Sun sextile Mercury; progressed ASC trine Pluto; transiting Jupiter trine MC; Pluto trine MC).

By 1962, Romania had begun to take a more independent stance and numerous reforms were made against the wishes of the hard-line Stalinists (progressed Sun inconjunct Uranus; progressed ASC inconjunct Mercury). In 1967, Nicolae Ceausescu took over (progressed Sun semisquare Jupiter; progressed MC sextile Uranus; progressed ASC inconjunct Sun semisquare Uranus). His reign lasted until late December 1989 when a revolt that began in Timisoara soon swept towards Bucharest. Ceausescu was toppled, thrown into prison and executed nine days later (progressed Sun trine Uranus opposition Saturn; progressed MC square Moon). Transiting Jupiter and Uranus were sitting on Mercury and squaring the MC and Pluto was squaring the Moon.

A new Constitution was framed in December 1991 (progressed Sun semisquare Sun; progressed ASC semisquare Neptune). Communists were swept from power and all state-owned companies were privatized in November 1996. King Michael returned to Romania in 2001 and had some of his former property returned (progressed Sun sextile Mercury; progressed ASC trine Mercury).

Romania is scheduled to become part of the European Union in January 2007 (progressed Ascendant trine Sun).

# Bucharest (Bucuresti)

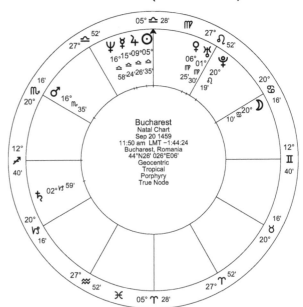

**September 20, l459, 11:50 a.m. LMT**
**Source: Mayor's Office**

The capital and largest city of Romania is known as the "Paris of the East" due to its spacious parks, numerous trees and broad boulevards, albeit a slightly shabbier version. Founded by Bucur in the 15th century and named for himself, the Turks first invaded in 1541. Capital of Wallachia since l659, it became the capital of Romania in 1859. Germans occupied the city in both World Wars and allied air raids ruined large parts of the city in 1944. A massive earthquake in 1978 caused extensive damage and the revolution in late 1989 saw massive street demonstrations as Ceausescu was ousted from office and executed.

The main sights in Bucharest are the Romanian Atheneum, one of the most grand concert halls in Europe; the Casa Republicii, the second-largest government building in the world after the Pentagon which has over 1000 rooms and the Voievodul Palace, a 13th century monument to such princes as Vlad Tepes, aka Dracula.

# Brasov (Kronstadt)

Romania's seventh-largest city and largest metropolis in Transylvania is situated 85 miles northwest of Bucharest against the backdrop of Mt. Timpa and Mt. Postavarni. Founded in 1211 by Teutonic Knights, it was a center for trade with the Orient. Only in 1918 was this region ceded to Romania as it was under Hungarian control for centuries. Nearby is the Bran Castle (also called Dracula's castle) and Sinaia, the summer home of Romanian monarchs.

## Cluj Napoca

Romania's fifth-largest city is located in Transylvania. Founded as Napoca by the Romans, it became a German settlement in the 13th century and capital of Transylvania in 1405. It became part of Romania in 1921.

The main sight is St. Michael's Cathedral, the largest Catholic church in the country. Cluj also has the second-largest university in Romania.

## Constanta

The second-largest city in Romania is located on the Black Sea some 125 miles east of Bucharest. Founded as Tomis by the Greeks in the 6th century BC, the present city was founded a thousand years later. Occupied by the Turks from 1413 until 1878, Constanta is the premier resort for the country. Inside the central city are remains of Roman walls and baths.

## Galati

Romania's sixth-largest city is situated on the Danube River 110 miles northeast of Bucharest. It's primarily an industrial city and a major oil refining and railroad transportation center.

## Iasi (Jassy)

The third-largest city in Romania is located in Moldavia and was its capital until 1862. Tatars attacked Iasi in 1513, as did the Turks in 1538. Russians besieged the city in 1686.

## Timisoara (Temesvar)

Romania's fourth-largest city lies in the southwest part of the country. Founded in the 13th century, it was occupied by the Turks from 1552 until 1716. After World War I, it was ceded by Hungary to Romania. It was here in December 1989 that the revolution began which toppled Ceausescu from his reign of terror.

# Russia
## Rossiyskaya Federatsiya

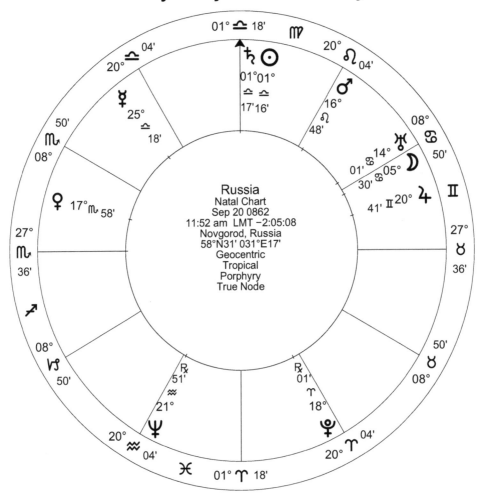

Russia
Natal Chart
Sep 20 0862
11:52 am LMT −2:05:08
Novgorod, Russia
58°N31' 031°E17'
Geocentric
Tropical
Porphyry
True Node

**Chart 1, September 20, 862 A.D., 11:52 a.m. LMT, Novgorod**
**Source: Lenin Library for the date; noontime presumed**

Russia is the largest country on earth, containing 11 percent of the world's land surface and spanning 11 time zones. Straddling two continents (Europe and Asia), the dividing lines are the Ural Mountains and the Caucasus Mountains. European Russia is a region of vast plains, wooded in the north and grassy further south. Here is the world's most fertile soil, called chernozem. East of the Urals lies Siberia, an area of frozen and marshy tundra near the Arctic which graduates to a forested region called the taiga and then to the steppes of Central Asia.

Russia has 21 semi-autonomous republics within its borders which run from the Gulf of Finland to the Black Sea and to the Pacific Ocean. Russia has the world's largest inland body of water, the Caspian Sea; its deepest freshwater lake, Baikal; and Europe's largest lake, Ladoga. The main rivers are the Volga, Don, Dvina, Dniester, Ob, Lena, Amur, Irtysh and Yenisei. Many volcanoes dot the region around the Kamchatka peninsula near Vladivostok in the Far East. Russia's coastline is 23,402 miles long and its highest point is Mt. Elbrus (elevation 18,481 feet) in the Caucasus region.

Population: 145,470,197; 81% Russian; 4% Belarussian; 4% Tatar; 3% Ukrainian (100 other nationalities)

Religion: 25% Orthodox; 60% atheist

Economy: Russia leads the world in production of coal, iron ore, petroleum, lead, manganese, platinum, barley, wheat, flax, potatoes and sugar beets. With the exception of tin and rubber, Russia is self-sufficient. It has 60 percent of the world's proven oil reserves, mines half of the world's iron ore and one-third of its coal. Russia also has 20 percent of the world's forests and large deposits of copper, zinc, gold, diamonds and uranium.

# Imperial Russia

On September 20, 862 A.D. (chart 1), Rurik founded the Russian state at Novgorod. He founded a dynasty that would last more than seven centuries. Rurik was a Varangian, a warrior tribe from Scandinavia. In 988, Prince Vladimir of Kiev accepted Christianity and gave birth to a state called Kievan Rus. By 1169, Kievan power began to decline as influence moved to the city of Vladimir (MC semisquare Jupiter). Mongols from Central Asia invaded in 1237 and killed half of the population (ASC sesquare Pluto); five years later, Alexander Nevsky defeated the Livonian Knights (MC sextile Mars; ASC inconjunct Moon). The Battle of Kulikovo weakened Tatar control in 1380 (MC trine Moon; ASC trine Venus square Pluto). Tamerlane conquered Moscow the following year. The Mongol empire of the Golden Horde fell in 1480 (ASC sextile Venus inconjunct Pluto) and increased the power of Muscovy.

In January 1547, Ivan the Terrible was crowned Czar of all the Russias (MC square Venus conjunct Mars semisquare Sun/Saturn) and during his reign, regions around the Volga, Kazan and Astrakhan became part of the emerging Russian empire. Ivan died in 1584 (MC inconjunct Neptune; ASC square Neptune). The Rurik dynasty ended in 1598, thus beginning what is known as the Time of Troubles (MC square Moon sesquare Neptune; ASC sextile Sun/Saturn). Over the next 15 years, drought, famine and epidemics were rampant. Sweden and Poland invaded Russia and Boris Gudonov was elected czar.

Michael Romanov was elected czar in March 1613 and was crowned in July (MC trine Jupiter and Neptune; ASC semisquare Mercury). The Ukraine was annexed into Russia in 1667 (MC inconjunct Uranus). Peter the Great in 1689 took the throne and threw his sister, Sophia, who was acting as regent, into a convent (MC semisquare Neptune). The boundary with China was finally established at the Amur River and Peter began to westernize Russia, by force when necessary. Peter laid the cornerstone for Saint Petersburg in May 1703 which was to be his capital and window to the sea (ASC semisquare Pluto). The 1709 Battle of Poltava routed the Swedes, who had been a thorn in Peter's side for years (ASC sextile Mars).

In November 1721, the Russian Empire was founded and Livonia and Estonia were annexed. This empire died with the end of Czardom in 1917 but was resurrected again when the USSR (Soviet Union) was established in 1922. Catherine the Great wrested the throne from her husband in July 1762 (MC square Jupiter). Russia received eastern Byelorussia from the first partition of Poland in 1772 (MC opposite Sun/Saturn). Pugachev began a peasant revolt the following year (ASC semisquare Jupiter) which threatened to overturn the monarchy. Russian ambition for territory crossed the Bering Sea when Alaska was settled in 1783. Russian lands now stretched from 20 degrees east of Greenwich eastward to 130 degrees west of Greenwich, a region which spanned 210 degrees of longitude. Russia annexed the Crimea in 1792 (MC sextile Jupiter) and in 1795 received Lithuania, Courland and the northwest part of the Ukraine in the third and final partition of Poland (MC sextile Neptune).

But Russian expansion continued. Georgia was annexed in 1801 (ASC sextile Jupiter) and Sweden ceded Finland to Russia in 1809 (ASC sextile Mercury). But Napoleon had designs to add the Russian Empire to his own. Napoleon entered Russian territory in the late summer of 1812, fought a battle at Borodino west of Moscow and then proceeded to lay siege to the capital of Moscow. Muscovites set fire to their city rather than let it fall to Napoleon, so when the French Emperor entered the city, it was in ruins and the storehouses of food and supplies were empty. Napoleon had to retreat back to France during the infamous Russian winter which killed a good percentage of his troops (ASC semisquare Uranus). Czar Alexander I was hailed as a hero by the Russians and was given a warm welcome in Paris as well. Alexander I died in December 1825 and the throne was up for grabs. This prompted the Decembrist revolt between those loyal to Alexander's brother, Constantine, and those loyal to his younger sibling, Nicholas. Nicholas II won (ASC sextile Moon). Azerbaijan was annexed in 1828 (MC inconjunct Mercury) and Armenia followed the next year.

Russia went to war against Turkey in April 1854 over the Crimea, but the largest country in the world was defeated two years later (MC conjunct Jupiter trine Neptune). With the ascension of Alexander II to the throne he set in motion a plan to free the serfs, a *fait accompli* by 1861. Four years later, in 1865, Russia began its conquest of central Asia (MC square Sun/Saturn; ASC conjunct Sun/Saturn). To balance the treasury, Russia sold Alaska to the United States of America in 1867 (ASC sesquare Mars; MC conjunct Moon). For all of his good works, Alexander II was assassinated by an anarchist in 1881 (MC square Pluto).

Russia began construction of the Trans-Siberian Railway which would run 5,780 miles from Moscow to Vladivostok (MC square Mercury; ASC sextile Mars opposite Pluto). The railroad would be completed by 1904, the same year that Russia went to war against Japan over the city of Port Arthur (ASC conjunct Mercury). Russia suffered a humiliating defeat at the Battle of Tsushima which led to the first Russian Revolution of January 1905. Father Gapon led a group of peasants to the Winter Palace in St. Petersburg, but the Czar was not there. Soldiers fired on the crowd and hundreds were killed. This was "Bloody Sunday," an event which forced Czar Nicholas II into granting Russia a Parliament, called the Duma which opened in late 1905. Russia was technically a Constitutional Monarchy, although somebody apparently forgot to remind the Czar as he still ruled with an iron hand.

The end for Czarist Russia began in August 1914 when Nicholas II went to war against Imperial Germany and Austria-Hungary. Ironically, the Kaiser of Germany, Wilhelm II, was his cousin. Russia entered the conflict on the side of the Allies but it suffered one defeat after another. Soldiers had little ammunition and after two very cold winters, began to mutiny against their officers. The Army began to retreat back to Russia (MC square Venus trine Pluto). It got so bad that Nicholas couldn't count on his generals. He was forced to abdicate his throne on March 15, 1917 at 3:00 p.m. in Pskov. Nicholas abdicated for not only himself but also for his hemophiliac son, the Tsarevitch Alexis. He left the monarchy to his brother, Michael, who carried on the dynasty. But Michael also gave up his right, and thus was the Russian monarchy finished and the Romanovs no longer in power after 300 years.

A Provisional Government had been formed in early March 1917 with Alexander Kerensky as its leader (MC semisquare Moon sextile Jupiter and Neptune). The government had a tenuous hold on power and revolts broke out in July. Meanwhile, the Royal Family had been placed under house arrest at the village of Tsarskoe Selo, but in August they were moved to the Siberian city of Tobolsk. Meanwhile, Nikolai Lenin had arrived back in Russia and made plans to usurp control of the country. The Bolshevik Revolution began at 2:00 a.m., November 7, 1917 (chart 2) and ended two days later.

## Bolshevik Russia

After analyzing the events of the October Revolution in which Lenin and his cronies seized power, the chart I use for Bolshevik Russia is for the time noted on Lenin's proclamation that the MRC (Military Revolutionary Committee) now controlled the government and that the Provisional Government had fallen. Some historians and astrologers might think

this document to be premature, but Kerensky had in fact left St. Petersburg. Power was in the hands of the Petrograd Soviet despite the fact that cabinet ministers were holed up in the Winter Palace. The first meeting of the Petrograd Soviet convened at 2:35 p.m. and the Second Congress of the Soviets opened at 10:40 p.m. On November 8, those cabinet ministers surrendered at 2:12 a.m. and at 8:40 p.m. Lenin took the podium and proclaimed, "we shall now proceed to construct the Socialist order." Early in the morning of November 9, the Land Decree and the Constitution of Power was read. But being an historian, I worked with all the aforementioned charts, and the 10:00 a.m. chart works best using both transits and progressions.

One should remember two things: Russia was using Local Mean Time in 1917 as Standard Time Zones were not put in use until the 1930s. Russia was also on Daylight Savings Time during the Revolution from July 1917 until January 1918. Russia was also using the Julian Calendar (OS), making the dates mentioned in Lenin's and Trotsky's diaries off by 13 days. Russia didn't start using the Gregorian calendar until February 1918. Thus all events occurring in those days in November 1917 (NS) used both DST and LMT. Subtract 2 hours and 1 minute to get the GMT to alleviate confusion.

The Bolshevik takeover of the government was a piece of cake compared to what followed. Lenin had promised to get Russia out of the war, but the price was steep when he signed the Treaty of Brest Litovsk in March 1918. Russia was forced to cede one-third of its territory to the Germans (progressed MC semisquare Mercury; progressed Moon square ASC; transiting Mars semisquare Sun and Saturn; Jupiter square Mars; Saturn conjunct Neptune). When the Civil War broke out in May 1918, Uranus was square the ASC. Two months later, in July 1918, the progressed Moon at 29 Leo was conjunct Regulus when Lenin had the Royal Family murdered at Ekaterinburg. The cost to Russia during the Great War and its Civil War was 16 million; no nation on earth had suffered more in so short a period of time.

Lenin also knew his economic system was at fault, so in March 1921 he unveiled the New Economic Plan as thousands were starving and millions more were existing close to the edge and disease was rampant. With the progressed Moon crossing the MC, Americans like Armand Hammer arranged to feed the Russians, thus saving millions from death. The progressed ASC was in the final degrees of Scorpio as well, the most difficult sector of the most intense and irrevocable sign there is.

The First Russian Empire was founded by Peter

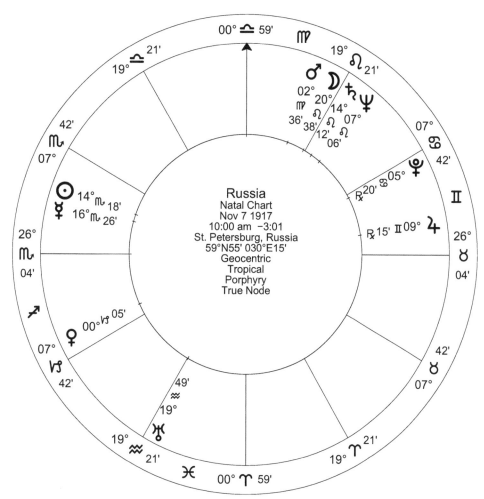

Russia
Natal Chart
Nov 7 1917
10:00 am  −3:01
St. Petersburg, Russia
59°N55' 030°E15'
Geocentric
Tropical
Porphyry
True Node

**Chart 2, November 7, 1917, 10:00 a.m. EEDT/LMT, 6:59 a.m. GMT; St. Petersburg**
Source: Lenin's proclamation states 10:00 a.m. Some astrologers prefer the time of 2:12 a.m., November 8, 1917, when the Provisional Government gave up; others prefer the time of 8:40 p.m. when Lenin said, "we shall now begin to construct the socialist order."

the Great in 1721. The Second Russian Empire was founded December 30, 1922 at 8:30 p.m. with Russia, the Ukraine, Byelorussia and the Trans-Caucasus as charter members. This would be known as the USSR, Soviet Union or Union of Soviet Socialistic Republics (progressed Sun was square Uranus, and the progressed MC square Pluto; progressed Venus opposition Pluto; transiting Mars sextile Sun; Saturn trine Uranus). Lenin's health deteriorated and he suffered a stroke in early 1922. Stalin wanted Lenin to name him successor, but Lenin didn't fully trust the "man of steel." Lenin died in January 1924 and some believe Stalin had him poisoned (progressed Sun square Moon sesquare Pluto; progressed MC sextile Neptune; Venus inconjunct Neptune; transiting Neptune opposition Uranus; Pluto sesquare ASC). Stalin then had to jockey for top dog with Leon Trotsky. Stalin had Trotsky exiled to Central Asia and by December 1929 was in full control of the government (progressed ASC square Mars). The first of the Five-Year Plans was also implemented which led to numerous

agricultural disasters down the road due to the collectivization of farms (transiting Jupiter conjunct Jupiter; Saturn square MC; Neptune conjunct Mars).

Stalin, always the paranoid, still believed he had adversaries in the Politburo and so he began a series of purges and phony trials to weed out dissidents. Kirov was one of the first to go in December 1934 (progressed Sun square Mars; progressed MC trine Uranus; progressed ASC trine Neptune; transiting Saturn square Sun opposition Saturn; Pluto trine ASC). It's believed that millions perished in Stalin's quest to purge Russia.

With Hitler's escalating power in Nazi Germany, Stalin thought it wise to make a pact with Hitler to avoid future confrontation. A non-aggression pact was signed between Hitler and Stalin only nine days before Hitler invaded Poland, which began World War II (progressed Sun inconjunct Pluto; progressed ASC opposition Jupiter; progressed Moon conjunct Jupiter but Jupiter was square the ASC; transiting Mars conjunct Moon in the ninth house). Russia was

135

allowed to annex the Baltic States of Estonia, Latvia and Lithuania in July 1940 (progressed Sun trine Neptune; transiting Uranus opposition ASC). Russia felt it was necessary to grab the Baltic states to protect itself from German ships then patrolling the Baltic.

But Hitler betrayed Stalin in June 1941 when he invaded Russia, capturing Kiev and laying siege to Leningrad and Stalingrad (progressed ASC opposition Jupiter; progressed Moon conjunct Pluto; transiting Saturn/Uranus opposition ASC). The Russians didn't give up without major resistance and the Nazis were finally repelled in early 1943 (progressed Sun opposition Jupiter). Soviet troops then "liberated" Eastern Europe from Nazi domination to replace with their own form of repression. Russians entered Berlin in late April 1945 just as Hitler was committing suicide (progressed ASC trine Saturn; transiting Pluto sextile Jupiter). The Russians also conquered Poland, Czechoslovakia, Hungary, Yugoslavia, Bulgaria, Romania and Albania before the 1940s had ended.

The Potsdam Conference, held outside Berlin in July 1945, laid the framework for the Cold War which followed. Russia had lost 6 million soldiers in World War II and another 14 million were wounded. Over 1 million alone died in the siege of Leningrad. Thus, the death toll from World War I, the Civil War, Stalin's purges and World War II cost Russia about 40 million lives either dead or wounded (transiting Mars opposition ASC; Neptune sesquare Uranus; Pluto sextile Jupiter).

Berlin became a sore spot for the Russians who occupied its eastern districts. The former German capital was more than 100 miles inside the West German border and its position was extremely vulnerable, a place associated with spies, double agents, intrigue and espionage. Russia decided to blockade Berlin in June 1948 over a currency dispute but the Allies formed an airlift to keep the city from starving (progressed MC sextile Mars; transiting Saturn conjunct Moon opposition Uranus; Pluto square Sun). The Soviets relinquished their blockade a year later, about the same time that Marshal Tito of Yugoslavia broke with the Kremlin.

Russia exploded its first Atomic Bomb in August 1949 (progressed Mercury opposition Pluto; transiting Sun sextile Pluto; Uranus sextile Mars; Pluto semisquare MC). In October 1949, the Soviet Union formed Comecon, a trade pact with her Eastern European satellites (transiting Saturn sextile Sun). A major goof occurred in late June 1950 when the Soviet delegate to the United Nations was absent when a vote was taken to send troops into Korea (progressed MC trine Pluto; transiting Mars square Pluto).

After ruling the Soviet Union for over a quarter of a century, Joseph Stalin died in March 1953 (progressed Sun trine Moon sextile Uranus; progressed MC square Neptune; progressed ASC square progressed Mars; transiting Uranus trine Sun; Pluto conjunct Moon). With aspects like these, it's possible that Stalin was poisoned just as he was reputed to have done to Lenin. Two men, Malenkov and Bulganin, then became joint leaders until 1955 when Nikita Khrushchev took the helm (progressed Sun sesquare Neptune; progressed MC inconjunct Jupiter; progressed ASC trine Moon sextile Uranus). The Warsaw Pact was also signed at this time. In May 1955, the Russians pulled out of Vienna (transiting Mars semisquare Neptune; Saturn square Moon/Saturn).

Nations in eastern Europe chafed under Soviet domination and some managed to gain a small measure of independence. The East Germans rose up in June 1953 and the Hungarians revolted in October 1956. Soviet tanks rolled down the streets of Budapest and thousands crossed the border into Austria (progressed Moon square Mars; Mars semisquare Neptune; ASC sextile progressed Uranus; Saturn square Mars in the ninth house). Ironically, transiting Pluto was trining natal Venus which should have been indicative of peace, but since those two planets oppose each other natally, it didn't work out that way at all.

The Soviets surprised the world in October 1957 when they sent up a space satellite, called Sputnik, and thus began the space race (progressed Moon trine MC; progressed ASC sesquare Neptune; transiting Mars square Pluto). The year of 1961 was a turning point in east-west relations. East Germans were escaping to West Berlin, which was a major embarrassment to the Russians, so they erected a wall around Berlin in August 1961 to stem the tide of refugees once and for all. Guards were told to shoot anyone attempting to flee. Thousands of East Berliners lost their jobs and the Cold War got much uglier (transiting Saturn sesquare Jupiter; Uranus square ASC). Russia was also having problems with Cuba. The Bay of Pigs invasion was a failure for America in March 1961 but the Kremlin couldn't afford to ignore events in Cuba, the only Communist country in the western hemisphere (progressed Sun semisquare Sun; progressed MC semisquare Venus; progressed Venus square Sun opposition Saturn). Progressed Jupiter also began an 18-year square to natal Mars which would last through the 1970s.

Cuba was becoming more and more of a hotbed so

the Soviets decided to send missiles to Cuba to expand its nuclear arsenal. In late October 1962, U.S. President Kennedy confronted Premier Khrushchev and demanded the Russians pull all their missiles out of Cuba or risk the consequences. The world lay on the brink of war but fortunately Khrushchev backed down (progressed Sun conjunct Venus, progressed MC conjunct Mercury; transiting Venus conjunct ASC; Jupiter opposition Mars). Khrushchev was ousted from power in October 1964 when Brezhnev took over (progressed Sun semisquare Mercury trine Mars; transiting Pluto sextile Sun). Ever since 1948, Russia's progressed Sun had been in the first house, a temporary anomaly that lasted until 1984. Russia was beginning to see the light and even though the Cold War continued, the Soviets were more amenable to compromise than confrontation, at least with the West.

When the Czechs revolted in August 1968, Brezhnev waited until the last minute before he sent in the troops (progressed Sun sesquare Moon semisquare Uranus opposition Pluto; transiting Saturn inconjunct ASC). Progress was also being made at the negotiation tables and the SALT treaty was signed in November 1969 (progressed Sun inconjunct Neptune; progressed ASC inconjunct progressed Jupiter). Over the next decade, Russia was comparatively peaceful and prosperous; internal dissent was the exception, not the norm.

Russia fooled the world when it invaded Afghanistan in late December 1979 (progressed Sun sextile Mercury sesquare Mars; progressed MC inconjunct Pluto; ASC sextile Sun inconjunct Saturn; transiting Jupiter square Jupiter; Neptune trine Moon). Soviet tanks met great resistance, millions fled across the borders and the Russians finally had to admit defeat. Afghanistan was the Soviet Union's "Vietnam."

Brezhnev died in November 1982 and was succeeded by Yuri Andropov, former head of the KGB (progressed Sun inconjunct Moon; progressed MC trine Neptune; progressed Venus square ASC; Mars finally entered Libra). Andropov wasn't very popular; 15 months later he was dead and Chernenko took over for 13 months until he died in March 1985. Then Mikhail Gorbachev took over as Russia's progressed Sun was again entering the twelfth house and it was time to clean out the closet, oil the rusty parts, open the windows and let in some fresh air before the Russians suffocated. Progressed Jupiter was also beginning a long trine to the natal MC, the progressed MC was opposing Jupiter as well.

Gorbachev began a program called Glasnost, meaning openness, and later he introduced perestroika, or freedom to experiment. Russia needed a shot in the arm just as progressed Mars was about to cross the natal MC. Gorbachev slackened government control of certain enterprises but the Russian economy was anything but rosy. In the midst of all this initial euphoria a nuclear reactor at Chernobyl in the Ukraine melted down in April 1986. Complete details were hidden from the world but the radioactive clouds which wafted across eastern Europe indicated something serious had occurred (progressed Sun sesquare Jupiter; progressed Moon conjunct Uranus; transiting Saturn opposition Jupiter; Neptune opposition Pluto; Pluto trine Pluto).

By the time Pluto was crossing the Russian Sun in late 1989, Russia and Communism were rotting to the core. Transiting Saturn conjuncted Uranus and shortly it would approach Neptune, the planet said to rule Communism. Four days before that conjunction, the Berlin Wall was breached on November 9, 1989, and within days other Eastern European satellites were throwing off the Soviet yoke (progressed MC trine Saturn; progressed ASC inconjunct Mars; progressed Moon sextile Jupiter and Mercury). Russia this time didn't send in her troops to quell the uprisings (transiting Venus opposition Pluto; Mars trine Uranus; Pluto square Saturn). Gorbachev knew the Soviet Union was a sick puppy and probably resigned himself to its eventual demise.

Gorbachev allowed the Russian Republic to elect its leader. The people chose Boris Yeltsin in June 1990, the first time in Russian history the people had ever elected anyone to govern themselves (progressed Sun at 29 Capricorn indicated an end to the old way of doing business). Few people inside or outside of the Soviet Union had any idea that a coup staged by ultra-rightwingers in August 1991 would eventually topple the Soviet Union. Within weeks, the republics of Estonia, Latvia, Lithuania, Belarus, Ukraine, Moldova, Georgia, Armenia, Azerbaijan, Kazakhstan, Uzbekistan, Tajikistan, Kirzhigstan and Turkmenistan had declared their independence (progressed ASC opposition Neptune; progressed Mercury opposition Pluto; progressed Mars at MC trine Jupiter). The Communist Party was discredited and its leaders banished. The KGB came under fire (transiting Saturn trine MC; Neptune inconjunct Saturn; Pluto semisquare MC). The coup that was designed to hold the line did in fact snap that line the old-timers had tried to preserve. One should remember that Mercury and Venus were retrograde when the coup took place.

With the Soviet Union breathing its last, several constituent republics met in Minsk to form what is today known as the Commonwealth of Independent States (CIS). This was the true "declaration of independence" of Russia from the Soviet Union, even though Boris Yeltsin was already acting as its President. The date was December 8, 1991, the time 7:45 p.m. EET (5:45 p.m. GMT) when the proclamation took place in Moscow. Gorbachev resigned as leader of the Soviet Union on Christmas Day 1991 at 7:45 p.m. EET (progressed ASC inconjunct Pluto). Many astrologers consider one of the two dates as the birth of modern Russia. I tend to disagree, for in December 1991, the Soviet Union, which to me was a government inside a government (an empire) disbanded, not the premise established in November 1917 when the Bolsheviks took over. Granted they were Communist and the new government is not. The real difference seems to be that the current Head of State is elected, not appointed as it was in Soviet days, or dynastic in Czarist times (progressed ASC opposition Neptune trine Jupiter).

One of the first items on Yeltsin's agenda was to repair the economy. Price controls were lifted, inflation was rampant and Russians were shocked by the cost of everyday items they had gotten for next to nothing, if they could get them at all in the olden days. Russia was no longer a superpower and for a while looked more like a Third-World country than a nation which had built itself up by its bootstraps over the previous half-century. With the progressed Sun trine the MC making good aspects to both progressed Mars and Jupiter, capitalism took off at record paces, but the crime rate also escalated.

Democracy was an untried concept for the Russians and Yeltsin had his hands full trying to manage members of Parliament. Yeltsin dissolved Parliament in September 1993 and then Parliament had him impeached (progressed ASC square Sun opposition Saturn; transiting Jupiter trine Uranus). A new Constitution was signed December 12, 1993 (transiting Jupiter trine Pluto).

Rebels in the province of Chechnya attacked Russian troops in December 1994, beginning a conflict that is still unresolved (progressed Sun inconjunct Mars; progressed ASC sextile Uranus; progressed ASC square Mercury). Russia had to borrow millions of dollars just to keep its fledgling economy afloat and the debt was piling up. Russia defaulted on its debt repayment in August 1998 (progressed MC sesquare Neptune in the eighth house, transiting Uranus opposition Saturn/Neptune in the eighth house and Pluto inconjuncted its own position). Yeltsin had endured many physical crises during his time in office, but his resignation on December 31, 1999 came as a shock to the world (progressed Sun opposition Neptune; progressed ASC trine Pluto; transiting Uranus square Sun). Vladimir Putin, a former KGB

chief, took over the helm. In 2001, private ownership of land was permitted (progressed Sun trine Jupiter; progressed ASC square Jupiter).

Russia seemed to be floating along, now that the crises of post-Soviet euphoria had calmed down. Russia's progressed ASC entered Aquarius in early 1989 and went into Pisces in mid-1998, where it will remain until mid-2006 when the MC goes into Capricorn and the ASC moves into Aries, the sign of pioneering and rebirth. Churchill once said that "Russia is a riddle wrapped in a mystery inside an enigma," so typical of a nation straddling the borders of the old and the new, Europe and Asia.

## Moscow (Moskva)

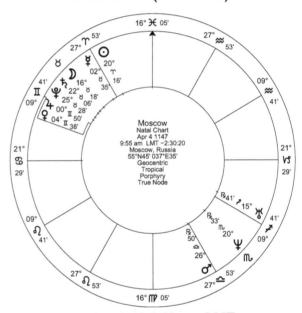

**April 4, 1147, 9:55 a.m. LMT**
**Source: Club Iskra cites the Ipatiev Chronicles**

The capital and largest city of Russia was settled in the late 10th century but dates its founding from a document written by Yuri Dolgoruky in April 1147. Nine years later (progressed MC sextile Pluto) a wooden wall was built around its fortress called the Kremlin. In 1237, the Mongols burned the community (progressed ASC square Uranus) and Tatars did the same in 1293 (ASC conjunct Mars). With its Sun in Aries and Mars in the fourth, Moscow has seen numerous fires: the great fire of 1331 (progressed ASC conjunct Neptune) and the blazes of 1392 (progressed ASC conjunct Pluto), 1480 (progressed ASC square Mars), 1571 (progressed ASC square Pluto) 1591 (progressed ASC square Jupiter) and 1737 (progressed MC conjunct Mars) were particularly bad.

In 1325, the Metropolitan (head of the Russian Orthodox Church) moved his headquarters to Moscow (progressed ASC opposition Moon) thus making Moscow the spiritual heart of the nation. After the fall of Constantinople in 1453, Russia was free from Byzantine control and was soon called "The Third Rome." In l459, the Grand Prince of Muscovy was elevated in status, making his power similar to that of the Greek Emperor in relation to the Patriarch (progressed MC trine Saturn; progressed ASC conjunct Jupiter). Within a century this led to the theocratic autocracy of the Tsars. In l485, Ivan the Great imported Italian architects to increase the glory of the Kremlin (progressed ASC trine Mars) and by 1534 they decided on stone rather than wood. The Time of Troubles began in 1598 (progressed ASC square Uranus) and in 1610 the Poles occupied the city (progressed ASC trine Pluto).

A settlement expressly for foreigners was established in 1652 (progressed MC sextile Jupiter; ASC inconjunct Saturn) which became one of Peter the Great's favorite haunts. In 1712, Russia's capital moved to St. Petersburg (progressed MC trine Jupiter; ASC opposition Jupiter) and for the next two centuries, Moscow sank to provincial status and lost 25 percent of its population. Moscow University was founded by Lomonosov in 1755 and remains the largest in the country (progressed ASC trine Mercury). Russian fears mounted as Napoleon invaded in 1812 (progressed MC square Pluto). Rather than let Napoleon savor a victory, Muscovites torched the city and left few, if any, food supplies. Napoleon thus had to retreat to France with only a fraction of his former Grand Armee.

By the mid 19th century, Moscow had 350,000 inhabitants and was connected by rail to St. Petersburg (progressed ASC sextile Mercury). Its population trebled in less than 50 years. Shortly after Lenin took over in 1917, Moscow became the scene of fighting between the Reds and the Whites and in March 1918. Lenin returned the capital to Moscow (progressed MC opposition Mars; ASC trine Uranus). Due to war and famine, Moscow had lost half its population during the war.

Under Stalin, Moscow built a subway in 1935 (progressed ASC sextile Mars square Pluto) known for its chandeliers and artwork, possibly the most beautiful underground railway system in the world. Moscow was placed under siege at the end of 1941 due to Hitler's invasion but the Germans were unable to conquer the city (progressed MC opposition Neptune; ASC square Jupiter). Rebuilding took place at a frantic pace after World War II and by 1951 a redevelopment plan covered a region of 340 square miles (progressed MC conjunct Venus). Metropolitan Moscow became law on August 18, 1960 and the Summer Olympics took place in 1980 despite the fact that the Americans boycotted the games (progressed ASC trine Pluto). Moscow witnessed the death of the Soviet Union in December 1991 and replaced flags atop the Kremlin with those of Russia (progressed ASC trine Venus).

Moscow is Europe's largest city in population and in area. The heart of the city is the Kremlin, a walled fortress of 10 acres lying 130 feet above the river. Inside the Kremlin are churches and palaces: the Facets Palace is the oldest (1487) and built in an Oriental style, while the Terem Palace (1635) was home to Peter the Great. The Great Kremlin Palace (t838) was built in the Classical style and the recently-built Palace of Congresses was home to the Supreme Soviet. Famous churches include the Uspenski or Assumption (1475), used for royal coronations; the Archangel (1505), used for royal burials; and the Annunciation (1484), used for royal weddings. The Kremlin walls contain 20 towers and gates.

Fronting one wall is Red Square, scene of May Day and Revolution Day parades. Measuring 2,300 by 430 feet, it's one of the world's largest open-air squares. Here is located Lenin's Tomb where the founder of the Soviet state lies mummified. Across the square is St. Basil's Cathedral (1555) built by Ivan the Terrible and probably the most famous edifice in Russia with its nine domes of varying sizes, shapes and colors. On the other side of Red Square is the massive GUM department store and the State Historical Museum.

A few blocks away is the gargantuan Lenin Library with more than 40 million volumes and nearby is the Bolshoi Theatre, famous for its ballet troupe. Further out is Lubyanka Square, which fronts the headquarters of the KGB. In Lenin Hills is the university with its main building towering 790 feet above the city.

A map reveals that Mosoow's main streets radiate like a spider web from the Kremlin. The first circle is called the Garden Ring which was built over the old city walls. Further out is the Forest Ring, a greenbelt which separates the old city from its newer suburbs. Moscow has five airports and several railroad stations, 120 museums, 35 theatres and 75 cinemas. Moscow is the industrial heart of Russia with major steel mills, automotive plants, chemical factories, electronic and machinery foundries. Its population is almost 9 million.

Moscow's chart has two major aspects: Sun opposition Mars, and Neptune opposition the Moon-Saturn-Pluto stellium. Moscow feels like a Moon in Taurus place, rather conservative, somber and gray in appearance and with those Plutonian vibes it seems rather oppressive and threatening. The Sun in Aries opposition Mars and square the ASC propelled this community from a sleepy backwater into the most powerful city in the region. The Sun trine Uranus but inconjunct Neptune could point not only to the aecretiveness but also to the unpredictability that often pulled Moscow from the brink of disaster. Neptune opposite the Moon indicates the powerful religious aura despite the fact that atheism was in vogue during the Communist era.

Compared to St. Petersburg, Moscow has a definite Oriental flavor. With Cancer rising, Moscow is the Mother City of Russia and the spiritual heart of the nation. Venus conjunct Jupiter illustrates the powerful artistic and cultural leanings as well as its wealth. Moscow's chart has a seesaw pattern indicating mood swings from one extreme to another. Before the outer planets were discovered, Moscow's chart had a bucket pattern with Mars as the handle. No wonder this city has a history of repeated invasions, fires and subsequent reconstruction.

## St. Petersburg

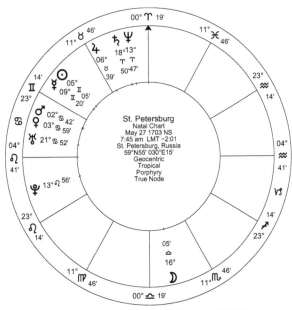

**May 27, 1703 (NS), 7:45 a.m. LMT**
**Source: Lenin Library for the date; time rectified from "early morning"**

Shortly after Peter the Great returned from Holland, he began to plan a great city to rival anything he had seen in Europe. He chose as his site the marshy delta of the Neva River which runs 45 miles from Lake Ladoga to the Gulf of Finland. On the morning of May 27, 1703, Peter laid the cornerstone of the city in the Peter and Paul fortress. Numerous problems arose including drainage, mosquitoes and cold weather. Most laborers were forcibly imported and

thousands died. In 1712, enough of the city had been completed that Peter moved the capital here from Moscow (progressed MC and ASC sextile Mercury). Work then was begun on other palaces outside the city. Peter died in 1725 and two years later the capital was temporarily moved back to Moscow (progressed MC square Uranus) where it remained until 1732 (progressed ASC trine Saturn). With its elevation only a few feet above sea level, St. Petersburg has suffered numerous inundations (about 250) since its founding. The floods of 1777, 1824 and 1924 were particularly devastating.

The political heart of Russia became an industrial center after 1801 when aa iron foundry was constructed (progressed MC conjunct Mars) and a seat of learning in 1819 when its University was founded (progressed ASC opposition Neptune, ruler of ninth). Russia's first railway was built in 1837 to nearby Tsarskoe Selo (progressed MC sextile Mercury) and to Moscow in 1851 (progressed ASC trine Mars). By the end of the 19th century, St. Petersburg had nearly 2 million residents. As capital of the largest country and empire on earth, it has seen numerous political demonstrations. The Decembrist Revolt of 1825 (progressed ASC opposition Saturn) brought Nicholas I to the throne instead of his brother, Constantine. The student revolt of 1876 founded the Nihilist movement (progressed MC conjunct Neptune), but the most massive demonstration took place on Bloody Sunday in January 1905 when Father Gapon went to the Winter Palace to petition the Czar for better working conditions for the peasants (progressed MC conjunct Moon opposition Saturn). The guards fired on the demonstrators and the First Russian Revolution erupted. The Czar was forced to allow a Duma (Parliament).

At the beginning of World War I in August 1914, St. Petersburg had more than 2 million people. Many thought its name sounded too German so it was changed to Petrograd (Peter's city). In late 1916, troops which had deserted their posts began coming home and bread riots broke out. The sentries refused to fire on the hungry and the government was in absolute chaos. In mid-March 1917, the Provisional Government was formed under Kerensky and the Czar was forced to abdicate. Another revolt in July 1917 erupted when conditions remained static. Lenin knew the time was ripe to take over the government; on November 7, 1917 (NS), the Bolsheviks took over important facilities and 24 hours later, the Provisional Government had surrendered (progressed ASC trine Neptune and Pluto). Transiting Sun and Mercury were sesquare the natal MC, transiting Venus squared the MC, Mars sextiled its natal position,

Jupiter sat on Mercury, Saturn trined natal Neptune. Transiting Neptune had gone over the ASC earlier that summer.

Lenin moved the capital back to Moscow early in 1918 and St. Petersburg lost power and influence and its population shrunk by 65 percent. Less than a week after Lenin's death in early 1924, the city was renamed in his honor (progressed MC inconjunct Sun opposite Jupiter). With its location, Leningrad was a prime target for the Nazis during their 1941 invasion of Russia (progressed ASC opposition Mars). By September 1941, Leningrad was under siege, its lifeline reduced to a timber road across Lake Ladoga. When the siege ended 900 days later in January 1944, nearly 1 million were dead, some 650,000 of them having starved to death (progressed ASC trine Jupiter). Reconstruction began soon after and by 1955, Leningrad had a subway line, a major feat in this swampy terrain. Workers had to excavate 500 feet down to reach bedrock; most commuters feel as if they're journeying into the bowels of the earth via some of the longest escalators in the world. Less than a month after the August 1991 coup, this city readopted its original name (progressed MC square Neptune).

St. Petersburg is a magnificent and regal-looking place. Often called the "Venice of the North" due to its numerous bridges and canals. This city is the world's most-northerly metropolis and one of the most northerly major cities (see Oslo, Helsinki and Reykjavik). The city is dominated by the 402-foot spire of the Church of St. Peter and Paul across the river from the Winter Palace. Nearby, the cruiser Aurora has been transformed into a museum. The heart of St. Petersburg is Palace Square, fronted by the Baroque Winter Palace, built in 1754 by the Empress Elizabeth, and the Admiralty which is the oldest government building in town. The Winter Palace is one of the largest royal residences on earth; it's been converted to a museum with more than 3 million artifacts in its 350 galleries. It ranks with the Louvre, Prado, Vatican and Metropolitan as one of the premier art museums.

The main artery of St. Petersburg is called the Nevsky Prospekt which connects the Winter Palace to the Alexander Nevsky Convent. Nearby are two huge churches: the Kazan Cathedral was designed as a miniature Saint Peter's with a 235-foot dome, and St. Isaac's Cathedral with its 330-foot dome is the third-largest domed place of worship in the world after St. Peter's in Rome and St. Paul's in London. With Leo rising, St. Petersburg has numerous palaces as well. The Mariinsky Palace is now the City Hall, the Tauride Palace once housed the Petrograd

Duma, and the palaces outside the city are even more spectacular. The palaces at Tsarskoe Selo include the huge Catherine and Alexander Palaces where the last of the Romanovs were confined. Nearby is Pavlovsk and Gatchina. The most spectacular royal residence is 20 miles west on the Baltic called Petrodvorets (aka Peterhof). The main building is 895 feet long and sits on a hill 65 feet above the water. Severely damaged by the Germans in World War II, it's been completely restored to its former glory. Three cascades of water flow down from the palace to the shoreline and on the grounds are 144 fountains, most of them illuminated at night.

St. Petersburg is a city of grandeur and elegance, neo-Classical and Baroque in style, pastel-painted with numerous spires and domes. It seems content today to revel in its former glory but its Aries MC does indicate an early pioneering spirit. With Saturn and Neptune in the tenth trine Pluto in the first and opposition the Moon in the fourth, building this city came at a steep price and with a heavy loss of life. Sun and Mercury in Gemini indicate the numerous cultural attractions, including the Kirov Theatre with its famous ballet corps. In many respects, this city reflects its namesake, Peter, who had Sun in Gemini in the third and Moon in Sagittarius in the ninth. Peter dearly loved the sea and spared no expense in building his "window to the west" due to Jupiter in Taurus square the ASC. Venus and Mars in Cancer square the MC point to the luxury-loving and hedonistic nature of this city during its time as the capital of the largest empire on earth. Those two traits also contributed to the eventual downfall of the monarchy. Today, St. Petersburg is the main port for Russia and a major shipbuilding center as well as the second-largest industrial and manufacturing center of the country.

## Chelyabinsk

Chelyabinsk is Russia's eighth-largest city and is situated on the eastern fringe of the Urals 125 miles south of the city of Ekaterinburg. Chelyabinsk grew dramatically after factories were relocated here from the west during the Nazi occupation. The main industries are oil refining, petrochemicals, automobiles and textiles.

## Ekaterinburg (Sverdlovsk)

Russia's fifth-largest city is located 870 miles east of Moscow on the eastern side of the Urals. Founded in 1721 by Peter the Great, it became a focal point for the Great Siberian Highway in 1783 and a major stopover on the Trans-Siberian Railway after 1878. It was here in Ekaterinburg that the Russian royal family (Nicholas II, Empress Alexandra, their son and four daughters) were executed by the Bolsheviks in July 1918. In 1924, the city was renamed to honor the Bolshevik leader, Yakov Sverdlov but it reverted to its old name in 1991. This city is located in the midst of one of the most mineral-rich areas on earth and is still today a major training center. It also makes heavy machinery, electrical equipment and chemicals.

## Kazan

Russia's ninth-largest city is situated three miles from the Volga River 435 miles east of Moscow. Founded by the Tatars as Bolgary in the 13th century, it was captured by Ivan the Terrible in 1552. A major industrial center and oil refiner, it also makes ships, leather, furs and silk.

## Nizhni Novgorod (Gorki)

Russia's fourth-largest city is located on the Volga River 235 miles east of Moscow. Founded as a fort in 1221, it became residence of the Grand Dukes of Suzdal in 1350. Nizhni Novgorod is famous for holding Russia's largest trade fair. Renamed in 1932 to honor the author, Maxim Gorky, it was a place of internal exile and banned to foreigners in Soviet days. This city makes automobiles, riverboats, hydrofoils, aircraft and diesel motors, and is also a major oil refining center.

## Novosibirsk

Russia's third-largest city is situated on the Ob River in central Siberia, 1,740 miles east of Moscow. Founded in 1893 when a way station was needed for the Trans-Siberian Railway, it prospered after World War II when factories were moved here from German-occupied Ukraine and Byelorussia. This city is also Siberia's largest scientific research center.

## Omsk

Omsk is Russia's seventh-largest metropolis, located in western Siberia 1,370 miles east of Moscow at the place where the Trans-Siberian Railway crosses the Irtysh River. Founded in 1716 as a fort, it's now an oil refining center and makes petrochemicals and cars.

## Perm (Molotov)

Russia's eleventh-largest city is situated on the Kama River in the Urals 175 miles northwest of Ekaterinburg and 700 miles east of Moscow. Founded in 1723 as a copper-smelting center, it was renamed Molotov in 1940 to honor Vyacheslav

Molotov, the Soviet foreign minister. It reverted to its old name in 1957. Perm is a steel center and makes automobiles, aircraft, chemicals, textiles and paper products.

## Rostov Na Donu

Russia's twelfth-largest city is located on the River Don at the northeast tip of the Sea of Azov, which is 30 miles away. Founded in 1750 as a customs port when Turkey still ruled the region, by the 19th century it was Russia's second-largest exporter of grain. Rostov on the Don makes agricultural machinery, electrical equipment, chemicals, barges, glass, wine and cigarettes.

## Samara (Kuybyshev)

Russia's sixth-largest city is situated on the Volga River 535 miles southeast of Moscow. Founded in 1586, it was renamed in 1935 to honor Valerian Kuybyshev, but reverted to its old name in 1991. Samara was the capital of the Soviet Union from 1941 to 1943 during the darkest days of World War II. A dam upstream on the Volga forms Russia's largest reservoir. Samara makes transportation equipment, petrochemicals, timber and food.

## Ufa

Russia's tenth-largest city is located on the western fringe of the Urals 225 miles south of Perm. Founded in 1574 as a fort to guard trade routes across the Urals, it grew tremendously in the 1950s, when oilfields were discovered. Ufa makes telecommunications, office and electrical equipment.

## Volgograd (Stalingrad)

Russia's thirteenth-largest city is situated on the Volga River 275 miles from the Caspian Sea. Founded in 1589 as Tsaritsyn, a fort designed to protect against Cossacks which marauded the region. Renamed in 1925 to honor the Soviet leader, Joseph Stalin, it was the focal point for the German invasion which took place from August 1941 until February 1943. More than 350,000 Nazi soldiers were cut off and many of them either killed or imprisoned. The city was almost destroyed in the process. Large monuments to the heroes of Stalingrad tower over the city, which returned to its old name in 1961 after Stalin's policies fell out of favor. The city makes agricultural machinery, ships and petrochemicals and is a major oil refining center.

# San Marino
## Serenissima Republica di San Marino

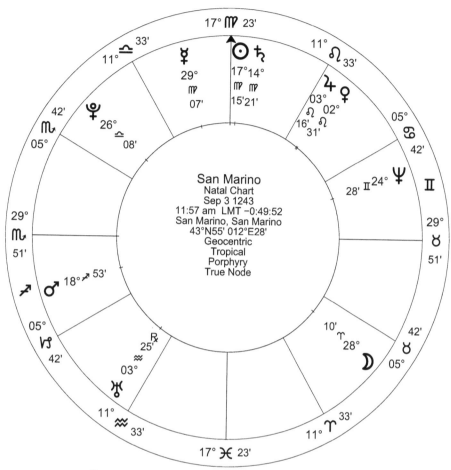

San Marino
Natal Chart
Sep 3 1243
11:57 am LMT −0:49:52
San Marino, San Marino
43°N55' 012°E28'
Geocentric
Tropical
Porphyry
True Node

**September 3, 1243, 11:47 a.m. LMT, San Marino**
**Source: *Los Angeles Times* for the date; noontime assumed**

San Marino is completely surrounded by Italy on the slopes of Mt. Titano (elevation 2,438 feet) a few miles from the Adriatic Sea.

Population: 27,336; 99% Sanmarinese

Religion: 99% Catholic

Area: 23 square miles (the size of the borough of Manhattan in New York City)

Economy: Tourism, postage stamps and coins are the main sources of income

According to legend, San Marino was founded February 3, 301 A.D. by a monk named Marinus who was fleeing Dalmatia. On September 3, 1243, San Marino became a republic, the oldest democratic republic in the world. The first constitution was framed in 1263 (progressed ASC square Saturn). The independence of San Marino was finally recognized by the Pope in 1631 (progressed ASC square Sun sesquare Venus and Jupiter). Ironically, armies from the Papal States invaded the country in 1739 (pro-gressed Sun sesquare Saturn).

A customs union was formed with Italy in 1862 (progressed Sun square Venus; progressed ASC semisquare Mercury). San Marino declared war on Germany in August 1914 (progressed ASC square Neptune). But it decided to remain neutral when World War II broke out in May 1940 (progressed Sun sextile Sun). Germans bombed the country anyway in July 1943 during the Allied invasion (progressed Sun inconjunct Mars).

After the war, Communists gained control of the government in 1947 (progressed ASC sextile Mars). Women were finally given the vote in 1960 (progressed ASC opposition Moon semisquare Saturn). Another Communist coalition ruled the country from 1978 to 1988. The European Union in 2001 planned to close loopholes for San Marino as a tax haven (progressed ASC conjunct Mars semisquare Uranus sesquare Jupiter).

# Seborga
## Antigo Principato de Seborga

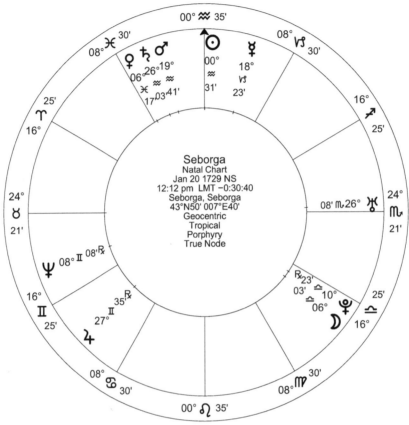

**January 20, 1729, 12:12 p.m. LMT, Seborga**
**Source: the Internet for the date; noontime presumed**

Seborga is situated on a hill, 1,600 feet above the Ligurian Sea just above the towns of San Remo and Bordighera, Italy. Monaco is 18 miles (27 km) southwest along the Riviera.

Population: 2,000

Area: 14 square miles (about two-thirds the size of New York's Manhattan Island)

Economy: Dependent upon postage stamps and coins

I had never heard of this place, even through my long career as a travel agent. *The Los Angeles Times* ran a cover story on Seborga in its May 4, 1997 travel section. Seborga is not mentioned in any history book or travelogue I've ever seen.

The Counts of Ventimiglia granted Seborga to Benedictine monks in 954 A.D. By 1079, it had become a principality of the Holy Roman Empire. In 1118, the first nine templars of the Knights of St. Bernard were ordained, and thus did Seborga become the first and only sovereign Cistercian state in history.

The principality was sold to Vittorio Amedeo II of Savoy, King of Sardinia, January 20, 1729, but the transfer of ownership was never registered with the House of Savoy, an oversight that would one day allow Seborga to retain its independence. Note that Pluto is sesquare the natal ASC and Pluto governs the seventh house of treaties and Pluto hides things. Seborga maintained its anonymity (Neptune in first house square Venus, ruler of the ASC) when a treaty with the Republic of Genoa failed to mention the place; it wasn't mentioned in the Treaty of Vienna in June 1815 either.

When Italy was unified in March 1861, Seborga again escaped mention and thus is not considered part of the current Italian Republic (progressed Sun sesquare Mercury; progressed ASC opposition Venus square Neptune), according to experts on international law. Ever since 1943, Seborgans have elected Giorgio as their leader, just to be democratic.

In April 1995, Seborgans voted for a constitution and on August 20, 1995, Seborga declared its independence on St. Bernard's Day (progressed Sun conjunct Pluto semisquare Uranus).

# Serbia
## Savezna Republika

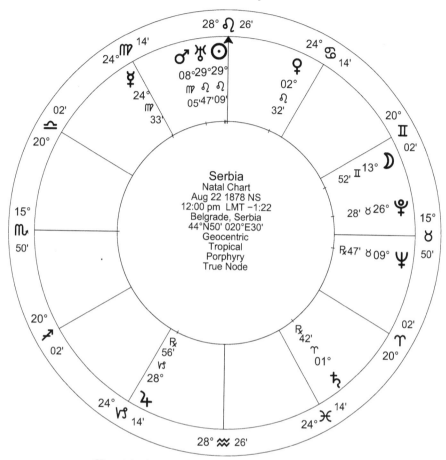

**Chart 1, August 22, 1878, noon LMT, Belgrade**
**Source: Yugoslavian Embassy for the date; noontime presumed**

This country is divided into three regions: Serbia proper, Vojdovina and Kosovo. In the north is the Pannonian plain, through which flows the Danube. Other main rivers are the Sava, Tisza and Morava. The southern part is rugged and mountainous.

Population: 10,047,290; 63% Serbian, 14% Albanian

Religion: 65% Orthodox; 20% Moslem; 4% Catholic

Area: 33,986 square miles (the size of Indiana or Hungary); 35% arable, 50% urban

Economy: Main exports are meat and foodstuffs, machinery, clothing and hardwoods. Chief resources are copper, lead, zinc, coal, antimony and bauxite.

Marshall Tito once said, "I'm a leader of a country which has two alphabets, three languages, four religions, five nationalities living in six republics, surrounded by seven neighbors." A lot has changed since he died, with the break-up of Yugoslavia.

Romans conquered this region in 9 A.D. which they called Pamionia. During the 5th century, barbarians under Attila the Hun invaded from the north and then came the Slavic tribes including the Serbs, Croats, Slovenes. During the 10th century, the Serbs accepted Christianity (Eastern Orthodox). The Kingdom of Serbia was first founded in the 12th century, uniting the states of Raska and Zeta. Serbia's most glorious period occurred during the reign of Stefan Dusan (1331-1355). Unfortunately, he died on his way to Constantinople to lay claim to the throne of Byzantium. Serbs were defeated by the Turks in 1371 on the Maritsa River in Bulgaria.

But the date which lives on in Serbian memory is June 28, 1389, when the Serbian leader, Czar Lazar, and the Ottoman leader, Sultan Murat, were both killed in the Battle of Kosovo. The Serbs lost, but ironically, Montenegro managed to remain free of Turkish rule for the next five centuries and its independence was recognized by Turkey in 1799.

In 1804, a farmer named Karageorge began a revolt against the Turks which, lasted until his death nine years later. The revolutionary fervor was rekindled in 1815 by Obrenovic and for the next 14 years, Serbia was allowed to be an autonomous part of the Ottoman Empire. Turkish troops finally left Serbia in 1877, and one year later, with the signing of the Treaty of Berlin in July 1878, Serbian independence was recognized. The King proclaimed independence August 22, 1878 (chart 1).

King Alexander and his wife, Queen Draga, were assassinated in June 1903 (progressed ASC trine Venus; transiting Saturn inconjunct Mars; Uranus inconjunct Mercury). The first Balkan war broke out in October 1912, when Serbia went to war with Bulgaria and Greece against the Turks (progressed MC opposition Saturn; progressed ASC inconjunct Neptune; transiting Jupiter conjunct Moon; Uranus conjunct Jupiter; Pluto sesquare ASC). The second Balkan war erupted in June 1913 when Serbia, Greece, Romania and Turkey fought against Bulgaria over the region called Macedonia (transiting Jupiter sextile ASC square Sun and Uranus; Saturn square Mars; Pluto sextile Sun and Uranus).

On June 28, 1914, the 525th anniversary of the Battle of Kosovo, Archduke Franz Ferdinand, heir to the throne of Austria-Hungary, and his wife, Sophie Chotek, were assassinated by Gavrilo Princip, a Serbian sympathizer working for the Black Hand. Austria was outraged and sent steep demands to Serbia that it knew Serbia could not comply with. At the end of July 1914, Austrians began bombing Belgrade and World War I had begun. At the time, the progressed MC was sextile Venus, which seems rather odd, considering Venus is supposed to be the planet of peace and harmony.

Looking at the Serbian chart, however, yields another picture entirely. Venus opposed Jupiter retrograde in the third house and trined Saturn, which was also retrograde in the fifth house. Using midpoint structures, the natal ASC sesquares Saturn, while on the 30-degree dial Venus is in aspect not only to the natal ASC but also to the Neptune/Pluto midpoint. Note also that the Moon sesquares Jupiter, Mars trines Pluto and the Sun conjuncts Uranus which squares Pluto. Using the 30-degree dial, these combinations become much clearer.

The transiting aspects weren't much better. Saturn was inconjunct Jupiter, Uranus squared Neptune, Neptune opposed Jupiter and Pluto was still sesquare the ASC when the Archduke was shot.

Serbia lost 25 percent of its population during the Great War. More than 45,000 died in battle and 133,000 were wounded. With the Austro-Hungarian Empire defunct by mid-November 1918, it was de-cided to form the Kingdom of Serbs, Croats and Slovenes with Belgrade as its capital. Bosnia, Macedonia and Montenegro were asked to join the union which was born on December 1, 1918 (chart 2) (progressed ASC opposition Moon semisquare Jupiter; Jupiter trine ASC semisquare Sun and Uranus; Saturn conjunct MC; Neptune square Neptune).

## Yugoslavia

In January 1929, King Alexander closed Parliament and began to rule as dictator. The name of the country was also changed to Yugoslavia, or land of the southern Slavs (progressed MC trine Saturn; progressed ASC trine Venus; transiting Jupiter square ASC; transiting Uranus trine ASC; transiting Pluto square MC). However, the King was assassinated in Marseille in October 1934 and as his heir, Prince Peter, was only 11 years old, his cousin, Paul, became Regent (progressed ASC inconjunct Mars; progressed Sun sextile Uranus sesquare Neptune).

In March 1941, Peter signed an alliance with Nazi Germany that so angered his countrymen that he was forced to abdicate one month later (progressed MC inconjunct Sun square Neptune; transiting Uranus square Uranus). In May 1941, German troops marched into Yugoslavia and a puppet state was established inside Croatia (transiting Jupiter square Uranus; transiting Saturn opposition Moon and Pluto conjunct ASC). Italy then occupied southern Slovenia and the entire province of Montenegro while Bulgaria, a German ally, occupied Macedonia.

By October 1944, Marshal Tito and his guerrilla fighters had rid his country of the Nazis (progressed Sun opposition Pluto; progressed MC semisquare Pluto; transiting Saturn conjunct Jupiter/Pluto; transiting Pluto trine Venus). Yugoslavia had lost 305,000 lives in battle and 425,000 had been wounded. But the country changed one fascist government for another as the Russians or Soviets now held sway. In late November 1945, the Kingdom of Yugoslavia came to an end and a People's Republic was proclaimed (progressed MC sextile Jupiter; progressed ASC opposition Uranus; transiting Mars conjunct ASC; transiting Neptune sextile Sun).

## Yugoslavia (Serbia)

The Republic was proclaimed November 29, 1945 (chart 3), with Marshal Tito as its leader. The Constitution was approved January 31, 1946. Yugo-

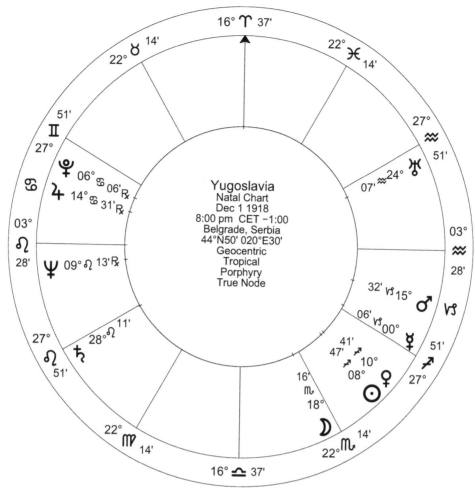

**Chart 2, December 1, 1918, 8:00 p.m. MET, Belgrade**
Source: *Serbian Horoscopes* by Branka Stamenkovic. The Times of London says "evening."

slavia was expelled from the Communist bloc in June 1948 due to Tito's views which differed radically from those of Stalin (progressed Sun sesquare Saturn; progressed MC inconjunct Neptune). Tito began to make even more radical reforms in September 1965, which included massive decentralization (progressed Sun and MC sesquare Pluto; transiting Neptune sesquare ASC).

After leading his country for 34 years, Tito died in May 1980 (progressed Sun inconjunct Pluto; progressed MC trine Pluto; progressed ASC semisquare Uranus; transiting Pluto sesquare MC conjunct Jupiter). Tito had managed to keep a lid on ethnic differences during his reign, but before long, Yugoslavia would, erupt into civil war and evaporate into petty squabbles.

Slobodan Milosevic took the helm in 1987 (progressed Sun square Jupiter; progressed MC opposition Jupiter; progressed ASC conjunct Mars) and promptly began to alienate ethnic groups. In late June 1991, Croatia and Slovenia seceded and, declared their independence, Macedonia followed suit in Sep-

tember and Bosnia did the same in October 1991 (progressed Sun opposition Saturn; progressed MC sesquare Sun trine Mercury; progressed ASC trine Sun sesquare Mercury). Serbia went to war against its former partners; Slovenia was ignored but Croatia took quite a pummeling. Bosnia was attacked in April 1992 (progressed ASC sextile Neptune) and the Serbs occupied 70 percent of that country by the end of the year. Inflation was running rampant (about 3,000 percent per month), unemployment was about 40 percent and the U.N. imposed sanctions on Serbia which made it a pariah nation throughout the civilized world. A peace accord was drawn up by the U.S. in November 1995, which finally brought to an end the internecine warfare that had lasted 4½ years (progressed ASC conjunct Pluto; transiting Jupiter sextile Jupiter; transiting Neptune inconjunct Saturn). U.N. sanctions were lifted in October 1996.

But Serbia wasn't finished being the "bad boy of the Balkans." In late 1998, the Serbian army began an extensive plan of ethnic cleansing in Kosovo, the southern part of the country which is mostly Moslem

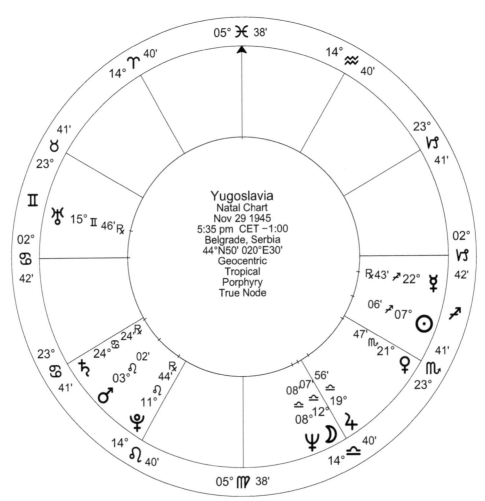

**Chart 3, Yugoslavia (Serbia), November 29, 1945, 5:35 p.m. MET, Belgrade**
**Source: *Knjiga Srpskih Horoskopa* by Branka Stamenkovic**

and Albanian. In March 1999, bombers under NATO's command began firing on Serbian military installations as well as on Belgrade. The bombing lasted for 2½ months before a U.N. peacekeeping force arrived to clean up the mess and hold the Serbs at bay. Russia even forced its way into the fracas as they deemed Serbia one of their allies (progressed Sun sesquare Uranus; progressed MC semisquare Uranus; progressed ASC sextile Moon; transiting Jupiter trine Sun; Uranus trine Uranus; Neptune opposition Mars).

The Serbians had had enough of Milosevic and he was voted out of office in October 2000 (progressed Sun opposition Mars; progressed ASC sextile Uranus; transiting Neptune opposition Mars; Pluto trine Pluto). Milosevic surrendered to authorities who wanted to place him on trial for war crimes and he was extradited to the Netherlands in July 2001.

Prime Minister Djindjic was gunned down in March 2003 (progressed MC sextile Sun; transiting Saturn opposition Mercury; Neptune opposition Pluto and Pluto sextile Jupiter). His assassins had links to Serbian paramilitary groups still loyal to Milosevic as well as to organized crime. Some also felt that Milosevic's wife may have had a hand in Djindjic's murder. Then to add insult to injury, the body of the former Serbian President, Stambolic, was found in March 2003. He had originally befriended Milosevic but was probably kidnaped in August 2000. Stambolic had planned to run against Milosevic in that year's elections.

In March 2006, Slobodan Milosevic, former leader of Yugoslavia during the tumultuous 1990s when former republics of Slovenia, Croatia, Bosnia and Macedonia broke away from his tyrannical and authoritarian rule, died in his prison cell in the Netherlands while he was awaiting his trial on "crimes against humanity." Two months later, in late May 2006, the last remaining province of Montenegro declared its independence. A movement also is underway to grant the region of Kosovo its freedom by the end of 2006, but Serbia refuses to even consider that a possibility (progressed MC inconjunct Sun square Mars/Pluto; progressed Saturn sesquare natal MC).

Meanwhile, Serbia has an annual inflation rate of more than 100 percent, an unemployment rate of 30 percent and half its people live in poverty.

# Belgrade (Beograd)

The capital and largest city of Serbia lies on bluffs overlooking the junction of the Danube and Sava rivers. Founded by Celts in ancient times, its name means "white citadel." Occupied over the centuries by Romans, Byzantines, Ottomans and Austrians, it became the capital of Serbia only in 1882. In April1941, the Germans came and stayed for three years. Many military installations and power plants were bombed by NATO planes during the spring of 1999 when the Serbs were "ethnically cleansing" the region of Kosovo.

# Slovakia
## Slovenska Republika

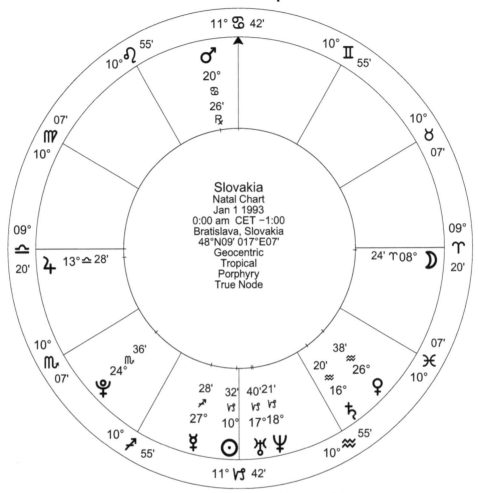

**January 1, 1993, 12:00 a.m. MET, Bratislava**
**Source:** *Los Angeles Times* **says midnight**

Situated in central Europe, Slovakia is a region of vast forests and rugged mountains. The Tatra Mountains sit on the border with Poland, while the Carpathian Alps flank its eastern border. The highest point is Gerlachovka (elevation 8,711 feet).

Population: 5,414,937; 86% Slovak, 11% Hungarian

Religion: 60% Catholic, 8% Protestant

Area: 18,859 square miles (the size of Estonia or New Hampshire); 30% arable, 57% urban

Economy: Main exports are timber, textiles, machinery and chemicals. Major resources are coal, lignite and salt.

Settled by the Slavs in the 5th century A.D., Slovakia merged with the Moravian Empire four centuries later. In 907, it was conquered by Germans and Magyars. In 1038, Slovakia became part of Hungary, which ruled the region for the next nine centuries.

On October 28, 1918, Slovakia united with Bohemia and Moravia to form the nation of Czechoslovakia. The Germans took over in March 1939 until the Soviet army liberated them from the Nazis in April 1945. A Communist government was formed in February 1948.

Talks began in July 1992 to discuss the possibility of Slovakia seceding from Czechoslovakia, and on January 1, 1993, Slovakia became an independent nation. During 1998, there was no president due to a standoff in Parliament (progressed MC inconjunct Saturn opposition Uranus; progressed ASC conjunct Jupiter). Slovakia became part of the European Union in May 2004 (progressed MC trine Pluto; progressed ASC square Neptune).

# Bratislava

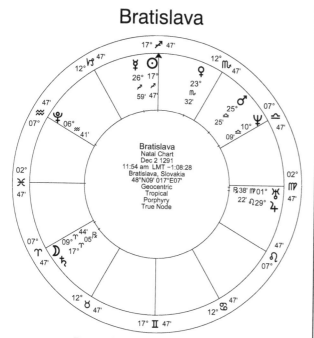

**December 2, 1291, 11:54 a.m.**
**Source: University Kniznica**

The capital and largest city of Slovakia is situated on the Danube River, about 40 miles down river from Vienna. Founded in the 5th century by Bretislav and named for himself, it was part of Hungary from 907 until 1918 when the Austro-Hungarian Empire collapsed after World War I. It was the capital of Hungary from 1541 until 1784 but still housed the Diet (Parliament) of Hungary until 1848 when revolutions across Europe moved the capital.

## Kosice

Slovakia's second-largest city is situated 15 miles from the Hungarian border. Due to its industrial importance, its population has quadrupled over the past five decades. The main sights are the 14th century Gothic cathedral and the Miklus prison, which has medieval instruments of torture.

# Slovenia
# Republica Slovenija

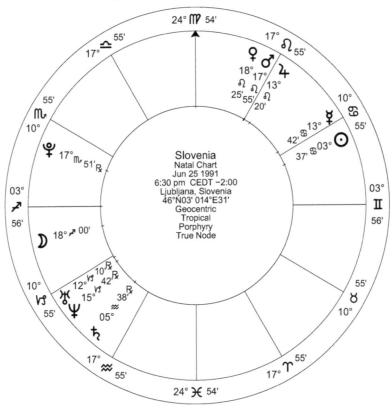

**June 25, 1991, 6:30 p.m. MEDT (4:30 p.m. GMT), Ljubljana**
**Source:** *Book of World Horoscopes* by Nicholas Campion cites British TV 4

Situated in the NW part of what was once Yugoslavia at the northern end of the Adriatic Sea, most of Slovenia is alpine and forested » the remainder has hilly plains. The coastline is only 20 miles long. The highest point is Mt. Triglav in the Julian Alps (elevation 9,393 feet).

Population: 1,930,132; 91% Slovenian, 3% Croatian

Religion: 71% Catholic, 2% Moslem

Area: 7,836 square miles (the size of Massachusetts or Macedonia); 1.2% arable, 50% urban

Economy: Main exports are machinery, timber, transportation equipment, chemicals and tobacco. Chief resources are coal, mercury, lignite, lead and zinc.

The Romans knew this region as Pannonia. The Slovenes, a Slavic tribe, arrived in the 6th century and the state of Samu was founded a century later, which dominated Hungary until 790. Slovenia accepted Austrian rule in 1526 to ward off future attacks by the Ottoman Turks and in February 1867, it became part of the vast Austro-Hungarian Empire.

Slovenia agreed to become part of the Kingdom of Serbs, Croats and Slovenes (aka Yugoslavia) in December 1918. Germans occupied the region from 1941 to 1944, and part of Slovenia was occupied by the Italians which had occupied its western districts since 1920.

On June 25, 1991, Slovenia declared its independence from Yugoslavia only 30 minutes after neighboring Croatia had done the same thing. Slovenia is the most advanced and prosperous of all former regions of Yugoslavia and the only one to have been asked to join NATO. Slovenia joined the European Union in May 2004 (progressed ASC trine Mercury and Jupiter).

## Ljubljana

The capital and largest city of Slovenia lies on the Ljubljana river. During the 1st century A.D., the Romans founded a city named Emona but it was destroyed by the end of the 5th century. First mentioned in 1144, it was called Luwigana. It was chartered around 1220. Ljubljana was capital of Illyria from 1809 to 1849 and capital of Slovenia only after 1918.

# Sovereign Military Order of Malta (SMOM)

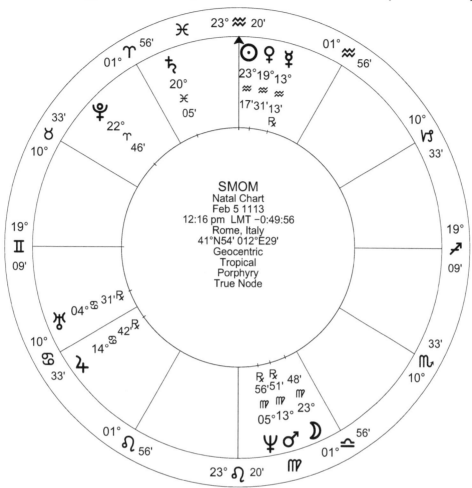

**SMOM, February 5, 1113, 12:16 p.m. LMT, Rome, Italy**
**Source: The Internet; noontime presumed**

SMOM is the world's smallest self-governing territory; it occupies an office building in downtown Rome, Italy. This country has a mailing address. SMOM issues its own passports, coins, postage stamps and license plates. It has diplomatic relations with 80 nations which regard SMOM as a sovereign state. Its full name is Sovereign Military Holy Order of St. John of Jerusalem, of Rhodes and of Malta.

The Order of St. John was founded in the late 11th century. With the Bull Pie Postulatio Voluntatis of February 5, 1113, the Papacy approved of the order which had established a hospital for pilgrims in Jerusalem. Military protection for those pilgrims journeying to the Holy Land to ward off bandits occurred sometime in the early 12th century. Members of this order required they be knights or sons of knights.

After the defeat of the Christian Kingdom of Jerusalem in 1291, the order transferred its headquarters to Cyprus (progressed MC semisquare Jupiter/Uranus; progressed ASC sextile Mars trine Jupiter). By

August 1310, the order had moved to the island of Rhodes (progressed MC conjunct Neptune; progressed ASC trine Saturn). The Turks expelled the order from Rhodes in December 1522 (progressed MC semisquare Sun inconjunct Neptune). On March 23, 1530, Malta was granted to the Knights of St. John as a fiefdom (progressed MC inconjunct Mars square Jupiter). During the summer of 1565, the Turks laid siege to Malta (progressed MC square Venus semisquare Uranus).

Grand Masters of the Knights of St. John of Malta were made princes of the Holy Roman Empire in 1607 and by 1630 had achieved the title of "eminence"(progressed MC trine Saturn; progressed ASC trine Venus). The French under Napoleon occupied Malta in June 1798 and expelled the Knights of St. John (progressed MC square Neptune sesquare Pluto). The British ousted the French in September 1800 (progressed ASC sextile Pluto). Britain made Malta a Crown Colony in 1814 (progressed MC sextile Sun trine Pluto).

The Order was recognized by the Treaty of Verona of December 14, 1822. The Order moved its headquarters to the Palazzo di Malta in Rome in 1834. A constitution was framed June 24, 1961 (progressed MC sextile Saturn square Venus) and autonomy was granted to the Order in 1966 (progressed MC trine Moon; progressed ASC semisquare Jupiter). The Sovereign Military Order of Malta was granted permanent observer status in the United Nations August 24, 1994 (progressed MC sextile Pluto; progressed ASC conjunct Moon inconjunct Sun and Pluto).

# Spain
## Reino de Espana

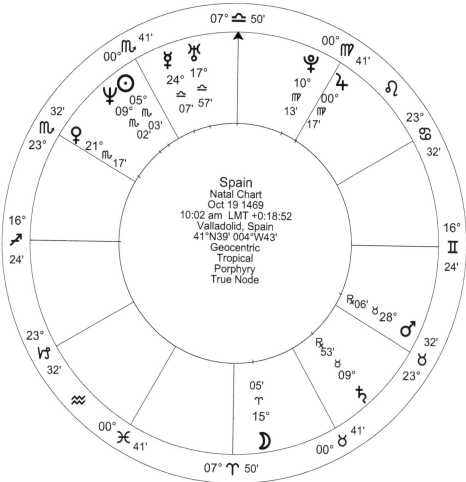

Spain
Natal Chart
Oct 19 1469
10:02 am  LMT +0:18:52
Valladolid, Spain
41°N39' 004°W43'
Geocentric
Tropical
Porphyry
True Node

**Chart 1, October 19, 1469, 10:02 a.m. LMT, Valladolid**
**Source: Spanish Royal Archives says 10:00 a.m.; chart rectified**

Spain occupies 85 percent of the Iberian peninsula in southwest Europe. It is bordered by the Atlantic Ocean in the northwest, the Bay of Biscay and the Pyrenees Mountains on its north and by the Mediterranean on its eastern and southern flanks. Gibraltar, a British colony, lies only 10 miles from North Africa. Spain's interior is called La Meseta, or Castile, a high plateau. The northern provinces are Galicia, Leon, Navarre, Asturias, Vizcaya, Guipizcoa and Catalonia. The Costa Brava runs from Barcelona to the French border. The southern regions are Valencia, Murcia, Extramadura and Andalusia, the hottest part of Spain and Europe. The main rivers are the Guadalquivir, Ebro, Duero, Tagus and Guadiana. Spain's coastline is 3,085 miles long. Main mountain ranges are the Pyrenees and the Sierra Nevada. The highest point is Mulhacen (elevation 11,477 feet). The Costa del Sol runs from Almeria to Algeciras.

Spain also has dominion over the Balearic Islands (1,936 square miles) which include Majorca, Minorca and Ibiza in the Mediterranean. The Canary Islands (2,808 square miles) lie 60 miles off the African coast. Spain also controls the enclaves of Ceuta and Melilla in the nation of Morocco.

Population: 40,037,995; 7% Castilian, 16% Galician, 3% Basque

Religion: 98% Catholic, 2% Moslem

Area: 194,884 square miles (about 25% smaller than France or 30% larger than California); 30% arable, 77% urban

Economy: Main exports are footwear, textiles, clothing, furniture, chemicals and transportation equipment. Spain is Europe's third-largest producer of wine and ranks number one in olives and citrus fruits. Spain has large reserves of iron ore, uranium and coal, and also has 35 percent of the world's supply of mercury.

Spain was settled around 3000 B.C. by the Iberians. Two thousand years later, the Phoenicians settled around Cadiz. During the 6th century B.C., Greeks began colonizing the Mediterranean coast about the same time the Celts first arrived. Romans conquered Iberia in 206 B.C. and drove out the Carthaginians and then ruled Iberia for the next six centuries.

Invasions by the Suevi, Alans, Vandals and Visigoths caused the Romans to flee in 411 A.D., and Toledo was made capital of their kingdom. After a dispute over the Visigothic right to succession in 711 A.D., Moslems (Moors) from North Africa were asked to quell the revolt. The Moors crossed the Straits of Gibraltar in the summer of 711 and invaded Andalusia before ousting the Visigoths entirely. Charles Martel stopped the Moslem advance at Tours in 732 A.D. or European history would have been considerably different.

Charlemagne conquered Barcelona in 801 A.D. and El Cid, Spain's national hero, drove the Moors from Toledo in 1085 and from Valencia nine years later. Portugal declared its independence from Spain in June 1128, but their sovereignty wasn't recognized until October 1143. Cordoba was captured from the Moors in 1236, Seville in 1248. The provinces of Castile and Leon were united in 1246 and Aragon and Valencia in 1309.

With the marriage of Ferdinand of Aragon to Isabella of Castile on October 19, 1469, those two kingdoms were united, thus forming the birth of modern Spain (chart 1). Their "Catholic Majesties" founded the infamous Inquisition in January 1480 (progressed Sun inconjunct Moon; progressed MC conjunct Uranus; progressed ASC sextile Mercury semisquare Neptune). The Moors were finally driven out of Spain with the surrender of Granada in January 1492 (progressed MC sextile Jupiter; progressed ASC sextile Sun). Jews were ordered to either convert to Catholicism or depart the country by August 3, 1492, the very day that Columbus sailed for the New World (progressed ASC semisquare Venus).

The Treaty of Tordesillas gave Spain all lands west of a line which ran 370 leagues west of the Azores. Portugal got all lands to the east of that line (progressed Sun square Jupiter). With the ascension of Charles I, a Hapsburg who had married Ferdinand and Isabella's daughter Juana, the Golden Age of Spain began in 1516. Charles became Holy Roman Emperor three years later, the same time that Cortes landed in Mexico and conquered the Aztecs (progressed Sun sesquare Saturn progressed MC opposition Mars; progressed ASC square Sun). Magellan also began his circumnavigation of the world that same year which would result in Spain gaining dominion over the Philippines. Pizarro conquered Peru in 1534 (progressed Sun trine Saturn and Pluto; progressed MC semisquare Mars; progressed ASC square Mars).

The Jesuit order was founded by Ignatius de Loyola in 1540 (progressed MC semisquare Sun; progressed ASC trine Neptune sextile Saturn opposition Pluto). During the reign of Philip II, Spain was the most powerful and wealthiest nation in Europe. The northern provinces of the Netherlands declared their independence in January 1579 (progressed MC trine Mars; progressed ASC opposition Venus) and the following year when the old Portuguese dynasty died out, Spain annexed Portugal for the next six decades. Philip II met his "Waterloo" when he sent an armada to England in the summer of 1588, but he was badly defeated. Philip II was once married to England's Queen Mary I but was truly incensed when her sister, Queen Elizabeth I, had her cousin, Mary Queen of Scots, beheaded for treason in 1587. The armada started with 131 ships and 25,000 seamen but when it sailed back to Spain, it had only 65 ships and 10,000 sailors (progressed Sun trine Sun; progressed MC square Neptune; progressed ASC sesquare Uranus).

Spain's fortunes began to decline dramatically as Britain became the power on the high seas. In 1609, nearly 1 million Moriscos (converted Moslems) were expelled from Spain (progressed MC opposition Jupiter semisquare Moon; progressed ASC trine Mercury semisquare Saturn sesquare Neptune). In 1640, Spain relinquished its hold over Portugal (progressed Sun sesquare Pluto; progressed MC inconjunct Jupiter; progressed ASC square Uranus). In May 1702, the War of the Spanish Succession began when King Louis XIV of France tried to place one of his relatives on the Spanish throne (progressed Sun semisquare Saturn; progressed MC conjunct Mars; progressed ASC semisquare Uranus). As a result of this conflict, the Hapsburgs were out and the Bourbons took over when the war ended in 1713 (progressed Sun sesquare Venus; progressed MC square Pluto).

Spanish supremacy sank to the depths in 1805 when Admiral Horatio Nelson of England trounced the Spaniards at the Battle of Trafalgar (progressed Sun semisquare Venus; progressed MC semisquare Mercury sextile Neptune). Rumblings in the colonies in Latin America began in August 1809 when Ecuador declared its independence (progressed ASC opposition Mars). Mexico followed suit in September 1810 (progressed Sun inconjunct Saturn) along with

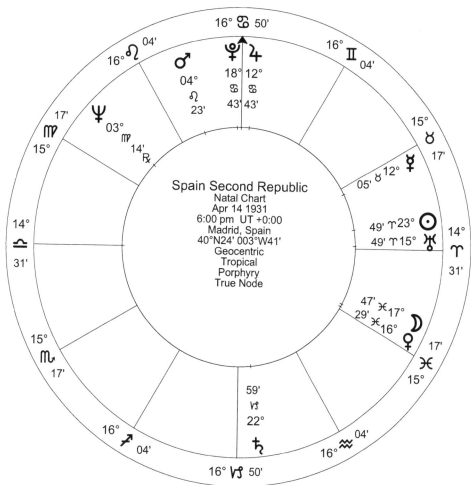

**Chart 2, April 14, 1931, 6:00 p.m. GMT, Madrid**
**Source: Local newspapers**

Argentina, Chile and Colombia. In 1811, Paraguay and Venezuela decided to sever ties with Spain (progressed MC inconjunct Moon; progressed ASC square Jupiter).

In 1814, the Duke of Wellington rid Spain from French domination (progressed Sun opposition Moon; progressed ASC sesquare Moon square Jupiter). In July 1821, Peru declared its independence and the regions of Guatemala, Honduras, El Salvador, Nicaragua and Costa Rica declared themselves free in September 1821 (progressed MC sesquare Saturn semisquare Neptune). With the independence of Bolivia and Uruguay in August 1825, Spain's empire in the New World had been reduced to Cuba and Puerto Rico (progressed Sun semisquare Pluto; progressed MC trine Mars; progressed ASC semisquare Mercury inconjunct Saturn).

In 1833, the Carlist War erupted over monarchial succession (progressed MC semisquare Venus; progressed ASC trine Moon). All church lands were confiscated in 1836 (progressed MC inconjunct Saturn; progressed ASC sextile Uranus) and by 1848,

more reforms were demanded (progressed ASC inconjunct Mars). Military rule ended in Spain in 1868 (progressed ASC square Moon sesquare Jupiter). On February 11, 1873 the first Spanish Republic was born (progressed ASC sextile Venus) but it lasted only one year.

Jose Marti began the Cuban revolution in 1895 (progressed Sun semisquare Venus; progressed MC inconjunct Saturn square Pluto; progressed ASC square Venus). After a brief war with the United States in 1898, Spain lost Cuba, Puerto Rico, Guam and the Philippines to the Americans (progressed Sun sextile Neptune; progressed ASC square Mars). Spain's empire in the Americas was finished.

Spain decided to remain neutral in August 1914 when World War I began (progressed Sun sesquare Pluto; progressed MC inconjunct Mars; progressed ASC sextile Mars; transiting Uranus square Saturn; Neptune trine MC; Neptune trine Mars). Primo de Rivera declared himself dictator in 1923 and was unopposed by the King Alfonso XIII (progressed Sun square Sun). The second Spanish Republic was declared on April l4, 1931 and the new government attempted to exile the Jesuits and to separate the church from the state (transiting Uranus conjunct Moon).

## Spain Second Republic

The Republic (chart 2) destroyed all parochial, or religious, education and removed the Army from the political arena. It also founded modern labor conditions, made much-needed agrarian reforms and gave autonomy to Catalonia, Galicia and the Basques. Anarchists found the reforms too mild and numerous churches were set ablaze. Strikes became more and more frequent.

Note the difficulty in the chart for the Republic. The Sun squares Saturn, indicative of hatred or aversion to old ways and outmoded authority demigods. Jupiter (religion) and Pluto (renovation or destruction) bracket the MC which squares Uranus (revolution). The Moon (ruler of the MC) and Venus (ruler of the ASC) conjunct each other and trine the MC and Pluto, but they're made weak by their placement in a cadent house. Note also that Neptune (idealism) semisquares Pluto (radicalism) and sesquares the Sun/Uranus midpoint, and the Moon sesquares Mars (violence) as well.

Elections were held in February 1936, which promoted an alliance between Socialists, Liberals and Communists (progressed MC opposition Saturn; progressed ASC square Pluto semisquare Neptune). In July 1936, the Spanish Civil War began with a military coup led by Generalissimo Francisco Franco (transiting Mars square ASC; Saturn trine Uranus). The coup was supported by the Carlists, rich landowners, the Church and the Falangists. Republicans and most workers were against the war. Franco received military support from Nazi Germany, Fascist Italy and Communist Russia. The civil war ended in March 1939 (progressed Sun semisquare Venus; progressed MC square Sun). More than 300,000 Spaniards had lost their lives (100,000 were murdered and 200,000 were starved), 240,000 were imprisoned and over 300,000 Republicans were exiled. Over 4 percent of Spain's people were no more as Franco took over the reins of power. With such disaster and calamity, it was no surprise when Spain decided to stay out of World War II when it broke out in September 1939 (transiting Jupiter trine Mars; transiting Neptune trine Saturn; Pluto sesquare Moon and Venus).

A referendum was held in July 1947 which approved a return to the Spanish monarchy when Franco passed away (progressed MC sesquare Moon and Venus; transiting Jupiter trine Moon and Pluto;

Uranus sextile Sun). Spain ended its protectorate over Morocco in March 1956 (progressed MC square Mercury; progressed ASC square Mars sextile Neptune). In July 1969, Juan Carlos was designated to be the future monarch when the "provisional government" passed into oblivion. That occurred in November 1975 when Franco died and the monarchy was restored (progressed Sun sesquare Saturn; progressed MC sesquare Uranus; progressed ASC sesquare Mars inconjunct Pluto; transiting Jupiter opposition ASC conjunct Uranus; Uranus square Mars).

The Spanish monarchy was restored November 22, 1975 at 12:45 p.m. MET in Madrid when Juan Carlos ascended the throne (Source: *New York Times* and the *Guardian*). Progressing the angles of the 1469 horoscope shows the Sun sextile Mars and the MC was semisquare the Moon and opposing Jupiter. In 1978, Spain was made a Parliamentary Monarchy. In January 1980, the regions of Catalonia, Galicia and the Basque provinces became autonomous (progressed MC trine Sun; progressed ASC sextile Jupiter).

Spain joined the European Union in January 1986 (progressed MC opposition Pluto; progressed ASC trine Sun; transiting Mars opposition Saturn; Jupiter trine Uranus). To honor the 500th anniversary of Columbus' discovery of the New World, Spain hosted both the Summer Olympics in Barcelona and a World's Fair in Seville during the summer of 1992 (progressed Sun semisquare Mars; progressed ASC sextile Saturn and Pluto and trine Neptune). In 2000, race riots broke out in Andalusia against the Moslems and the Basques renewed attacks for complete independence.

In March 2004, terrorists belonging to Al Qaeda blew up commuter trains in Madrid during the morning rush hour (progressed MC trine Mars; progressed ASC square Uranus). Two years later, in March 2006, the Basque terrorist group (ETA) declared a permanent cease-fire (progressed MC inconunct Jupiter).

## Madrid

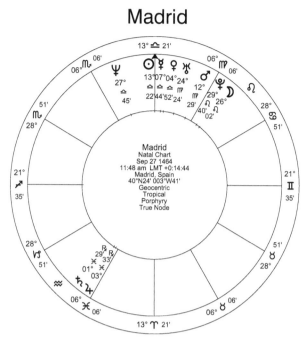

**September 27, 1464, 11:48 a.m. LMT**
**Source: Archivo Historical Nacional**

## Barcelona

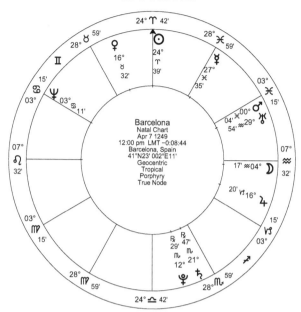

**April 7, 1249, noon LMT**
**Source: Ayuntamiento**

The capital and largest city of Spain is located in the center of the country in the province of Castile. Founded as a Moorish fortress in the 9th century and called Medshrid, the Castillians ousted the Moors in 1083 under Alfonso VI. Only in 1561 did Madrid become the capital of Spain. Occupied by the French in 1808, it boomed soon after with the arrival of the railroads. During the 1930s, Madrid was the heart of the Second Spanish Republic and a major battlefield for control of the country during the Spanish Civil War.

The chief sights in Madrid are the Plaza Mayor, completed in 1620, and The Prado, an art museum second to none. The Palacio Real and the Parque del Retiro are also popular. The Centro de Arte Reina Sofia houses Picasso's huge mural of Guernica which describes the Nazi bombing of that town during the Civil War. The Museum Thyssen Bornemisza is also popular with art lovers.

Near Madrid is a structure called El Escorial where King Philip II resided during the glory days of the 16th century. Toledo, made famous by El Greco, lies south of the city and manages to retain its medieval appearance. Segovia with its Roman aqueduct is northwest of Madrid.

Madrid is Spain's second-largest industrial center (after Barcelona) and is a major aircraft center.

Spain's second-largest city and greatest seaport lies on the Mediterranean coast in northeast Spain near the French border. It's also the capital of Catalonia. Founded more than 2,000 years ago by Barca from Carthage, during the Spanish Civil War it was a bastion of Republicanism. In 1992, it hosted the Summer Olympics.

The heart of Barcelona is the Barrio Gotico constructed in the Middle Ages. Between the old city and the newer sections of town are the Ramblas, a series of five streets lined with numerous cafes and bookstalls. The most famous parks are Cuitadella, in which the Parliament and Modern Art Museum are located, and Montjuic, a high hill housing the Castel. Barcelona was the home of noted architect, Antonio Gaudi, whose Catedral Sagrada Familia, begun in 1883 and still uncompleted, is the most famous monument in Barcelona. Outside the city is the monastery of Montserrat and the mountain called Tibidado. Barcelona is the number-one industrial and manufacturing center of Spain and is a major oil refining center.

# Bilbao

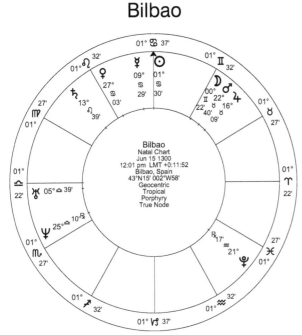

**June 15, 1300, 12:01 p.m. LMT**
**Source: Ayuntamiento**

Located seven miles south of the Bay of Biscay, Bilbao is the largest port of northern Spain as well as its leading banking center. Bilbao is the capital of the province of Vizcaya and is a major shipbuilding center.

# Granada

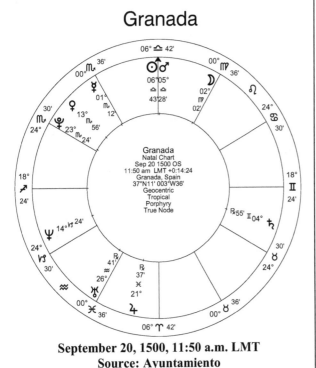

**September 20, 1500, 11:50 a.m. LMT**
**Source: Ayuntamiento**

Granada is situated 120 miles northeast of Gibraltar in Andalusia. Famous for its Moorish architecture such as the Alhambra, built in 1248, and the Generalife, a summer palace. From the 11th century until January 3, 1492, Granada was capital of the longest-lasting Moorish empire in Europe. Its 16th-century Cathedral once had the tombs of Ferdinand and Isabella in the Capilla Real. Granada is heart of flamenco, a style of dance introduced centuries ago by the Arabs.

## Malaga

Located on the southern Mediterranean coast near the resorts of Torremolinos and Marbella, it was founded by the Phoenicians. The Romans called it Malaca. The main attraction is the 11th-century fortress of Alcazaba. Malaga is primarily a port city.

## Murcia

Located 110 miles south of Valencia, to the Romans it was known as Vergilia. The Moors were ousted in 1263 after two centuries of rule. Murcia is today an industrial city and mines iron ore and zinc.

## Seville

Seville is Spain's fourth-largest city, the largest port and industrial center of Andalusia. Located on the Guadalquivir river, it was known to the ancients as Hispalis. The Visigoths who had ruled the region were ousted by the Arabs in 712 who then held sway for half a millennium. By the 16th century, Seville had a monopoly on trade with the New World. The most famous site in town is the 13th-century cathedral, the largest Gothic structure in the world. Its tower, called the Giralda, is nearly 400 feet high. The Alcazar, which was rebuilt in the 14th century, and the Jewish quarter of Santa Cruz are also popular. The best time to visit Seville is during Semana Santa (Holy Week) while the worst time is in the summer as Seville has the highest temperatures in Europe. Seville hosted a World's Fair in 1992 to honor Columbus' discovery of the New World.

# Valencia

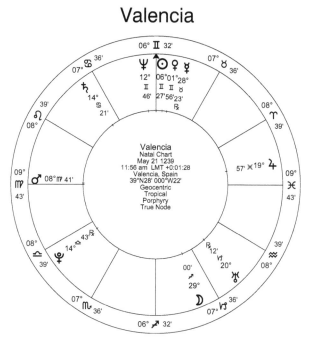

**May 21, 1239, 11:56 a.m. LMT**
**Source: Archivo del Reino**

# Zaragosa

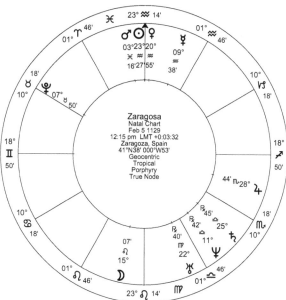

**February 5, 1129, 12:15 p.m.**
**Source: El Alcalde**

Spain's third-largest city lies on the Mediterranean and is a popular seaside resort with miles of beaches and seven famous gardens. Valencia was captured by El Cid from the Moors in 1094 but the Moors retook it eight years later. The Moors were finally ousted in 1253. Between 1238 and 1469 it was the capital of the Kingdom of Valencia and it was the last Republican city to fall to Franco in 1939. Valencia is also a cultural center with 18 museums as well as a major center for iron and steel, shipbuilding, railways, chemicals and food processing.

Situated on the Ebro River 170 miles northeast of Madrid, Zaragosa is Spain's fifth-largest city. The Phoenicians settled the region and called it Salduba while the Romans named it Caesaraugusta. From 712 until 1118 it was under Arab (Moorish) rule and called Saraqustah. From the time in 1469 when Ferdinand and Isabella's marriage united Spain into one country until 1561, Zaragosa was the capital of Spain until the Court moved to Madrid.

# Sweden
## Konungariket Sverige

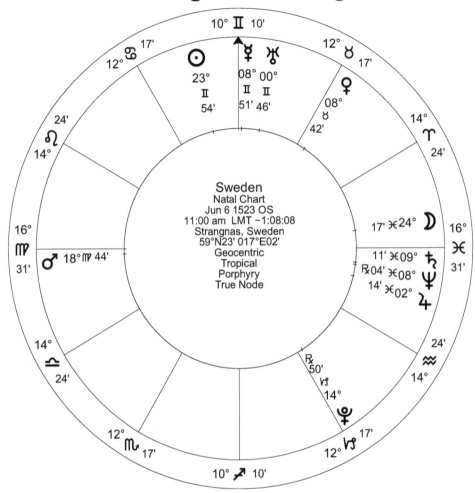

**June 6, 1523, 11:00 a.m. LMT, Strangnas**
**Source: Astrologer Monica Werneman says between 10:30 and 11:00 a.m.**

Occupying the eastern half of the Scandinavian peninsula, Sweden is bordered by the Seas of Bothnia and the Baltic. Mountains cover the north, while the center, called Svealand, is flat and rolling terrain. The south, called Gotland, is highly forested. Sweden has more than 10,000 lakes, the largest being Vanern, Vattern and Malaren. Sweden's coastline is more than 2,000 miles long and offshore lie 20,000 islands. The highest point is Kebnekaise (elevation 6,946 feet).

Religion: 94% Lutheran, 4% Moslem

Population: 8,875,053; 89% Swedish; 2% Finnish; 1% Lapp

Area: 173,731 square miles (the size of Spain or California); 83% urban, 7% arable

Economy: Main exports are lumber and paper products, (10 percent of world), iron ore, steel, automobiles and furniture. Chief resources are zinc, lead, copper and silver. Sweden is also the world's second-largest shipbuilder.

Viking raids along the northern shores of Europe began in the 8th century and in 826 A.D., Ansgar introduced Christianity to Sweden. By 862 A.D., Varangians had established the first Russian state. Finland was conquered by Sweden in 1155 and a century later, in 1250, Birger Jarl made peace with the Hanseatic League and founded Stockholm. Sweden was joined to Norway from 1319 to 1365 and then with Denmark after the Union of Kalmar was founded in 1397.

Sweden revolted against Danish rule in 1435 and established its own Parliament, the Riksdag. The King of Denmark executed many Swedish nationalists in 1520 in what has come to be known as the Stockholm massacre.

On June 6, 1523, Sweden seceded from the Union

of Kalmar and elected Gustavus Vasa as its first monarch. Four years later, Lutheranism became the state religion (progressed ASC conjunct Mars). In 1537, Sweden was victorious against the Hanseatic of Lubeck thus ending that league's monopoly on trade in the Baltic (progressed Sun trine Neptune, progressed MC conjunct Sun and progressed ASC square Moon). Beginning in 1563, Sweden went to war against Denmark for the next 97 years (progressed Sun inconjunct Jupiter; progressed MC sextile Mars and sesquare Jupiter).

The Thirty Years War pitted Catholic against Protestant in 1618 (progressed Sun opposition Moon; progressed ASC sextile Pluto). Gustavus Adolphus began his drive to conquer the Baltic in 1621 (progressed MC trine Pluto; progressed ASC sesquare Uranus). The first Swedish settlement in America was based in Delaware in April 1638 (progressed Sun square Pluto; progressed MC trine Uranus; progressed ASC trine Moon). By the end of the 30 years War in 1648, Sweden was indeed the dominant power in the Baltic and was given Pomerania, now in northern Poland (progressed Sun trine Sun inconjunct Moon sesquare Mercury and Saturn; progressed ASC square Jupiter). The conflict with Denmark ended in 1660 (progressed MC sesquare Neptune; progressed ASC square Saturn).

With the rise of Peter the Great of Russia, Sweden felt threatened as Peter wanted ports on the Baltic that belonged to Sweden. The Great Nordic War began in 1697 with Sweden against Russia, Denmark, Norway and Poland (progressed MC opposition Uranus semisquare Pluto). In 1700, a coalition between Russia, Poland and Denmark forced Sweden to cede Estonia and Livonia to Russia (progressed MC square Jupiter; progressed ASC conjunct Pluto). Sweden lost further territory in 1709 after Russia won the Battle of Poltava (progressed ASC trine Uranus). Sweden lost Finland to Russia in 1716 (progressed MC square Mars) but Sweden regained Finland in 1788 (progressed MC conjunct Jupiter). But Russia took back Finland in September 1809 (progressed MC square Sun; progressed ASC sextile Uranus).

In 1810, internal dissent over the question of monarchial succession forced Sweden to import Count Bernadotte, one of Napoleon's marshals, to be the future King of Sweden (progressed Sun sextile Mercury; progressed MC square Moon). In January 1814, Sweden was granted dominion over Norway as punishment to the Danes which sided with Napoleon against the British (progressed ASC semisquare Mars inconjunct Jupiter). From that point to this day, Sweden has remained neutral in all conflicts, European or otherwise, Count Bernadotte "became King in 1818.

Primary schools were established in 1842 (progressed Sun trine Saturn conjunct Venus). Sweden's labor party was founded in 1888 (progressed Sun conjunct Sun square Moon). Sweden lost Norway in June 1905 when Norway decided to sever its union with Sweden (progressed Sun sextile Venus trine Saturn). Old age pensions, unemployment insurance and other welfare measures were first enacted in 1911 (progressed Sun opposition Pluto; progressed MC trine Jupiter; progressed ASC trine Uranus).

Sweden remained neutral when World War I broke out in August 1914 (progressed Sun sextile Mars; transiting Uranus square Venus; Pluto trine Jupiter). Sweden also remained neutral in May 1940 despite the fact that its neighbors, Denmark and Norway, were being overrun by German troops (progressed MC sextile Uranus; transiting Neptune square Sun; Pluto semisquare ASC). Sweden profited handsomely by supplying materials to both the Allied and the Axis sides.

The Salic Law of Primogeniture was abrogated in 1978 to allow future monarchs to reign if no male heir survived. In February 1986, Prime Minister Olav Palme was assassinated on the streets of Stockholm (progressed ASC equals Saturn/Pluto midpoint; transiting Saturn square Saturn opposition Mercury; Uranus square Sun/Mars). Voters in 1991 demanded that the government cut taxes and limit welfare benefits; Sweden had the highest tax rate in the world at that time (progressed Sun inconjunct Jupiter, progressed MC conjunct Mars; progressed ASC sextile Mars).

Sweden finally agreed to join the European Union in January 1995 (progressed MC square Sun sesquare Venus; transiting Jupiter opposition Mercury/Uranus; Saturn sextile Venus square Mercury; Pluto semisquare Pluto). Sweden began to shut down its nuclear power plants two years later. In 2001, Sweden decided not to convert its currency to the Euro.

## Goteborg

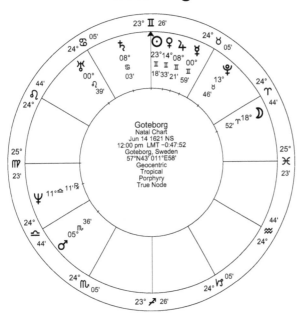

**June 14, 1621 (NS), noon LMT**
**Source: City Library**

Sweden's second-largest city and the largest port in Scandinavia lies on the Kattegat at the mouth of the Gota River. Founded by King Carl IX in 1603, it was designed with numerous canals, possibly to please its numerous Dutch settlers. Goteborg is an ice-free port and a center for ferry traffic from neighboring Denmark. It also has Europe's largest indoor mall and second-largest indoor arena and Scandinavia's largest amusement park.

## Malmo

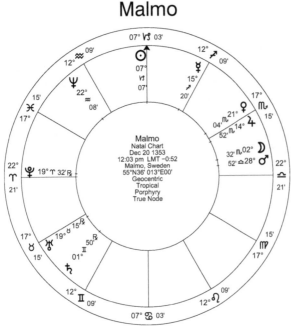

**December 20, 1353, 12:03 p.m. LMT**
**Source: Stadsarkivet**

Sweden's third-largest city lies on the Oresund, a short hop from Denmark which once owned this part of Sweden. Founded in the 12th century as a trading post, Danish rule ended in 1658. Malmo was the place where the Union of Kalmar formally ended in 1524, having united Scandinavia for 127 years.

## Stockholm

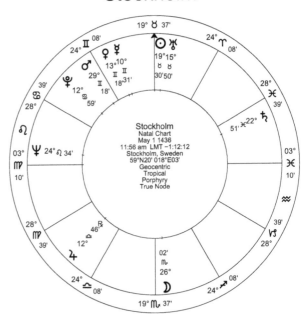

**May 1, 1436, 11:56 a.m. LMT**
**Source: Stadsarkivet**

Stockholm is the capital and largest city of Sweden. Situated on 20 islands in the midst of Lake Malaren in what is termed the Stockholm Archipelago, it's a pleasant blend of urban sophistication next door to rustic lands so dear to the natives. Founded by Birger Jarl in 1250, the central city is composed of the districts of Ostermalm, Norrmalm, Sodermalm and the Gamla Stan.

Stockholm has many museums, the most interesting being the Vasa which displays a ship sunk in 1628 and raised 333 years later. The Drottingholm Palace is the royal residence but the Royal Palace in town is used for formal royal affairs. The Riddarholm Church contains tombs of 200 Swedish kings and nobles and is one of the oldest structures in the city being constructed in 1270. The most distinctive building in Stockholm is the Stadhuset (City Hall) a modern edifice where the Nobel Prizes are awarded each year. Stockholm is surrounded by a greenbelt and parks such as Millesgarden and the Skansen are not to be missed.

# Switzerland
## Schweiz; Suisse; Svizzera

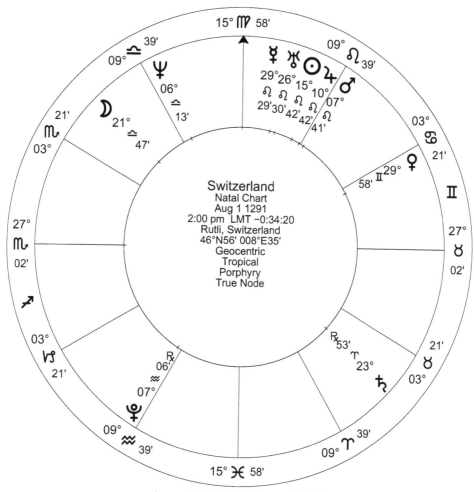

**August 1, 1291, 2:00 p.m. LMT**
Source: *Encyclopedia Britannica* for the date; time is rectified from statements by local historians
which state "during a picnic"

Switzerland is situated in the heart of central Europe, a country famous for the Alps which cover 60 percent of its area. The highest point is Monte Rosa (elevation 15,203 feet) near the Italian border. The Jura Mountains border France; the only flat land, called the Midlands, lies between Lucerne and Geneva. This country has numerous glaciers and more than 1,000 lakes, the largest being Lakes Geneva, Konstanz and Maggiore. Switzerland is also the source of the Rhine and Rhone Rivers. Its most famous peaks include the Eiger, Jungfrau and the most famous peak of all, the Matterhorn.

Switzerland has 23 cantons, all sovereign, while the national government handles the Army, railroads and postal facilities.

Population: 7,283,274; 65% German, 18% French, 10% Italian

Religion: 46% Catholic, 40% Protestant

Area: 15,942 square miles (the size of the Netherlands or New Hampshire and Vermont combined); 68% urban, 10% arable

Economy: Main exports are machinery, chemicals and textiles, watches, clocks, cheese and chocolates. Tourism and 500 banking institutions are the chief sources of income.

In ancient times, this region was known as Helvetia. It was conquered by Julius Caesar in 58 B.C. and when the natives tried to leave, the Romans told them to stay put. Roman occupation ended in 401 A.D. when the Allemanis took the east and the Burgundians took the west. Helvetia was divided between Burgundy and Germany in 814 after the death of Charlemagne, and in 1032, the entire region was inherited by the Holy Roman Empire. Rudolf von

Habsburg was elected Holy Roman Emperor in August 1273, and thus a native son was elected to the highest post in Europe at the time.

On August 1, 1291 the Eternal Pact was signed by delegates from Uri, Schwyz and Unterwalden during a picnic overlooking Lake Lucerne. They rebelled against the Holy Roman Empire which held the region to feudal obligations. It was a favorable time as Rudolf had just died and they decided to take action before another Emperor was elected. The Swiss defended their liberties at the Battle of Morgarten in 1315 (progressed Sun semisquare Saturn) and in 1386, the Holy Roman Empire was fought and in 1388 at the Battle of Nafels, the Austrians were defeated (progressed Sun semisquare Neptune; progressed MC sextile Moon semisquare Pluto). From 1474 to 1477, Switzerland warred against Burgundy (progressed ASC semisquare Mercury).

In 1481, a hermit named Nicholas of Flue suggested that the cantons might try to settle their differences by compromise instead of warfare (progressed Sun opposition Uranus; progressed MC sesquare Jupiter inconjunct Uranus). In 1499, Swiss cantons defeated the Holy Roman Empire and Habsburg rule finally came to an end (progressed MC sesquare Mercury). Swiss troops invaded Italy in 1512 and drove the French from Lombardy (progressed Sun inconjunct Uranus sesquare Jupiter; progressed MC trine Uranus; progressed ASC conjunct Jupiter).

Zwingli established the Swiss Reformation in 1519 (progressed ASC conjunct Sun). The Savoyards were driven out of Geneva in 1530 (progressed Sun sesquare Mercury progressed MC semisquare Venus; progressed ASC trine Saturn). A religious war erupted in 1520 between Protestants and Catholics and Zwingli was killed (progressed MC square Sun). Geneva finally accepted Protestantism in 1536 (progressed MC sesquare Neptune) and John Calvin, an emigre from France, formed a dictatorship over Geneva in 1541 (progressed Sun opposition Saturn).

The Thirty Years War began in 1618, further inflaming religious rivalry (progressed MC conjunct Jupiter). Three decades later when the Treaty of Westphalia was signed, Swiss independence was finally recognized and permanent neutrality assured (progressed Sun conjunct Mars opposition Pluto; progressed MC semisquare Moon sesquare Saturn; progressed ASC semisquare Neptune). An internal religious war, however, broke out in 1656 (progressed Sun conjunct Sun; progressed ASC square Uranus). Hugenots from France emigrated to the western part of Switzerland in 1685 when Louis XIV revoked the Edict of Nantes. Another religious war broke out in 1712 and this time the Protestants won

(progressed Sun sextile Jupiter - progressed MC square Jupiter).

French troops occupied Bern in 1798 and the Helvetic Republic was formed (progressed Sun square Neptune; progressed MC conjunct Pluto opposition Mars; progressed ASC trine Neptune). In 1815, the final cantons around Geneva joined the Swiss Confederation (progressed Sun square Saturn; progressed MC sextile Saturn). The country was politically unified in September 1848 when a Constitution was framed (progressed Sun opposition Uranus; progressed ASC square Moon). A revised Constitution in 1874 gave more power to the central government (progressed Sun sesquare Mars; progressed MC conjunct Saturn).

Due to its topography, Switzerland was isolated from the rest of southern Europe. In 1872, the St. Gotthard tunnel was begun through the Alps and the Simplon Tunnel to Italy was completed in 1906. Switzerland remained neutral in August 1914 when World War I began (progressed ASC sesquare Saturn; transiting Saturn conjunct Venus; Neptune trine ASC; Pluto semisquare Sun). After the Treaty of Versailles was signed in 1919, the League of Nations was formed with its headquarters in Geneva (progressed Sun square Mars). In 1934, the Bank Secrecy Law was enacted (progressed Sun inconjunct Moon square Neptune; progressed MC trine Moon semisquare Mars sesquare Pluto; progressed ASC semisquare Mars inconjunct Saturn).

When World War II erupted in September 1939, Switzerland again decided to remain neutral (progressed Sun square Uranus; progressed MC sextile Uranus). Unknown to the Allies, Swiss banks were funding the Nazis and hoarding deposits made by Jews inside Germany, thinking their funds would be safe in Switzerland. True to its Scorpio nature, Swiss bankers played dumb and refused to answer queries about those deposits.

Women were finally given the right to vote in 1971 (progressed Sun sextile Uranus; progressed ASC conjunct Moon). In August 1990, the Bank Secrecy Act was overturned, thus enabling foreign governments to more easily track the flow of funds from individuals and countries seeking to launder their profits through secretive Swiss banks (progressed MC conjunct Sun; progressed ASC square Pluto). A law in 1994 banned heavy trucks on Swiss highways and put a moratorium on highway construction for a decade (progressed ASC square Mars and Pluto). Switzerland also rejected participation in U.N. peacekeeping forces.

The Swiss/Nazi collaboration scandal broke in February 1997 and many Holocaust survivors sought compensation for deposits made prior to and during World War II (progressed Sun square Moon; progressed MC sextile Moon semisquare Neptune; progressed ASC square Jupiter). By August 1998, Switzerland agreed to pay $1.5 billion in reparations (transiting Jupiter and Uranus conjunct Pluto opposition Mars trine Neptune; Pluto sextile Neptune). In March 2001, Switzerland said no to joining the European Union (progressed MC conjunct Uranus) but it did agree to becoming the 190th member of the United Nations in September 2002 (progressed ASC sesquare Venus). The Swiss army was also reduced by 40 percent at this time and immigration to Switzerland became more restricted.

## Basel (Basle)

The second-largest city in Switzerland is located on the Rhine River and is thus the nation's largest port. Founded by the Romans as Basilia, the first university in Switzerland was founded here in 1460. The main sights are the Munster, a huge 12th-century cathedral and the Markplatz which fronts the Rathaus (City Hall).

## Bern (Berne)

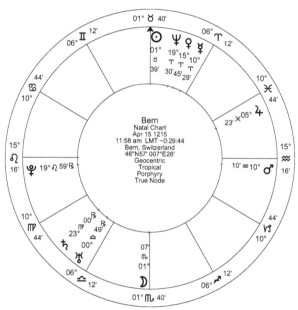

**April 15, 1215, 11:58 a.m.**
**Source: Stadtarchiv**

The capital and fourth-largest city of Switzerland is located on a bend in the Aare River. Founded as a fortress in 1191, it was made a free Imperial town in 1218. Capital of Switzerland only since 1848, its most famous sights are the famed Clock Tower, the bear pit (the city's name means bear) and the Munster, the biggest church in town. There's also the

house where in 1905 Einstein formulated his first theory of relativity while working as a civil servant.

## Geneva (Geneve, Genf)

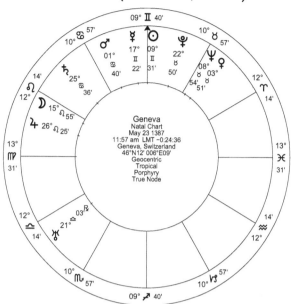

**May 23, 1387, 11:57 a.m. LMT**
**Source: Archives de l'Etat**

Switzerland's third-largest city and center for its French-speaking populace is situated at the western end of Lac Leman (Geneva) where the Rhone River drains the lake. Founded by the Romans in the 1st century A.D., it was an independent community during the Middle Ages. During the 15th century, it became a financial center due to the power of its merchant class. Over the following century at the birth of the Reformation, Geneva became home to reformers like Zwingli and Calvin. From 1401 to 1603, Geneva was part of the Kingdom of Savoy and was seized by the French in 1798; it joined the Swiss Confederation only in 1815.

After World War I, Geneva assumed international importance as headquarters for the League of Nations; it's also the second home to the United Nations. The World Health Organization and the International Labor Organization are also based here. Geneva's also the home to the International Red Cross founded here in 1864.

The main attractions in Geneva are the Jardin Anglais with its huge flower clock and the 12th-century Cathedral of St. Pierre. The symbol of Geneva, however, is the Jet d'Eau, a fountain that shoots water 475 feet into the air. The drive along the shores of Lake Geneva will allow you to see some of the most opulent and majestic mansions in the country and on clear days, one may also see Mont Blanc, the highest peak in western Europe just over the border with France.

# Zurich

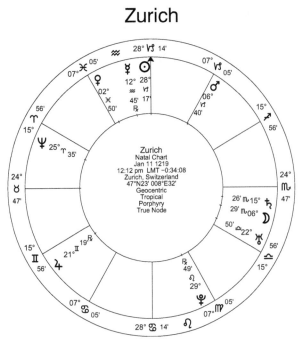

**January 11, 1219, 12:12 p.m. LMT**
**Source: Stadtarchiv**

The largest city in Switzerland and heart of its German-speaking residents lies at the north end of Lake Zurich where it meets the Limmat River. Founded by the Romans in 15 B.C. and known as Turicum, it became part of the Swiss Confederation in 1351. During the Protestant Reformation, Zwingli was based here before he was killed. Zurich is the financial and commercial heart of the country if not of Europe as well. The main sights in Zurich are the Grossmunster with its two towers and the Fraumunster. The 12th century Town Hall is quite impressive as is the Peterskirche with the largest clock dial in Europe. For museum lovers, there's the Kunsthaus and the Swiss National Museum.

# Turkey
# Turkiye Cumhuriyeti

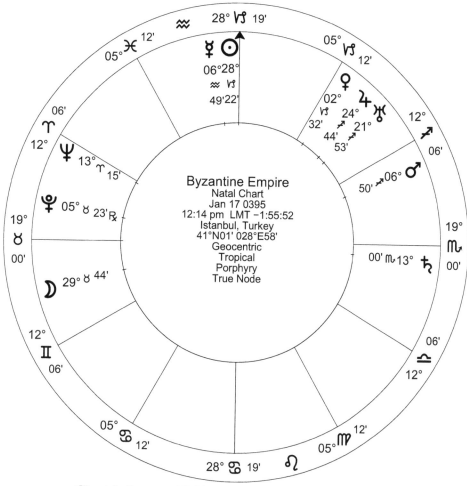

Chart 1, January 17, 395 A.D., 12:14 p.m. LMT, Istanbul
Source: Encyclopedia Britannica for the date; noon assumed

## Byzantine Empire

Located at the juncture of Europe and Asia, Turkey is bordered by the Black Sea on the north, the Aegean Sea on the west and the Mediterranean Sea on the south. Continentally, it's separated by the Bosporous, the Sea of Marmara and the Dardanelles (Hellespont). The coastline is 4,471 miles long. The European part of Turkey is called Thrace (9,121 square miles) while its Asian part is called Anatolia, or Asia Minor, a wide and treeless plateau surrounded by mountains. The highest point is Mt. Ararat (elevation 16,945 feet).

Population: 66,493,970; 80% Turkish, 13% Kurdish

Religion: 99% Moslem

Area: 301,382 square miles (larger than Texas and 50% larger than France); 34% arable, 74% urban

Economy: Main exports are cotton, tobacco, citrus, olives and carpets. Main resources are antimony, coal, chromium, mercury and copper. Unfortunately, the largest cash crop are illegal drugs like hashish and heroin.

By the 20th century B.C., Asia Minor had become the seat of the vast Hittite empire which lasted until the Assyrians conquered it in the 14th century B.C. By 687 B.C., Anatolia had become part of the Persian empire under Cyrus the Great and Darius. Greeks came in 334 B.C., when Alexander the Great of Macedon conquered the area on his way to the Orient. By the 1st century A.D., most of Anatolia was part of the Roman Empire.

Emperor Constantine decided to build a new capital for the Roman Empire on the site of the ancient Greek city of Byzantium. The foundation stone was laid in November 326 A.D. and this new city which

169

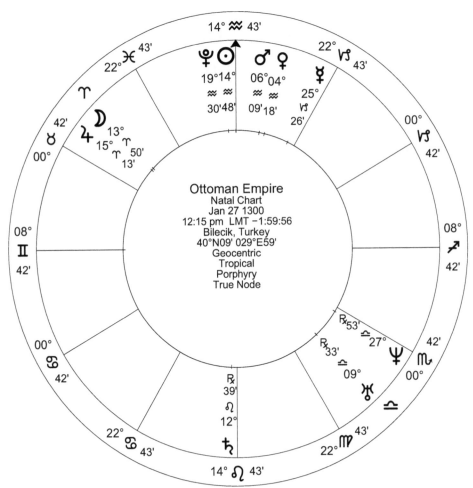

**Chart 2, January 27, 1300, 12:15 p.m. LMT, Bilecik, Turkey**
**Source: Astrologer Hakan Kirkoglu, from Istanbul**

he named after himself, called Constantinople, was dedicated in May 330 A.D. As the Roman Empire was simply too vast and unwieldy, it was divided on January 17, 395 A.D. and thus was the Byzantine Empire founded which would last for more than a thousand years until it was overrun by the Ottomans.

Moslems invaded Turkey in the 7th century and converted its churches into mosques. Anatolia was taken by the Seljuk Turks in 1038 and the Byzantines surrendered to them in 1071. Meanwhile, there was dissent inside the Roman Church, and those differences resulted in the Great Schism of July 1054 which permanently separated the Roman Catholic Church from the Eastern Orthodox whose influence extended throughout the Balkans into Russia and Anatolia.

In 1204, Crusaders attacked Constantinople on their way to the Holy Land, looting and pillaging everything in sight. Shortly after, Mongols invaded from the steppes of Asia. Inside Turkey, a man named Osman was beginning to conquer lands previously held by the Byzantines by the end of the 13th century.

## Ottoman Empire

(chart 2) The Ottomans captured the city of Bursa April 6, 1326 and made it their capital (MC semisquare Mercury; ASC sesquare Pluto). The capital was moved to Edirne in 1361 (MC conjunct Jupiter). Turks fought the Serbs at the battle of Kosovo in June 1389 (MC square Sun) and four years later, Bulgaria became part of their emerging empire (ASC opposition Mercury semisquare Uranus). The Byzantine Empire finally capitulated to the Ottomans on May 29, 1453 when the city of Constantinople surrendered (MC square Jupiter; ASC opposition Moon). No longer would Europe be the bastion of Christianity as Muslims were now taking over the Balkans.

Greece fell in 1460 (ASC trine Pluto) Bosnia in 1463 (MC opposition Mercury) Albania in 1468 (ASC square Mercury) and Wallachia (modern Romania) in 1476. In 1526, the Ottomans captured Hungary and laid siege to Vienna (MC trine Mercury), threatening the Hapsburg domains. The Ottoman naval fleet was defeated at Lepanto in October

1571 and Ottoman power waned afterwards. The Turks again laid siege to Vienna in July 1683 and would have captured that city had not troops arrived from Poland at the last minute (ASC semisquare Saturn trine Neptune). Upon their departure, the Ottomans left behind sacks of a new beverage to Europeans called coffee, and the rest as they say is history. The Ottomans were finally ousted from Hungary in 1699 (MG semisquare Venus; ASC square Uranus).

Catherine the Great, Tsarina of Russia, was also seeking to expand her empire when she went to war with the Turks in 1774 (ASC inconjunct Mars) and The Ottomans lost the Crimea. The Serbs revolted in 1804 and the Greeks declared their independence in April 1821 (ASC opposition Jupiter). Nine years later in 1830, their freedom was guaranteed (MC square Neptune).

The Crimean War began in April 1853 against Russia (MC opposition Pluto). With British and French assistance, Turkey regained the Crimea and Russia lost its right of passage through the Bosporous from the Black Sea to the Mediterranean. A constitution was framed in 1876 and Turkey got its first Parliament, but the following year, things returned to normal and the Constitution was torn up (MC sesquare Mercury; ASC sesquare Moon). The Russo-Turkish War of 1877 over Bulgaria was occurring at the same time that the Romanians were declaring their independence. The Treaty of Berlin in July 1878 granted independence to Serbia, Bulgaria, and Romania (MC semisquare Neptune; ASC sesquare Moon/Jupiter). Only tiny Albania remained an Ottoman province in Europe.

A student uprising in 1908 restored the Constitution (MC sextile Saturn; ASC semisquare Mars). War against Italy erupted in 1911 (MC trine Sun) and in late November 1912, Albania broke loose from Ottoman control (ASC semisquare Mars/Saturn). Meanwhile, the First Balkan War broke out in October 1912 against its former European provinces and the Second Balkan War erupted in June 1913.

World War I began in August 1914 with Turkey on the Axis side with Germany, Austria and Bulgaria against the rest of Europe (MC trine Pluto). The Turks defended the peninsula of Gallipoli in April 1915 against the Allies, many of whom were from Australia and New Zealand. Deportation of Armenians in eastern Turkey also began in April 1915 which many believe was an attempt to annihilate the Armenians. The British began to free many Middle Eastern countries under Ottoman control in 1916, with the help of Lawrence of Arabia (ASC sesquare Saturn sextile Neptune).

The Turks were still fighting when the Germans signed the Armistice in November 1918. Kemal Ataturk resisted any attempt at Allied occupation of his homeland, much more so after the Greeks invaded Smyrna in September 1919 (ASC semisquare Sun). In August 1920, Ataturk became president of Turkey and the Greeks were driven out of Smyrna and other coastal communities (MG square Mercury). Ataturk separated the religious sector (Caliphate) and the political sector (Sultanate) in November 1922. The Treaty of Lausanne was signed in 1923, ending Turkey's involvement in World War I. Turkey became a Republic in October 1923 (MC conjunct Neptune; ASC semisquare Pluto) ending over six centuries of Ottoman rule.

## Turkey

With the proclamation of the Turkish Republic October 29, 1923 (chart 3), Kemal Ataturk became its first leader. The new capital was now Ankara, the Caliphate was abolished in 1924 and the Greeks and Bulgarians repatriated (progressed MC trine Venus; progressed ASC square Mars sesquare Jupiter). Over the next few years Ataturk completely redesigned Turkish life in his attempt to bring his country into the modern world (progressed ASC conjunct Pluto). Ataturk made the Latin alphabet requisite for writing Turkish, he banned the fez and veil and prohibited religious political parties from having any voice in the government. Like Lenin in Russia, Ataturk pushed Turkey full-force into the 20th century. He also banned polygamy and proclaimed that all religious beliefs would be tolerated and Islam would not become the state religion. Ataturk died in November 1938 (progressed Sun square Neptune; transiting Jupiter square Jupiter; Saturn square Pluto; Pluto sesquare MC).

When World War II began in September 1939, Turkey decided to remain neutral—a wise decision considering its disaster in the previous war (progressed Sun semisquare Mars; progressed MC sesquare Venus; transiting Jupiter inconjunct Sun). In order to become a charter member of the U.N., however, Turkey was forced to declare war on Germany, which it did in February 1945; but Turkey saw no action on the battlefield (progressed Sun sesquare Pluto; progressed MC opposition Mars; progressed ASC trine Jupiter square Mercury and Saturn). In 1950, Turkey joined NATO (progressed MC square Pluto; progressed ASC sesquare Uranus).

Riots broke out on Cyprus in 1955. Britain ruled the island which had a large Greek population with a sizeable Turkish minority (progressed Sun sextile Mars; progressed MC inconjunct Venus). Britain

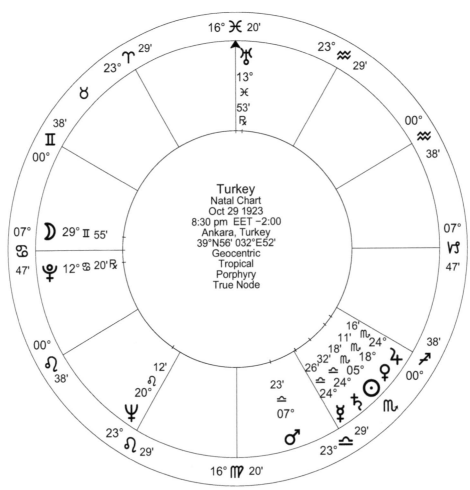

**Chart 3, October 29, 1923, 8:30 p.m. EET, Ankara**
**Source:** *Emergence of Modern Turkey* by Lewis says 8:30 p.m.

granted Cyprus its independence in August 1960 and a military coup executed the old leaders of Turkey (progressed Sun inconjunct Pluto; progressed ASC square Sun; transiting Saturn opposition Pluto; Uranus conjunct Neptune; Pluto sextile Sun; Neptune trine ASC). Martial law was in effect for one year (progressed Sun square Uranus; progressed MC opposition Saturn and Mercury). In 1964, Turkey became an associate member of the European Union (progressed ASC sextile Mars).

After the removal of Archbishop Makarios of Cyprus in July 1974, Turkey invaded that island and gained control of 40 percent of its territory (progressed MC inconjunct Mars; transiting Saturn conjunct Pluto/ASC; Uranus conjunct Mercury/Saturn; Neptune sextile Mars; Pluto semisquare Neptune). Turkish Cypriots established a separate state on the northern part of Cyprus and Turkey took over most of the U.S. bases on that island (progressed ASC square Venus).

Turkey was placed under martial law in 1978 (progressed MC sextile Pluto; progressed ASC conjunct Neptune) and a military government took the helm in September 1980 (transiting Uranus sesquare ASC). The press was censored and over 20,000 Turks became political prisoners (progressed Sun semisquare Venus; progressed ASC semisquare Mars; progressed MC sextile Uranus). Martial law was rescinded in 1984 (progressed Sun square Mars; progressed MC opposition Venus; progressed ASC square Jupiter sextile Mercury and Saturn).

In June 1993, Kurdish rebels demanded an independent state in the eastern part of Turkey and Turkey also got its first female prime minister (progressed MC semisquare Pluto; transiting Mars opposition Jupiter; Jupiter conjunct Sun; Saturn trine Pluto). In June 1997, the pro-Islamic government was forced to resign under pressure from the military (progressed Sun inconjunct Neptune; transiting Mars square Moon; Uranus inconjunct ASC). The Kurdish rebellion ceased after February 1999 when its leader, Ocalan, was captured and sentenced to death (transiting Mars trine ASC; Jupiter square Moon). In 2001, Turkey went through a major financial crisis and the IMF stepped in. The Civil Code was expanded for more rights for women at the same time (progressed Sun sextile Jupiter; progressed ASC semisquare Mercury and Saturn).

In order for Turkey to eventually join the European Union, it will have to adhere more strictly to human rights protocols and to eliminate torturing of suspects and criminals. Turkey will also have to reform the military which has staged three coups in recent years and still dominates the government. Journalists will also have to be freed in a country which has only limited right of free speech and the press. And lastly, the question of its occupation of northern Cyprus will have to be addressed. Turkey has made a few reforms in mid-2003 by increasing freedoms for the minority Kurdish population which can now broadcast their own language over the radio and TV channels. Kurds will also be allowed to give their children Kurdish names and another law was repealed which gave reduced sentences to those who committed "honor crimes," i.e. the killing of women who are accused of bringing shame to their families.

## Istanbul

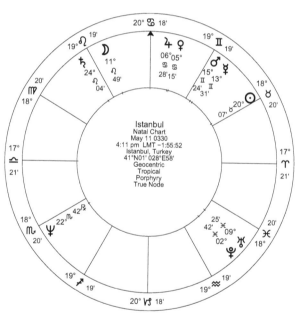

Istanbul
Natal Chart
May 11 0330
4:11 pm LMT –1:55:52
Istanbul, Turkey
41°N01' 028°E58'
Geocentric
Tropical
Porphyry
True Node

**May 11, 330, 4:11 p.m. LMT**
**Source: Istanbul University Library gives**
**the date and time; *Encyclopedia Britannica***
**gives the time of 4:00 p.m.**

Founded in 659 B.C. by Byzas, the city known as Byzantium grew to be the largest city in the eastern Mediterranean by the time Emperor Constantine decided to make it capital of the Roman Empire in 324 A.D. Named after himself, the foundation stone was laid during the hour of the Crab on November 4, 328 and dedicated May 11, 330 at 4:00 p.m. In 381, this city became the seat of Patricarch (progressed ASC square Uranus). In 413, walls were built surrounding

the city on the Golden Horn and in 439 a seawall was constructed. By 537 the fabled Cathedral of St. Sophia was completed but five years later a plague wiped out 20 percent of the populace (ASC square Sun). The Arabs in 675 (MC semisquare Moon) lost their fleet, and Bulgarians tried in 813 to capture the city, as did the Russians three times over the next two centuries.

With the Great Schism in the Church in 1054 (ASC trine Mercury), Constantinople became headquarters for the Eastern Orthodox Church, the Second Rome. In 1097, the First Crusade passed through this city on its way to the Holy Land and in1204, Crusaders sacked and pillaged this glorious port (MC square Uranus; ASC square Sun). By 1302, the district of Galata became a walled fortress.

The chief turning point in the history of modern Constantinople occurred May 29,1453 when the siege by the Ottoman Turks ended (ASC trine Pluto), thus making this a Moslem city and capital of their empire. Santa Sophia was turned into a mosque and Christians left for friendlier climes. Under Suleiman the Magnificent (1520-66), Constantinople rose to new heights of power and glory due to the establishment of the Caliphate (ASC trine Saturn). Over the next four centuries, life was relatively peaceful in this city of nearly a million people. In 1838, the first bridge across the Golden Horn was completed and by 1885, water and sewage line were completed. In 1912, electric lights finally lighted this fabled city that spans two continents.

During World War I, Constantinople was blockaded by the Allies (MC opposition Sun; ASC semisquare Pluto). In 1920, the Sultanate was abolished with the collapse of the Ottoman Empire. The capital was moved to Ankara in 1923 and the Calipate eliminated the following year (ASC inconjunct Jupiter). On March 28,1930, Constantinople was renamed Istanbul which means "downtown" in Greek (MC square Uranus; ASC square Sun). In 1973, the first suspension bridge across the Bosporus was opened (MC trine Sun; ASC sextile Jupiter) thus linking the European side of this city to that on the Asian continent.

Istanbul is located on the Bosporus, the narrow strait which links the Black Sea (19 miles to the north) to the Sea of Marmara which eventually empties into the Aegean Sea after passing through the Dardanelles. Over its long history, this city has been witness to more than 50 earthquakes and 60 fires, although most of its important structures were left intact. Towering over Istanbul are three mosques: Hagia Sophia, the Blue Mosque and the Suleimaniye. At the tip of the Golden Horn lies the

Topkapi Palace containing the famous Seraglio of the Sultans.

Despite the majority of Istanbul lying on the European continent, this city has a decided Oriental flavor. Natives love to sit at the numerous coffee houses sipping the beverage they introduced to the Europeans three centuries ago when they besieged Vienna. Like most eastern cities, Istanbul has a terrible traffic problem as most of its streets are little wider than alleys. The Galata Bridge is the most heavily-used in the world but over the din may be heard the muezzins calling the faithful to prayer four times a day. If ever a city deserved to be called "the Crossroads of the World," Istanbul should be placed close to the top of the list. The Old City has nine square miles, while the New City which spans the Bosporus is 98 square miles in area. The population is close to 3.5 million, most of them Turks but also with a sizeable Greek minority.

# Ankara

Capital and second-largest city of Turkey, Ankara is located in the center of the Anatolian plateau 220 miles east of Istanbul. Founded in the 8th century B.C. as Angora by the Phrygians, it was the capital of the Roman province of Galatia. Capital of Turkey only since 1923, it has grown from a town of 30,000 to a metropolis 100 times that size.

A huge monument to the founder of modern Turkey, Kemal Ataturk, towers over the city. A few structures still remain from Roman times which contrast sharply with the very modern appearance of Ankara. The Archaeological Museum is a treasure trove of Hittite artifacts from a kingdom that ruled this region millenniums ago. Ankara is also famous for its leatherwork and its mohair which comes from the Angora goat for which this city is named.

# Ukraine
## Ukrayina

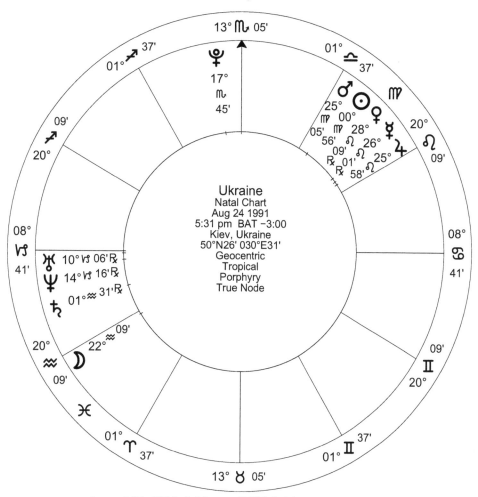

Ukraine
Natal Chart
Aug 24 1991
5:31 pm BAT −3:00
Kiev, Ukraine
50°N26' 030°E31'
Geocentric
Tropical
Porphyry
True Node

**August 24, 1991, 5:31 p.m. BGT, 2:31 p.m. GMT, Kiev**
**Source: AURA, an astrological group in the Ukraine**

Ukraine lies south of Russia bordering the Black Sea. This region has the richest soil on earth, called chernozem, making the Ukraine the breadbasket of the former Soviet Union. The southern part is called Crimea, which is tropical and mediterranean in climate, and in the southwest are the Carpathian Mountains which border Romania. Its west is called Podolia and in the southeast on the border with Russia is the Sea of Azov. The highest point is 6,762 feet above sea level.

Population: 48,760,474; 73% Ukrainian; 22% Russian

Religion: 60% Orthodox; 15% Catholic; 8% Moslem; 2% Jewish

Area: 233,089 square miles (Europe's second-largest and 10% smaller than Texas); 60% arable, 70% urban

Economy: Main exports are iron and steel, food, coal, machinery. Ukraine has large resources of manganese, petroleum and natural gas.

Settled by Ukrainians in the 1st century A.D., this land was invaded by Huns and Avars over the next five centuries. During the 9th century, a major political and cultural center emerged known as the Kievan Rus. In 988 A.D., Vladimir I accepted Christianity thus bringing the Byzantine influence to the vast plains and steppes to the north. The Mongols (Tatars) invaded the region in 1240 and laid waste to the area thus allowing Polish encroachment from the west. In 1653, the Ukraine asked Russia for protection against the Poles, but by 1667, Ukraine had been absorbed into the Russian Empire.

In October 1853, the Crimean War broke out between Russia and the Ottoman Empire over protection rights of Christian holy places in Palestine which the Sultan had agreed to enforce. Britain and France also got involved trying to intercede with the Russians and Turks, but in March 1854, Britain and France had sided with Turkey against Russia. The western allies sent their navies to capture Sevastopol, thus ending Russia's domination of the Black Sea. In December 1855 when Austria threatened to join the conflict on the side of the Allies, Tsar Alexander II agreed to negotiations which ended the Crimean War in March 1856. Russia was forced to give up its Black Sea fleet and to cede southern Bessarabia to Moldavia which was then part of Romania.

In January 1918, the Ukraine declared its independence from Russia but two years later, the Soviet army occupied the region during a war with Poland. In late December 1922, the Ukraine became a charter member of the Soviet Union (USSR). A man-made famine in 1932 caused between 7 and 10 million deaths as a result of forced collectivization of farms under Stalin's edict.

In March 1939, the Ukraine declared war on Germany but in June 1941, German troops tore through the region on their way to Stalingrad and laid waste to the country. In February 1945, the Yalta Conference was held in the Crimea shortly before the end of World War II. Ukraine lost nearly 5 million people during the war with uncounted millions wounded and homeless.

The most devastating event to befall Ukraine occurred in late April 1986 when a nuclear reactor at Chernobyl melted down. As the fallout cloud crossed eastern Europe, untold panic and anxiety resulted. In the local dialect, the name Chernobyl means "wormwood" which was mentioned in the Bible. To this day, the region north of Kiev is still unfit for human habitation. Chernobyl was finally shut down in December 2000.

On August 24, 1991, the Ukraine proclaimed its independence from the Soviet Union. Debates with Russia broke out immediately over division of the Black Sea naval fleet and nuclear weaponry (MC sextile Neptune; ASC sesquare Jupiter). In February 1994, Crimeans voted to become part of Russia which ironically it had given back to the Ukraine in 1954 (transiting Pluto square Moon). Ukraine's nuclear arsenal was also sent back to Russia at this time.

A new Constitution in June 1996 granted the people the right to own private property, something banned for years under the Soviets (progressed MC conjunct Pluto; transiting Pluto square Venus). A tainted election in November 2004 pitted one candidate supported by the Russians against the local favorite (Yushenko), who was poisoned (progressed Sun trine Neptune; progressed MC square Mercury and Jupiter; transiting Neptune square MC).

# Kiev (Kiyev)

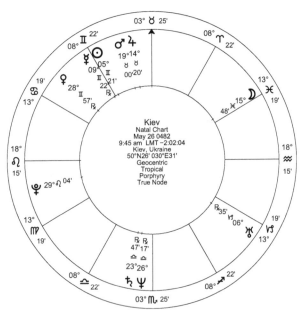

**May 26, 482 A.D., 9:45 a.m. LMT**
**Source: Lenin Library gives the date**
**of May 482, but no specific date;**
**chart rectified as to date and time**

Kiev is called the "Mother City of Russia" and was founded by three brothers and named for the eldest, Kiy. Varangians captured the city in April 862 (progressed MC sextile Moon) and in 882 the Kievan Rus dynasty was founded and went on to rule Russia for the next seven centuries (progressed MC conjunct Sun). In 988, Prince Vladimir converted to Christianity in order to marry the daughter of the Patriarch of Byzantium (progressed MC trine Mars). Due to its location on major trade routes, Kiev was invaded numerous times in its early history the most devastating occurring in 1240 when the Mongols completely leveled Kiev, leaving 90 percent of it in ruins (progressed MC square Pluto, progressed ASC square Sun). In 1320, the region west of Kiev was absorbed by Lithuania (progressed MC square Jupiter) but by 1569, Kiev came under Polish rule (progressed MC opposition Saturn). Because of harsh Polish rule, the Kievans asked Russia for protection in 1654 (progressed MC trine Moon) and 13 years later, the entire Ukraine came under Russian domination (progressed ASC conjunct Saturn).

A suspension bridge was built across the Dnieper in 1848, and the railroads came in 1869. In January 1918, Kiev was placed under German domination for the duration of World War I (progressed MC square Uranus). The Poles came again in 1920 but were ousted a month later by the Soviet army (progressed MC sextile Mercury). The government of the

Ukraine moved from Kharkov to Kiev in 1934 (progressed MC opposition Saturn).

Three months after the German invasion of Russia in June 1941, Kiev became an occupied city and over the next two years, more than 100,000 Jews were captured and shipped to Babi Yar (progressed MC semisquare Moon). The Nazis left Kiev in ruins and it wasn't until 1965 that the suspension bridge was rebuilt (progressed MC inconjunct Saturn). In April 1986, the nuclear plant at Chernobyl melted down causing 130,000 people to be evacuated from this region north of Kiev (progressed MC sesquare Neptune, progressed ASC square Moon). It may be years before we know the full extent of this accident, both biologically and genetically.

With Jupiter at the MC it comes as no surprise that Kiev became the birthplace of the Russian Orthodox Church. In medieval times, Kiev had over 400 churches, most in Byzantine or Romanesque styles. One of the main sights is the Golden Gate, a fortress built 300 feet. above the river and the oldest monastery (the Cave Monastery) in Russia or the Ukraine.

## Odessa

Odessa
Natal Chart
Sep 2 1794 NS
1:15 pm LMT −2:02:56
Odessa, Ukraine
46°N28' 030°E44'
Geocentric
Tropical
Porphyry
True Node

**September 2, 1794, 1:15 p.m. LMT**
**Source: *Odessa* by Kononova for the date;**
**time speculative**

The region around Odessa, the fifth-largest city in the Ukraine, was first settled by the Greeks. During the Middle Ages it was ruled by the Tatars, or Mongols. Russian troops captured the fortress in 1774, and two decades later, they enlarged the fortress, expanded the port and built a naval base. Catherine the Great feminized its original name of Odessus. From 1819 (progressed MC trine Pluto sextile Mercury and Pluto) until 1849 (progressed MC square Mercury and Pluto) Odessa was a free port with no customs duties. By the end of the 19th century, it was the second-largest port in Russia and its fourth-largest city. The railroad came in 1866 (progressed ASC opposition Mercury).

During the first Russian Revolution in 1905, Odessa witnessed the famous mutiny on the Potemkin after which 15 percent of the populace fled to safer climes (progressed ASC trine Sun inconjunct Moon). After the second Russian Revolution in early 1918, Odessa was occupied for three years alternately by Ukrainian, German, Austrian and French troops (progressed MC square Neptune, progressed ASC conjunct Saturn opposition Mars). During World War II, Odessa was briefly occupied by the Germans until liberation by the Soviets shortly before the Yalta Conference in early 1945 (progressed MC conjunct Pluto, progressed ASC opposition Jupiter).

With Sagittarius rising, Jupiter in the first house sextile Pluto and trine Mercury and the Sun in the ninth, it's no accident that Odessa is probably the most international city of the Ukraine. The climate is certainly more agreeable and its surroundings are very Mediterranean. Unlike most other cities of the former Soviet Union, Odessa really likes foreigners due to Venus, ruler of the MC, making harmonious aspects to the rulers of the ASC and DESC. There seems to be little of the xenophobia or distrust of anything western that is prevalent in cities like Moscow or Kiev.

## Donetsk

Ukraine's third-largest city was founded by an Englishman, John Hughes, in 1872 to make rails for the Russian transportation industry. It's the chief city of the Donets basin.

## Dnepropetrovsk (Ekaterinoslav)

Ukraine's fourth-largest city is situated on the Dnieper River. Founded by Grigori Potemkin (Catherine the Great's lover and possible husband) in 1778, it was renamed in 1926. It's the center for iron and steel mills.

## Kharkov

Ukraine's second-largest city was founded in 1655 as a fort against the Cossacks. From 1780 until 1918 it was the capital of the Ukraine. After 1880 it became a major industrial center.

## Lvov (Lviv)

Ukraine's sixth-largest city was founded in 1256 by the Duke of Galicia who named it after his son, Leo. Until 1918, it was part of Poland.

# The United Kingdom of Great Britain and Northern Ireland

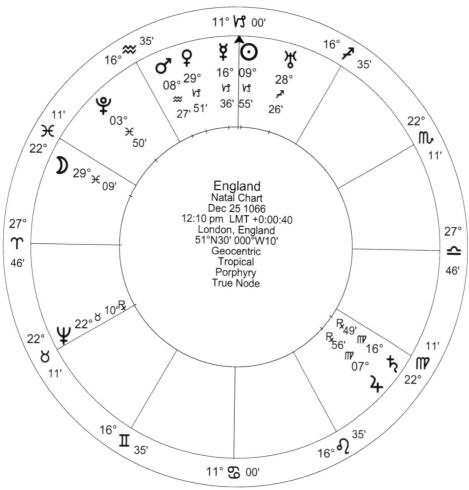

**December 25, 1066, 12:10 p.m. LMT, London**
**Source: Coronations usually take place at mid-day; chart rectified to shortly after noon**

## England

The island of Great Britain lies off the coast of France and is separated from the European continent by the English Channel, also known as the Straits of Dover or La Manche. Bordered on the east by the North Sea, on the west by the Irish Sea and on the south by the Atlantic Ocean, this island contains the countries of England, Scotland and Wales.

England is a land of rolling plains in the south which rise upwards toward the Midlands, the industrial heart of the country. The coasts of Devon and Cornwall in the southwest have towering cliffs and rocky headlands while the coastline in the southeast is famed for its white cliffs. England's Lake District is situated west of the Pennine Mountains and in Yorkshire are the moors made famous by writers and poets. The Cheviot Hills separate England from Scotland while the Cambrian Mountains. separate England from Wales.

Scotland is a rugged land more suited to industry than agriculture. In the south are the uplands while the center of the country around Edinburgh and Glasgow has most of the farmland and industry. The highlands of the north are mountainous with plateaus and deep valleys, a land unsuited to farming but agreeable to grazing.

Wales has rugged mountains and deep valleys bordering the Irish Sea. Northern Ireland, also called Ulster, has rolling plains and low mountains which ring its coastline.

The highest point is Ben Nevis in Scotland (elevation 4,406 feet).

The coastline of the United Kingdom is 7,723 miles long and no spot is more than 120 miles from the sea. Several islands lie off the coast: the Channel

Islands (Jersey, Guernsey, Aldemey and Sark) lie off the coast of France while the Shetlands and Orkneys lie just north of Scotland.

| Region | Area | Population |
|--------|------|-----------|
| England | 50,331 sq. mi. | 49,946,790 |
| Scotland | 30,418 sq. mi. | 5,111,000 |
| Wales | 8,019 sq. mi. | 2,927,000 |
| N. Ireland | 5,452 sq. mi. | 1,663,000 |
| | 94,220 sq. mi. | 59,647,790 |

The United Kingdom is the size of Oregon or Romania; 89 percent live in urban areas, and 25 percent of the land is arable. About 81 percent are English, 10 percent Scottish, 2 percent Welsh, 2 percent Irish, 2 percent Caribbean and 3 percent East Indian or Pakistani. 55 percent are Protestant (mostly Anglican), 10 percent are Catholic, 3 percent Moslem and 1 percent Jewish. The main exports are automobiles, engineering equipment, aircraft, petroleum, chemicals, electrical goods, textiles and wool. The main resources are coal and peat. Shipbuilding is a major industry in Northern Ireland, and fishing is important to Scotland, along with its vast petroleum reserves in the North Sea.

# United Kingdom Timeline

| | |
|---|---|
| 55 B.C. | Julius Caesar invades the island of Britain |
| 43 A.D. | Emperor Claudius conquers Britain |
| 122 | Hadrian builds a wall to keep out the Plots from Scotland |
| 408 | Roman occupation ends and Britain is invaded by Angles, Jutes and Saxons. The native Celts, Gaels and Brythons move farther west and in from the North Sea coastline |
| 597 | St. Augustine converts King Ethelbert to Christianity |
| 793 | The Danes begin their invasion along the North Sea |
| 1016-3 | King Knut (Canute) of Denmark governs England |
| 1066, October | William of Normandy defeats King Harold at Hastings |
| 1066, December 25 | William the Conqueror is crowned King of England in Westminster Abbey |
| 1085, December | The Domesday Survey (census) is completed (MC conjunct Venus sextile Moon; ASC square Pluto) |
| 1139 | Civil war breaks out over the royal succession (MC sextile Neptune semisquare Mars; ASC sextile Neptune semisquare Jupiter) |
| 1170, December | Thomas a Becket, the Archbishop of Canterbury, is murdered (Sun sesquare Jupiter; ASC sesquare Uranus) |
| 1192, December | King Richard I is held for ransom while returning from a Crusade in the Holy Land (Sun semisquare Moon; MC trine Mercury and Saturn; ASC trine Uranus) |
| 1209 | King John is excommunicated over his choice for the Archbishop of Canterbury (Sun sesquare Mercury; ASC trine Sun inconjunct Mars |
| 1215, June 15 | King John is forced to sign the Magna Carta by his barons who are tired of high taxes and abuses by the monarchy (MC trine Mars square Jupiter) |
| 1258 | The Great Council meets in Oxford and demands a larger role in government (Sun opposition Mercury sextile Saturn; MC sesquare Pluto) |
| 1265, January | England's first Parliament opens |
| 1282 | English armies conquer Wales (Sun inconjunct Sun; ASC square Venus) |
| 1290 | All Jews are expelled from England |
| 1314, June | Robert the Bruce of Scotland defeats the British at the Battle of Bannockburn thus assuring Scottish independence (ASC opposition Neptune) |
| 1327, January | Edward II is deposed by his wife and then executed (Sun sesquare Mars) |
| 1337 | The 100 Years War begins over English claims to the French throne (Sun inconjunct Pluto; ASC sextile Mars square Jupiter) |
| 1348 | The Black Death kills over one-third of England's population (MC square Mercury; ASC semisquare Venus) |
| 1399, September | King Richard II is deposed by Henry Bolingbroke (MC sextile Mars square Jupiter; ASC conjunct Mars) |
| 1415, October | The English defeat the French at Agincourt (Sun inconjunct Neptune; MC semisquare Mars; ASC semisquare Venus) |
| 1453 | England loses all its holdings in France except Calais as the 100 Years War ends (Sun sesquare Saturn) |
| 1455, May | The War of the Roses begins between the houses of York and Lancaster over succession rights (ASC trine Mars) |
| 1483, June | Edward V is deposed by his uncle, Richard III and later murdered (Sun semisquare Mercury; MC conjunct Pluto; ASC sextile Jupiter semisquare Neptune) |
| 1485, August | Richard III is slain by Henry Tudor on the field at Bosworth thus bringing an end to the War of the Roses (Sun conjunct Pluto; ASC opposite Sun inconjunct Mars) |
| 1509, April | Henry VIII comes to the throne (Sun square Uranus; MC conjunct Moon) |
| 1534, November | Henry VIII becomes head of the Church of England and thus establishes the English Reformation (MC sesquare Jupiter) |
| 1536, February | Wales becomes part of Britain (ASC sesquare Uranus) |
| 1553, July | Mary Tudor ascends the throne and begins persecuting Protestants (ASC |

| | sesquare Sun) |
|---|---|
| 1558, November | Elizabeth I comes to power and the Golden Age of Britain begins (Sun trine Mercury and Saturn; ASC trine Uranus) |
| 1577, December | Francis Drake begins his circumnavigation of the globe (Sun square Pluto) |
| 1588, August | The Spanish armada is defeated ensuring British safety on the high seas (Sun sesquare Venus) |
| 1600, December | The East India Company is founded (ASC square Uranus) |
| 1603, March | Elizabeth I dies and ends the Tudor line and is succeeded by her archenemy Mary Stuart's son, James VI of Scotland. Thus are England and Scotland united under one crown (Sun opposite Uranus; MC square Moon inconjunct Venus; ASC opposite Moon trine Venus) |
| 1607, May | England's first settlement in America, Jamestown, founded (MC trine Pluto) |
| 1611 | The King James Bible is printed (MC sextile Jupiter) |
| 1629, March | King Charles I disbands Parliament and rules through advisors for the next eleven years (Sun sextile Neptune; MC semisquare Jupiter; ASC sesquare Pluto) |
| 1642, August | The English Civil War breaks out between the Royalists and supporters of Parliament, led by Oliver Cromwell (ASC sextile Uranus) |
| 1649, February | Charles I is beheaded for treason and England becomes a Commonwealth with Cromwell as its leader (MC sesquare Moon and Uranus; ASC semisquare Saturn) |
| 1660, June | The Stuart monarchy is restored (ASC sextile Sun square Mars) |
| 1665 | The plague kills thousands in London (Sun trine Uranus; MC inconjunct Moon; ASC semisquare Uranus) |
| 1685, February | James II, a Catholic, comes to the throne (Sun conjunct Saturn trine Mercury; ASC semisquare Sun) |
| 1689, February | James II fled to Europe and William III and his wife, Mary, agree to rule jointly and sign the Bill of Rights (MC trine Neptune; ASC trine Moon) |
| 1701 | The Succession Act is passed banning future Catholic sovereigns (MC inconjunct Pluto) |
| 1702, May | The War of the Spanish Succession begins and lasts for the next 11 years (Sun inconjunct Pluto) |
| 1707, May | The Act of Union unites England and Scotland (Sun trine Mars; MC square Sun) |
| 1714, August | Queen Anne dies, ending the Stuart line; the throne passes to the Hanovers from Germany (Sun square Mercury; ASC semisquare Venus) |
| 1721 | Horace Walpole becomes England's first Prime Minister (Sun inconjunct Neptune; MC semisquare Jupiter) |
| 1756 | The Seven Years War begins against France (Sun trine Moon; MC sextile Venus) |
| 1759, September | England defeats the French at Quebec, thus gaining Canada (Sun semisquare Mercury) |
| 1764 | James Watt invents the steam engine, thus beginning the Industrial Revolution (MC square Jupiter; ASC conjunct Mars) |
| 1776, July | The American colonies proclaim their independence (ASC conjunct Pluto) |
| 1781, October | Britain is defeated at Yorktown, Virginia and Cornwallis surrenders to George Washington (Sun semisquare Mars; ASC sextile Mercury opposition Saturn) |
| 1788, January | Australia is settled as a penal colony (Sun square Moon) |
| 1793, February | England goes to war against Republican France (MC sesquare Neptune; ASC square Mercury inconjunct Saturn) |
| 1801, January 1 | The Union of Great Britain and Ireland is established (midnight) |
| 1812, June | Britain wars against America over impressment of seamen (ASC inconjunct Uranus) |
| 1815, June | Wellington defeats Napoleon at Waterloo (MC conjunct Venus sextile Moon; ASC sesquare Mercury) |
| 1837, June | Victoria ascends the throne (MC square Neptune; ASC opposite Uranus) |
| 1842, August | The Treaty of Nanking is signed with China over trading rights and opium trafficking (MC semisquare Sun) |

| | |
|---|---|
| 1854, April | Britain fights against Russia in the Crimea (Sun opposition Jupiter) |
| 1858, November | The Indian Empire is founded |
| 1867, July | Canada becomes a self-governing dominion (MC and ASC sextile Neptune) |
| 1882, September | Britain purchases controlling interest in the Suez Canal (MC semisquare Neptune; ASC semisquare Saturn) |
| 1899, October | The Boer War begins in South Africa (MC sesquare Jupiter) |
| 1901, January | Australia receives its independence and Queen Victoria die (ASC sesquare Uranus) |
| 1910, May | South Africa is granted independence (MC sesquare Saturn; MC sextile Pluto) |
| 1914, August | World War I begins against Austria-Hungary and Germany (MC square Mars trine Jupiter; ASC square Neptune) |
| 1918, November | World War I comes to an end with the signing of the Armistice. Britain lost 900,000 soldiers and over 2 million have been wounded. Women are also given the vote (Sun trine Sun; ASC sesquare Sun) |
| 1921, December | Ireland is partitioned and the Irish Free State is born (Sun sesquare Uranus; MC semisquare Moon) |
| 1929, November | The Great Depression begins (MC conjunct Neptune; ASC sesquare Mercury) |
| 1931, December | The Treaty of Westminster is signed creating the British Commonwealth (Sun conjunct Neptune; MC sesquare Sun; ASC opposition Pluto) |
| 1936, December | Edward VIII is forced to abdicate so he can marry an American divorcee (MC inconjunct Uranus sextile Moon trine Venus) |
| 1939, September | World War II begins against Germany (Sun trine Venus; MC sesquare Mercury; ASC inconjunct Mars conjunct Jupiter) |
| 1945, May | World War II ends with Britain in dire financial straits (MC square Jupiter) with 357,000 soldiers dead and 369,000 on the wounded list |
| 1947, August | Britain pulls out of India which is partitioned (Sun trine Mars; MC inconjunct Sun; ASC sesquare Venus) |
| 1957, March | Ghana is the first colony in Africa to gain its freedom (Sun inconjunct Mercury square Saturn; ASC trine Neptune) |
| 1969, August | Violence erupts in Northern Ireland between Catholics and Protestants over English occupation and desired reunion with Ireland (Sun square Moon and Uranus; ASC trine Venus) |
| 1973, January | Great Britain joins the European Common Market (MC trine Pluto) |
| 1979 | Margaret Thatcher becomes England's first female Prime Minister (Sun inconjunct Mars sextile Jupiter; MC opposition Sun; ASC sesquare Neptune) |
| 1982, April | Britain goes to war against Argentina over the Falkland Islands (ASC square Sun) |
| 1992, December | Prince Charles and Diana decide to separate after 11 years of marriage; they are formally divorced four years later (Sun sextile Neptune; MC semisquare Jupiter; ASC square Mercury) |
| 1994, May | The Chunnel under the English Channel is completed, thus linking Great Britain to the European continent |
| 1999, July | The Scottish Parliament is reconvened and Scotland gains limited autonomy (Sun inconjunct Uranus; MC opposition Venus trine Moon; ASC inconunct Neptune semisquare Jupiter sesquare Pluto) |
| 1999, October | The Labor government under Tony Blair abolished the right of more than 700 hereditary peers to sit and vote in the House of Lords |
| 2005, July | Native-born terrorists attacked the London subway system (progressed MC inconjunct Pluto) |

# London

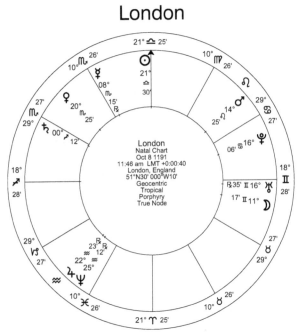

**October 8, 1191, 11:46 a.m. LMT**
**Source: The Guildhall**

London is the capital and largest city in the United Kingdom. There are in fact many Londons. The City of London occupies 677 acres near the Tower of London and St. Paul's Cathedral, while the County of London contains 32 boroughs more than 116 square miles with 3.5 million people. Greater London has more than 6.5 million people in 610 square miles. While the City of London was chartered in 1191, the County was established April 1, 1889 and the Greater London Council which manages metropolitan London was founded April 1, 1965. During the 19th century, London was the largest city in the world.

Located on the Thames River just upriver from where it empties into the English Channel or North Sea, it was founded by Romans in the spring of 43 A.D. and named Londonium. In 449, the Angles arrived and renamed it Lundencaster. Danes laid siege to the city in 994. London became a royal city in 1066 when William the Conqueror made it his capital. The two greatest disasters to befall London occurred almost simultaneously: the plague of 1665 killed 68,000 people and the following year, in September 1666, the Great Fire burned 13,000 homes and necessitated the rebuilding of the entire city. Christopher Wren was one of the more noted architects who contributed to the rebuilding of London during the late 17th century.

The world's first underground railway (subway) was completed in 1853 and its stations offered shelter during the German air raids of World War II. For decades, port facilities along the Thames had been threatened by rising waters of the sea, but in 1984 a flood barrier was completed at Woolwich to prevent future inundations. London once had the worst air pollution on the planet due to the combination of its famous fog with coal soot; now London has some of the cleanest air in Europe.

London has numerous attractions, including world-class museums like the National Gallery, Tate Gallery and the Victoria and Albert museum. The British Museum and Library is one of the finest places for research on the planet. The Houses of Parliament (aka the Palace of Westminster) and its clock tower, called Big Ben, are London's most-famous buildings and the view across the Thames is breathtaking. Next to the government buildings is Westminster Abbey where British sovereigns are crowned. Further down the river is St. Paul's Cathedral, designed by Wren after the fire, with the second-highest dome in the world. Further east is the Tower of London built by William the Conqueror, and the Tower Bridge, completed in 1894. Most of the government offices line Whitehall, a broad avenue running north from Parliament along the Thames. A bit west at the end of the Mall is Buckingham Palace, home to the monarch and down the street is Trafalgar Square and Picadilly Circus, the two centers of London.

London has many famous neighborhoods. The most famous are Mayfair, home to the wealthy as well as numerous playhouses and fashion boutiques. Then there's Chelsea and Kensington near Hyde Park, the largest park in central London. Along with Regent's Park (home to the zoo), Green Park and St. James' Park, these areas of greenery encircle the heart of royal London. Further out in the suburbs is Hampton Court, Kew Gardens and Greenwich, home to the Royal Observatory from where all time is measured.

London is probably the leading banking center, after New York, and the fulcrum of international trade and commerce. Its docks are some of the busiest in the world and its two airports are the busiest in Europe.

# Bath

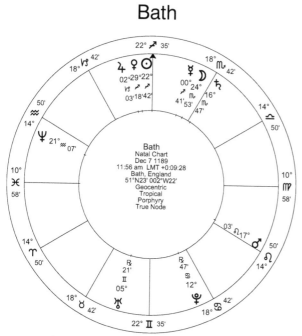

**December 7, 1189, 11:56 a.m. LMT**
**Source: Wigglesworth**

Situated on the River Avon 12 miles southeast of Bristol, the Romans built baths atop the numerous hot springs during the 1st century A.D. They called it "Aquae Sulis." In 577, the Saxons renamed it "Aet Bathum" and it was here that Edgar was crowned the first King of England in May 973. Beginning in 1702 with the visit of Queen Anne, Bath began its Golden Age due to people like Beau Nash who surrounded himself with the creme of society. During the 18th century, most of Bath was transformed into the finest example of Georgian architecture on the planet. The Royal Crescent and the Pump Room above the baths are the most famous examples. Bath has 11 parks and as a center of style and fasion, its Museum of Costume should not be missed.

# Birmingham

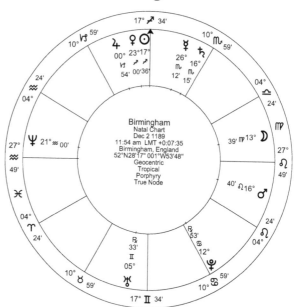

**December 2, 1189, 11:54 a.m. LMT**
**Source: Lord Mayor**

England's second-largest city lies in the heart of the Midlands, a vast industrial region comparable to the Ruhr. Known originally as Bermengeham, it was a small market town until James Watt's invention of the steam engine in the 1760s created the Industrial revolution. During the Victorian Age, Birmingham was the leading commercial and industrial center of England. The chief sights are the Town Hall and the Law Courts. Its main products include autos, firearms, jewelry and brassware.

# Blackpool

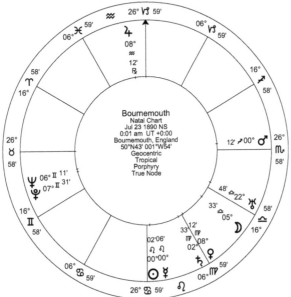

**January 21, 1876, 12:01 a.m. GMT**
**Source: Wigglesworth**

Situated on the Irish Sea 40 miles northwest of Manchester, Blackpool is England's premiere resort city and largest amusement center. A seven-mile promenade fronts the sea and passes by a 515-foot tower which is a small-scale reproduction of the Eiffel Tower.

# Bournemouth

**July 23, 1890, 12:01 a.m. GMT**
**Source: Wigglesworth**

Situated on the English Channel 50 miles south of London, Bournemouth is one of England's finest seaside resorts. First settled in 1810, its first pier was constructed in 1861. More than six miles of beaches and five miles of promenades cater to thousands of tourists annually.

# Bradford

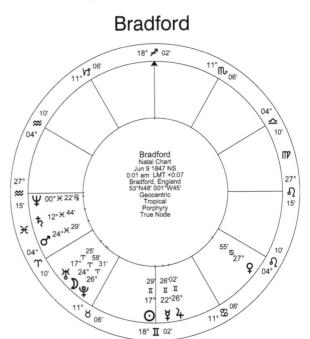

**June 9, 1847, 12:01 a.m. LMT**
**Source: West Yorkshire Archives**

England's seventh-largest city is located 30 miles northeast of Manchester. Originally the property of the Earls of Lincoln from 1086 until 1311 when woollen manufacturing began, the mainstay of its economy for centuries.

# Brighton

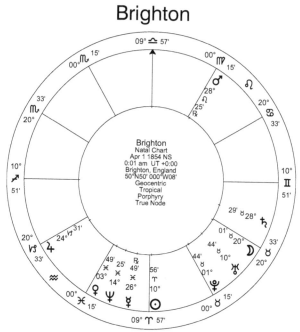

**April 1, 1854, 12:01 a.m. GMT**
**Source: Wigglesworth**

Located on the English Channel 45 miles south of London, it was known as Bristelmestune in the 11th century. Its reputation as a fashionable resort began in the late 18th century when the Prince of Wales (later George IV) began to spend time in Brighton. He constructed the Royal Pavilion which was completed in 1822. Its interior is extravagant and gaudy in a Chinese and Indian motif. Brighton is today a liberal city with the second-largest gay and lesbian community in England. The Palace Pier is one of the largest in the world.

# Bristol

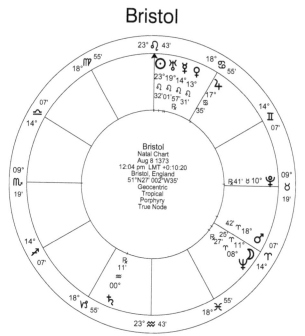

**August 8, 1373, 12:04 p.m. LMT**
**Source: City of Bristol**

England's eighth largest city is situated on the River Avon 105 miles west of London. Known as Bricgstowe in the 11th century, by the 15th century it was the chief port of western England and was captured by Parliamentarians during the Civil War in 1645. The famed glassworks were founded in the 18th century and its floating harbor was completed in 1809. The Germans bombed Bristol in 1940. Bristol had England's first free-library and newspaper outside London as well as its first savings bank. Its main industry is aircraft manufacture.

# Cambridge

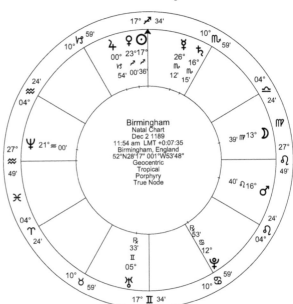

**May 8, 1207, 11:55 a.m. LMT**
**Source: Mayor of Cambridge**

Located on the River Cam 50 miles north of London, this city was known as Cantabrigia when it was first settled in the 9th century. The first college was founded in 1281 by disgruntled students from nearby Oxford. Ever since, Cambridge has been a center for study of science and math. Its main colleges are Kings, Queens, Peterhouse, St. John's, Emmanuel, Magdalene, Christ's and Trinity College with its famed Wren Library.

# Coventry

**January 20, 1345, 12:14 p.m. LMT**
**Source: The Library, Coventry**

Situated 20 miles southeast of Birmingham, Coventry was founded by Saxons in the 7th century. It was here that Lady Godiva rode naked through town protesting high taxes in the 11th century. Coventry gained fame as a cloth-making center four centuries later. Captured by Parliamentarians during the Civil War of the 1640s, it was heavily-bombed by the Germans from November 1940 to April 1941. More than 50,000 houses burned. Coventry is famous for being the chief automaker of England and has a massive new cathedral completed in 1962.

# Derby

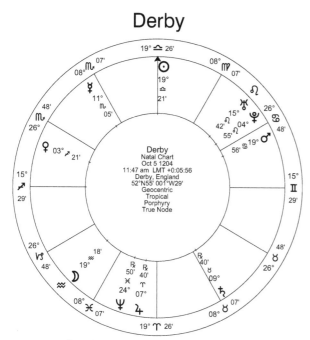

**October 5, 1204, 11:47 a.m. LMT**
**Source: City of Derby**

Situated 35 miles northeast of Birmingham, Derby is noted for its porcelain works and the home of the finest cars on earth, Rolls Royce.

# Exeter

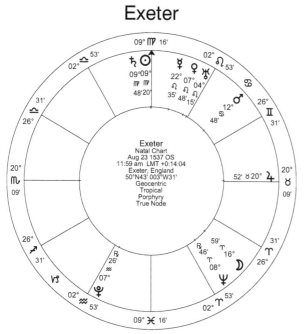

**August 23, 1537, 11:59 a.m. LMT**
**Source: Wigglesworth**

Located on the River Exe 155 miles southwest of London, it was founded by the Romans as Isca Dumnomiorum. Danish invasions began in the late 9th century and the Vikings completely destroyed the town in 1003. A ship canal was completed in 1564, and the city was heavily-bombed by the Germans during World War II. The main attraction in town is St. Peter's Cathedral which has the longest unbroken Gothic vault in Europe. The main industry in Exeter is making wool.

# Gloucester

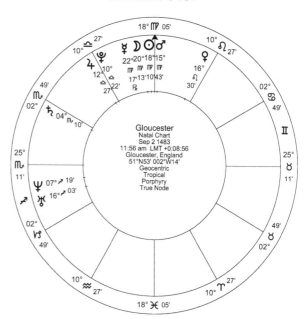

**September 2, 1483, 11:56 a.m. LMT**
**Source: Wigglesworth**

Located on the Severn River 95 miles west of London, it was founded as Glevium by Roman Emperor Nerva.

## Huddersfield

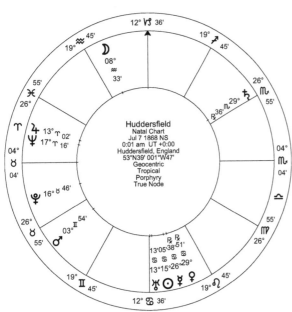

**July 7, 1868, 12:01 a.m. GMT**
**Source: Wigglesworth**

This industrial city is located 15 miles southwest of Leeds and is famous for its textiles, hand-woven cloth and its wool trade.

## Ipswich

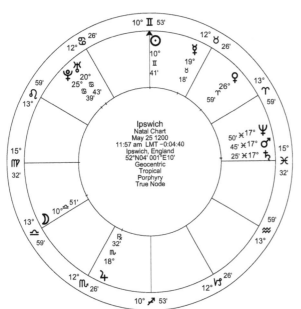

**May 25, 1200, 11:57 a.m. LMT**
**Source: Wigglesworth**

Located on the River Orwell 70 miles northeast of London, Ipswich is a center for the wool industry and is also a major port, its docks being situated at Harwich.

## Kingston Upon Hull

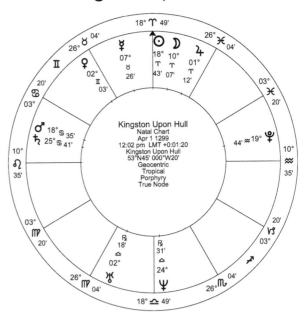

**April 1, 1299, 12:02 p.m. LMT**
**Source: Mayor of Kingston**

Situated on the Humber estuary, Kingston upon Hull is a major port on the North Sea. Its first docks were constructed in 1293 the same year it changed its name from Hull to Kingston. It endured a six-week siege during the Civil War in 1643 and it was bombed by the Germans during World War II. During the late 18th century, Kingston upon Hull was the third-largest whaling port in England.

## Leeds

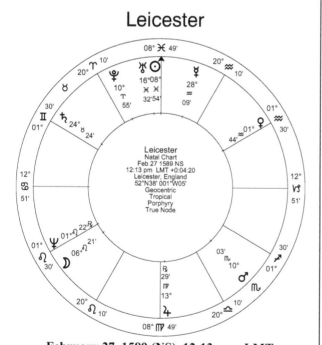

**July 23, 1626 (NS), 12:06 p.m. LMT**
**Source: Lord Mayor**

England's third-largest city is situated 35 miles northeast of Manchester. During the 14th century, Leeds became the center of the wool trade and five centuries later the leading wholesale clothing manufacturer. Textiles and railroad equipment are the main industries today and the main attraction is the massive Town Hall completed in 1858.

## Leicester

**February 27, 1589 (NS), 12:13 p.m. LMT**
**Source: Leicestershire Archives**

Located 85 miles northeast of London, this indus-trial city was founded by the Romans and named Ratae Coritanorum, and the central part of town still has Roman baths. Its main industries are hosiery, knitwear and shoes.

## Liverpool

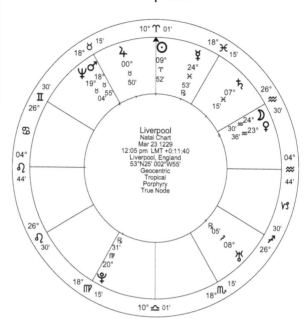

**March 23, 1229, 12:05 p.m. LMT**
**Source: Lord Mayor**

England's fifth-largest city is located on the estuary of the Mersey River. Settled by Norsemen in the 8th century as Hlithar-pollr, it was refounded by King John in August 1207. During the 17th and 18th centuries, trade with America and Africa increased its fortunes through slaves, cotton and sugar. During the 19th century, Liverpool was the main port of embarkation for emigrants to the New World. A tunnel under the Mersey, completed in 1934, connected Liverpool to Birkenhead, and German air raids during 1940-41 bombed a large portion of the city.

Liverpool witnessed a renaissance during the 1960s when musicians like the Beatles put Liverpool on the map. Since then, however, many docks are vacant and unemployment is high. This is a football-crazy town and its fans are rowdier than most. The main sights are the two cathedrals, especially the newer one which was begun in 1904 and is as yet uncompleted. When it's finished, it will be one of the largest places of worship on earth.

## Manchester

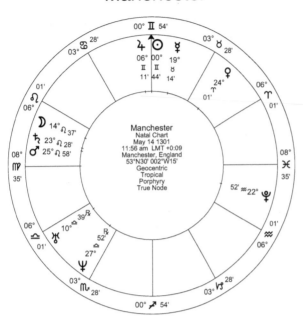

**May 14, 1301, 11:56 a.m. LMT**
**Source: Lord Mayor**

## Newcastle Upon Tyne

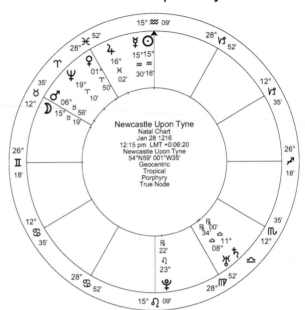

**January 28, 1216, 12:15 p.m. LMT**
**Source: Lord Mayor**

England's sixth-largest city is located in the Midlands 35 miles from the Irish Sea. Founded in 79 A.D. by the Romans and called Mancunium, the Danes destroyed the settlement in 870. During the 14th century, Flemish weavers arrived and four centuries later, Manchester was the center of the cotton milling industry. In 1821, the Manchester Guardian was first published and remains one of the most influential and respected journals in Europe. A canal to the sea was opened in 1894 and in 1940 the Germans bombed the city.

Manchester is home to the largest university in Europe and declared itself a nuclear-free zone in 1980. Manchester was also the birthplace of the English suffragette movement and where English labor unions first took root. The world's first computer was built here and Manchester is also the second-largest banking center in England with its own Royal Exchange. Manchester is quite liberal and has a large gay and lesbian community. It's a soccer-mad town whose chief attraction is its Town Hall.

Located on the North Sea, it was founded by the Romans and named Pons Aelli, Scots occupied Newcastle in 1646 during the English Civil War and shortly afterward, this city became synonymous with coal. Over the next two centuries, Newcastle was the largest coal port in the world. The Great Depression of the 1930s hit Newcastle quite hard and in many respects it's still on the road to recovery. The main attraction is nearby Hadrian's Wall, which runs for 173 miles, and was built during the 2nd century A.D. to protect England from the Picts in Scotland.

## Northampton

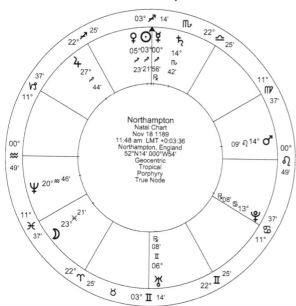

**November 18, 1189, 11:48 a.m. LMT**
**Source: Mayor's Parlour**

Located 65 miles north of London, this is an industrial city whose chief claim to fame is the manufacture of shoes and boots. Northampton is also a steel-making center.

## Norwich

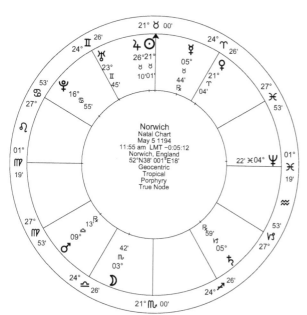

**May 5, 1194, 11:55 a.m. LMT**
**Source: Lord Mayor**

Located 100 miles northeast of London and 20 miles from the North Sea on the Wensum River, a fort was built here in 570 A.D. by King Uffa and a mint was founded in 940. During the Middle Ages,

Norwich was England's second-largest city due to its prominence in the wool trade. Norwich has 30 churches, the largest of which is the Anglican Cathedral with its 315-foot spire.

## Nottingham

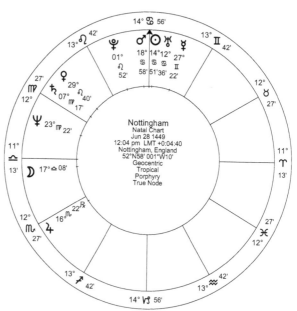

**June 28, l449, 12:04 p.m. LMT**
**Source: Lord Mayor**

Located on the River Trent 45 miles northeast of Birmingham, Nottingham was founded in the 6th century by the Saxons and called Snotingahan. King Charles I began the English Civil War here in 1642, and during the 19th century the industrial revolution took over making lace, hosiery, clothing, textiles, as well as bicycles and tobacco. Nearby is Sherwood Forest, the home of the mythical Robin Hood who was the bane of the Sheriff of Nottingham in the days of Richard the Lion-Hearted.

# Oxford

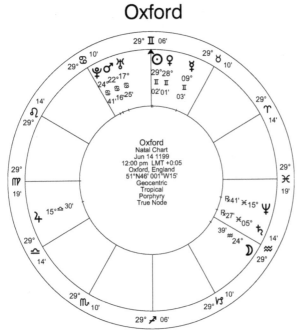

**June 14, 1199, noon LMT**
**Source: Lord Mayor**

Oxford is located at the junction of the Thames and Cherwell rivers 50 miles northwest of London. Its fame comes from being the home to 29 undergraduate colleges and six graduate schools. During the 12th century, the first college was founded, the oldest in England. Women were admitted in 1879 but could not hold degrees until 1920. Besides the colleges of note, the most noted sights are the Ashmolean Museum and the Bodleian Library. The colleges excel in the humanities and the sciences. The more prominent institutions of learning are University, Balliol, Merton, Exeter, Queens, Magdalen, Trinity, Christ Church, Corpus Christi and New Colleges.

# Plymouth

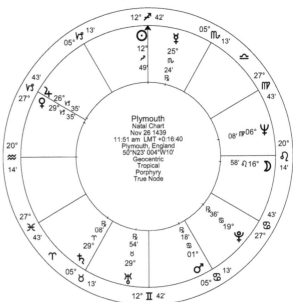

**November 26, 1439, 11:51 a.m. LMT**
**Source: Lord Mayor's Parlour**

Located on the south coast of England where the River Tamar meets the sea, some 190 miles southwest of London. Founded as Sutton, its name was changed in 1439 when it was chartered. It was from here that the Mayflower sailed to the New World in September 1620. Germans bombed its numerous docks during World War II. Plymouth also has shipyards and is a major seaport.

# Portsmouth

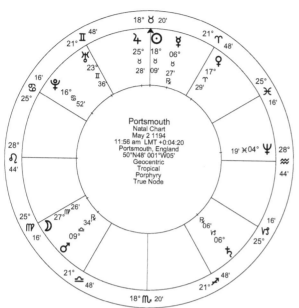

**May 2, 1194, 11:56 a.m. LMT**
**Source: The Library**

Located on the sea 65 miles southwest of London on the Spithead, this city was founded by Richard I the Lion-Hearted. Portsmouth constructed its first naval dock in 1540 and has been England's premier navy town ever since. German air raids during 1940 destroyed almost 90 percent of the city. Nearby is the resort town of South Sea.

# Reading

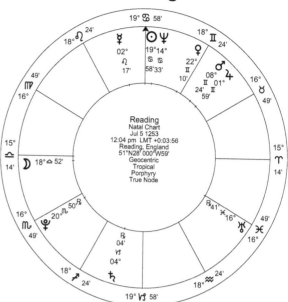

**July 5, 1253, 12:04 p.m. LMT**
**Source: Central Library**

Located on the River Thames 35 miles west of London, it was first settled in the 9th century by the Danes. Reading is an industrial town with many electronic and engineering firms.

# Sheffield

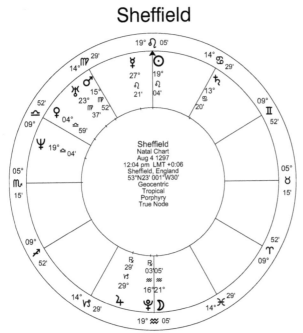

**August 4, 1297, 12:04 p.m. LMT**
**Source: City Library**

# Southampton

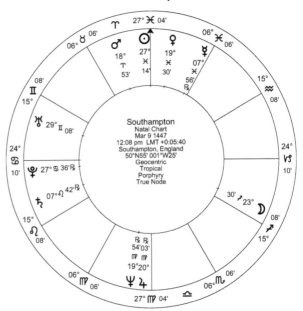

**March 9, 1447, 12:08 p.m. LMT**
**Source: Mayor's Parlour**

Located 35 miles east of Manchester in the Midlands, this is England's fourth-largest city. During the 11th century it was known as Hallam, but its fame didn't really begin until the 18th century when it gained a monopoly on the manufacture of cutlery. In 1830, Sheffield became a steel center and its mills were further enlarged in 1856 when Bessemer arrived. German air raids in 1940 destroyed much of the city and today, Sheffield is still famous for its manufacture of cutlery, steel and plate.

Located on the English Channel 70 miles southwest of London, it was known as Hantune during Saxon times and Clausentum to the Romans. In 1803, the Harbour Commission was founded and in 1831, the Royal Pier was built. Southampton is today the main passenger port for steamer traffic across the Atlantic and is a major freighter-container port as well. It was from here that the Titanic sailed on its ill-fated maiden voyage to America, despite the fact that it was built in Belfast and had the name of Liverpool under its name on the stern. Oil refineries were constructed beginning in 1951.

## Stoke on Trent

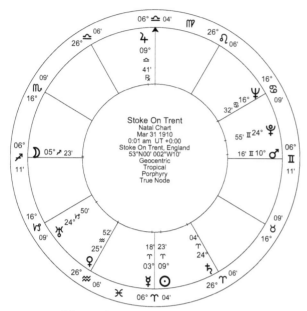

**March 31, 1910, 12:01 a.m. GMT**
**Source: Lord Mayor's Parlour**

This industrial city is located 40 miles north of Birmingham in the Midlands and is famous for its manufacture of porcelain, china and Wedgwood.

## Teeside

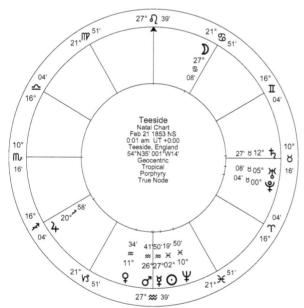

**February 21, 1853, 12:01 a.m. GMT**
**Source: Borough Council**

Teeside is located on the River Tees 45 miles north of York on the North Sea. As English cities go, this is a relatively modern community having been founded in 1830 with the arrival of the railroad. Middlesborough, as it was then known, made over one-third of England's pig iron and it's still a major iron and steel center. Middlesborough merged with several other surrounding towns in April 1968 to form the city of Teeside.

## Torquay

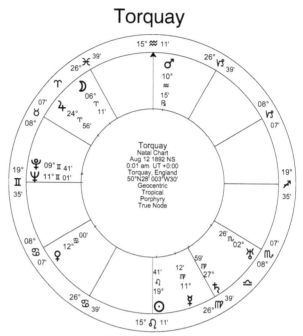

**August 12, 1892, 12:01 a.m. GMT**
**Source: Borough Council**

Located on Tor Bay 30 miles east of Plymouth on the Atlantic Ocean, an abbey was founded here in the 12th century and known as Torre. Today this city is a resort center due to its mild climate and warm waters coming from the Gulf Stream. Torquay has a sub-tropical feel and is the only place in England where palm trees grow naturally.

# Wolverhampton

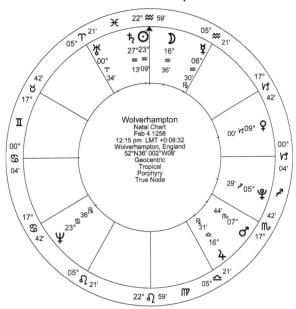

**February 4, 1258, 12:15 p.m. LMT**
**Source: Metropolitan Borough Council**

Located 15 miles northwest of Birmingham, a monastery was founded at Werogona Caste in the 10th century. A fire in 1590 lasted for five days and ruined the town; another fire in 1696 did extensive damage as well. Famous for its manufacture of bicycles since 1897, it also makes locks and safes.

# York

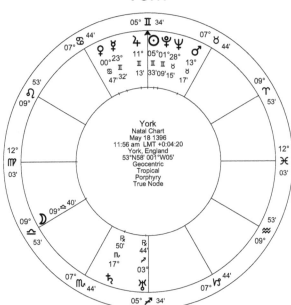

**May 18, 1396, 11:56 a.m. LMT**
**Source: Lord Mayor**

York is located on the River Ouse in Yorkshire, the largest county in England. Founded in 74 A.D. as Eboracum by the Romans, it was here in 306 that Constantine was proclaimed Emperor of the Roman Empire. An archbishopric was founded in 627, and in 867, the Danes occupied York. The darkest moment in York's history came in 1290 when its large Jewish community was expelled. York's most popular attraction is its massive Cathedral, begun in 1220 and completed in 1470. York Minster is the largest Gothic church in northern Europe. A fire in July 1984 severely damaged the building. York's ancient walls surround the city for three miles. York is famous for its manufacture of chocolates.

Other British cities for which you may wish to calculate a chart:

Bedford: 0W29, 52N08, April 23, 1166, 11:57 a.m. LMT

Chester: 2W54, 53N12, April 6, 1506, 12 noon LMT

Durham: 1W34, 54N47, September 21, 1602 (OS); October 1, 1602 (NS), 11:50 a.m. LMT

Hastings, 0E36, 50N51, February 15, 1588 (OS); February 25, 1588 (NS), 12:13 p.m. LMT

Lancaster: 2W48, 54N03, June 12, 1193, 12 noon LMT

Lincoln: 0W33, 53N14, November 30, 1409, 11:53 a.m. LMT

Salisbury: 1W48, 51N05, January 30, 1227, 12:15 p.m. LMT

Stafford: 2W07, 52N48, May 1, 1206, 11:56 a.m. LMT

Winchester: 1W19, 51N04, January 23, 1588 (OS); February 2, 1588 (NS), 12:14 p.m. LMT

Windsor: 0W38, 51N29, May 28, 1277, 11:58 a.m. LMT

Worcester: 2W13, 52N11, November 12, 1189, 11:46 a.m. LMT

The times given are for Local Mean Time which was not in use prior to the beginning of the 19th century. Local Apparent (or Sundial) Time was the norm, so I have converted from one system to another to keep your computer from losing its sanity.

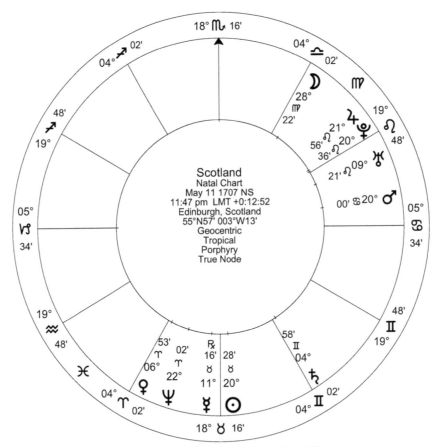

**May 1, 1707 (OS), May 12, 1707 (NS)**
**Source: Acts of Parliament says midnight; chart relocated to Edinburgh**

## Scotland

| | |
|---|---|
| 80 A.D. | The Romans conquer Caledonia and subdue the native Picts |
| 122 | Hadrian builds a wall between Scotland and England |
| 211 | Roman occupation ends |
| 6th century | Scots invade from Ireland and Norsemen conquer the Shetland and Orkney islands; St. Columba converts the Scots to Christianity |
| 843 | Kenneth McAlpin establishes the Scottish monarchy |
| 1018 | Malcolm II defeats the English and annexes Lothian |
| 1040-57 | Macbeth, a Dane, becomes King of Scotland |
| 1100 | Henry I of England marries Matilda of Scotland, uniting England and Scotland |
| 1297 | William Wallace (Braveheart) defeats the English |
| 1314, June | Robert the Bruce defeats the English at Bannockburn |
| 1328 | England recognizes Scottish independence |
| 1542, December | Mary Stuart becomes Queen of Scotland and later weds the King of France |
| 1587 | Mary Stuart is beheaded by the English which so riles Spain's Philip II that he sends an armada to England |
| 1603, March | James VI, son of Mary Stuart, becomes King of England and jointly rules both countries |
| 1707, May 12 | The Act of Union formally unites England with Scotland and the Scottish Parliament is dissolved |
| 1715, December | A revolt erupts for the son of James II, father of Bonnie Prince Charlie whom the Scots feel is the legal heir to the British throne |
| 1745, July | Bonnie Prince Charlie is defeated in battle at Culloden |
| 1973 | Oil is discovered off the North Sea coastline |
| 1999, July 1 | The Scots regain their Parliament and limited autonomy |

# Aberdeen

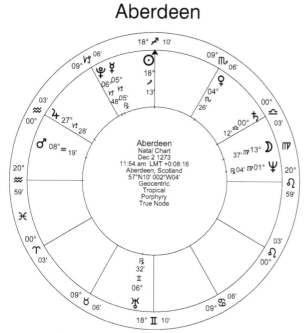

**December 2, 1273, 11:54 a.m. LMT**
**Source: City Library**

Aberdeen lies on the east coast of Scotland and is the center of the North Sea petroleum industry and is also a major fishing port.

# Dundee

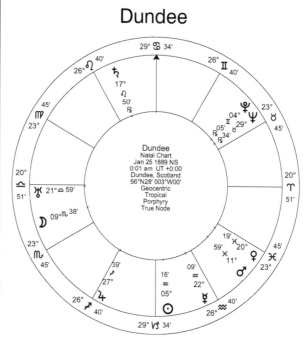

**January 25, 1889, 12:01 a.m. GMT**
**Source: Mayor's Office**

Located on the Firth of Tay 35 miles north of Edinburgh, Dundee was founded by William the Lion around 1200 as a fort. Dundee is famous for its rich cakes and orange marmalade. Other industries include shipbuilding and jute mills.

# Edinburgh

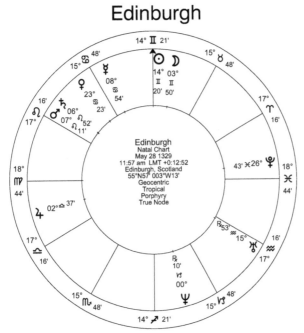

**May 28, 1329, 11:57 a.m. LMT**
**Source: National Library**

The capital of Scotland and its second-largest city is located near the south shore of the Firth of Forth. A castle built here in the 7th century by Edwin of Northumbria gave this city its name "Eadwine's burgh." Capital of Scotland since 1450, a new city was built during the 18th and 19th centuries below the Castle and laid out in typically Georgian style with straight streets, squares and crescents. The main feature of Edinburgh is its Castle, which towers over the city; the surrounding old town dates back to the 16th century. The Holyrood Palace sits at the end of the Royal Mile and is used when the English monarch visits the city. Princes Street is bordered by gardens is one of the most beautiful avenues in the world. Due to its high level of sophistication and cultural attractions, Edinburgh has been called the "Athens of the North" due to its three universities. Excellent vantage points to view the city are Gallon Hill and Arthur's Seat which rises to an elevation of 825 feet.

# Glasgow

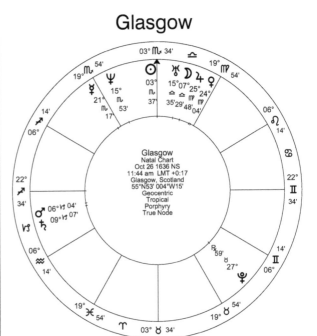

**October 26, 1636 (NS), 11:44 a.m. LMT**
**Source: District Library**

Glasgow is the largest city and chief port of Scotland and located on the River Clyde. Founded in 543 A.D., it was chartered as a burgh in 1178. During the 12th century, Glasgow began to grow west towards the sea some 15 miles away. Glasgow University was founded in 1451. Overseas trade accelerated in the 18th century and shipyards were constructed. The passenger liners, Queen Mary and Queen Elizabeth, were built here at Clydebank during the 1930s. Glasgow is also a center for rail transport and is the chief industrial region in Scotland.

Downtown Glasgow surrounds George Square, an excellent example of modern town planning. The Cathedral is one of the few to escape destruction during the Reformation. Glasgow is also a major art center and the Hunterian and Kelvingrove galleries are world famous.

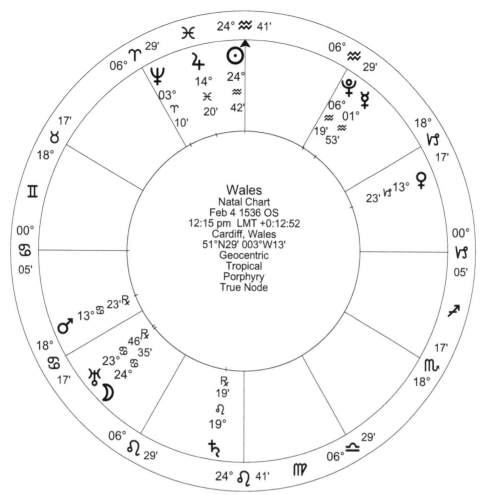

**February 4, 1536, 12:15 p.m. LMT, Cardiff**
**Source: Encyclopedia Britannica for the date; noontime assumed**

# Wales

| | |
|---|---|
| 4th century A.D. | Christianity is introduced from Ireland |
| 9th century | Vikings plunder seacoast towns |
| 1071 | William the Conqueror becomes Lord of Wales |
| 1246 | Llewellyn takes the title of Prince of Wales |
| 1256-67 | The Welsh endeavour to expel the English |
| 1282, December 11 | Edward I of England conquers Wales |
| 1284 | Statute of Wales annexes Wales to England |
| 1301, February | Edward II becomes the first Prince of Wales |
| 1402-09 | Owen Glendower sets up an independent state of Wales |
| 1485, August | Henry Tudor, a Welshman, becomes King of England |
| 1536, February | Henry VIII unites Wales with England |

# Cardiff

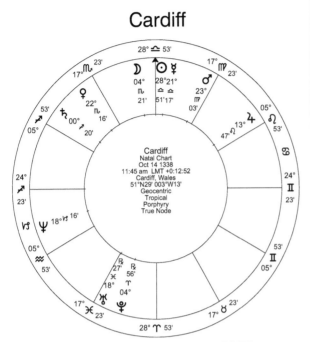

**October 14, 1338, 11:45 a.m. LMT**
**Source: Glamorgan Archives**

The capital and largest city of Wales is located on the Bristol Channel. Founded as a fort in Roman times, it was the world's greatest coal port during the 19th century. The main attractions are Cardiff Castle, which was renovated in the 19th century, and the National Museum of Wales.

# Swansea

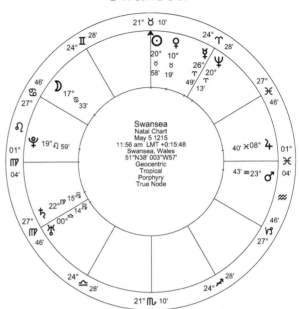

**May 5, 1215, 11:56 a.m. LMT**
**Source: Guildhall**

The second-largest city in Wales is situated on the River Tawe 35 miles west of Cardiff. During the 19th century, it was a major coal port and tin-plating center.

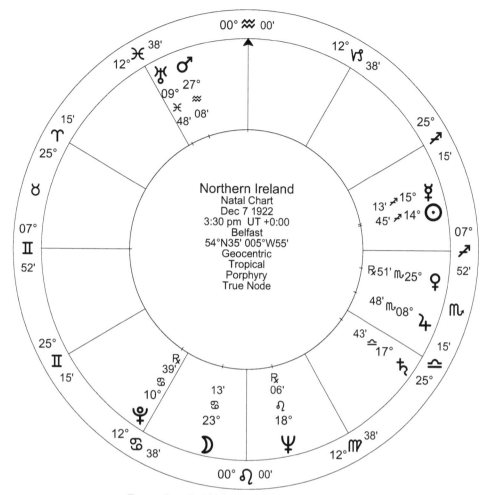

**December 7, 1922, 3:30 p.m. GMT, Belfast**
**Source: James Russell;** *Mundane Astrology* **by Baigent; Campion and Harvey state 3:28 p.m.**

## Northern Ireland

| | |
|---|---|
| 16th century A.D. | The English crown confiscates Catholic land after three rebellions |
| 17th century | Scots Presbyterians are moved in to oust the Catholics |
| 1651 | Anglicans are brought in, putting Catholics at further disadvantage |
| 1886 | Prime Minister Gladstone proposes Home Rule for Ulster |
| 1920, December | Northern Ireland's Parliament opens |
| 1921, December 6 | Home Rule is accepted and Ireland is partitioned |
| 1922, December 7 | King George V signs a bill creating Northern Ireland |
| 1966 | Riots begin in Londonderry |
| 1969, August | Terrorism against English occupation escalates with the IRA assistance but even more English troops are brought in |
| 1972, March | Great Britain suspends the Parliament of Northern Ireland |
| 1994, September | A short-lived truce begins after more than 3,200 have been killed in a quarter century of violence |

# Belfast

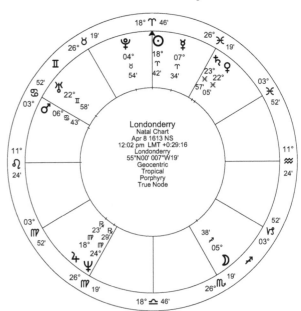

Belfast
Natal Chart
May 7 1613 NS
11:56 am LMT +0:23:40
Belfast
54°N35' 005°W55'
Geocentric
Tropical
Porphyry
True Node

**May 7, 1613 (NS), 11:56 a.m. LMT**
**Source: Education Board**

The capital and largest city in Northern Ireland is located on the River Lagan near the Irish Sea. Its name, "Beal Feirsde," refers to a sandbank. Founded in the 7th century A.D., Scottish settlers began to arrive in 1604 and soon outnumbered the native Catholics. Rivalry between the two religious groups began to escalate in the 19th century and by 1919 the IRA was established here in Belfast. Their reign of terror began anew in August 1969 and continues unabated to this day, despite a tenuous cease-fire which was enacted in late 1994. Many refer to this city as "Little Beirut" as the presence of British troops and tanks gives an impression of a war zone. Much of Belfast has been gutted by bombs and Catholics and Protestants tend to stay in their own areas. The chief sight in Belfast is City Hall, one of the most impressive government buildings in the British Isles. Its 175-foot dome towers over the city; nearby is the Customs House, another architectural gem.

Belfast's main industries include shipbuilding, engineering, cotton and linen. It was here in the Harland and Wolff shipyards that the Olympic, Titanic and Brittanic were built, which in their day were the largest ships ever built.

# Londonderry

Londonderry
Natal Chart
Apr 8 1613 NS
12:02 pm LMT +0:29:16
Londonderry
55°N00' 007°W19'
Geocentric
Tropical
Porphyry
True Node

**April 8, 1613 (NS), 12:02 p.m. LMT**
**Source: City and County Library**

Situated on the River Foyle about 60 miles west of Belfast, St. Columba founded an abbey here in the Dark Ages and in 546, the town of Doire was established. Its name was changed when it was chartered to add the name of London to Derry to honor English permission to colonize the region. Londonderry has massive walls which surround the old city for over a mile.

St. Columba's Cathedral was one of the first Protestant churches to be erected in Great Britain after the Reformation.

# The Vatican
# Citta del Vaticano

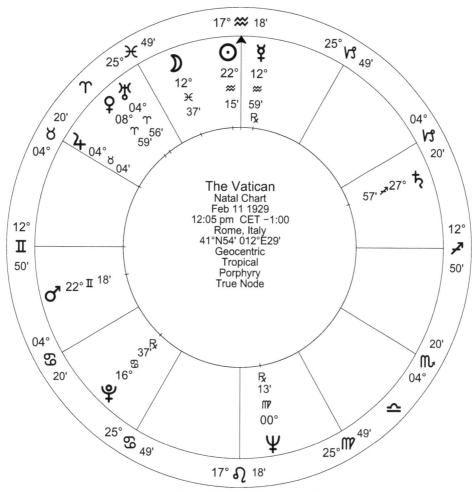

**February 11, 1929, 12:05 p.m. MET, Rome**
Source: *New York Times* says 12:05 p.m.

The Vatican, or Holy See, occupies 109 acres inside Rome, Italy. Besides the largest cathedral in the world, St. Peter's, and the famed Sistine Chapel and Vatican Library, the Holy See also has dominion over the Lateran Palace, Basilica of St. John Lateran, the churches of Santa Maria Maggiore and St. Paul's Outside the Walls, all inside the city of Rome. The Vatican also governs the Castel Gandolfo and the Palace of San Callisto outside Rome. The population of the Vatican is about 1,000. The Vatican also has its own radio station and newspaper.

The Vatican occupies the site of Nero's Circus, the place where St. Peter was crucified upside down and where thousands of Christians were either slain by gladiators or fed to the lions. The Popes began to use this area for their residence during the 5th century A.D. shortly before the first church of St. Peter was constructed. In that church, the Pope crowned Charlemagne as Emperor of the Romans on Christmas Day 800 A.D. Due to political strife, the Papacy moved to Avignon, France between 1309 and 1377.

When the nation of Italy was founded in March 1861, King Vittorio Emanuelle II ruled most of the Italian peninsula except for Venice and the Papal States. The Papal States were ceded to the Kingdom of Italy in 1870 and Pope Pius IX ended up being a prisoner inside the Vatican and never left it until his death in 1878. The capital of Italy was moved to Rome in July 1871 and the King moved into the Quirinale Palace. The Papal States consisted of 17,000 square miles in central Italy and had about four million inhabitants.

During the reign of Pope Pius XI, the Vatican was made a separate country when Benito Mussolini agreed to the Lateran Treaty in February 1929. Ratification of that treaty took place June 7, 1929.

Pope Pius XII took over in March 1939 (progressed Sun sesquare Pluto; progressed MC sextile Saturn; progressed ASC conjunct Mars). Pope Pius' refusal to directly confront Nazi aggression brought harsh criticism throughout the world as millions of Jews and other minorities were slaughtered. Some felt the Pope had made a secret pact with Hitler to remain neutral while others felt he was a secret Nazi sympathizer.

In October 1958, the much-loved Pope John XXIII took the reins of power (progressed Sun square Mars; progressed MC trine Pluto). He did his very best to bring the Roman Catholic Church into the modern age when he formed Vatican II to reform dogma and the liturgy in October 1962 (progressed MC square Mars; progressed ASC inconjunct Mercury).

Paul VI was elected Pope in June 1963 (progressed ASC conjunct Pluto) and his reign lasted until August 1978 when John Paul I came to the Papal throne. He died after a month in office (progressed MC semisquare Sun). Many believe he was murdered because he wanted to investigate and reform the Vatican Bank. His successor, John Paul II, was the first non-Italian Pope in over four centuries, a Polish Cardinal named Karol Wojtyla. Despite his overly-conservative viewpoints, he was much-loved and was the most widely-traveled Pope in history.

The Pope was shot in May 1981 by a terrorist working for either the Turks or the Bulgarians (progressed MC conjunct Venus). A Concordat between the Vatican and Italy was signed in June 1985 ending the status of Rome as a sacred city (progressed MC sextile Mercury). Religious education in schools was also removed. The Vatican opened relations with the U.S. in 1984 and with Israel in December 1993 (progressed Sun semisquare Moon; progressed MC sextile Sun and Mars). The Pope visited Israel in December 2000 (progressed Sun conjunct Jupiter; progressed MC trine Neptune).

After over a quarter century on the Papal throne, Pope John Paul II died in April 2005 (progressed Sun semisquare Mars; progressed ASC inconjunct Moon opposition Mercury sesquare Saturn). His replacement, Cardinal Joseph Ratzinger, took the name of Benedict XVI.

According to the prophecy of St. Malachy, a 12th century Irish bishop, there is one more Pope to sit on the throne of St. Peter. Some theologians believe these prophecies are a forgery and deciphering them is like trying to make sense from Nostradamus' quatrains. Regardless of whether they're real or false, the descriptions seem to fit the most recent Popes.

For example, Benedict XV (1914-1922) is described as "Religio Depopulata" which could relate to the Bolsheviks taking over Russia and the establishment of atheism.

Pius XI (1922-1939) is described as "Fides Intrepida" possibly for standing up to Fascism and Nazism which increased during his reign.

Pius XII (1939-1958) is described as "Pastor Angelicus" which might relate to his seeming serenity and. mystical manner during the trying times of his reign with the rise of Hitler, Stalin and Mussolini and his leadership during the early days of the Cold War.

John XXIII (1958-1963) is called "Pastor et Nauta" or pastor and sailor. This Pope was the patriarch of Venice, a former maritime power.

Paul VI (1963-1978) is called "Flos Florum" and on his coat of arms three lilies are shown..

John Paul I (1978) is called "De Medietate Lunae" or a, half moon. His brief reign lasted from one new moon to another.

John Paul II (1978-2005) is described as "De Lahore Soils" or the labor of the Sun. This Pope was born under an eclipse and was ironically buried under a Solar Eclipse as well.

Benedict XVI (2005- ) is called "Gloria Olivae" or the glory of the olive. To me, this speaks of a Pope who will try to mend fences around the world, especially between various religions.

According to St. Malachy, the last Pope will be Peter the Roman who will be persecuted during the time of tribulations before Rome is destroyed. Whether Benedict XVI is the next-to-the-last Pope or not remains for history to unveil.

The present Pontiff will have to deal with many important issues to Catholics around the world. Issues as to whether priests will ever be allowed to marry and whether women will be allowed to become priests must be addressed. The sexual scandals involving priests and young boys and girls must not be swept under the carpet by transferring priests from one locale to another. Issues as to the inclusion of homosexuals into the fold. must also be addressed as well as abortion and contraception.

The Church has buried its head for entirely too long and must adapt to modern morality and not adhere to something that might have worked two millennia ago. Church members in North America and Europe "pick and choose" the doctrines they will accept, while members in Latin America are leaving the fold to embrace more evangelical institutions.

# Appendix A
# Charts of the European Union

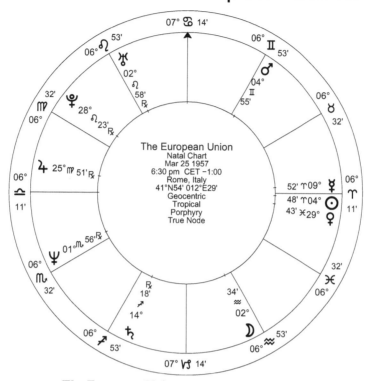

**The European Union, or the Treaty of Rome**
**March 25, 1957, 6:30 p.m. MET, 5:30 p.m. GMT, Rome, Italy**
**Source: Letter from Secretary General to James Russell**

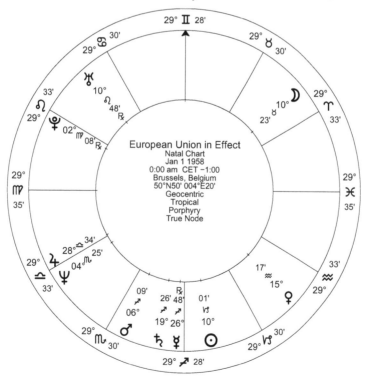

**European Union in Effect**
**January 1, 1958, 12:00 a.m. MET, Brussels, Belgium**
**Source: *The Times* of London says midnight**

# European Union

| Country | Admission Date | Time | Place |
|---|---|---|---|
| Belgium | January 1, 1958 | 12:00 a.m. CET | Brussels |
| France | January 1, 1958 | 12:00 a.m. CET | Paris |
| Germany | January 1, 1958 | 12:00 a.m. CET | Bonn |
| Italy | January 1, 1958 | 12:00 a.m. CET | Rome |
| Luxembourg | January 1, 1958 | 12:00 a.m. CET | Luxembourg |
| Netherlands | January 1, 1958 | 12:00 a.m. CET | Amsterdam |
| United Kingdom | January 1, 1973 | 12:00 a.m. GMT | London |
| Denmark | January 1, 1973 | 12:00 a.m. CET | Copenhagen |
| Ireland | January 1, 1973 | 12:00 a.m. GMT | Dublin |
| Greece | January 1, 1981 | 12:00 a.m. EET | Athens |
| Portugal | January 1, 1986 | 12:00 a.m. GMT | Lisbon |
| Spain | January 1, 1986 | 12:00 a.m. CET | Madrid |
| Austria | January 1, 1995 | 12:00 a.m. CET | Vienna |
| Finland | January 1, 1995 | 12:00 a.m. EET | Helsinki |
| Sweden | January 1, 1995 | 12:00 a.m. CET | Stockholm |
| Cyprus | May 1, 2004 | 12:00 a.m. EET | Nicosia |
| Czech Republic | May 1, 2004 | 12:00 a.m. CET | Prague |
| Estonia | May 1, 2004 | 12:00 a.m. EET | Tallinn |
| Hungary | May 1, 2004 | 12:00 a.m. CET | Budapest |
| Latvia | May 1, 2004 | 12:00 a.m. EET | Riga |
| Lithuania | May 1, 2004 | 12:00 a.m. EET | Vilnius |
| Malta | May 1, 2004 | 12:00 a.m. CET | Valletta |
| Poland | May 1, 2004 | 12:00 a.m. CET | Warsaw |
| Slovakia | May 1, 2004 | 12:00 a.m. CET | Bratislava |
| Slovenia | May 1, 2004 | 12:00 a.m. CET | Ljubljana |

*Scheduled to Join:*

| | | | |
|---|---|---|---|
| Bulgaria | January 1, 2007 | 12:00 a.m. EET | Sofia |
| Romania | January 1, 2007 | 12:00 a.m. EET | Bucharest |

Charts for these events, including the scheduled joining of Bulgaria and Romania, are shown on the following pages.

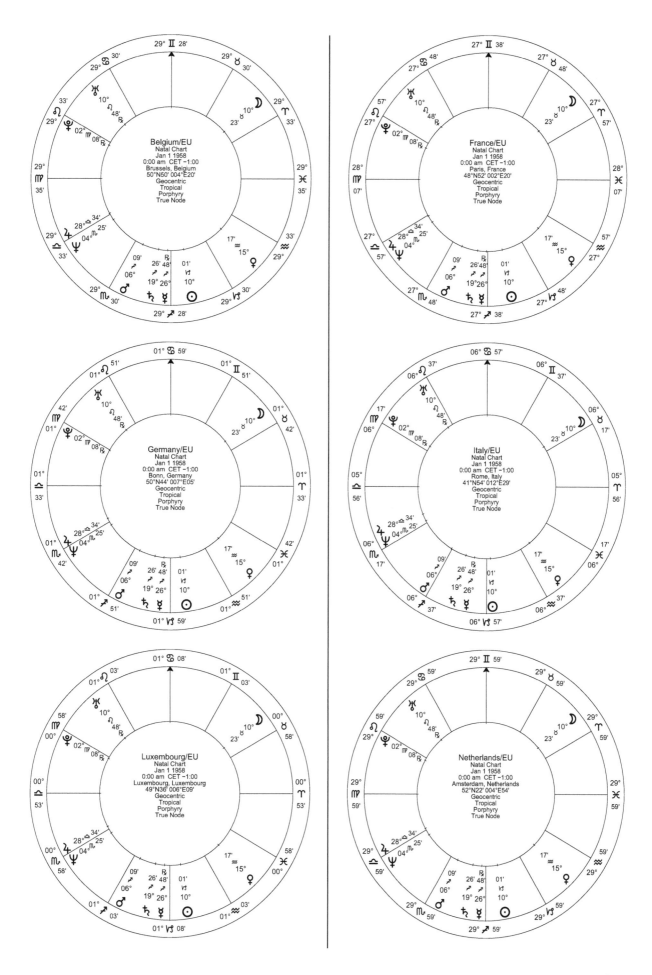

211

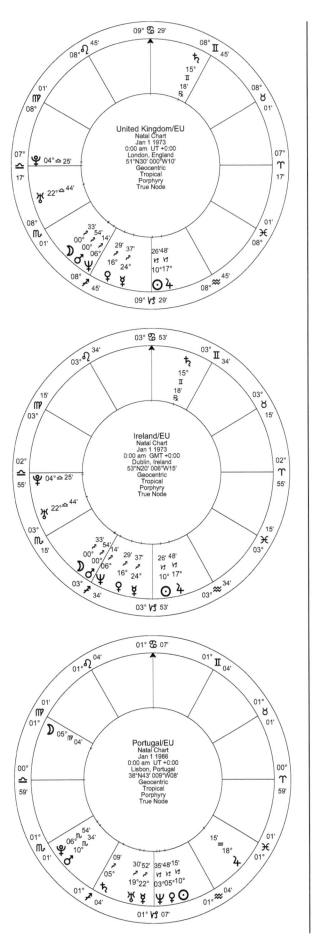
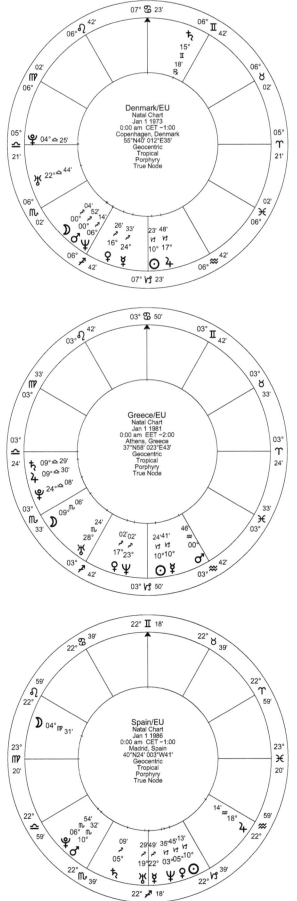

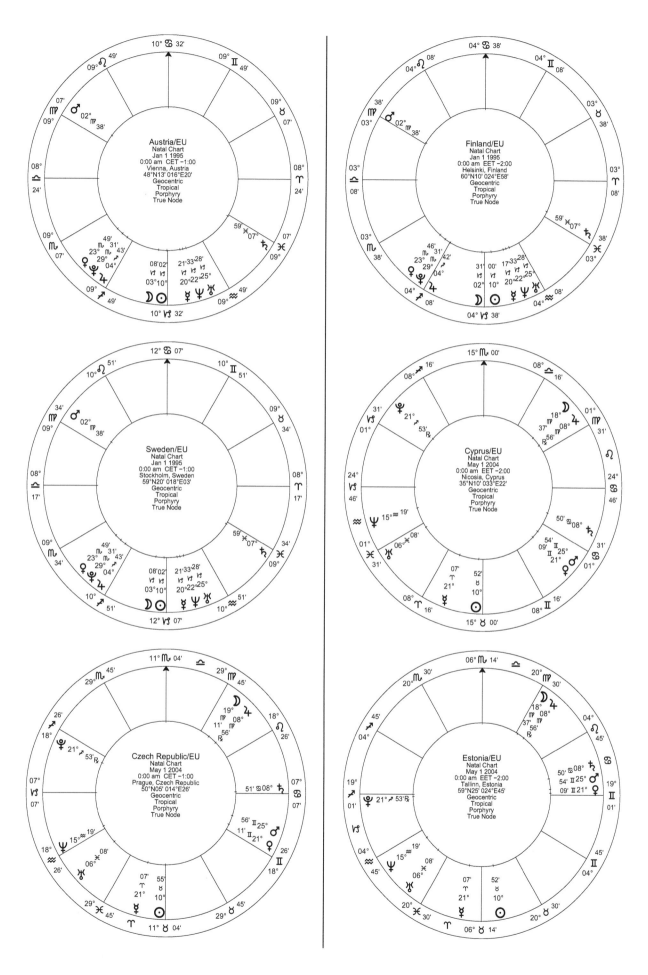

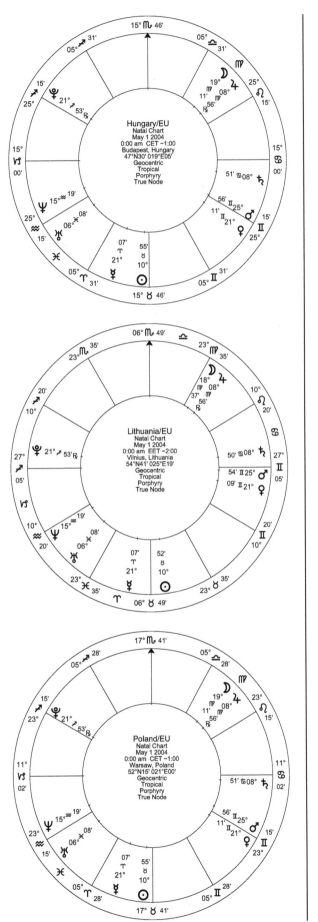
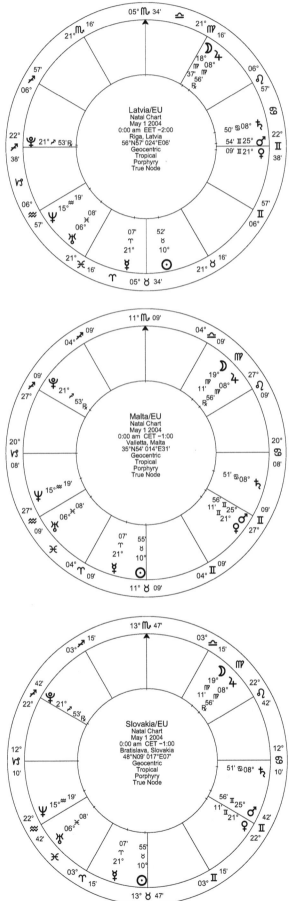

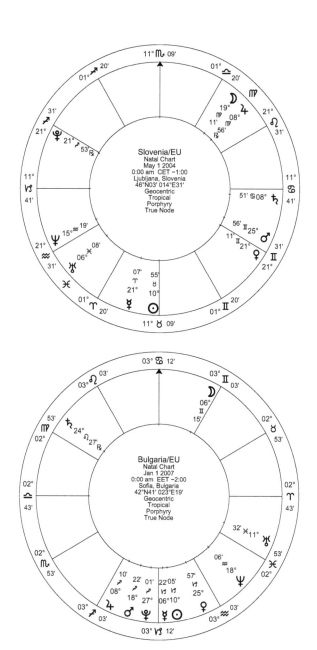

Slovenia/EU
Natal Chart
May 1 2004
0:00 am CET −1:00
Ljubljana, Slovenia
46°N03' 014°E31'
Geocentric
Tropical
Porphyry
True Node

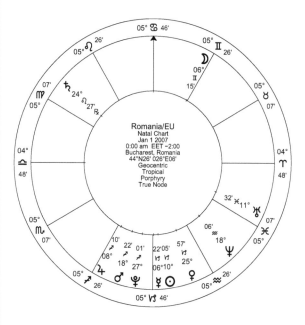

Bulgaria/EU
Natal Chart
Jan 1 2007
0:00 am EET −2:00
Sofia, Bulgaria
42°N41' 023°E19'
Geocentric
Tropical
Porphyry
True Node

Romania/EU
Natal Chart
Jan 1 2007
0:00 am EET −2:00
Bucharest, Romania
44°N26' 026°E06'
Geocentric
Tropical
Porphyry
True Node

# Appendix B
# Alternative Birth Times for Selected Cities

The majority of birth dates for cities listed in this book are for the moment when some local or national authority (king, prince, duke, etc.) granted certain rights to a community, i.e., a charter or incorporation. These charts have been drawn for noon LAT (sundial time) for the sake of consistency, and the LMT has been calculated for the reader.

Over the years I have toyed with these charts and have chosen alternate "birth times" for many places listed in this book. The following list thus represented my rectified birth times and does not represent the final authority on the matter, only my opinion. All times given below are given in LMT.

| Country | City | Birth Time | Ascendant |
|---|---|---|---|
| Austria | Innsbruck | 12:35 p.m. | 2 Libra |
|  | Linz | 1:10 p.m. | 27 Cancer |
|  | Vienna | 1:30 p.m. | 0 Aquarius |
| Belgium | Antwerp | 5:00 p.m. | 17 Virgo |
|  | Brussels | 3:45 p.m. | 7 Scorpio |
|  | Liege | 4:30 p.m. | 10 Scorpio |
| Croatia | Zagreb | 2:17 p.m. | 10 Libra |
| Czech Republic | Brno | 10:55 a.m. | 7 Taurus |
| Denmark | Arhus | 3:10 p.m. | 12 Scorpio |
|  | Copenhagen | 11:25 a.m. | 22 Cancer |
|  | Odense | 3:10 p.m. | 24 Leo |
| Estonia | Tallinn | 9:15 a.m. | 16 Leo |
| Finland | Helsinki | 10:50 a.m. | 19 Virgo |
|  | Tampere | 12:20 P.M. | 2 Sagittarius |
|  | Turku | 8:55 a.m. | 26 Libra |
| France | Bordeaux | 12:22 p.m. | 16 Libra |
|  | Clermont-Ferrand | 12:50 p.m. | 19 Leo |
|  | Le Havre | 4:30 p.m. | 15 Leo |
|  | Lyon | 3:15 p.m. | 12 Scorpio |
|  | Nancy | 12:40 p.. | 8 Libra |
|  | Nantes | 2:50 p.m. | 17 Aquarius |
|  | Nice | 1:05 p.m. | 18 Libra |
|  | Paris | 10:10 a.m. | 5 Leo |
|  | Rouen | 3:25 p.m. | 22 Sagittarius |
|  | Strasbourg | 5:10 p.m. | 17 Libra |
|  | Toulouse | 1:50 p.m. | 15 Gemini |
| Germany | Berlin | 12:55 p.m. | 25 Capricorn |
|  | Bonn | 4:25 p.m. | 22 Virgo |
|  | Bremen | 1:35 p.m. | 20 Virgo |
|  | Chemnitz | 12:45 p.m. | 1 Capricorn |
|  | Cologne (Koln) | 5:55 p.m. | 27 Scorpio |
|  | Dortmund | 1:40 p.m. | 8 Capricorn |

| | Dresden | 1:25 p.m. | 1 Cancer |
| | Dusseldorf | 2:00 p.m. | 4 Sagittarius |
| | Frankfurt | 3:35 p.m. | 9 Sagittarius |
| | Hamburg | 8:35 a.m. | 29 Cancer |
| | Hannover | 12:50 p.m. | 17 Libra |
| | Leipzig | 2:50 p.m. | 22 Aquarius |
| | Mainz | 2:25 p.m. | 14 Aries |
| | Mannheim | 1:10 p.m. | 1 Cancer |
| | Munich | 3:05 p.m. | 3 Scorpio |
| | Nuremberg | 4:25 p.m. | 9 Sagittarius |
| Iceland | Reykjavik | 5:20 p.m. | 15 Scorpio |
| Ireland | Cork | 1:25 p.m. | 13 Gemini |
| | Dublin | 11:00 a.m. | 27 Pisces |
| Italy | Turin | 4:00 p.m. | 6 Sagittarius |
| Liechtenstein | Vaduz | 8:55 a.m. | 25 Cancer |
| Luxembourg | Luxembourg | 12:30 p.m. | 19 Leo |
| Netherlands | Amsterdam | 2:30 p.m. | 6 Pisces |
| | The Hague | 1:50 p.m. | 8 Sagittarius |
| | Rotterdam | 10:40 a.m. | 13 Cancer |
| | Utrecht | 11:30 a.m. | 16 Virgo |
| Norway | Bergen | 11:05 a.m. | 12 Gemini |
| | Oslo | 5:15 p.m. | 18 Libra |
| Poland | Krakow | 2:30 p.m. | 21 Libra |
| | Lodz | 2:55 p.m. | 3 Capricorn |
| | Poznan | 11:15 a.m. | 26 Gemini |
| | Stettin | 1:45 p.m. | 28 Leo |
| | Warsaw | 3:25 p.m. | 5 Sagittarius |
| | Wroclaw | 12:55 p.m. | 6 Taurus |
| Portugal | Lisbon | 3:40 p.m. | 28 Libra |
| | Oporto | 1:35 p.m. | 25 Libra |
| Romania | Bucharest | 1:40 p.m. | 7 Capricorn |
| Slovakia | Bratislava | 2:25 p.m. | 17 Taurus |
| Spain | Barcelona | 9:45 a.m. | 10 Cancer |
| | Bilbao | 1:45 p.m. | 21 Libra |
| | Granada | 2:10 p.m. | 21 Capricorn |
| | Madrid | 11:50 a.m. | 21 Sagittarius |
| | Valencia | 4:55 p.m. | 9 Scorpio |
| | Zaragosa | 2:35 p.m. | 20 Cancer |
| Sweden | Goteborg | 1:50 p.m. | 13 Libra |
| | Malmo | 1:45 p.m. | 11 Gemini |
| | Stockholm | 1:20 p.m. | 16 Virgo |

| | | | |
|---|---|---|---|
| Switzerland | Berne | 12:30 p.m. | 21 Leo |
| | Geneva | 2:45 p.m. | 15 Libra |
| | Zurich | 10:55 a.m. | 23 Aries |
| | | | |
| United Kingdom (England) | Bath | 12:25 p.m. | 5 Aries |
| | Birmingham | 12:55 p.m. | 4 Aries |
| | Bristol | 3:20 p.m. | 15 Sagittarius |
| | Cambridge | 12:26 p.m. | 8 Virgo |
| | Coventry | 3:00 p.m. | 22 Cancer |
| | Derby | 2:15 p.m. | 21 Capricorn |
| | Exeter | 1:10 p.m. | 3 Sagittarius |
| | Gloucester | 12:35 p.m. | 2 Sagittarius |
| | Ipswich | 1:35 p.m. | 2 Libra |
| | Kingston upon Hull | 1:30 p.m. | 5 Leo |
| | Leicester | 1:15 p.m. | 24 Cancer |
| | Liverpool | 2:20 p.m. | 28 Leo |
| | Manchester | 11:35 a.m. | 5 Virgo |
| | Newcastle upon Tyne | 1:15 p.m. | 9 Cancer |
| | Northampton | 12:35 p.m. | 20 Aquarius |
| | Norwich | 1:55 p.m. | 22 Virgo |
| | Nottingham | 1:10 p.m. | 22 Libra |
| | Oxford | 12:50 p.m. | 8 Libra |
| | Plymouth | 1:10 p.m. | 19 Virgo |
| | Portsmouth | 1:55 p.m. | 2 Aries |
| | Reading | 2:35 p.m. | 11 Scorpio |
| | Sheffield | 12:30 p.m. | 9 Scorpio |
| | Southampton | 2:45 p.m. | 22 Leo |
| | Wolverhampton | 1:20 p.m. | 13 Cancer |
| | York | 3:20 p.m. | 16 Libra |
| | | | |
| United Kingdom (Scotland) | Aberdeen | 10:40 a.m. | 17 Capricorn |
| | Edinburgh | 12:25 p.m. | 23 Virgo |
| | | | |
| United Kingdom (Wales) | Cardiff | 11:30 a.m. | 21 Sagittarius |
| | Swansea | 11:45 a.m. | 29 Leo |

Please remember that charter or incorporation charts cannot take the place of a founding chart. But since practically all cities in Europe are so old, there is no way one can ascertain the actual founding date of a community without extensive rectification, and even then it's an educated guess at best.


On the next page are charts for my personal rectifications
for the founding dates of London and Paris.

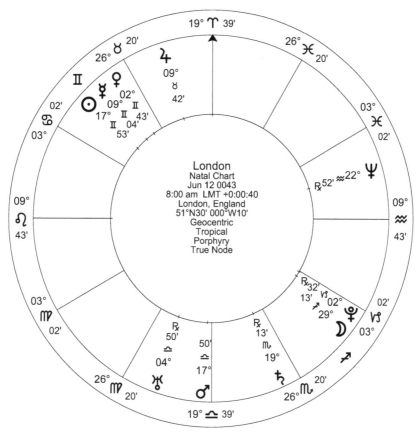

**London, June 12, 43 A.D., 8:00 a.m. LMT**
**Source: Rectified by reading journals of the Claudian conquest of Britain**

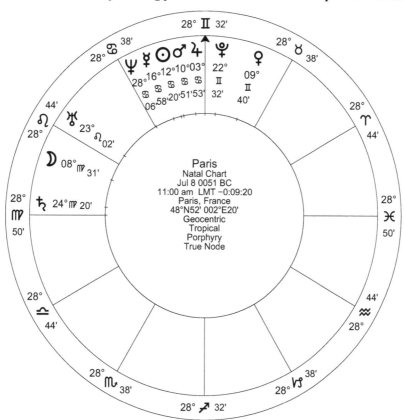

**Paris, July 8, 51 B.C., 11:00 a.m. LMT**
**Source: Bibliotheque Nationale in Paris cites a newspaper report that Paris would celebrate its 2000th anniversary on July 8, 1951**

Lightning Source UK Ltd.
Milton Keynes UK
UKHW050834040122
396588UK00001B/4